War 2.0

War 2.0

Irregular Warfare in the Information Age

Thomas Rid and Marc Hecker

PRAEGER SECURITY INTERNATIONAL
Westport, Connecticut • London

Library of Congress Cataloging-in-Publication Data

Rid, Thomas, 1975-
   War 2.0 : irregular warfare in the information age / Thomas Rid and Marc Hecker
     p. cm.
   Includes bibliographical references and index.
   ISBN 978-0-313-36470-9 (hard copy : alk. paper) — ISBN 978-0-313-36471-6 (ebook)
   1. Asymmetric warfare—Case studies. 2. Guerrilla warfare—Case studies. 3. Military
telecommunication—Case studies. 4. Information technology—Case studies. 5. Digital
media—Case studies. 6. Insurgency—Case studies. 7. Counterinsurgency—Case studies.
8. Military art and science—History—21st century. 9. Military history, Modern—21st
century. I. Hecker, Marc. II. Title.
   U240.R54 2009
   355.02'18—dc22   2009010466

British Library Cataloguing in Publication Data is available.

Library of Congress Catalog Card Number: 2009010466
ISBN-13: 978-0-313-36470-9

First published in 2009

Praeger Security International, 88 Post Road West, Westport, CT 06881
An imprint of Greenwood Publishing Group, Inc.
www.praeger.com

Printed in the United States of America

The paper used in this book complies with the
Permanent Paper Standard issued by the National
Information Standards Organization (Z39.48-1984).

10 9 8 7 6 5 4 3 2 1

Contents

Preface

Two sweeping changes have occurred in the past decade. Life now has a digital touch: we search new jobs online, find old friends on the Web, and plan vacations; we spot new restaurants, read the news and our favorite blogs, shop, and keep in touch with parents, children, and colleagues through mobile phones, texting, and video-chat. We send them digital images of our weddings and getaways. We collaborate, engage others, and sometimes flirt by instant messaging. Arcane communities meet online, for example, young Mormon families in Utah or amateur butchers in England. Even fraud and crime and hate are hooked up. Once in front of a screen, be it on a desktop, laptop, or increasingly a handheld device, we "log in"—not into a system, but into a community. The new media, in short, have become social.

The second revolution concerns armed conflict: only a few years back, the world's best armies saw themselves as lethal fighting machines, networked at the joints through signals and satellites. Such forces were capable of striking down on any foe rapidly and with crippling firepower, anywhere, even piercing through sandstorms and thick clouds, thanks to the wonders of modern sensor technology. Then came a surprising kink: new irregular enemies were hiding among the people, where sensors could not find them. Here religious motivations mattered, as well as ideology, sectarian hatred, close-knit social ties, language, dialects, cultural affinities, trust, and deep-seated grievances. These were pushing fighters to join the resistance, to form cells, to commit suicide attacks, and to lay roadside bombs. The new wars, in short, have become more social.

The first trend, we argue, is affecting the second. Historically, military applications gave birth to novel media technologies, such as radio, television, and even the Web. And these innovations have widened the corridor of action for the state and its regular armed forces more than they did for irregular bands of rebels. Sophisticated information infrastructure was simply too expensive for mutineers.

That asymmetry has been reversed. Now it is the new media that shape warfare, and technology has increased the options for irregulars more than it has for governments and armies. But it does so in rather counterintuitive ways. For some groups, irregular warfare in the information age is becoming less, not more, "population-centric." Not only the benefits, but also the costs have increased immensely for the irregular side. Successful insurgency, as a result, may be more difficult to pull off today than in the past. And counterinsurgency, as presently understood, may not offer the best methods to tackle irregular political violence in the twenty-first century.

War 2.0 is written for a general audience as well as for experts. Scholars of modern armed conflict, political advisors, officers, and journalists will, we hope, benefit from its analysis and the details it provides. The book opens by adding much-needed historical depth to the "new media." The reader is taken back to the beginnings of telecommunication at the end of the eighteenth century. Only a long historical view can keep a calm eye on current uses of media technology by both militants and militaries. The opening chapter can be read as a stand-alone essay on the much-neglected question of how guerrillas have used telecommunication over time (first as a target, then as a weapon, and now as a platform). Then we introduce two competing visions of how information technology can be used on the battlefield, by both regular and irregular forces: one is centered on technological grids, fast strikes, and military power; the other is focused on cultural links, protracted resilience, and political power. "War 1.0"—as we shall call the first ideal—guided regular armies in their relationship to the use of force and the public, as we show in three detail-rich case studies on the United States, the United Kingdom, and Israel. Numerous interviews in these countries and access to many unpublished documents were essential to write the three chapters. Yet that paradigm crashed into the dry desert of Iraq—and later in Afghanistan— when these conflicts morphed into nasty "guerrilla-type" operations. For non-state irregular fighters, and to a certain extent for regular officers, too, the competing template of battle then became what we call "War 2.0." Hezbollah, the Taliban, and al-Qaeda approximate this template to a varying extent. The three case studies are based on government and policy reports, extensive research in French, German, Dutch, and Arabic, as well as numerous expert interviews. The conclusion offers a novel angle on new media trends and their relevance for armed conflict, an assessment of the media operations and "strategic communication" of both sides, and a set of fresh recommendations. A chronology at the end gives a combined overview of landmark events in the recent history of telecommunication as well as irregular warfare.

Without the help of a lot of dedicated people this book would not have been possible. Many individuals and several institutions provided funding, vital advice and critique, intellectual inspiration, platforms to discuss the book's arguments, and that most crucial raw material: details we would not have found otherwise. First and foremost, we would like to thank the more than one hundred people who took the time to meet us in Paris, London, Berlin, Tel Aviv, Jerusalem, Washington, and at lesser-known places to critique our thinking and to share their experiences and ideas with us. Most interview sources are named in the text; some, however, chose to speak with us only on background for professional reasons. They are therefore not identified by name and affiliation. The authors accept full responsibility for errors of fact or interpretation.

Dominique David, Etienne de Durand, Philippe Coquet, Aline Leboeuf, Laurent Fromaget, Corentin Brustlein, and others at the Institut français des relations internationales (Ifri), led by Thierry de Montbrial, have created a truly inspirational intellectual atmosphere and an impressive strategic debate, which was essential for writing this book. The Ministère de la Défense and its social science research arm, the Centre d'Études en Sciences Sociales de la Défense (C2SD), have provided the core funding for this project. The empirical chapters of *War 2.0* are based on two Ifri reports commissioned by the C2SD in 2007 and 2008. The authors would like to thank the ministry for its permission to use some of the research in these pages and specifically Frédéric Charillon, director of C2SD, for his personal support.

A number of colleagues have helped to make the text more vigorous, either by pointing out weaknesses or by providing superior arguments, in particular Christofer Burger, Christopher Chivvis, Andrew Exum, Mike Dahan, Laurent Gayer, Daniel Kimmage, Patrick Müller, Yassin Musharbash, Nadia Oweidat, Angel Rabasa, Philipp Rotmann, Benjamin Schreer, Christoph Schwegmann, and Guido Steinberg. Several persons provided platforms to discuss the book's ideas: Wolfgang Seibel and Julian Junk at the University of Konstanz; Rafal Rohozinski at the Army War College in Carlisle; and Mike Birmingham at the U.S. Defense Information School at Fort Meade.

Thomas Rid would like to express gratitude to Volker Perthes at the Stiftung Wissenschaft und Politik—who initiated the TAPIR-Fellowship, a transatlantic postdoctoral program—as well as to Dan Hamilton at the Center for Transatlantic Relations at Johns Hopkins University/SAIS and Jim Dobbins, Steve Larrabee, and Nora Bensahel at the RAND Corporation. The authors would not have met without this program. We also appreciated the stimulating environment at the Centre de Recherche Français de Jérusalem and would like to thank Pierre de Miroschedji and Lyse Baer. In addition, several individuals deserve to be mentioned for their succor: Lawrence Lessig for his encouragement at an earlier stage; Françoise Thomas for her helping hand; Meriam Daadouche for her translations; Eric Sangar, Aurélie Cerisot, Katrin Wittig, Nicolas Buchon, Louise Romet, and Elie Tenenbaum for their research assistance; Natasha, Marie-Françoise, and Brother Elio at Ratisbonne for their cordial hospitality—and Cédric Parizot, an accomplished Franco-Bedouin chef in Jerusalem, for a dazzling *chameau bourguignon*.

Shorter and less enlightened versions of the argument were published in *Policy Review,* in *Die Zeit,* and in *Le Figaro.* Readers of these publications may appreciate a fresh look at this book. We are grateful to our editor, Robert Hutchinson at Greenwood, for taking on the project at an early stage.

Washington and Paris, January 2009

Introduction

Today's fiercest wars are fought by states against non-state actors. By the U.S. Army and Marine Corps, the world's most powerful land forces, against insurgents in Iraq and Afghanistan. By the Israel Defense Forces, one of the most formidable and nimble armies, against Hezbollah and Hamas. By NATO, the world's largest and longest-standing military alliance, against Taliban and al-Qaeda fighters. These are truly unequal battles. The most professional and advanced military forces have a breathtaking material superiority over any conventional enemy, let alone rough and ready bands of partisans with frail or no state support, with poor professional training and education, whose signature weapons are the bodies of desperate suicide bombers and makeshift explosive devices—a stark contrast to their adversary's Predator drones and F16s, to highly trained and superbly equipped Special Forces, and to the full resolve of Western nation-states. That conventional supremacy was spectacularly demonstrated in October 2001 and again in March 2003, when a predominantly U.S.-British–led joint force obliterated the Taliban regime in Afghanistan and then Iraq's regular army formations in a veritable twenty-first-century blitzkrieg.

Yet for all their conventional superiority, these forces soon discovered that they had two soft spots, one at home and one in the field. Both concern popular support. An insurgency, first, is a competition for the trust and the support of the local civilian population. During an insurgency the population falls into three groups: a small and disenfranchised fringe group initially supports the insurgency; on the other side are those who want to see the counterinsurgent and the government succeed; in the middle between the two is the largest group, which is neutral, uncommitted, and apolitical. Both the insurgent and the counterinsurgent compete for this group's support, for their acceptance of authority, for legitimacy. The insurgent's most valuable resource, therefore, is a political cause that can mobilize the uncommitted masses. Every suicide attack, every bomb, makes

a potent argument to these neutral observers that the government and the counterinsurgent police and military forces are weak, that they cannot fulfill their
promise to protect, and that they may be running out of time. If the insurgent
succeeds with this strategy, the counterinsurgent loses the population's goodwill.
And if the population is lost, the counterinsurgency is lost.

The second vulnerability is domestic support. Modern¹ armies have an open
flank: their nation's electorate and domestic public opinion. It is a constitutional
cornerstone of democracies that flag officers follow the orders of politicians—
that presidents, prime ministers, and chancellors are commanders-in-chief in
times of war. It is also a constitutional cornerstone of democracies that these
politicians are elected universally, be it directly or indirectly, and that governments pay attention to the public's expression of will, in national elections, but
also during the subsequent legislative period. Parliamentary systems are designed
to represent the people, to articulate and amplify the public's criticism and its discontent with the government's policy. That also applies to the executive's management of an ongoing war. As a consequence, when elections approach,
incumbents start worrying more and more about losing their jobs than about losing a distant war while their democratic challengers may be more concerned
about winning the elections: then a democracy is exposing its open flank without
protective armor.

This book examines the relevance of the changes in the media environment
for the conduct of armed conflict and war. How do the new media affect irregular warfare? Do the new media favor one particular side? How should states and
their conventional forces react? Recent innovations in information technology,
we argue, level the playing field and give a relative advantage to irregulars. But the
same trends also increase costs and uncertainty for the most sophisticated armed
groups. The reactions of governments and armies will therefore determine
whether the present changes in the conduct of irregular warfare—amplified by
the new media—will favor one side or the other.

Today's irregular forces have spotted both vulnerabilities, at home and in the
field. And they have learned to mount appropriate charges with great skill. From
the insurgent's point of view, it is important to note in this context, there is no
principal differentiation between military and civilian targets. Civilian dead or
hostages, in fact, may serve the irregular's purpose more efficiently and effectively: the physical risk for the attacker is smaller, and the psychological benefit—
the shock and outrage in the targeted community, whether in Afghanistan, Iraq,
Europe, or the United States—is larger. Both in the "near" theater and in the "far"
theater the purpose is essentially identical: to undermine popular support for the
counterinsurgent's cause. The bombings in Madrid on 11 March 2004 and newly
elected Prime Minister José Luis Zapatero's subsequent withdrawal of Spanish
troops from Iraq spectacularly illustrate this vulnerability. The episode is perhaps
the most dramatic one in recent years, but it is by no means an exception. The
large numbers of roadside bombs and suicide attacks against local civilian and foreign military targets in Afghanistan have provoked more aggressive action by

NATO. As inadvertent civilian casualties have risen, the Taliban has gained authority and legitimacy among the population.

Regular armies, as a result, are forced to refocus their attention. An enemy regime could be targeted exclusively and often secretly; the public, both at home and in theater, can, by contrast, only be "targeted" publicly. Armies consequently struggle with the "informational dimension," as military documents often put it.[2] The U.S. Army's capstone Field Manual 3-0, "Operations," is one of the most important military publications of the United States, updated for the first time since 9/11 and released in February 2008.[3] It redefines how the Army views public information *and* counterinsurgency. The document's significance can hardly be underestimated. For the first time in its history, the United States put civil support operations on the same level with offense and defense. New doctrine and new technology therefore go hand in hand in their main thrust: the public, especially the way public opinion is formed through the media, is paramount. "The impact of the information environment on operations continues to increase," FM 3-0 says in the sober language of doctrine.

But for an occupying force it can be difficult to manage a benevolent public image while being engaged in combat operations. For the insurgent, by contrast, it is easy to appear successful on the public stage: irregular fighters may score by simply blowing up a government building; the regular force has the difficult task of building up a government. Counterinsurgents quietly drink hundreds of cups of tea with local leaders to create trust and legitimacy; insurgents blast restaurants and markets to shatter that confidence. The destruction wrought by irregular fighters has an immediate impact; the government's reconstruction projects are slow to show effect. The insurgent may kill innocent civilians in one event, and thus undermine the authority's pledges to guarantee security for everybody; the counterinsurgent, in excruciatingly painstaking and invisible intelligence and law-enforcement work, may merely prevent such events. The costs for the counterinsurgent to maintain order and legitimacy are disproportionately higher than the costs for the insurgent to undermine that order and legitimacy. In sum, effective counterinsurgency is a game much less attention-grabbing and much more resource-consuming than effective insurgency. It is, therefore, much easier for irregular fighters to get "good" graphic media coverage, and to exploit an increasingly competitive journalistic profession. And they do. In the years after 9/11, al-Qaeda's leadership, often its number two, Ayman al-Zawahiri, kept appearing regularly on major Arab news channels to comment on current events and shape its radical followers' opinion. At the height of unrest in Iraq, the insurgency published more press releases than the American forces in the Middle East.[4] When the resistance in Afghanistan regained strength, the Taliban's spokesman, Qari Yousuf Ahmadi, became ubiquitous in Western media outlets, claiming responsibility for kidnappings and accusing NATO of killing innocent civilians. And Hassan Nasrallah, Hezbollah's point man and secretary general, is widely seen as having out-communicated the Israeli leadership during the 2006 Lebanon War.

The difference between internal and external communication is essential for understanding the impact of communication technology on warfare. The significance of this difference cannot be overstated. Modern Western armed forces have enthusiastically embraced information technology for their internal use. Improved digital technology, military planners reasoned, would enable real-time command-and-control under conditions of near-perfect situational awareness. A modern "network-centric" force would reign over the digitized battlespace through mutually interconnected units, weapon systems, and entire service branches. Proponents of "transformation" long held the futuristic vision of a forward observer on horseback, laser-pinpointing satellite-guided munitions from a B-52 bomber precisely into an al-Qaeda training camp. That vision, Secretary of Defense Donald Rumsfeld boasted in *Foreign Affairs*, had become reality in Afghanistan in 2001. Optimists hopefully declared a "revolution in military affairs," which culminated in the 2003 invasion of Iraq. Thanks to "information superiority" the joint force could minimize casualties among the troops and collateral damage among civilians. Thanks to modern technology, warfare would be faster, more accurate, more precise, more lethal, and ultimately less controversial.

In external communication the opposite applied: modern armed forces have long struggled to properly deal with information in the public domain. For a long time the press and other forms of journalism were the only vehicles of public information emanating from a conflict zone. Throughout the 1990s war coverage became more graphic and more immediate. Journalists were now a ubiquitous feature of the battlefield, equipped with mobile phones, e-mail, and digital cameras that made them effectively independent of military help in getting the message out. Military decision makers saw that improved flow of public information as a set of huge problems: journalists don't understand the business of war; they compromise operational security by unknowingly giving away secrets valuable to the enemy; and gruesome images of inadvertent mistakes and casualties undermine public resolve, making it even harder to fight and win wars. Officers observed with concern that military control, be it in the form of censorship or so-called security at the source, was being eroded by intrusive technologies. Institutional skepticism vis-à-vis the media was seemingly reinforced by historical lessons: young U.S. officers after Vietnam, for instance, were heavily biased against the press because the "scribblers" allegedly lost the war for them by breaking the support by the American people. Vietnam created a whole generation of "embittered officers" who "despised" the press, in the words of Henry Gole, an instructor at the Army War College in the 1980s. "They reserved a special venomous attitude for 'the media,' a term more sneered than spoken."[5] The press, and in fact all public external communication, was seen as a threat and as a problem, not as an opportunity to show the nation at home—or the enemy in the field—how well equipped and trained the army was. Even worse, it was not seen as a proper problem, but as a side problem that was not part of the more difficult operational planning tasks. Commanders regarded the press as a distraction and a nuisance, not as an integral part of military operations. Successful media operations were not seen as a precondition for military success, but rather as an ornament. To the extent that public affairs were seen as a problem, transformation erased that problem: civilian collateral damage would be minimized through the use of precision-guided munitions and any enemy would be destroyed more rapidly than the press coverage could undermine public support. In short: internally IT was embraced; externally it was shunned.

In the early twenty-first century two trends converged to shatter this mindset and reverse the order of importance between internal and external communications. First, irregular war became the center of attention, and with it the public perception of the war. Battlefields ceased to be a meeting ground of professionally trained officers and their specialized enlisted ranks. Irregular adversaries knew that they would stand no chance in a regular confrontation and chose guerrilla tactics instead: they hid among the population, recruited and trained amateur fighters from the ranks of the sympathetic locals, and fought for the allegiance of those who remained neutral or hostile. The new type of war—or rather a rejuvenated older kind of conflict—was population-centric for the insurgent. And soon counterinsurgent forces realized that this lesson also applied to them: the population was the key. External communication and public affairs vis-à-vis these key constituencies suddenly became just as important as optimized command-and-control and the digitized battlespace; external communication, in short, acquired the same operational relevance as internal communication, or perhaps an ever greater relevance, at least in doctrine—a significant recognition on the side of change-averse conventional armies.

Second, an entirely different trend in the media environment coincided with this doctrinal shift: traditional journalism began to lose its near-monopoly over the publication of news. Leading "old" media organizations such as CNN, the *New York Times*, and the BBC retain undisputed agenda-setting power and most likely will continue to do so. Yet the emergence of widespread Internet penetration around the world, particularly in North America, Europe, and Asia, coupled with innovative Web-based software, has opened up new venues for public interaction: blogs, image- and video-sharing sites, issue-specific discussion forums, wikis, social-networking sites, listservs, message boards, and regular Web sites. The number of nonprofessional participants in mass communication has increased significantly, and the barrier of entry to participate in that conversation has been lowered for amateur contributors. The "new media" serve as platforms in their own right, as many new sites have cultivated regular readerships that rival those of traditional media in size, and they offer inspiration and research sources for journalists. The expression "new media environment," for the purposes of this book, refers to the generally more dynamic publishing landscape that is the result of both professional journalism and Web 2.0's popular mass communication. In both the media and at war, therefore, a new social dimension has very quickly, in the span of several years, gained unexpected importance.

To understand the drivers of change, it is important to keep in mind the bigger picture. Two separate trends in the history of telecommunications converged in the year 2000: mass monologue and digital dialogue. More than two centuries ago, telecommunications had divorced the message from the messenger. No longer was it necessary to physically *transport* a message from sender to receiver; it could be *transmitted*. Anton Huurdeman, a historian of telecommunications, sees this development in an optimistic spirit typical of the innovators he studied: "Telecommunications eliminated a master-to-servant relationship: replacing the service of a messenger by mechanical telegraph in 1794, by copper wires in 1837, by electromagnetic waves in 1896, and by optical fiber in 1973."[6] More than in other fields, innovations in communication technology can cast a seductive spell. Those who experience the magic of "instant" communication are usually seized by entrepreneurial optimism and point out the benevolent effects of this development, an observation that applies to contemporaries and later historians alike. "What a playball has this planet of ours become!" the writer Jack London exclaimed in a political essay written in 1900. "The telegraph annihilates space and time. Each morning every part knows what every other part is thinking, contemplating, or doing."[7] Technologically enhanced communication, one historian concluded a century later, "improves human relationships."[8] In today's brave new world of digital intimacy, to use the title of a *New York Times Magazine* story on the subject, human relationships might not be improved, but they surely are more intense.[9]

Radio became a mass medium after World War I and television after World War II. Soon it was not improved, but deteriorated, human relationships that moved to the top of journalism's agenda. War used the media, but the media also used war: it sold. The Vietnam War is widely regarded as the first television war, although the moving images arrived in America's living rooms with considerable delay, depriving the footage of much of the graphic immediacy that characterizes the coverage of today's conflicts. One of the key moments in the history of war reportage came in 1991, when CNN's Peter Arnett broadcast live from the roof of the al-Rashid hotel in Baghdad. The city's bombardment and the tracers of the Iraqi air defense could indeed be witnessed in real time all over this planet of ours. In 1992, after an allegedly media-driven U.S. foreign policy intervention in Somalia, there was much talk about the so-called "CNN-effect." The media, it was argued, would drive military interventions, inbound, and outbound again, through the compelling use of images—images respectively of starving children and dead soldiers in Mogadishu.[10] During the next decade, print, radio, and TV-journalism entered into a period of rapid change: competition became tougher, deadlines became tighter, the thirst for sensations and human-interest stories became stronger. By 1994, the Internet had emerged as a popular medium.

As a consequence, the traditional "old" media came under additional pressure. Until only a few years ago, the printing press, radio, television, and even the Internet remained a public platform to receive information; sending information was a different story. Using telecommunications to send information in a dialogue was largely limited to other formats: telegraphy, telefax, telephone, and eventually e-mail and cellphones. Only in the year 2000, after the Dot-com bubble had burst and a new crop of companies had arisen from the financial market's ashes, did the two trends converge. New Web-based companies and services boasted "interactivity" and "user-generated content." The costs for both the private and public use of mass communication were radically lowered. The number of passive and active participants, as a consequence, radically shot up, and it continues to do so. Only in the early twenty-first century were the conditions for a permanent public dialogue created, or, more precisely, for a myriad of public dialogues of varying degrees of openness. Users were now able to contribute and publish by the push of a button, to blog, to discuss issues on Web forums, advertise and sell goods and services, find partners for work and play online, contribute to knowledge creation, engage in social movements—and take political action. The sum of all these parts was something new, something in need of a word and a name: "Web 2.0" was coined as a term to capture the Web's interactive revolution. It promised to turn passive consumers into active citizens and to reverse a century-old specialization: not only professionals would be in a position to mass-communicate; everybody would be able to do so. Eventually technology would improve human relationships. But the coin had a flip side. Technology also improved how humans abused relationships and how they ultimately engaged in violent organized conflict. Google's corporate motto may be "don't be evil," yet its users might well be inclined to do evil, and many of the new Web's firms inadvertently and unintentionally help them to be far more efficient at it than ever before.

In the summer of 2003, the insurgency in Iraq began to grow in strength. Initially there was resistance in the Pentagon and the U.S. government to call the new phase of the war by its name. Eventually the new head of Central Command, Army General John P. Abizaid, in his first press conference pronounced the operation a "classical guerrilla-type" war.[11] Conventional armies in Iraq and Afghanistan soon found themselves engaged in a long-term struggle against irregular enemies. Network-centric warfare was of little use against such subversive movements that employed classical guerrilla tactics. As a consequence, the two most important armies fighting in Iraq and Afghanistan began to revise their counterinsurgency doctrine in order to adapt to the new but rather unexpected operational realities that were demanding such a high toll in lives and treasure. The local population was recognized as the critical "center of gravity," or as the key terrain that needed to be gained. Both the insurgent and the counterinsurgent were competing for the trust, the loyalty, and the allegiance of the neutral local population. "The 'terrain' we are clearing is human terrain, not physical terrain," said David Kilcullen, one of General David Petraeus's key advisers at the time when the new counterinsurgency doctrine was developed.[12] Yet the human terrain did not remain confined by the same physical borders as the theater of operations.

For the first time in the history of armed conflict, the media environment allowed a potentially worldwide audience to witness what happened. One unexpected effect was that a local insurgency could have a globally dispersed audience—and not only a passive but also an active audience. That audience equally falls into three broad groups: neutrals and supporters of each side. The difference between the theater of operations and domestic audiences, as a consequence, became blurry. An excellent illustration is Younis Tsouli, better know as Irhabi007, a self-recruited cyber-terrorist (the word *irhabi* means terrorist in Arabic). The IT-skilled twenty-two-year-old son of a Moroccan tourism board official, and a resident of Shepherd's Bush in west London, was a ubiquitous figure of al-Qaeda's online activity.[13] He administered several radical Internet sites and pioneered new tactics, techniques, and procedures in the electronic jihad. Tsouli knew well that his online activism was a far cry from actually fighting the enemy in Iraq. In one encrypted chat conversation he openly struggled with the dilemma of matching words with deeds. "Dude," Tsouli complained to another online-jihadist, who chose the pseudonym Abuthaabit, "my heart is in Iraq." A telling dialogue ensued:

> *Abuthaabit:* How are you going to have enough to go there?
> *Irhabi007:* I suppose someone gotta be here!
> *Abuthaabit:* This media work, I am telling you, is very important. Very, very, very, very.
> *Irhabi007:* I know, I know.
> *Abuthaabit:* Because a lot of the funds brothers are getting is because they are seeing stuff like this coming out. Imagine how many people have gone [to Iraq] after seeing the situation because of the videos. Imagine how many of them could have been shaheed [martyrs] as well.[14]

This brief exchange illustrates well the tie between online organization and offline action, between domestic audiences and audiences in theater. Tsouli was far away from the battlefield in London, and, like many, badly wanted to have an impact on what was happening in Iraq and Afghanistan. Yet his was a struggle to inspire other potential extremists to fight, mounted from Europe and targeting the Middle East.

The Taliban offer a reverse example: their frequent kidnapping-assaults and attacks on aid-workers, foreigners, and coalition troops in Afghanistan are shrewd attempts to stop moderate citizens from supporting the operation, orchestrated from Central Asia and aimed at Europe's and North America's electorates. Yet both carry on the insurgency in the media, enhanced by the Internet in all its forms. As a result, Western militaries are caught between a rock and a hard place: in Afghanistan, Iraq, and elsewhere they face an international corps of inspired and stunningly creative radicals; at home they face a political leadership and a public media discourse highly susceptible to kidnapping of Westerners, particularly in Europe, and to violence against innocent civilians. It is not new that European activists of Muslim origin support local insurgencies in Africa or Asia. Algeria's *Groupe Islamique Armée* (GIA), for instance, relied on a largely Europe-based production and distribution network for its own magazine in the 1990s, *al-Ansar*. Yet, as we outline in chapter 6, both new technologies and competition for news are playing into the radicals' and the insurgents' hands in ways that were hardly imaginable only a few years ago.

In today's irregular wars, modern armies face two simultaneous generational challenges that amplify the consequences of this shift. Those below the rank of lieutenant colonel and major are likely to have a superior understanding of counterinsurgency, and they are likely to have a superior understanding of the new media. Those at the top are less likely to be aware. Particularly in hierarchical and bureaucratic organizations such as governments and armies, senior decision makers have risen to the top slowly. Many a senior official or general discovered e-mail, chat, text messaging, or podcasting for the first time when younger colleagues or their own children showed it to them. They continue to read newspapers in hard copy as their main source of information. Marc Prensky of games2train, a company that promotes the educational use of video games, calls these newcomers to the new media environment "digital immigrants."[15] Digital immigrants, for instance, speak with an "accent" when they talk about the technology and its use. Senator John McCain's famous remarks about "the Google" and "the internets" during the 2008 presidential campaign illustrate the point.[16] Many of today's majors, captains, and lieutenants, however, and surely the younger NCOs and the enlisted ranks, are "digital natives."[17] For many of them it is normal to have MySpace profiles, watch YouTube, chat, subscribe to podcasts, read blogs, use wikis, skype, twitter, and share stories, images, and videos online.

On the other hand, there is a generational disagreement regarding the use of force within many Western armies. Officers who were trained, educated, and professionally socialized after Vietnam favor big conventional operations of the Persian Gulf War type as an ideal. They tend to be more inclined to believe in conventional superiority of modern firepower in joint operations. Younger officers, who had their baptism of fire in Iraq and Afghanistan, recognize the limitations of firepower and understand counterinsurgency intuitively. They poke fun at the kill-and-capture guys, those who still hold dear the conventional approach to the use of force. Instead, particularly in Anglo-American forces, they highlight the role of civil affairs and population-centric operations. "Everybody below the rank of lieutenant colonel understands that," said Lieutenant Colonel John Nagl, then commander of the 1st battalion of the 34th armored regiment at Fort Riley, Kansas, who was involved in the rewrite and implementation of the U.S. Army's and Marine Corps' current counterinsurgency doctrine.[18] Despite the wide dissemination of the much-talked-about document, lieutenants and captains continue to be frustrated with the institutional army and its unwillingness to learn and adapt. Together with the high stress of back-to-back deployments, their considerable frustration with the senior officer corps was one important reason for alarmingly low retention rates among the Army's most promising young officers. Of the nearly 1,000 graduating cadets of West Point's class of 2002, 58 percent were no longer on active duty in 2007.[19] "A lieutenant can't put pressure on the Army; he just leaves," Nagl said. Those who leave, potentially the best and the brightest of a next generation of military leaders, are those best positioned to understand the significance of the new media.

But the digital media and irregular warfare have more in common than just dividing generations of officers; taken together they increasingly separate two types of warfare, or two competing paradigms of armed conflict. Change in communication technology in military and militant organizations, it should be noted with a grain of historical caution, has affected armed conflict since antiquity. But only in the past decade have the digital media had two novel effects: Web 2.0 is affecting the relationship between conventional and unconventional military force, and it is providing a new prism through which to perceive this relationship. Two competing ideals can be identified that drive and help to recognize modern war in clearer contours. Both are heavily inspired by technological innovations. "War 1.0," as we shall call the first paradigm, is centered on weapons technology, uses complex automated systems, is a predominantly military exercise, focuses on enemy formations, aims to interrupt decision cycles, has short duration, progresses quickly, ends in clear victory, uses destructive methods, uses intelligence primarily based on signals, and is run by top-down initiatives with a clear chain of command. The media and the public, in War 1.0, are a side problem, to be ignored. Information is protected, secret, and used primarily for internal purposes. At the same time information technology has an enhancing effect on this type of war: it makes the clash of military force more lethal, more destructive, more complex, faster, and technologically more sophisticated, opening up more possibilities to act against the enemy. The driver behind this development is a genuinely modern phenomenon: a specialization and professionalization that characterized Western armed forces from the Industrial Revolution to the present. It is the division of labor between military affairs and political affairs that is the hallmark of War 1.0.

A long-established division of labor between military force and political and economic action is almost absent from the contrasting vision, "War 2.0": a highly political exercise, it is social, revolving around complex cultural systems. Its focus is on the population, its aim to establish alternative decision cycles, its duration long, its progress slow, its end a diffuse success at best, its methods productive (such as nation-building), its most important intelligence based on humans. Its initiatives often come from the bottom up, with decentralized structures of authority. The media and the public, in War 2.0, are the central battleground, and they have the highest priority. Information is predominantly public, open-source, and intended for external consumption. At the same time, information technology has an enhancing effect: it makes the conflict more devastating, more violent, more complex, more resilient, more drawn out; and it opens up a broader spectrum of military and political action. But it also opens up a new range of vulnerabilities, costs, and perhaps insurmountable problems—for both regular forces and non-state militants.

The methodology of this differentiation is inspired by Carl von Clausewitz's mode of thinking: the distinction is an ideal one, and "War 1.0" and "War 2.0" are abstract notions, analogous to Clausewitz's concept of absolute war. The two paradigms are not types of real conflict that succeed each other chronologically or

historically. To the contrary: elements of each may be observed in the same conflict and even on the same side, as we shall see in later chapters. Yet it is the "obligation of theory," in Clausewitz's words, to serve as a "general gauge." That point
of reference can be approximated by reality, but it can never be reached in its pure
form. For the Prussian thinker it was, among other things, "friction" that always
intervened in "real war."[20] In real war, friction would indeed be one of the moderating factors that prevent the conflict from reaching one of the two extreme
forms outlined above. A similar figure of thought was used by the sociologist Max
Weber, who wrote about "ideal types." Weber even applied these ideal types to
war (Helmuth von Moltke's 1866 campaign) and also considered the relevance of
moderating factors, such as human error or incorrect information.[21] The method
of idealized concepts can be a powerful heuristic vehicle to understand a complex
phenomenon in a rapidly shifting sociotechnological environment, as was the
case in the early nineteenth century—and again 200 years later.

The differentiation into two principal, abstract types of war, consequently, will
be used to organize the book's argument. The first part looks at the counterinsurgent and War 1.0, the second part at the insurgent and War 2.0. This order
might seem counterintuitive, as an insurgent movement necessarily predates any
attempt to stop it. Yet at second glance the chronology is reversed: the organizations that have to quell rebellions, regular armed forces, predate their adversaries.
An insurgent movement, by contrast, has to improvise and organize its armed
militias as it matures; it is therefore always younger than the counterinsurgent it
faces. Focusing on the counterinsurgent first also reflects the usual approach of
regular armies when they confront an insurgency: they first know themselves,
their procedures, and the operational plan that landed them in the midst of a budding and rising and unexpected insurgency, to which the soldiers are only then
introduced.

But before looking at regular armed services and their reaction to a fast-
changing and evolving media environment, the latter phenomenon needs to be
understood. The first chapter, Wired at War, puts current developments in
telecommunications technology concisely into historical perspective. Insurgents,
we argue, have historically used their opponent's telecommunications facilities
first as a target, then as a weapon, and more recently as a platform. The second
chapter, War 1.0, shows that armies have a track record of embracing telecommunications technology for their internal use while neglecting both its public and
interactive dimension. But the conditions of twenty-first-century irregular warfare
have forced these armies to reluctantly recognize the limitations of this approach.
Chapter 3, The United States, reviews how the Pentagon and America's armed
forces have reacted to the new challenges during the invasion and occupation of
Iraq. Chapter 4, The United Kingdom, looks at Britain's recent lessons learned in
dealing with a fast-changing media environment in their most current operations.
Chapter 5, Israel, analyzes the Israel Defense Force's experience in the war against
Hezbollah during the summer of 2006. All three cases will show that the world's
most active armies have struggled, because of their professionalism and their high

degree of specialization, to give public affairs the appropriate priority in modern warfare.

Chapter 6, War 2.0, switches the perspective to the other side, that of the insurgent. It argues that changes in information technology affect the conditions of insurgency in a way that is, at first glance, beneficial for resistance movements. It outlines the spectrum of utilities, or functions, that can be harnessed through media operations in the public domain, and the altered relevance of the local population. The following three chapters then apply these ideas in three distinctly different but highly instructive cases. Chapter 7, Hezbollah, looks at the evolution of the Lebanese resistance movement's highly sophisticated media operations; chapter 8, Taliban, analyzes how the Afghanistan-based radicals developed their use of information technology from 1996; and chapter 9, Al-Qaeda, probes the global terrorist movement's use of the media both old and new. The three cases reveal that, relative to conventional armies, the media operations of irregular movements have improved faster and that insurgents have embraced new technologies with remarkable sophistication. But the sheer speed of change is also overwhelming these groups and brings its own set of unanticipated risks and costs—particularly for al-Qaeda, perhaps the most media-savvy terrorist movement in history. The consequences, as we show in the conclusion, are counterintuitive: Political violence in the age of Web 2.0 may be more resilient and militant groups more difficult to crush; but ultimately they are less dangerous and less threatening than they were in the past.

1

Wired at War

How do the new media affect war? Any serious attempt to answer this question will have to first understand the "new" media. Particularly in political conflict, all parties and actors are affected: technology has made journalism more intrusive, faster, and independent from military logistics even in remote areas. Deepening Internet penetration everywhere has turned the civilian populations at home and in theater first into keen observers and then into commentators of military action. And improved "network-enabled" command-and-control technology has made regular armies far more efficient and lethal.[1] But changes in telecommunication have an even more revolutionary impact on irregular forces.[2] To understand the Web's and wireless technology's significance at war, it is necessary to put into historical context what managers refer to as the "information revolution,"[3] and what military officers like to call the "new information environment."[4]

The history of irregular media operations is complex and fractured; generalizations are difficult. Yet it is possible to isolate three large and overlapping historical phases: First, throughout the nineteenth century, irregular forces saw the state's telecommunication facilities as a target that could be physically attacked to weaken the armies and the authority of states and empires. Second, for most of the twentieth century after the world wars, irregulars slowly but successfully began using the mass media as a weapon. Telecommunications, and more specifically the press, were used to attack the moral support and cohesion of opposing political entities. Then, in the early part of the twenty-first century, a third phase began: irregular movements started using commoditized information technologies as an extended operating platform. The form and the trajectory of the overarching information revolution, from the Industrial Revolution until today, historically benefited the nation-state and increased the power of regular armies. But this trend was reversed in the year 2000 when the New Economy's Dot-com bubble burst, an event that changed the face of the Web. What came thereafter, a second-generation Internet, or "Web 2.0," does not favor the state, large firms, and big armies any more; instead the new Web, in an abstract but highly relevant way, resembles—and inadvertently mimics—the principles of subversion and irregular war. The unintended consequence for armed conflicts is that non-state insurgents benefit far more from the new media than do governments and counterinsurgents, a trend that is set to continue in the future.

The historical approach chosen here to understand the new media is necessarily brief and superficial. Yet only a historical approach can hedge against two risks, against over- and underrating the problem at hand. The long view helps the reader (as well as the authors) to remain balanced and not blow technology's significance out of proportion, such as has happened initially in the IT industry and in the financial markets with the Dot-com bubble and in the defense establishment with the debate on "transformation." At the same time a historical approach highlights the true nature of the change we are observing: a change that is more cultural than technological.

TARGET

On 23 August 1793, the *levée en masse*, or conscription, was decreed in revolutionary France by the National Convention.[5] The law was a milestone in the creation of modern armies.[6] Exactly one year later, another and perhaps more important milestone in human history was reached: transport and communication were divorced, marking the birth of modern telecommunication. Since ancient times the most common form of long-distance communication was to send messages or letters by carriers and dispatch riders. The optical telegraph, or semaphore, first broke the physical link between messenger and message. The semaphore's idea was to convey information through visual signals, such as smoke, fires, lights, and flashes created by pivoting shutters and blades. The first modern system was built in 1794 by Claude Chappe and his three brothers, initially for military purposes. The first line, with nineteen stations across a distance of 190 kilometers, was completed on 16 July 1794. Then, on 15 August 1794, the era of telecommunications began: the new telegraph was used for the first time to report that the French general Armand Samuel de Marescot had liberated the city of Le Quesnoy, about 200 kilometers north of Paris, from Austrian troops after nearly one year of occupation. The Convention received the news only one hour after the battle's end.[7]

Napoleon developed the system and used the telegraph to stay in touch with Paris from places as far away as Russia.[8] Already in 1810, fixed installations ran west from Paris to Brest, north to Amsterdam, east to Mainz in Germany, and southeast to Lyons and then across northern Italy to Milan and Venice.[9] Operators in the towers waited for semaphore signals from their neighboring tower, took notes, checked for errors, and quickly passed the encrypted signals on to the next tower. The French government used the system until it was superseded by the electric telegraph in 1852. Optical telegraphy had several downsides. It was clumsy and slow to operate, with one character consuming about thirty seconds, the speed and viability heavily affected by snow and rain; it was limited by geography, it was an easy military target, and the signals could simply be intercepted— but most importantly it was exceedingly expensive to build, operate, and maintain. Optical telegraphy could be afforded only by the state and only for the most urgent and important military or political purposes, a trend that would persist for the next two hundred years.

The electrical telegraph ended the use of semaphores (except in naval affairs). The telegraph's history is also closely tied to revolution and war. It was developed and patented in the United States by Samuel Morse in 1837 and first operated between Baltimore and Washington, DC, on 24 May 1844. "What hath god wrought?" was the world's first electric memo. The new machine's messages became known as telegrams, cablegrams, or just "wires." The volatile political situation in Europe at that time, with the revolutions of 1848, made it clear to governments that the telegraph needed to be controlled. In Germany, the king in Berlin invested heavily in two lines from Berlin to Cologne and Frankfurt. When the first German national assembly convened in the *Paulskirche*, the church of St. Paul, in Frankfurt, the news that King Friedrich Wilhelm was elected the first emperor of Germany traveled to Berlin within an hour. Soon the idea was born to connect America and Europe by cable across the Atlantic, a bold project that boggled the mind of contemporaries. In 1858, even before the cable's installation was finished, the *Scientific American* praised the Atlantic Telegraph as "that instantaneous highway of thought between the Old and the New Worlds."[10] By 27 July 1866 the engineers had succeeded: a cable connected Follhummerum Bay in Ireland to the Newfoundland village of Heart's Content. The first message sent, again, concerned a conflict between two of the world's greatest powers at the time: "A treaty of peace has been signed between Austria and Prussia," it read. But not unlike optical telegraphy, the electrical messaging was exceedingly expensive, particularly across large distances. Sending a message on the Atlantic cable initially cost one dollar for each letter, at a time when the monthly wage for a regular worker was perhaps twenty dollars. The telegraph would remain in use for more than a century. In 1945, the year the Second World War ended, the number of telegraph messages sent in the United States exceeded 236 billions.

At war, the telegraph empowered the government and high command. In May 1855 the French and British armies in the Crimea had already begun wiring and receiving dispatches to and from capitals. Before the Battle of Königgrätz, the decisive battle of the Austro-Prussian war of 1866, Prussia's Chief of the General Staff Helmuth von Moltke used the telegraph to direct and arrange large marches from Berlin prior to the battle. He had arrived in the theater only four days earlier. The two major innovations of the German wars of unification, all won under Moltke's apt leadership, the railway and the telegraph, accelerated the mobilization of large armies and might have premeditated the German victory. "The telegraph has made the command of large armies significantly easier," Albrecht von Boguslawski, a prolific German lieutenant colonel, wrote in 1881.[11]

But the new technology had unwanted side effects, even in armies that had a legacy of colonial warfare, which emphasized the exercise of responsibility by the men on the spot. The British government began to bother its generals with suggestions, recommendations, and useless requests, such as inquiries into the well-being of individual officers. It also became possible to micromanage war from capitals: Napoleon III attempted to direct tactics and strategy from Versailles.[12] Having a delegate from supreme headquarters visit the commander in the field was bad enough, Moltke wrote when he was on the receiving end of the chain-of-command, but a "telegraph wire in the back" was even worse.[13] The permanent changes the technology brought were profound. The telegraph heralded the area of centralized control and command—the operational or theater level of war was born.[14] The telegraph, however, could only facilitate operational command; it was too static and not suited for tactical control.

In irregular conflicts, it should be stressed, these technologies almost without exception were used only by one side, by the state and by big armies. Bands of rebels couldn't even dream of maintaining a telegraph or telephone network for their own advantage. Instead, they turned it into a disadvantage for their enemies and attacked their telegraph posts and wires. Examples abound. In the district of the 10th German division, just outside Paris in 1870, a Dragoner-patrol caught a civilian trying to sabotage telegraph wires. The man, who was from the wealthy class of landowners, was instantly court-martialed. When he was asked for his motivation, he said, "in the most dignified posture," in the words of a German officer who was present, "because I am a Frenchman!" When the judge wanted to know what he had hoped to achieve, the man said he wanted to give an example to his compatriots so that they all would rise. He kept the noblest countenance when he faced the firing squad.[15]

At that time the telegraph network in North America was expanded as well. The first transcontinental line had been completed on 24 October 1861 between Omaha, Nebraska, and Sacramento, California. Soon Native Americans found out that the "talking wire" was used to pass on military information, and attacked it. When the Cheyenne were on a warpath in 1864 and 1865 in Nebraska and Wyoming, the government could not protect the lines, poles and station were burned, and wires ripped down. Station operators, often alone in remote areas with only a horse and a dog, were easy targets. Some could do nothing but helplessly cable about the impending deadly attacks on their shacks.[16] Quite ironically, the talking wire was not yet used for talking. Sound capability was added only later. In the same year, 1871, Moltke and Bismarck conquered Paris, Antonio Meucci filed a patent for the "sound telegraph" in the U.S. Patent Office. The first transmission in clear and comprehensible speech is recorded to have taken place five years later, on 10 March 1876, when Alexander Graham Bell shouted in his experimental device: "Mr Watson, come here, I want to see you."[17] Several inventors claim to have invented the telephone, but Bell was the first to patent "[t]he method of and apparatus for transmitting vocal or other sounds telegraphically."[18] He filed the specification on 14 February 1876.

The classical telegraph also played an important role in one of the classic counterinsurgencies at the end of the Gilded Age, the Philippine War from 1899 to 1902. By the end of July 1900, the U.S. government had laid 2,931 miles of land telegraph and telephone lines, and more than 200 miles of cable. Built primarily for use by the U.S. Army, the system was operated and maintained by the Signal Corps. Some 450 telegraph offices had been opened, sparsely staffed with just 25 officers and their men. Insurgents constantly attacked the lines. In the northern Luzon province, rebels cut wires, removed large sections, and felled the poles. In July alone, the lines were cut thirteen times and nearly 6,000 yards of wire was removed by the insurgents, reported Lieutenant Colonel James Allen, the Chief Signal Officer of the Division of the Philippines.[19] Attacking and removing telegraph wires was a common tactic among insurgents, from the Cuban War of Independence against the Spanish after 1895 to the Macedonian Insurrection against the Turks in 1903.

Even in the war that ended the Belle Époque in Europe, the First World War, the telegraph remained a target of irregular forces. T.E. Lawrence—as Lawrence of Arabia, one of the world's best-known insurgents—masterfully used the Ottomans' technological superiority against them. By 1914 the Turks made heavy use of telegraph links for the strategic command of their forces. Yet the system, not unlike some of today's most sophisticated command-and-control systems, had negative side effects. In Lawrence's prose:

> Young and I cut the telegraph, here an important network of trunk and local lines, indeed the Palestine army's main link with their homeland. It was pleasant to imagine Linan von Sandars' fresh curse, in Nazareth, as each severed wire tangled back from the clippers. We did them slowly, with ceremony, to draw out the indignation. The Turks' hopeless lack of initiative made their army a 'directed' one, so that by destroying the telegraphs we went far towards turning them into a leaderless mob.[20]

Garland, a British officer and specialist for explosives, taught Feisal's army to cut the Ottomans' lines, with his "own devices for mining trains and felling telegraphs and cutting metals." Lawrence himself occasionally climbed poles and cut cables—one time nearly falling down—then took the loose wire endings, tied them to camels, and rode on, ripping down the wire and dragging the poles behind them, until the weight got too heavy for the animals to pull.[21]

Yet the larger picture is more nuanced. Technology was at a problematic stage in the First World War. At the Western Front the telegraph often could not keep pace with fast maneuvers and moving forces. The technology's replacement by the telephone had begun in 1905, but was by no means completed in 1914.[22] Landlines were difficult to set up and even more difficult to maintain in mobile large-scale warfare. Radios, the most powerful communication tool for tactical command-and-control in subsequent years, were still at an early state of development and thus unreliable and cumbersome. In 1912 the Great German General Staff organized a corps exercise involving the new information technologies, telephones and radios and motorized cars. "When these inventions of the devil work, then what they achieve is more than amazing; when they do not work, then they achieve less than nothing," Erich von Falkenhayn, chief of the German general staff, concluded.[23] For the moment the old methods of communication had to be maintained as backup options. Yet a "modern Alexander," Alfred von Schlieffen wrote, should make full use of modern communication technology to command from distant headquarters, "telegraph, wireless, telephones, . . . automobiles and motorcycles."[24] As the war ground on through to 1919, more and more telegraph and telephone lines were installed, later even by American engineers in France. But the telegraph was not the future. The next big step in the evolution of information technology was only achieved with radio, the transmission of signals through electromagnetic waves. Already in 1893 Nikola Tesla pioneered wireless communications and demonstrated its feasibility. The technology was first called wireless telegraphy, and it was used to send Morse signals as text without the physically limiting copper wires. It was not capable of transmitting speech yet. One of the first long-distance Morse radio connections was established across the Norton Sound in Alaska, between Nome and St. Michel. In August 1904, the U.S. Army's Signal Corps started to operate a long-distance radio circuit, also to handle commercial business.[25] The U.S. Army's operation in the Philippines in 1908 was one of the first wartime tests of a new portable radio station, of the induction coil type (a predecessor technology to vacuum tubes), which could be carried as a wagon set and a pack set, mobile on three animals.[26]

The Canadian Reginald Fessenden was the first inventor to transmit speech by high-frequency radio signal. The first audio transmission succeeded on 23 December 1900 over a distance of about 1.6 kilometers. The First World War was the first major conflict in which telephony and wireless technology were combined into the "voice radio." The development was driven by the need for plane-to-plane communication in aerial dogfights, or for reconnaissance such as artillery spotting. Yet as late as 1917, British airplanes were still not technically able to send and receive voice. That problem was solved only when Ernst Alexanderson, an American radio inventor, devised the transceiver, a twin-valve radio telephony device that could both receive and send at the flick of a switch.[27] Nearly 10,000 radio sets had been produced for the Signal Corps and the Air Service, mostly airborne radiotelegraphs. In the war's later phases aircraft on both sides were outfitted with radio. The pilots used the new technology innovatively to report on enemy positions, or even to deceive the enemy through faked details that were intercepted by the enemy.[28] But the costs still outweighed the benefits, even quite literally: field radios had a huge need for energy and came with their own generator, bringing the set's weight to more than a ton that could be drawn only by horse wagon. Advanced sets that could be carried by men were rare.

Wireless technology was slow to catch on, and even during the course of a long war that witnessed the innovative use of many technologies, tactical radio remained in its awkward age. European armies remained insufficiently equipped with the new technology, and did not realize its potential yet.[29] Armies in particular were hardly enthusiastic about the unwieldy machines. The British Army Corps of Signals, for instance, had heavily invested in telephone and telegraph cables at the Western Front. The war's static battle conditions in France made it possible to lay a grid of wires back from British lines. As a result the struggle has been described as the "most wired-up war in history."[30] Allegedly British civilians, if they had the right connections in every sense of the word, were even able to ring relatives serving in the support trenches. Although the war saw radio brought to use in innovative ways, it ended before the technology could make a decisive difference for any one party.

Yet the combination of wireless technology and speech created an immensely powerful communication tool that would change the way armies operated in the field. These changes were already becoming apparent toward the end of the war. Static telegraph and telephone wires were able to establish communication only between fixed points, most likely between higher nonmobile headquarters on a strategic or operational command level. Radio, by contrast, was more flexible and transportable, and the use of the electromagnetic spectrum enabled multiple receivers, reflecting the organizational requirements of mobile small-unit warfare. Radio therefore was the optimal tactical communication instrument.

The technology's sender-receiver logic soon opened up new applications. Radio was an ideal instrument not only down on a tactical level, but also up on a political level: when receivers became widespread among the civilian populations as well as among troops—and only receivers, not transmitters—radio technology emerged as a mass-media phenomenon. The invention of radio eventually extended the government's persuasive power to the masses. In the Second World War radio, then as a channel to reach mass audiences through radio receivers, was employed as a propaganda tool to undermine the adversary's popular will as well as to rally public support at home. In the First World War, by contrast, it still had been the printed word that possessed an unrivaled power that it never had before and would never have thereafter. Growing literacy created a market, railway fast delivery, and the war a great demand and stories. The outbreak of the Great War and the high-flying nationalism it produced skyrocketed circulation numbers among newspapers across Europe.

WEAPON

In the twentieth century, insurgents and irregular fighters still saw their adversary's telecommunication facilities as an Achilles' heel, although attacking it would become progressively more difficult. Wooden telegraph posts were easy targets even for primitive fighters. That did not apply to the technology that succeeded the telegraph—energy emitted on the electromagnetic spectrum's radio-frequency range, the vehicle for the early wireless communication, could not be burned, felled, or torn down. The way insurgents took advantage of telecommunications forcibly began to change: they largely stopped attacking telecommunication installations, and began using the emerging mass media as a weapon.

Europe and America were mostly focused on big state-on-state war from 1914 to 1945. When colonial empires began to crumble after the Second World War, irregular movements had the chance to experiment with the new conditions of mass communication. The new technological possibilities, in terms of both propaganda and command-and-control, were attractive for insurgents, too. But it initially remained too resource intensive and costly for most resistance fighters to get their hand on the novel machines. There are, of course, exceptions: Irgun and Lehi, two militant Zionist groups during the 1930s and 1940s, operated radio stations to bolster their cause against the British authorities in Palestine. Nasser's "Sawt al-Arab," or Voice of the Arabs, became a popular outlet in the mid-1950s when inexpensive transistor radios spread to the illiterate poor even in more remote cities and villages across the Arabic world. By 1957, Cairo, with a stronger transmitter, started to tailor its messages to regional audiences and blared a constant stream of inflammatory anticolonialist propaganda into the Maghreb, fueling the insurgency in Algeria against the French.[31] In stark contrast to regular forces, irregulars did, by and large, not use radio tactically with great skill.[32] If radio was used, it was mostly used as a tool to communicate with friendly constituencies. Although less efficiently, radio was sometimes used by well-organized insurgent forces as a military command-and-control device, such as the Viet Minh and General Vo Nguyen Giap's use of radio to coordinate an impressively large force in the Battle of Dien Bien Phu.

But far more important than radio propaganda were images. The Crimean War and the American Civil War were the two first major conflicts documented by photographers. The British semiofficial photographer Roger Fenton and the American Mathew Brady, a pupil of Morse, are the two best-known pioneers. In the Civil War, photographers were literally "embedded" and assigned to specific military units or with particular headquarters; Brady, for instance, was with General Grant's headquarters and officially commissioned by President Abraham Lincoln to document the war; his presidential portraits have become icons. Yet photography was not of significant use for either military or naval operations in either war. Neither was photography significant for the reporting of the war in the press, as the technology to print pictures was invented and implemented only decades later, although photographs served as templates for lithographers and wood engravers. "Aeronauts" such as T. C. Lowe planned to use balloon-mounted cameras for reconnaissance purposes; yet it is unlikely that photography was actually used for military purposes in the Civil War.[33]

But Lowe's plans were prescient. Aerial reconnaissance soon became one of the most important military applications of photography. The first attempt to take pictures from balloons was allegedly made in the Austro-Italian War of 1859. But armies' use of photography evolved only after cameras could be mounted on airplanes—which seems to have happened for the first time about one hundred years ago, in 1909. On 24 April 1909 Wilbur Wright flew in Centocelle near

Rome with a photographer on board. During the next five years, inventors and technicians worked hard to bring a new technology with a high military potential up to operational standards. Their apparatuses were soon put to test in the First World War.

In the great European war, the public was much impressed by dog fights, combat between flying heroes, and bombardment from the air. But the airplane, it should be stressed, was chiefly used for reconnaissance, and thus "totally changed the nature of warfare," one contemporary expert pointed out. "It has almost eliminated the element of surprise."[34] In the war's early phases, the pilots, "the eye of the army,"[35] chiefly relied on what they could see and report for artillery fire control, not on the camera. Yet soon the idea to use the camera to supplement the eye was contemplated. Interpreting aerial photographs, like interpreting X-ray images, became a task for specialists, who would "read" the landscape. With the help of the camera it was possible to decipher previous enemy movements; locate trench formations, gun and mortar positions, "pill boxes," and listening posts. The new technology allowed one to assess the damage done, explore the possibilities of an attack, and to map unknown areas, particularly in colonies and overseas territory such as Palestine and Egypt, but also of Turkish positions. Toward the conclusion of the war, nearly all operations were planned with the help of photographs. Photographic airborne intelligence had revolutionized military intelligence, and supplemented reports of spies, interrogators, and intercepts. The undiscovered movement of major troop formations during the day was nearly impossible by 1917. In 1918 the German army alone, who started heating the cameras for more efficient performance in high altitude, was taking about 4,000 pictures a day, particularly on the Western Front. Aerial photography had become "a military activity of primary importance."[36] By the time of the Armistice, the camera was the "indispensable eye of a modern army."[37]

The First World War made war photography in the air more useful, but on the ground it became more violent, more graphic, and ultimately more problematic. Photography, in combination with vastly more destructive weapon systems, contributed to war's changing image; armed struggle was less and less seen as a noble calling but instead appeared as the brutal and bloody violence that it was. Yet, despite photography's being a ripe technology, it was not harnessed for operational military purposes, particularly not from the insurgent's point of view. That changed only when television technology came of age. Although the "theatrical use" of moving images long predated television, cinematography never unfolded the same political impact. The BBC operated the world's first regular, public, "high-definition" system from 1936 to 1939. During the Second World War, however, the commercial experiments were replaced by military ones. The allies and the axis powers experimented with airborne TV as a reconnaissance and bomb guiding tool.[38] During the war the U.S. Navy developed airborne television cameras that could transmit pictures from up to 200 miles. The system was used to guide pilotless aircraft, surface boats, aerial bombs, and assault drones.[39] Fifteen stations of public television went back to regular programs after the war, but in the entire United States there were only a few thousand receivers.[40] TV remained in its infancy during the War in Korea in the early 1950s, when sets were still too expensive for ordinary Americans and Europeans.

After the Second World War decolonization gained pace, and a number of irregular wars pitched professional armies against improvised popular resistance movements. In these expeditionary operations, often fought in lands distant from Europe and America, the public both in theater but more so at home increasingly became an operational variable. Already in the Malayan Emergency after 1948, public opinion gained importance in the war theater, although telecommunication was mostly used by the British authorities while the communists relied on posters and leaflets.[41] A similar dynamic can be observed in the French war in Algeria after 1954.[42]

Among the first and most dramatic examples of this new trend is the Tet Offensive in Vietnam in January and February 1968.[43] William Westmoreland had declared in a speech at the National Press Club in November 1967 that the enemy could no longer conduct major operations near South Vietnam's cities. "[Success] lies within our grasp," he had predicted somewhat optimistically.[44] Less than three months later the Vietcong, supported by the North Vietnamese Army, attacked with an estimated strength of 67,000 troops. For a brief but chaotic moment the onslaught turned Saigon into a war zone, and a small group of enemy troops even penetrated the U.S. embassy in Saigon. Although approximately 14,000 South Vietnamese and 4,000 American soldiers were killed, the attack was a massive defeat for the North. After a few weeks the North's units were driven out of every city they attacked, and their military infrastructure and equipment was destroyed. The attackers suffered horrendous human losses, probably between 45,000 and 84,000 men.

But the political outcome contradicted the military one. On the morning of 1 February 1968, in Fort Leavenworth, a young officer named Colin Powell, who later would become the chairman of the Joint Chiefs of Staff, came out of his bedroom, put on the coffeepot, turned on the TV news, and was shocked—as were many of his compatriots. The screen showed U.S. marines as they were fighting in the American embassy in Saigon, and Vietnamese forces battling in front of the presidential palace in the heart of the ally's capital. The attack on the embassy received intense TV coverage, and it was probably the first battle in Vietnam that made sense to many Americans. Eventually they could see the adversary. "The images beamed into American living rooms of a once faceless enemy suddenly popping up in the middle of South Vietnam's capital had a profound effect on public opinion," Powell remarked later, and he added, with respect to the consequences of the newscasts: "Tet marked a turning point, raising doubts in the minds of moderate Americans, not just hippies and campus radicals, about the worth of this conflict, and the antiwar movement intensified."[45] Probably more than anyone else Walter Cronkite spoke for moderate, ordinary Americans. He was host of *CBS Evening News*, the first consistently popular half-hour news show; President John F. Kennedy himself had inaugurated the first edition. Cronkite was equally shocked by the events in Vietnam of that early February. The anchorman remembers reading the news agency tapes in the newsroom in New York after the reports were coming in: "What the hell is going on? I thought we were winning the war?"[46] Cronkite, a veteran correspondent of the Second World War, decided to travel to Vietnam to inspect the situation. He toured the country and met with senior officers, even with Creighton Abrams, Westmoreland's successor, whom he knew as a colonel from the Battle of the Bulge. He was still shocked by what he saw in Vietnam and became convinced that the war was lost. When Cronkite returned from the trip, he commented in heavy and memorable words on Tet in a CBS News Special, *Report from Vietnam by Walter Cronkite*: "The only national way out then will be to negotiate, not as victors, but as an honorable people who lived up to their pledge to defend democracy, and did the best they could."[47] This was Walter Cronkite calling to accept defeat in Vietnam. After his remarks, the impact of which cannot be underestimated, President Lyndon B. Johnson reportedly concluded, "If I've lost Cronkite, I've lost Middle America."[48] A few weeks later the incumbent announced that he would not run for the presidency a second time.

The Tet offensive was the idea of General Nguyen Chi Thanh. He realized that the U.S. troops were fighting in an alien environment, and that Westmoreland was overconfident and "arrogant."[49] The North Vietnamese were also overconfident when they launched the Tet offensive; they failed to achieve many military objectives and suffered heavy losses. But they succeeded in one critical point: "in Saigon we planned to create a 'big bang' by occupying the U.S. Embassy," Bui Tin, a North Vietnamese colonel, wrote in his memoirs. "Tet was designed to influence American public opinion."[50]

A second example is the escalation of the conflict in Northern Ireland shortly thereafter. It produced equally iconic events and illustrates the explosive potential of mass communication when military operations are conducted among the people. Operation Banner, as it is known in the Army, was the longest and largest British campaign since the Second World War. In 1972 approximately 28,000 troops had been sent to Northern Ireland, more than twice the British peak strength of Afghanistan and Iraq in 2007 combined.[51] In total, more than 250,000 members of the Regular Army served in Ulster during the campaign; over 600 were killed, 102 in 1972 alone. Although the word "war" was rarely used during the campaign, more than 10,000 terrorist suspects were arrested, and more than 3,100 people perished. The mass media played an important role in that conflict. The level of violence began to rise at the end of the 1960s when an Orange Order March on 5 October 1968 escalated into large-scale riots in Londonderry. The incident became the first fully televised event of this kind in the United Kingdom. The cameras caught the Royal Ulster Constabulary using excessive force, thereby paving the way for an escalation of the conflict. "The Troubles," as the violent conflict between the two groups became known, erupted in the summer of 1969 during a march in Londonderry when the first deaths were caused, at a time when the province had 1.8 million inhabitants.

The British army soon introduced harsh interrogation techniques that were developed in colonial theaters during the 1950s and 1960s. Operation Demetrius, as the large-scale internment policy became known, produced some tactical benefits. But "the information operations opportunity handed to the republican movement was enormous," a study for the Chief of the General Staff noted in 2006. And the lesson of Demetrius was clear: the internment of large numbers of suspects, and their harsh treatment, had "a major impact on popular opinion across Ireland, in Europe and the US," the lessons-learned review stated "it was a major mistake."[52] The insurgents, the British authorities slowly understood, were rooted in Northern Ireland's local culture and were far better connected to the ordinary population than the counterinsurgents. The IRA just as easily took advantage of the violent incidents, most prominently a fateful January 1972 Sunday in Londonderry when thirteen civil rights protesters were fatally shot by British forces, famously known as "Bloody Sunday." "The events of Bloody Sunday were immediately exploited by a Republican information operation," the Army reported.[53]

A third example shows how quickly the media may break the will of a physically superior opponent, if political resolve is absent. On 3 October 1993, in the afternoon, a force of 160 U.S. troops, nineteen aircraft, and twelve vehicles set out from their base close to Mogadishu airport to "snatch and grab" leading figures of Mohamed Aideed's Habr Gidr clan and possibly the strongman himself. Their target was the Olympic Hotel in downtown Mogadishu. When the Americans had stormed the hotel and captured several enemy fighters, the situation quickly got out of hand. The task force encountered small arms fire, and two Black Hawk helicopters were downed. The operation escalated into a pitched battle in a typical developing world urban environment: narrow streets, civilians intermingling with enemy combatants armed with AK47 and RPGs. Delta Force, Air Force combat search and rescue assets, Navy Seals, and Army Rangers experienced more than 50 percent casualties in eighteen hours fighting against Somali paramilitaries without formal training. When the battle was over, eighteen American soldiers were killed, eighty-four wounded, and one—Chief Warrant Officer Michael Durant, the pilot of one of the downed Black Hawk helicopters—was captured. Aideed's troops celebrated their victory by desecrating the naked body of a dead U.S. Ranger and dragging it through the dirty streets of Mogadishu. Initial hearsay reports had it that an angry mob was showing body parts as "trophies," but these were dismissed by the Pentagon. After images of the events in Mogadishu's narrow streets emerged in the news, the story spun equally out of control on Washington's Pennsylvania Avenue. Paul Watson, a print reporter from the *Toronto Star*, photographed the Ranger's abuse as he happened to be on the scene with his 35-mm pocket camera. The reporter later won a Pulitzer Prize for his picture.

What followed was intentioned. Although the still photos of the battle were taken by an independent Western journalist, the moving images shown on CNN came from a questionable source. The Somali driver and stringer Mohamoud Hassan—allegedly associated with Aideed and a former freelancer for

Reuters[54]—recorded the video of the soldier's corpse being dragged and kicked through the dirt as well as footage of Durant's interrogation. Hassan had recorded the video early on 4 October and transmitted the Hi-8 cartridge through Nairobi to London, from where CNN relayed the footage electronically to Atlanta.[55] Soon the grisly pictures of the dead Ranger's humiliation and the frightened face of the interrogated Durant were broadcast across the United States and the rest of the world. Given that Hassan was able to obtain the video of Durant's interrogation, where presumably no independent local journalist was present, the assumption seems valid that the warlord had an interest in getting the images out. It is thus a plausible and probable assumption that Aideed and his colonels had an information operations calculus in mind: they intended to penetrate their adversary's decision loop and break America's will. The images were highly successful.

Images of the naked corpse of a U.S. soldier and the battered face and fright-ened voice of another captured soldier sent shockwaves through the American body politic: "The people who are dragging American bodies don't look very hungry to the people of Texas," commented Republican Senator Phil Gramm, reacting to thousands of telephone calls to Capitol Hill demanding the with-drawal of U.S. forces.[56] John McCain, an Arizona Republican on the Armed Services Committee, demanded that "Clinton's got to bring them home."[57] Not only did Congress put pressure on the President to consider a pullout from Somalia; the images had their own direct effect in the White House. National Security Advisor Anthony Lake commented later on the TV footage of the Battle of Mogadishu. The "pictures helped make us recognize that the military situation in Mogadishu had deteriorated in a way that we had not frankly rec-ognized," the President's advisor confessed.[58] Bill Clinton eventually decided to withdraw.[59] The incident undermined the credibility of American military might in the eyes of its opponents for years to come: if confronted with casual-ties, they concluded, the Americans would cut and run "with their tail between their legs."[60] Irregular fighters facing the world's most powerful military had come a long way indeed since its predecessors had burned telegraph poles a cen-tury or so earlier.

WEB 1.0

Text, sound, and still and moving images are genuinely different formats of information, illustrated by such distinct and products as books, music, photo, and film. The computer, and by extension the Internet, married these different for-mats. Digitalization and constantly increasing computing power allowed cram-ming all previous formats into the same device. What previously was done by separate apparatuses has migrated onto the same platform: personal computers, first desktop, then laptop, and finally handheld; first stand-alone, then as local area networks, and eventually as cloud-computing. The emergence of the Internet is arguably the most significant technological development in communication in human history. The Web's evolution can be structured into two main phases.

The first discussion of social interactions that could be enabled through the personal computer was initiated in 1962 by J. C. R. Licklider, at the time a scientist at MIT. Licklider's vision was a "symbiotic man-computer partnership."[61] Military officers were the first who would have an interest in such a relationship, he argued. And indeed, at the time Secretary of Defense Robert McNamara was keen to use data analysis to master an escalating jungle war in Vietnam. A psychologist by education, Licklider became the first head of the Advanced Research Projects Agency's (ARPA) computer research program in October 1962. ARPA had been created by the U.S. Department of Defense only four years before as a reaction to the Sputnik shock. Its mission was to keep America's military technologically ahead of its time, and ahead of its adversaries. Only a decade later, in 1972, the agency would add a "D" to its name, for defense, thus becoming DARPA. Other researchers joined the agency's computer team, and in 1967 efforts got off the ground to create ARPANET, the precursor of the Internet. The University of California in Los Angeles was chosen to be the first node on the ARPANET. By 1969—Nixon was now speaking of "Vietnamization"—an initial four computers were connected. In October 1972 Robert Kahn, an Internet pioneer also working at ARPA, presented the new network to the public at the International Computer Communication Conference (ICCC). Earlier that year, Ray Tomlinson had written the first email software, to meet the developers' need for better coordination.

"The Internet as we now know it embodies a key underlying technical idea, namely that of open architecture networking," wrote some of the Internet's founders in a joint article.[62] In such an architecture, individual networks can be designed and set up separately, each with its own user interface. Kahn realized that a new version of the computer protocol was needed, one that would meet the demands of an open network. That protocol would eventually, after Kahn had brought Stanford University's Vint Cerf on board, be named the Transmission Control Protocol/Internet Protocol (TCP/IP). It embodied a pragmatic spirit: First, communication had to work on a best-effort basis; if one packet of information didn't make it to its destination, the source would retransmit it. Second, technically simple "black boxes"—today's routers or gateways—would be used to connect the networks. Third, there would be no global control of the Web.

ARPANET, a packet-switching rather than a circuit-switching system grew into a transcontinental, high-speed computer network that linked hundreds of research institutions, laboratories, and universities with the U.S. defense establishment. From here, things were developing fast: the first e-mail was sent in 1971, file transfer was added in 1973, and Local Area Networks, or LANs, appeared in the late 1970s. By 1983, in the year Reagan invaded Grenada, after ARPA had handed over the project to the Department of Defense and adopted a new protocol, TCI/IP, the military components, MILNET, were severed from the remaining civilian part with 68 nodes, separating operational requirements from research and development. At that time computer communication was well established and e-mail was common among the pioneers. The U.S. National Science Foundation created a university network backbone. The network, still in its infancy, was used for commerce and educational purposes in the 1980s, when the British scientist Tim Berners-Lee had begun creating the html language, the early building block of the World Wide Web. He published a proposal for the World Wide Web in late 1990, suggesting a browser-based system. On 6 August 1991, Berner-Lee, based at the Swiss research institute CERN, sent a message to the *alt.hypertext* newsgroup, explaining the WorldWideWeb project:

> The project started with the philosophy that much academic information should be freely available to anyone. It aims to allow information sharing within internationally dispersed teams, and the dissemination of information by support groups.[63]

In his message he also asked the members of the group to "try it" and provided the link to the world's first Web page.[64] A perhaps more significant turning point in the history of the Internet came on 22 April 1993 when the Mosaic web browser was introduced, a graphical browser developed by a team at the University of Illinois's National Center for Supercomputing Applications. The browser's easy-to-use graphic interface—an early version of what is the standard today—turned the HyperText Transfer Protocol, or http, into the most widely used Internet protocol. One week later CERN put its Web-enabling software officially on the public domain, explicitly relinquishing any intellectual property rights to the code. From there several key developments followed in short succession: on 22 April 1993 the world's first popular Web browser, Mosaic 1.0, was released at the National Center for Supercomputing Applications (NCSA) at the University of Illinois. At first there were only twelve users, said Marc Andreessen, who co-developed the browser, "and I knew them all twelve."[65] At the time—in a year when the United States suffered a highly visible blunder in Somalia in the Battle of Mogadishu—there were only about fifty Internet pages, each mostly a single site file. But more and more research institutes were equipping their databases and files with Internet access. Soon the Netscape Navigator was developed, the first browser with a graphic interface. The software was released on 13 October 1994, free for everybody to test and use. Netscape's entrepreneurs were convinced that "this thing will just grow and grow and grow."[66] They were right. The vision of the Internet pioneers of a free information exchange and collaboration was tantalizing, not only for geeks and researchers. The Pentagon launched its Web site, www.defenselink.mil, in the same month. Netscape went public on 9 August 1995, and its stocks soared on the first day. By 1996 the word "Internet" entered daily usage in the United States and ordinary people began to have "e-mail" addresses. Increasingly venture capitalists and entrepreneurs sensed the revolutionary potential. Foreshadowing a future trend, some irregular militants had been among the earliest adopters: by the end of August 1996, only days after its publication in a London newspaper, Osama bin Laden's first *fatwa* against the United States was available online.

Soon one of the most remarkable developments in the Internet's history unfolded: the Dot-com bubble. From 1995 to approximately 2001, the global stock markets heavily invested in the Web and all related industries. During these euphoric and hopeful years, communication providers were convinced that the celebrated New Economy would require a sturdy infrastructure of broadband access with demand doubling every three months. So they massively invested in new hardware: copper wires were already being replaced by the more efficient and faster fiber-optic cables in the 1970s, and now a virtual fiber-optic boom ensued. The abundance of venture capital and the widespread excitement made it possible for companies such as Global Crossing to invest gigantic sums in fiber infrastructure. The telecom companies bankrolled about $1 trillion in "wiring the world."[67]

Soon after the turn of the millennium the euphoria came to an abrupt end. On 10 March 2000 the NASDAQ Composite technology index peaked at 5,132.52 points, more than doubling its value in less than a year. That Friday, in hindsight, marks the date of the Dot-com bubble burst, with the NASDAQ Composite giving way more than 9 percent in three days. In the following two years a huge number of companies went bust, including Global Crossing. But investment in hardware was crucially different from investment in software: nobody would "dig up" the cables and eliminate overcapacity. To the contrary, improved switching technology even kept increasing the cables' data transfer capability. The unused cable capacity became known as "dark" fiber, and analysts predicted that in the coming decades only a small section of the cables will be "lit." After the stock market bubble had burst, and an estimated sum of $5 trillion was burned, the developed world entered a mild yet protracted recession during the early 2000s.[68]

Yet the investments' overall effects were largely positive. For consumer and small businesses, "[t]he broad overinvestment in fiber cable is a gift that keeps on giving," Thomas Friedman wrote.[69] The infrastructure of telecommunication backbones around the world led to a downward spiral in prices for Internet and telephony services. Global participation became not only affordable, but cheap. In 2009 nearly 1.5 billion people worldwide had Internet access; more than one-third of all users were in Asia, while Africa and the Middle East had the fastest growth rates.[70] In North America around 73 percent of all households had Internet access; in the European Union the penetration ranged from 30 to 88 percent.

The Dot-com bubble commoditized telecommunication. Previously only states and large companies were able to build optical telegraph chains, to shoulder the investments of laying copper wires, to create and maintain telephone networks, or to operate radio transmitters. Particularly under the adverse conditions of warfare, the benefits of modern communication were confined to highly specialized and resourced regular armies—insurgents had almost no possibility to benefit operationally from telecommunications. Only large media organizations had the means and the resources to run radio or television stations, and to publish newspapers and magazines. The state control of communication in times of war began to erode with the advent of modern journalism that made use of the telegraph, photographs, radio, the TV. Yet it collapsed nearly completely when several trends coincided: a fall in prices for computing, improved digital technology, over-capacity in bandwidth, and the expansion of Internet penetration and mobile phones in rich countries, emerging markets, and even in poor regions. Still the Internet, up until 2001, like the old media, remained a platform for mass mono-logue, albeit with a growing number of corporate senders and individual receivers. When the demand for participation and interactivity in mass communication began to soar, the companies who survived the stock markets' wrath began to churn out the software that enabled a veritable reincarnation of the Web.

WEB 2.0—PLATFORM

Peter Drucker, a well-known management writer, made an instructive com-parison in a 1999 article in *The Atlantic*: "The steam engine was to the Industrial Revolution what the computer has been to the Information Revolution—its trig-ger."[71] At the time Drucker wrote these lines, the computer was just starting to trigger a massive cultural and social change, not merely a technological one: the new media. This cultural change continues to affect human collaboration in all fields: business, the arts, leisure, travel, politics—and warfare. A number of simul-taneous changes associated with the digitalization of various products and serv-ices are usually lumped together under the term new media: widespread personal computers, online music distribution, MP3 players, DVDs, digital TV, mobile phones, PDAs, blogs, video-sharing, photo-sharing, social networking, online publications of all sorts, and all innovative Web-based communication projects and businesses. Yet the talk of the new media as a catchall phrase might distract from its genuinely new characteristics.

Time magazine's Person of the Year 2007 was "you," the individual. In nearly all countries Web sites that boast so-called "user-generated content" had climbed to the very top of the traffic ranking lists.[72] Such peer-to-peer technologies empower activist individuals, a trend known as Web 2.0. The term, coined by the entrepre-neur Tim O'Reilly,[73] describes a second-generation Internet where contributions of private individuals and self-organized communities compete with those of companies and governments: YouTube, a video sharing site; MySpace or Face-book, two social networking sites; Wikipedia, a collaborative encyclopedia; eBay, a person-to-person auction site; and countless so-called forums that allow indi-viduals to publish their comments and distribute text, image, or video files. The new Web connects people directly and enables dialogue. The contrast to the old media could hardly be sharper, where news companies (and in some countries the state) were the masters over a public monologue. New media, as Wikipedia put it rather elegantly, is "the marriage of mediated communication technologies with digital computers."[74] The former used to be public, the latter private.

The expression new media is apt for three reasons. First, the phenomenon is genuinely new: mass media and social interaction were merged for the first time in history. Second, the term "media" (as opposed to just Internet) hints at a new relationship between its two meanings: on the one hand the plural of *medium*, which refers to a vehicle or channel that conveys information in any single communicative act, and on the other hand a public and professional journalistic outlet. It is one key characteristic of the new media that both dimensions are merged and blurred. Third, and most significant, the cost of physical capital, from the invention of the optical telegraph in 1794 to the launch of satellites, was the central organizing feature of information and cultural production. The immense infrastructure costs made production capital-intensive, to the benefit of large entities. That changed in the early twenty-first century: the declining price of computation and connectivity inverted the capital structure of communication and cultural production and massively increased the number of participants. The changes triggered a cascade of effects that were not limited to peaceful human interaction, but affected extremism, irregular war, and terrorism in a way that is only beginning to be registered by the world's most advanced military forces. Particularly for security agencies it is absolutely essential to understand that the resulting changes in modern irregular warfare are deeply embedded into—and resulting from—much broader sociotechnological changes of our time.

One key aspect is that Web 2.0 gave rise to alternative production models that applied in a range of areas—including militancy and the production of violence, as we will show later. These novel dynamics are not market-based, not firm-based, and not governmental, but based on nonproprietary commons, a model that has become known as peer-production. Yochai Benkler, who spelled out the idea in 2002, identified the conditions that can give rise to peer-production:

> Where physical capital costs for fixation and communication are low and widely distributed, and where existing information is itself a public good, the primary remaining scarce resource is human creativity. And it is under these conditions that the relative advantages of peer production emerge to much greater glory than possible before.[75]

Academia and scientific research are examples of a mix of proprietary production logic and nonproprietary peer-production; examples from software development are more emblematic, with Linux being probably the best known.[76] Wikipedia is an example of pure commons-based cultural or knowledge production. A critical mass of participation in such projects cannot be explained by an immediate monetary incentive, as in market-based production, or by direct command, as in firm-based production. Other sociopsychological rewards come into play, such as professional reputation, a belief in social progress, the ideal of education, political and spiritual motivations, and even addiction.

Another concept, the long tail, describes the niche strategy of many Web-based businesses, such as Amazon.com, Audible, the iTunes Store, Google, eBay, or Netflix. Low distribution costs and inventory expenses allow such businesses to make a profit from selling a small number of specific and slow-selling items to a large number of customers. The demographic of buyers that purchase the hard-to-find and (previously) hard-to-sell items is called the "Long Tail."[77] The requirements are a large population of customers (or, in irregular war, potential supporters and activists), easy product search, and cost-effective delivery. The principle of the long and flat end of the distribution curve essentially harnesses Web-enabled economies of scale.

As a result of these novel dynamics, the barriers of entry for new businesses were lowered. The long-tail logic makes it easier for a highly specialized company to be viable as a business and enter a market, even without a locally concentrated customer base. The range of products that are either sold or downloaded from the Web is growing, and with more customers entering online markets, more and more industries are affected by this trend. Even the film industry benefits: "If there's 1m people around the world who are interested in ice-fishing," said Jeremy Zimmer, cofounder of a Hollywood-based production firm, "we can make a movie for them."[78] Icefishing is a random example, but it shows the Web-driven increase in opportunities. The Web opens up niches that previously did not exist for producers and retailers, not even in large urban conglomerates and population centers. This logic can, of course, be expanded to the nonproprietary world: the barrier for entry for new noncommercial movements is lowered too, be it for leisure, politics, or violent conflict.

Driven by the aforementioned technological trends and the ensuing production principles, innovation has been decentralized. If a larger number of people tackle the same problem independently of each other, it is likely that they will come up with a larger number of possible solutions to choose from. User innovation communities existed long before computers, in communities within professions or certain sports, for instance.[79] The management literature has a massive body of literature on "communities-of-practice," a name for small groups of motivated individuals who share a passion for their job and a willingness to invest resources and take risk for the good cause. Such like-minded communities are self-emerging rather than created in a top-down manner. Their members perceive themselves in like situations, share a common mindset, foster a cooperative spirit; they most often share similar practical experiences, and they encourage out-of-the-box thinking. The communities are informal rather than formal, cut across departmental or unit boundaries, and focus on the output. The problem exposure enables them to recognize changes in their immediate environment well before senior leaders in hierarchical structures can. Communities-of-practice, moreover, can span organizational boundaries and even include outside actors, and are in a better position to ignore established patterns, precepts, and traditional expectations.

The changes under way in the new media enhance these effects not merely because the number of participants is vastly increased. Several cultural effects come into play as well.

The new media blur the public and the private domain. The interactive Web has begun to distort the distinction in public and private information, and therefore the distinction between mass media and personal conversations.

Some blogs and social-networking sites with their message boards (Facebook's "wall," for instance) and semipublic conversations inside social groups and in member-only Web forums are the most visible expression of an ongoing redefinition of what is considered private and what is public.

A widespread culture of pseudonymity has evolved. Using no name or a nickname is accepted practice on the Web, and not frowned upon. In any brick-and-mortar public forum such as a Q&A session, in roundtable discussions, or in business meetings, refusing to provide a name, or using an obvious pseudonym, would be considered awkward. Only specific settings, such as Alcoholics Anonymous, encourage anonymity. Yet online the social conventions are different: issue-specific discussion boards (for instance, on how to handle a specific software), listservs, networking sites, dating sites, auction sites, blogs, even the mainstream media and newspapers tolerate and encourage online conversation where most participants use pseudonyms.

Trust can be established online. Ordinary people all over the world use anonymous online forums to enter into transactions with other private individuals: for auctions, sales of used cars, real estate rentals, and furniture trade. Sports, group activities, and even online dating have become ubiquitous mainstream activities. In most but not all of these cases individuals will reveal their real identity at some point during the transaction or activity. All of these interactions require some level of trust before that happens.

The aforementioned dynamics apply unevenly in today's societies. This points to a digital divide that works for the benefit of newcomers. The divide is not between the rich world with a high Internet penetration and poor countries with low penetration. At first glance this divide appears to be a *generational divide*—particularly so for hierarchical and bureaucratic organizations such as governments and armies, whose senior decision makers have risen slowly through the ranks to the top. Many a senior official or general discovered email, chat, text messaging, and podcasting for the first time when younger colleagues or their own children showed it to them. They continue to read newspapers in hard copy as their main source of information. These senior officials can be seen as "digital immigrants"; when they speak about the Web, they have an accent.[80] On the other side are the members of the so-called Generation Y, sometimes also called the "Net Generation," born after the mid-1970s: most of today's majors, captains, and lieutenants, the younger NCOs and the enlisted ranks are "digital natives." For most of them it is normal to have MySpace profiles, watch YouTube, chat, subscribe to podcasts and feeds, blog, write wikis, skype, google, use IM, and share stories, images, and videos online—and, of course, to text. At second glance, however, the picture is different: the new media have only temporarily opened a generational gap; today's captains will be tomorrow's generals. The more significant divide with respect to the use of violence in the new information environment is an *organizational divide*.

The interactive Web's organizational principles resemble and inadvertently mimic the organizational principles of some modern insurgent movements: initiative, anonymity, self-recruitment, varying levels of participations, self-motivated participants, often self-funded, fueled by idealism, not by orders. We argue, therefore that Web 2.0—understood in both a metaphorical and a cultural sense, not in a technological one—initially benefits insurgents more than counterinsurgents. To highlight this asymmetry, the following chapter, War 1.0, will look at the conventional armies and the modern media, and then zoom into detail in three case studies. Chapter 6, War 2.0, and the subsequent case studies will repeat the exercise for irregulars.

War 1.0

Modern armies, throughout their history, have embraced modern technology to enhance their combat power. The previous chapter showed that this is particularly true of telecommunication technology. Technology, therefore, had—and continues to have—a profound influence on modern warfare. This chapter will look in more detail at War 1.0 and thus prepare the ground for the following three case studies. Armed forces that prepare for War 1.0 see themselves as standalone armies focusing on military transformation, not political transformation; they are enemy-centric, not population-centric; they emphasize instead clandestine psychological operations (PSYOPs) and hidden information operations (IO), not the public side of strategic communication; they highlight military capabilities, not political systems; they look at hard measures of effectiveness and rational interests, not at subtle cultural perceptions; they take a short historical view, not a long one. These dichotomies are the result of a division of labor between military affairs and political affairs. That division of labor is the hallmark of War 1.0.

The division of labor is tied to information technology, particularly in the context of today's irregular wars. The connection becomes visible when briefly viewed against its historic context. Since the invention of optical telegraphy during the revolutionary period in France, communication technologies have created both new benefits and new costs for military organizations. For the past 200 years, only two types of actors had the means to systematically use telecommunications—that is, access to the technological infrastructure—during armed conflict: the government (including the armed forces) and large media organizations.[1] But the two sides have diametrically opposed interests during times of war: officers, with their minds firmly focused on the enemy, prefer secrecy; journalists, with the news-consuming home audience on their mind, prefer publicity. A conflict between the media and the military, therefore, became a permanent side effect of modern warfare.[2] Throughout the history of industrial state-on-state wars—from the Crimean War, the American Civil War, the wars of German Unification, the two World Wars, the Korean War, to the Persian Gulf War—that applied to both sides of the conflict. The adversary's press was studied scrupulously as an important source of intelligence, particularly if the adversary was a democratic political entity with a thriving public debate.[3] New communication technology in the hands of one's own press, therefore, was generally seen as a problem. Novel information technologies in the hand of one's own army, navy, or air force, by contrast, were seen as a source of strength as it improved command-and-control and the agility of the force. In conventional, "symmetric" confrontations, communication technology became an additional element of competition between the opposing armies or alliances.

The coincidence of two simultaneous trends has opened the view on a limitation of conventional armies: the simultaneous rise of modern telecommunication technology and the rise of insurgencies have ended the military's and the media's shared monopoly of information, and elevated the public domain's importance at war. The insurgent's interest, in an unexpected way, began to coincide with the prerogatives of the media, first old then new. Publicity and openness are in the interest of irregular violent movements, both strategically and, as we shall see in later chapters, doctrinally and operationally. As a consequence publicity, not secrecy, is also in the interest of the counterinsurgent. If taken seriously, this argument would amount to a veritable cultural revolution for big regular armies. In unconventional operations and counterinsurgency (COIN), the goal is to win the locals' hearts and minds, to gain trust and legitimacy, to advertise gains and progress in reconstruction, and to maintain support at the home front. In COIN, openness and public relations are both more difficult and more important than in conventional war.

The argument is organized in four steps: first we will outline how the world's most modern armed forces embraced "transformation" and the use of new information technologies to become more efficient and more lethal. Second, the same principle of professional specialization, a division of labor, that drove the evolution of modern armies also shaped their relationship vis-à-vis the mass media and the public; the result was that the internal discipline of public affairs moved to the bottom of the priority list of modern war. Third, insurgencies deny that division of labor and consequently make it more difficult for the counterinsurgent, specialized on the use of military force, to understand the political causes and shape the perceptions of the local population. Fourth, the means for the counterinsurgent are especially limited in expeditionary campaigns in foreign countries, such as in Afghanistan and Iraq, where time, the use of force, and local knowledge are constrained.

TRANSFORMATION

Just as French rulers had embraced the optical telegraph in 1794 to communicate internally faster and more efficiently to transmit orders and information, the U.S. military was quick to use the computer two hundred years later for the same purpose. The Pentagon and America's defense intellectuals initially focused their attention on a so-called Revolution in Military Affairs, what eventually became known as "Transformation." Its essence was speed and precision. The same developments that mesmerized entrepreneurs in the private sector at the end of the twentieth century showed their seductive effect on officers, soldiers, sailors, airmen, and marines in the public sector. The Dot-com bubble epitomized the investors' inability to accurately understand and interpret the long-term economic significance of the Web's sociotechnological changes; many heralded the advent of a "new economy" that would redefine basic economic laws. The U.S. defense establishment, correspondingly, invested heavily in network-centric warfare and heralded a "new way of war" that equally hoped to redefine the laws of armed conflict. The eternal uncertainty and friction that had made warfare so unpredictable for centuries, Clausewitz's fog of war, could eventually be lifted. "Never in history—not in Napoleon's time, and not in the Balkans today—has a military commander been granted an omniscient view of the battlefield in real time, by day and night, and in all weather conditions," wrote Admiral Bill Owens, one of the U.S. Navy's enthusiasts.[4] "Today's technology promises to make that possible," Owen wrote, only one year before the United States invaded Afghanistan. The "new revolution," the admiral enthused, "challenged the hoary dictums about the fog and friction of war, and all the tactics, operational concepts, and doctrine pertaining to them."[5]

This revolution in military thinking tantalizingly started in the skies above Iraq in 1991 and received a sobering reality check in Baghdad's urban sprawl beginning in late 2003.[6] The intermediary years deserve a quick examination. The U.S. victory against Saddam Hussein in the Persian Gulf War was stunning. President George H. W. Bush summed up the prevailing excitement in Western military circles when he said that the "specter of Vietnam has been buried forever in the desert sands of the Arabian peninsula."[7] The Cold War had just ended, and the coalition's battlefield successes in Iraq, achieved with the help of precision-guided munitions, superior satellite communications, and the sophisticated use of air power, highlighted the breathtaking potential of modernized forces at the dawn of the twenty-first century. The driving force of this development was the computer and modern information technology. "Information" became a nearly irresistible prefix and buzzword, with the effect that its meaning has been blurred: the debate revolved around information war, information effects, and information superiority. The U.S. armed forces felt it increasingly necessary to come up with a separate doctrine on "information operations." One of the earliest publicly accessible military documents on information operations was Pamphlet 525–69, published by the U.S. Training and Doctrine Command, TRADOC. The document's title, "Concept for Information Operations," illustrated the novelty of the ideas it contained. It vowed to create an "information age army," capable of striking fast and precisely. Speed and precision were the dominant motives early on in "info ops," reflecting its roots in command-and-control warfare, dashingly abbreviated as C2. General William W. Hartzog, then the TRADOC commander and a Vietnam veteran, was adamant that the new "information age paradigm" he observed would change the nature of war. "Only the best soldiers, leaders, staffs, and organizations, who understand the importance of speed and precision in information processing and applications, will be able to be fully successful in this kind of environment," Hartzog wrote in the foreword to the study published on 1 August 1995. The pamphlet foreshadowed many of the arguments that would dominate the strategic and doctrinal thinking for nearly a decade. Blending romanticism with futurism, the new force was called "Force 21" in Roman numbers:

> This shared situational awareness, coupled with the ability to conduct continuous operations, will allow Force XXI armies to observe, decide, and act faster, more correctly, and more precisely than their enemies. All dimensions of battlespace (land, sea, air, and space) and all battlefield operating systems (command and control, maneuver, fire support, etc.) will be linked digitally in future Information Age armies. Today's Army has asymmetrical capabilities.[8]

Asymmetry was here considered to be a competitive advantage, as no country and hence no army could possibly compete with America's lead in the information revolution. "By using and protecting the use of information infrastructures (people, electromagnetic spectrum, computers) while influencing or denying a potential adversary's use, the Army will gain an unprecedented advantage on the battlefield and in OOTW." That abbreviation stood for "operations other than war," a term that was fashionable in the mid-1990s to describe what is called small wars or counterinsurgency today. In the mid-1990s it was nearly inconceivable that the United States, the country that was home to Microsoft and IBM, could ever lose its dominance in the digital battlespace. Yet the document already referred to and distinguished two fundamentally different elements, the relationship of which would be discussed in much detail in the years to come: computers and people, or automated and human systems, as information operations doctrine would put it later.

Transformation had two closely intertwined main components, one technical and one cultural: information technology and jointness, with the former enabling the latter. Admiral Owens, then vice chairman of the Joint Chiefs of Staff, wrote about a "system-of-systems," a grid of interconnected sensors located in satellites hovering in space—in unmanned aerial vehicles in the sky—ship-borne radar at sea, and land-based acoustic sensors. The admiral's vision of a "digitized battlefield" was to amass and evaluate huge quantities of information about any given battle arena, with sensor-to-weapon connectivity enabling fast and precise strikes. The resulting system, Owens was convinced, constituted a qualitatively different military potential. "In part because of earlier investments, particularly in electronic and computational technologies, the things which give military forces their fighting capability are changing, and these changes point toward a qualitative jump in our ability to use military force effectively," the vice chairman wrote.[9] Soon other concepts came to dominate the strategic debate. Network-centric warfare was more intuitive and operational than the abstract talk of a revolution and soon captured the imagination and the procurement portfolios of America's armed forces. Its essence was to translate an information advantage into a decisive warfighting advantage. As a consequence, America's NATO allies felt the pressure to follow the world's most powerful force down its path of modernization in order to remain "interoperable," to be able to plug into the networked joint fighting force and participate in the fast fight on the digitized battlespace.

Consequently, the technology led to a necessary cultural adaptation. As services, agencies, and suborganizations—or "systems"—that did not directly work together in the past were more and more connected, the training, the education, and the doctrine of operations needed to be adapted as well. Former U.S. Secretary of Defense Donald Rumsfeld had a key role in driving the cultural change in the American military. In an article in *Foreign Affairs* he spelled out how a transformed military would fight the wars of the future. The secretary reported from a visit to Afghanistan, where U.S. Special Forces in real-time cooperation with the U.S. Air Force conducted the world's first truly network-centric operations. Rumsfeld, awed by his own organization's high-tech spectacle, recounted how American Special Forces troopers, sporting beards and on horseback, called in air support to obliterate enemy positions:

> "Two minutes." "Thirty seconds." "Fifteen seconds." Then, out of nowhere, a hail of precision-guided bombs began to land on Taliban and al Qaeda positions. The explosions were deafening, and the timing so precise that, as the soldiers described it, hundreds of Afghan horsemen emerged, literally, out of the smoke, riding down on the enemy through clouds of dust and flying shrapnel.[10]

Transformation, Rumsfeld pointed out, cannot be seen as a temporary reform project, to be finished after a couple of years. It could only be seen as an ongoing and permanent process of change. "[W]e must make the leap into the information age, which is the critical foundation of all our transformation efforts," Rumsfeld wrote.[11] Modern communication equipment enabled independent forward observers, be it Special Forces troops, CIA operatives, or even indigenous troops, to coordinate remote strikes delivered by the Navy, the Air Force, or the Marine Corps. The revolution in military affairs, senior officers pointed out, could not be brought about by merely introducing new technologies to gather real-time information about the battlespace, but operators needed to be trained accordingly. The ability to communicate seamlessly on the battlefield was seen as critical for success.

Phase one of Operation Iraqi Freedom, the invasion, implemented many of these principles. In contrast to the first Iraq War of 1991, operations in both Afghanistan and Iraq were nonlinear; there was no front line and even large mechanized formations moved with high velocity in enemy territory. This increased mobility of a large number of individual units made situational awareness essential, awareness of both the position of friendly troops and that of adversarial formations. Various communication systems were employed to guarantee situational awareness, such as tactical satellite communication, terrestrial systems, or UAVs. A transformed military, in essence, can strike its enemies more precisely, make maximum use of its own sensor grid to locate and move "blue" friendly forces, use signal intelligence to assemble a near-instantaneous picture of "red" hostile forces, and rapidly devastate adversarial command-and-control nodes. In short, it can win faster. The public dimension of warfighting was nearly irrelevant.

SPECIALIZATION

As internal communication and command-and-control became a more sophisticated and specialized field, a similar development played out in the field of external communication, one important element of which was media relations. But the institutional setup of communication specialists in regular armies continued to reflect their historic mission: to fight and win big industrial wars. The conventional setup of media operations in modern armies had a major shortcoming that emerges forcefully in counterinsurgency operations: its military component and its political component are disconnected. The analysis of organizational setups is a dry exercise, but a necessary one in order to appreciate how far the practice in counterinsurgency operations deviates from the doctrinal prescriptions and from bureaucratic norms. Western armies, and the ministries or departments that control them, are large bureaucracies. Bureaucracies create divisions and specialized units to deal with new problems and opportunities. As modern information technology steadily improved, the communication tools at the disposal of governments and their military forces proliferated. As a consequence, Western armed forces have created a set of functionally different specializations, career tracks, departments, and stand-alone agencies to deal with public information in conflict.

From many an ordinary Iraqi's or Afghan's point of view, there is only one major group he or she is dealing with in the reconstruction effort: Westerners. These foreigners could be from any coalition country; they could be working for a civilian government, for an NGO, for a company, or for a military organization. If they wear a uniform, they will most likely have a particular military specialization. Depending on their affiliation, they will have a very different mindset, training, and responsibility. Within the armed forces, three specializations, in theory, deal with one of the core tasks of communicating with local constituencies in a counterinsurgency campaign in order to gain the trust of the populations, and thus ultimately to bolster the government's authority and legitimacy.

First, public affairs officers are trained to communicate information about military operations to domestic audiences, both external and internal to the Department of Defense, and to the international media. In many NATO countries, the military field of public affairs is abbreviated as PA. In most Western armies, almost every unit from company-size upward has its own public affairs officer. It is his responsibility to establish ground rules for journalists, register and provide services to media representatives in the area of operations, manage the release of news material, organize press pools or the embedding of reporters, and monitor and assess media coverage. In the day-to-day practice of counterinsurgency operations in Iraq and Afghanistan, public affairs officers more and more work with the local public and the local media.

The second field is psychological operations. PSYOPs officers, in theory, are trained to influence the thinking and the decisions of adversarial target audiences, political decision makers, officers, and neutral civilians. Psychological operations are designed to "influence"—a word that is rarely used by public affairs officers to describe their work—the "emotions, motives, objective reasoning, and ultimately the behavior of foreign governments, groups, and individuals."[12] Third, and most important, civil affairs officers are designated active or reserve forces and units that are specifically trained and equipped to work with local civil authorities, government officials, and nongovernmental community leaders. "Civil-military operations may include performance by military forces of activities and functions normally the responsibility of the local, regional, or national government," U.S. doctrine says.[13]

All three areas fall under the extended umbrella of information operations, or IO. Information operations officers are taught in American staff colleges to influence, disrupt, corrupt, or usurp adversarial decisions and decision-making processes. At the same time friendly decision making is protected from enemy interference. The tools to do that can be physical or cognitive. The core capabilities of information operations are electronic warfare, computer network operations, deception, operational security, and PSYOPs. The joint staff sees capabilities that "operate in the information environment" and have a military purpose different from information operations as supporting activities. Combat camera or intelligence operations are examples. "Related" capabilities are those that are less aggressive and less focused on interrupting decision making, such as public affairs—which by definition deals with home constituencies—and civil affairs. In other NATO countries, the concepts are largely similar, although it is highly debated among these groups of officers whether information operations and psychological operations should conceptually or institutionally be linked to public affairs or not.

Several specializations in communication policy transcend the armed forces. Two are noteworthy. Public diplomacy is the overarching term for information activities by the U.S. government, particularly the State Department. The objective of public diplomacy is to support and promote U.S. foreign policy objectives vis-à-vis foreign audiences. In counterinsurgency and reconstruction operations, U.S. government agencies other than the military engage in public diplomacy to promote the local understanding of the reconstruction effort, the rule of law, and civic culture.[14] An alternative term that is increasingly used for government-wide information policies in many NATO countries is "strategic communications."

This sophisticated division of labor has several implicit assumptions: that military action and perception can be managed separately; that target audiences can be informed separately; that the adversary's level of bureaucratic setup is remotely comparable to one's own; and, if technologically more sophisticated offensive information operations are part of the game plan, that the adversary's communication infrastructure has the technological sophistication that makes him vulnerable to these operations. All of these assumptions have always been questionable in irregular wars; they are even more questionable in a twenty-first-century media environment.

Yet the major shortfall is not organizational, but conceptual. Conventional war is an enemy-focused undertaking: its imperative is to use whatever it takes to strafe enemy formations and to break the leadership's will, while carefully managing the information that is reported from battle. Under such conditions victory was perhaps easier to achieve in secrecy and surprise. Conventional public affairs operations, as a consequence, were an annex to the real show of force—irrespective of whether they were restrictive, like the pool arrangement of the 1991 Persian Gulf War, or open-access, like the embedded media program of the 2003 Iraq War. "You gotta remember," the 3rd Infantry Division's chief public affairs officer, Lieutenant Colonel Mike Birmingham, explained a year after the invasion of Iraq, "[the] media wasn't on the mind of the brigade commanders. What's on their mind is: they're warfighting. That's why they hire public affairs officers."[15] The ideal situation the system is designed for looks something like this: at war, when diplomats would take a step back and make place for gunners, the raw use of firepower—now "transformed" and more lethal—would be the main message vis-à-vis the adversary; press officers would only turn around and talk to the journalists and explain the front-line action; the press would then report the news home. Public affairs, therefore, was a career specialization that did not attract the most ambitious and the brightest officers (perhaps the Marine Corps has been an exception to this rule). Conventional public affairs officers didn't have to know the languages of other cultures, their history, their mores, their customs, and their sensibilities.

In counterinsurgency that is very different. Secret tactical operational surprise is still possible and sometimes necessary, such as the elimination of an insurgent stronghold or an improvised explosive device (IED) cell. But even tactical surprise has to be reported to the appropriate local audiences to have a wider effect. In population-centric operations, strategic surprise and secrecy are by definition impossible: if the population is the prize, it needs to know that it was won (or at least its views need to change). Public affairs operations in counterinsurgency, therefore, need to be more sophisticated and more aggressive than in conventional war.

THE LIMITS OF SPECIALIZATION

When the United States and its allies realized that they were facing insurgencies using classical guerrilla tactics in Iraq and Afghanistan, the American and British land forces were ill-prepared to counter them. The lessons from previous counterinsurgencies—Vietnam and Malaya stand out respectively—had been neglected in the Cold War frenzy for force modernization. As NATO countries were facing the numerically superior Red Army across the Fulda Gap, artillery and surface-to-air missiles were considered more important than understanding Russian culture and Soviet grievances. The latter clearly were not the prerogative of armies, but rather that of academics and planning staffs. Thus, faced with an entirely unexpected kind of conflict in Afghanistan and Iraq, the American land forces had trouble adapting to the new realities, and initially relied on heavy firepower[16] and a harsh treatment of prisoners.[17]

Perhaps the most characteristic difference between regular armies and insurgent movements is their responsibility for the cause—and the lack thereof. Modern armies are not responsible for the reasons of going to war; civilian superiors hand the cause and the objective of war down to the generals, who merely execute. Politicians craft the language and the arguments that justify the costs and sacrifices of going to war, and they allocate the resources for a nation's armed services; military spokespersons strictly and narrowly stick to their predefined political talking points and focus on the tactical aspects of operations in their work.[18] Not so in an insurgency, where there is no division of labor between professional politicians and professional warfighters (and within the army between commanders and public affairs officers). Fighters, at least in an insurgency's early stages, have to execute, justify, and fund action on their own. This feature of modern war, not surprisingly, has not been sufficiently appreciated by the classic theorists, such as Carl von Clausewitz, Antoine-Henri de Jomini, Alfred Thayer Mahan, Sir Julian Corbett, or Basil Liddell Hart. These writers were trained as specialists in the use of organized military force between industrial states. Their governments and armies were characterized by the very division of labor that is denied to those and by those attempting to overthrow established authority.

The prerequisite for any insurgency is a cause. The cause is a necessary requirement that distinguishes a rebellion and political violence from being merely a plot or organized crime. The cause is the answer to the question of how to mobilize both active and passive support. Causes come in many forms: gaining independence from foreign oppression, fighting for freedom against an authoritarian government, or ending the discrimination of one ethnic or religious group by others, to give just a few examples. Throughout the nineteenth and twentieth centuries, three species of insurgencies could be observed according to their cause. Separatist movements were insurgencies in which a minority group fought for autonomy and independence against a central government. Examples are the IRA's attempt to break Northern Ireland away from the UK, Internal Macedonian Revolutionary Organization in their struggle against the Ottoman Empire, Eritrean Liberation Front wishing to be independent from Ethiopia, ETA demanding Basque independence from Spain, the PKK's fight against Turkey, and the wars in Chechnya. The second type of guerrilla war targeted native incumbent governments. It was widespread in Latin America, in Thailand, in Burma, and most significantly in the Muslim world, such as the Syrian Vanguard Organization against the Assad regime, al-Jihad against the government of Egypt, and the Marsh Arabs against Saddam Hussein. When domestic rulers were confronted, the patriotic, nationalistic, or religious-fundamentalist cause was stressed. The third, and for the present study most relevant group, were insurgencies against what was perceived as foreign occupiers, either in the setting of a general war against colonial or other occupation or in the aftermath of a defeat against a regular army. It often happened that a war of "liberation" enabled the mobilization and training of guerrilla forces, and after the occupier had been defeated, the previously opposing groups turned on each other in a civil war. This happened in China, Algeria, Vietnam, Yugoslavia, Albania, Greece, the Philippines, Malaya, and Afghanistan.

A collective feeling of grievance is at the bottom of every protest movement. The cause is an insurgent movement's instrument for tapping into the general population as a recruitment pool. A successful cause has to meet several criteria. First, it needs to maximize the number of supporters while minimizing the number of opponents in the population.[19] Second, a cause has to be strong. It needs to self-motivate fighters, as they cannot be recruited, conscripted, paid, or simply called to duty for king or country. Third, the cause must be taboo for the counterinsurgent. If the government can espouse the insurgency's cause without losing its authority and cutting back too much on its interests, it is in a position to take away the insurgency's most valuable asset. This is what happened to the Malayan Communist Party after Britain credibly announced it would release the colony into independence after the insurgency was subdued; Britain effectively orchestrated a political countercause operation. Finally, a cause has to be of long duration. Economic disparities between classes, for instance, are a source of revolutionary energy only as long as class inequalities with an unjust income distribution continue to feed the grievance of the deprived. If political and economic change affects the cause, it may cease to be one. Some of these requirements might become contradictory: the first requirement and the second requirement may be in contradiction when maximizing the zeal of a smaller set of supporters is working against maximizing that of the overall number of supporters; such is the case with Islamic militants in Afghanistan and Iraq. If the cause's power to mobilize masses is inferior to its power to radicalize minorities, insurgent movements might resort to force to get recruits to join their ranks.

On a more general level, the consequences of this lack of specialization in asymmetric conflicts—or, inversely put, the consequences of their political nature—are best illustrated by the common use of language. In any insurrection, where a weak side is engaged in violent action against stronger government authority, words, ideas, and perceptions become politically charged in a way that is rarely the case in state-on-state wars. Language becomes a recruiting tool, a call for support, a rallying cry. The particular words and terms that are used to describe the opponent, oneself, the type of conflict, and its history are highly contested; it can even be stated as a rule that the insurgent and the counterinsurgent never agree on terminology, and it is difficult to imagine how this could be otherwise.[20]

The stronger side commonly referred to its adversaries as partisans, *francs tireurs*, *Freischärler*, pirates, "savages," traitors, saboteurs, mutineers, criminals, bandits, brigands, rebels, militants, irregulars, terrorists, fanatics, extremists, and insurgents. These terms stand for illegitimate and illegal agency. The state's organized units, by contrast, are referred to as the government forces, the authorities, the police, law-enforcement agencies, soldiers, officers, troops, and, of course, the full litany of professional military terms: armies, divisions, brigades, as well as generals, colonels, down to sergeants and privates. The type of conflicts that see the use of government forces against nongovernment forces are unconventional wars, campaigns of pacification, irregular wars, counterinsurgencies, asymmetric conflict, small wars, internal wars, low-intensity conflicts, and sometimes counterterrorism, or in earlier times "savage wars"— terms that are meant to express that these conflicts deviate from the norm of regular conflict.

From the point of view of the weak, this vocabulary and these interpretations are politically unacceptable. The weaker side is engaged, in its self-description, in revolutionary war, anticolonial war, people's war, a struggle against oppression or for independence, liberation, resistance, and holy war. The ones taking up arms (or pikes, scythes, and suicide belts) to defend their ethnic group, their race, their country, or their religion refer to themselves as resistance fighters, freedom fighters, loyalists, defenders of the people, holy warriors, mujahideen, martyrs; they might use all-inclusive terms, such as "Kurds" or "Muslims," often with adjectives like "real" or "true," in order to stress a larger group's patriotic or moral obligation to take up arms. And, of course, they try to appropriate the terminology of professionals, and refer to their own organizations as armies or brigades and to their fighters as soldiers and commanders. Their opponents, by contrast, are referred to as enemies of the people, mercenaries, colonizers, fascists, infidels, oppressors, and crusaders.

Enumerating all of these terms and views does not add precision to the understanding of the phenomenon. Yet it serves to make a more general point. There is no neutral ground in this war of words, no vocabulary all sides could agree on, not just normatively but also descriptively. The level and the extent to which language is partisan and politically charged is, in itself, a distinctive feature of irregular war. In state-on-state wars, both sides have more or less the same organizational setup, training, equipment, rules of engagement, and terminology to measure and compare their strength: mechanized infantry divisions are tallied against other mechanized formations, air defense installations against the strength of an air force's offensive capabilities. Even in political terms it is comparatively easy to agree on a settlement and on the terms of victory and defeat. No such simplicity exists in irregular war. As a result, even a strictly analytical approach seems doomed to take a side.[21] The possibility of precision is severely limited.

POLITICAL WARFARE

In popular wars, each side aims to gain the people's trust and the acceptance of its competing governance. That competition for legitimacy is a zero-sum game. The language used as described is intended to bolster one's own legitimacy and to sabotage that of the adversary. But language is only one element. Insurgents use all available tools to overthrow existing authority, military and paramilitary, political, economic, and media affairs. In an insurgency's early phase, when existing authority needs to be undermined, intimidation and terrorism are particularly effective instruments to demonstrate in the most vivid and graphic way that the government does not have the monopoly of force, and that it cannot keep its institutional promise to protect its subjects.[22] The counterinsurgent equally uses all available means to maintain government authority and legitimacy, military, political, economic and public affairs. "Isn't war," Clausewitz asked, "just another way of writing and speaking [the people's and the government's] thoughts?"[23] In irregular war, this phrase is more pertinent than Clausewitz might have envisioned.

Already in Clausewitz's age, a countertrend to professional military specialization had started in European colonies. Among the first modern armies who were forced to adapt to irregular warfare were the French. In 1840, only a few years after *On War* had been published, the Prussian General-Major Carl von Decker of the Kriegsschule in Berlin traveled to Africa to observe the ongoing French campaign against Ab del-Kader's insurrection. Decker was one of his time's brightest generals. "Hopefully you left all your European ideas over there in Toulon," a French officer greeted the Prussian as he debarked from his vessel in Algiers. Methods of specialized, professional, and industrial war were pointless in what was essentially a political conflict from the beginning. In the same year Thomas-Robert Bugeaud became commander in chief of all French forces in North Africa and instituted a highly successful new counterinsurgency strategy. To conceptualize that new strategy, French officers—not unlike contemporary American doctrine writers—used a space metaphor to come to grips with the role of the population. Magnificent public works had been accomplished, one of Bugeaud's best officers analyzed, and the physical terrain and its material topography had been remodeled successfully. But the population's moral topography remained unchanged. The reason, Charles Richard wrote, was simple: "If one sets out to conquer a country, in the word's true sense, there are two sorts of conquests to realize: that of the land is the material conquest, and that of the people is the moral conquest."[24] The first is executed by the force of arms, and sometimes it takes only the time of four or five large battles; the second is executed by ideas, and it can take centuries, he wrote, particularly "if the conquering people is Christian and the conquered people is Muslim." Some of Bugeaud's methods proved highly successful, such as the *Bureaux arabes*. It would serve as a template for later generations of French army officers especially trained to deal with the local population, so-called "indigenous affairs officers."[25]

In Tonkin and in Madagascar toward the end of the nineteenth century, Joseph-Simon Galliéni pioneered the so-called oil-spot method, "la méthode de la tache d'huile,"[26] what was alternatively called *progressive occupation*. The new thinking rested on a distinction between slow and fast action. "The pirate"—the expression was commonly used at the time for irregular fighters—"is a plant that grows only in certain terrains," Lyautey wrote many years before Mao used a similar and much-quoted metaphor, that of the insurgent swimming like fish in the water. The soil stands for the population, which the insurgents need as victims and supporters. "And the surest method is to render that terrain refractory," Lyautey advised.[27] Attacking an insurgency's foundation, or its soil, meant to "turn the population into our foremost helper," he wrote elsewhere.[28] These lessons had occupied scholars and practitioners of colonial warfare for well more than a century, and by the end of their most costly war, the War in Algeria of 1954 to 1962, no officer corps had accumulated more experience in it than the French. The set of instruments necessary to succeed in such operations extended far beyond military means and included political, economic, and social action.

To understand the nature of political warfare in Iraq, the U.S. military drew on a surprising source: David Galula, a French lieutenant colonel who fought—and lost—in Algeria from 1958 to 1960, wrote two books that were highly significant for the American doctrinal reorientation that began in 2005. Both captured insights that had been common knowledge in the French forces for many decades.[29] When some of the Army's most talented leaders realized the need to change course in Iraq and reorient the force for counterinsurgency operations, they recognized the lack of doctrine. Lieutenant General David Petraeus was instrumental in drafting and publishing a much-praised field manual, *Counterinsurgency*, or FM 3-24 in the Army's publication code system, to fill that void. Petraeus, who holds a Princeton PhD, successfully commanded the 101st Airborne Division in Northern Iraq. After leading the Multi-National Security Transition Command-Iraq he moved on to become the commanding general of the Combined Arms Center in Fort Leavenworth, the Army's intellectual hub. There he initiated the overhaul of America's counterinsurgency doctrine.

With the Army in dire need of guidance and orientation, Galula's writings were eagerly absorbed. Little did it matter that Galula held only a minor and unimportant role in the war, first as an Army captain and later as a lieutenant colonel; that his sector wasn't central to success or defeat; that his writings were almost unknown in France (he published only one book, a little-known novel in French under the pseudonym of Jean Caran, *Les moustaches du tigre*, a raunchy novel about a strip club).[30] Galula's military writings build on more than a century of French experience in North Africa.[31] Galula's books went unnoticed in France and Europe for decades, but were eagerly absorbed in the United States (in fact Galula was published in French only in 2008). "Of the many books that were influential in the writing of Field Manual 3-24," the foreword of the manual's commercial edition explains, "perhaps none was as important as David Galula's *Counterinsurgency Warfare: Theory and Practice*."[32] One commentator even called

Galula the "Clausewitz of counterinsurgency."[33] But unlike Clausewitz, Galula did not assume that war—counterinsurgency warfare in his case—had an intrinsic drive toward escalation, thereby approximating the model of absolute war. Instead counterinsurgency was characterized by the opposite: limitations.

LIMITED MEANS

In modern irregular war, the means at the disposal of the counterinsurgent are more limited than in the past while the reverse is true for the insurgent. A principal distinction of two fundamentally different types of counterinsurgencies is important in this regard. Counterinsurgents can be endogenous or exogenous to an insurgency. If the government or the authority that tries to quell a revolt is imposed from the outside, by a colonial power, by an international interim administration, or by an invading occupying force, the counterinsurgent is exogenous. If the government and the dominant military forces conducting the campaign are indigenous, the counterinsurgent is endogenous. The outcome of small wars in the nineteenth and twentieth centuries demonstrates that the odds for insurgents to succeed are much higher when they face foreign domination rather than native governments—a difference that is particularly pronounced in the twentieth century. In the nineteenth century, colonial powers sometimes managed to squash insurgent movements fuelled by the ideology of jihad, sometimes with ghastly brutality, for instance the French against Abd el-Kader in Algeria or the Russians against Shamyl in the Caucasus.[34] Long-term success in modern exogenous counterinsurgency operations, such as in Indochina, Vietnam, Afghanistan (both for the Soviets and NATO), and even in Iraq, is by far more difficult for three reasons.

The first limitation is that the stakes for the counterinsurgent are limited. The potential for escalation is greatest in endogenous counterinsurgency campaigns where both the insurgent and the counterinsurgent see their objective as nonnegotiable and even existential. Chechnya is an example. The Kremlin as well as the Russian military leadership regarded the province as an integral part of Russia; Dzhokhar Dudayev's All-National Congress of the Chechen People considered the province occupied and wanted to end an illegitimate post-Soviet aggression that was, in their view, the continuation of a 150-year-old struggle for independence against Russian oppression. Another example was France in Algeria in the 1950s. The declining empire was not willing to lose its three 120-year-old French départements: from a French point of view it was dealing with an internal insurgency. French political leaders and even more so the French military elite, until de Gaulle started to speak of *autodétermination*, had regarded Algeria as French, particularly since it had created a sizeable settler population of significantly more than 1 million Europeans at the country's Mediterranean coast. The FLN, by contrast, saw itself fighting an external and illegitimate occupying force. In Iraq or Afghanistan, the situation was different. A coalition of Western democracies with no territorial ambitions was fighting a local insurgency (with only modest global dimensions). The intervening forces view themselves as temporary guests in an insecure and war-torn country with a limited mission: to stabilize the security situation in order to enable political and economic progress—and ultimately prevent that country from becoming a launch-pad for global terrorist attacks. Although the stakes in Afghanistan and Iraq are high, a defeat would probably not affect the constitutional stability and the political systems of the NATO countries involved.

The second limitation is time. It has already been pointed out that insurgents tend to take a long view of history whereas counterinsurgents take a short view. This difference in approach is particularly pronounced if liberal democracies are engaged in a counterinsurgency campaign in Islamic countries. Modern democracies have a shortened attention span: driven by the new media, news cycles have accelerated, markets swiftly react to political crises, and voter preferences may be more volatile. A democratic political entity therefore is likely to lose patience with a permanently costly foreign policy faster than in the past. But it is noteworthy that it is in the interest of the counterinsurgent to take a short historical view: the level of carnage and havoc caused by disruptive attacks is often described as new and unprecedented in its cruelty and its disregard for human life, an anti-status quo assault on long-established authority and cherished traditions that has to be opposed swiftly and decisively.

Insurgents, in marked contrast to their opponents, tend to take a long historical view, claiming that their resistance or their objective is rooted in ancient narratives, that it is sanctioned by holy scriptures or directly by God, or that one ethnic or national or religious group has been suffering for generations already, waiting to be liberated by the present crop of leaders, eager to heap upon them the accumulated glory of generations for their heroism and martyrdom. The ideology of global jihad refers to its enemies as "crusaders," suggesting that the United States and its European allies are not engaged in an isolated conflict, but instead wage a long war against Muslims. The recurrence to ancient history helps build up a grandiose cause that justifies grandiose sacrifice. This difference may be particularly pronounced in Islamic narratives, especially if interpreted by radical Islamists. The U.S. president is seen as the successor of a long line of "unbelievers," or *kaffir*, imposing their power upon holy Muslim lands: the Byzantine emperors of Constantinople, the Holy Roman emperors in Vienna, the imperial rulers in Britain and France, and now Zionists and Americans.[35]

External counterinsurgents face a crucial disadvantage as a result: their opponents believe that it is comparatively easy to outlast them. And the experience with most insurgencies in the second half of the twentieth century proves them right. This view can be exploited by an insurgency's communication policy vis-à-vis the local population. And indeed, modern interventions without territorial ambitions are nearly always limited for the intervening power, limited in time and investment. Foreign counterinsurgents have a reduced interest in success, finite resilience, and exhaustible staying power, and therefore a limited tolerance for the use of extensive force. Internal struggles, by contrast, are potentially unlimited: domestic counterinsurgents may have an existential interest in success and unlimited staying power, and therefore may utilize extreme force to crush resistance if all else fails to work. Liberal democracies and ineffective authoritarian regimes during the 1950s and 1960s found it difficult to cope with colonial insurrections.[36] Authoritarian governments, by contrast, often managed to crush budding insurgencies by applying extraordinarily harsh tactics, both militarily and in prisons: Syria's destruction of an emerging Islamist insurrection in Hama in 1982[37] and Egypt's crackdown on the Muslim Brotherhood perhaps stand out both in their brutality and in their continued relevance as sources of grievance among radical Islamists.

The final limitation concerns cultural and linguistic knowledge. It is closely related to the sequence of events, and therefore to time. It is always the insurgency that takes the initiative, at least initially, to use force or provoke its adversaries to use force. By the time of its taking initiative, a resistance movement will likely be consolidating. The government's reaction therefore comes at a point in time when the insurgency has already gained strength. Counterinsurgents, therefore, often have to "come from behind," Petraeus wrote in his introduction to the reworked U.S. counterinsurgency manual.[38] One of the most problematic consequences of this sequence is that the counterinsurgent also has to "come from behind" regarding his knowledge about the grievances, motivations, causes, and organizational structures that underlie and drive a resistance movement. The larger the geographical, historical, cultural, and linguistic barriers between the two political entities engaged in the effort—between the intervening force and the resisting one—the larger is the counterinsurgent's challenge to comprehend. The context and framework for any strategic communication or public affairs activity in exogenous asymmetric wars, therefore, is indefinitely more complex than in conventional wars. Not only does it become complicated to describe tactical and operational events from a neutral standpoint with neutral language, even if positive stories were reported. The weak side perceives the entire conflict and its news coverage through a filter—the cause. And any information emanating from the wrong side is likely to be seen as untrustworthy, as part of a plot, a conspiracy.

Modern counterinsurgency was, in many respects, the opposite of the transformed war the Pentagon leadership envisioned: the best-case scenario for outcome was not a clear-cut military victory, but rather a more ambiguous political success; the aim was not the devastation of the enemy, but the reconstruction of the host nation; military action was not swift and rapid, but drawn-out and long; high-tech equipment was not pivotal, but highly trained humans were; warfare was less dependent on jointly connected sensors and signal intelligence, but more on human intelligence and tribal relations; interrupting decision cycles was not decisive, but getting into the local populations' hearts-and-minds was. Counterinsurgency in many ways was a polar opposite to regular war; it was not secretive and enemy-centric, but highly visible and population-centric. Against this background, the relative gains created by modern technology seem to be larger for the insurgent than they are for the counterinsurgent. This asymmetry in benefit can be observed in a variety of areas, but it is particularly pronounced where information, be it technical or political information, is traded publicly. But, as we shall see in the second half of this book, the changes described have also resulted in significant relative costs for the insurgent.

3

The United States

America's push into Baghdad early April 2003, culminating in several so-called Thunder Runs, was one of the fastest advances of major mechanized formations in military history. Yet for the next half-decade there was almost no progress. A never-ending trickle of small arms attacks, suicide bombings, and improvised explosive devices (IED) ambushes crippled the U.S. forces in Iraq. But that standstill on the battlefield belies a rapid conceptual turnaround in the world's most advanced land forces. The U.S. Army that entered Baghdad on 9 April 2003 saw itself as one of the most lethal fighting machines in military history. The U.S. Army that still stood in Baghdad in April 2008, by contrast, saw its mission as "armed social work," as its revised field manual FM 3-24, *Counterinsurgency*, put it. Its objective had changed from regime removal to "nation building."

How does this turnaround affect the U.S. military's policy vis-à-vis the media? What role do media operations play in wars "amongst the people"? Irregular war and counterinsurgency caught the U.S. Army by surprise. Old concepts for the use of force had to be adapted to new realities on Iraq's battlefields, and very quickly. That shock, or the mismatch of concepts and reality, was particularly brutal for those who dealt with information at war. The population increasingly was seen as the center of gravity, and the critical terrain was human, not geographical. Public information, as a consequence, became mission critical.

This, to be sure, was not so in the past. The career field and the military specialization of information operations was seen more as a technical exercise in high-tech maneuver warfare, where situational awareness was critical—the ability to destroy the enemy's communication networks and decision-making processes through command-and-control warfare. Public affairs was not only a side show, or a "related activity" in the language of doctrine, with a low order of resources and priority; it was also focused on the home front, not on the war front. Historically and by definition public affairs centered largely on the U.S. public: the electorate, the taxpayers, and the relatives of military personnel had priority for military spokespersons, not what some local Iraqis or Afghans may see, hear, read, or say.

This chapter is organized in three sections.[1] To understand the complex instructional setup of military communications in the United States today, the evolution of two separate organizational strains has to be outlined: first, that of information operations (IO), a military discipline traditionally focused on information's secret and technological side; and second, public affairs (PA), which is focused on the public and human side of information. As the war in Iraq progressed, commanders and doctrine writers realized that the two largely separate strains—separated both conceptually and, more importantly, institutionally—had to be brought together and integrated. Third, the de facto attempt to merge IO with PA created a significant amount of institutional confusion and competition between and within the different services.

THE EVOLUTION OF INFORMATION OPERATIONS

In early May 2007 Rupert Murdoch, one of the world's most successful media moguls, stood before sixty of his most senior executives in a California resort. The meeting was set up as a brainstorming to discuss opportunities of the news business in print and on television. The publishing industry found itself under heavy pressure to adapt to new technologies. Murdoch's News Corp controlled some of the world's most successful media companies, such as Fox News, 20th Century Fox, HarperCollins, MySpace, *The Sun*, and, since 2007, the *Wall Street Journal*. Murdoch opened the session by asking his executives to raise a hand if they knew how news would work in an era dominated by the Internet. None shot up.

If, in May 2007, the U.S. Secretary of Defense would have summoned sixty of his most senior generals and admirals to discuss the future challenges of warfare in the early twenty-first century, and if Robert Gates would have asked them how war worked in an era dominated by the Internet, no hands would have shot up either. If Gates would have waited and the rising tension in the room would have pushed the first general to volunteer his view—thus prompting others to join in—the secretary would have heard a set of entirely different, even contradictory, recommendations. That is the most salient feature of the American security establishment's reaction to the new information environment: confusion. That confusion, to a large extent, is caused by the fact that senior generals and admirals are in charge of new technologies they themselves have not been socialized in; they therefore tend to either over- or underrate their significance. Yet this state of affairs was not new. The Pentagon has a solid historical track record of misunderstanding and misinterpreting the sociotechnological changes in its operating environment. Three different mindsets, or philosophies, on the nature of "information operations" can be tracked in the Department of Defense: command-and-control; cyberspace; and what recently was called "information engagement." These three schools of thought are chronologically, conceptually, and institutionally distinct, yet overlapping.

Command-and-control was historically the first field to benefit from novel machines that helped to receive and process information. To exercise authority and accomplish an objective, a commander needed to manage a set of complex logistical tasks: move equipment into theater, manage large numbers of personnel, assign specific tasks, direct maneuver movements from a distance, assess current developments, adjust ongoing operations, review progress, and facilitate a myriad of decisions along the way. The Internet itself, as an offshoot of the military's ARPANET, was initially intended to be a command-and-control network. Throughout military history, new telecommunication technologies had long been used to improve military command-and-control capabilities. Only later were these technologies adopted by the press, by business, and eventually by the public. It is not surprising that in the early days of computer networks, the U.S. military was optimistic that it could use and exploit the emerging technologies for its own and exclusive advantage. Particularly the Air Force was—and remains—at the forefront of this line of thinking. In both World Wars, air commanders could do little more than send the aircrews off into a mission and pray for their success and safe return. In the Gulf War in 1991, for the first time in military history, aircrews were equipped with sophisticated communication systems that allowed them not only to implement a concept of operations, but also to adapt it in real time to suit unexpected developments. "The potential this mode of command gives to air units is tremendous," the Gulf War Air Power Survey pointed out after the war.[2] The same optimistic and hopeful spirit permeated DoD Directive TS-3600.1, *Information Warfare (U)*, the first joint directive that mentioned information warfare in the context of command-and-control. The directive was issued on 21 December 1992, more than a year after the first public Web site had already been published at CERN.

As a result of the military's focus on command-and-control, the public dimension of information warfare was virtually absent in the 1990s. Only occasionally did open-minded officers use their own communications grid to help get the story out. The Marines, accustomed to publicly presenting themselves as a small elite force, were apt at this game. Molly Moore, a defense correspondent, recalled her excitement when she was allowed to use the Marines' brand-new e-mail system during the 1991 Gulf War.

> Now, I could sit in my tent, run an extension cord to an electrical line that snaked through the tent, and tap out my story on the laptop computer. I could then take the floppy disk to the camp communications tent, where a computer-whiz sergeant would insert it into his computer, punch in a few code letters, and zap the story by electronic mail to a base at Jubail.[3]

Moore, thanks to the U.S. Marine Corps, was able to use e-mail years before it became fashionable commercially in media organizations, businesses, and private interactions.

A dozen years later, when America decided to invade Iraq, this time to get rid of the Saddam regime for good, command-and-control technology again had reached a historic milestone. Donald Rumsfeld's and the military's bold vision of a "transformed" joint force had been, to a large extent, turned into reality. "Sensor coverage was exceptional," an official Army study prepared by the RAND Corporation reported. A range of new technologies made this possible: for instance, the Global Hawk, a unmanned airplane; JSTARS, flying reconnaissance platforms able to pierce even through sand storms; Predator, a drone; and particularly Blue Force Tracker (BFT), a system that allowed the tracking of the position of friendly forces mainly through satellite-based GPS transmitters. More than 1,300 Blue Force Tracker units were in use among coalition forces, giving operational commanders the ability to track far-flung friendly units in an otherwise confused tactical environment. Major General Buford Blount, the commanding general of the 3rd Infantry Division, one of the Army's spearhead formations during the invasion, said he couldn't image how he would have been able to monitor the more than 10,000 vehicles under his control without Blue Force Tracker. That system was even more capable than its name implied. It could not only track forces, but also communicate with them via a rudimentary e-mail system. BFT was also used for navigation when visibility was poor. Its ability to place friendly forces on a high-resolution digitized map on large plasma screens created unprecedented levels of situational awareness. Unit commanders were even able to direct their forces through built-up areas at night. The Blue Force Tracker was an effective coordination instrument, mainly because of its ability to receive and transmit both terrestrial and non-line-of-sight signals.

But early on, defense intellectuals and operators sensed that interconnected computers would not only be a strength, but also a weakness. Inspired by experiences in the 1991 Gulf War, the Pentagon's Defense Information Systems Agency (DISA), based in Arlington, staged a mock attack on DoD computer systems. The results were eye-opening: the mock government hackers seized control of 88 percent of the 8,900 Pentagon computers they attacked, and only a tiny number of the attacks were detected by administrators. Robert Ayers, chief of DISA's information warfare division, warned with a historical analogy that has caught on since: "We are not prepared for an electronic version of Pearl Harbor," he said in July 1995. "Our infrastructure is not safe and not secure."[4] That same year the Air Force released its "Cornerstones of Information Warfare," a document that viewed information for the first time both as a weapon and as a target. For a military publication it was a rather philosophical paper that attempted to define information and "information functions."[5] Although somewhat clumsy, it laid the intellectual foundations for many doctrinal publications to come, including those of other services and also joint publications. It distinguished between offensive and defensive information operations and even applied John Boyd's OODA-Loop to information warfare. Then, on 4 October 1995, when the public use of the Web was still in its infancy, the U.S. Department of Defense established its first task force to examine the threats to national interest posed by information warfare, the Defense Science Board Task Force.

The first Joint Doctrine on Information Operations followed soon, on 1 October 1998. It established a definition that still stood ten years later: information operations are actions, the doctrine said, to affect adversary information and information systems while defending one's own information and information systems. The document's authors used a broad concept of information system and information-based process, "whether human and automated," ranging from national political decision making to America's commercial information and energy infrastructure.[6] Joint Publication 3-13, as it is known, also introduced the concept of "information superiority," the ability to use information while interrupting the adversary's use of information. In sum, the overwhelming focus on command-and-control absorbed the utility of information technology, largely blinding the military to its uses in the public domain. The slow rise of another new idea, one with even more futuristic undertones, increased this obfuscation: cyberspace.

Cyberspace is a concept distinctly different from command-and-control. Much broader, it reflects the insight that the "space" created inside and by computer networks—space in a metaphorical sense—could not be seen comprehensively as merely two adversaries who tried to degrade the other's ability to decide and act on the battlefield. A vast and growing amount of data, residing in a veritable thicket of unknown and often anonymous servers and personal computers, in times of war and in times of peace, had an incomprehensible, almost mystical aspect. Cyberspace captured this ambiguity, a quality the term retains to this day. The origins of cyberspace are telling in this respect. The word first appeared in a 1984 science fiction novel by William Gibson, *Neuromancer*. The author's inspiration came from watching teenagers who seemed to drift into a dream world as they played video games in a Vancouver shopping arcade. Gibson employed what he said seemed "evocative and essentially meaningless" to describe a "consensual hallucination experienced daily by billions of legitimate operators."[7] Users, Gibson wrote, would "jack in" and navigate through a universe of information displayed as shapes, colors, and characters in a three-dimensional space. As the Internet evolved, the term caught on in the nonfiction world and was used more and more as a synonym for the Web. Yet it retained its essential fictional feature: it still was used as a smokescreen to project new opportunities and latent fears.

When the military first started talking about cyberspace, it was actually in that original playful sense. That was in the early 1990s, when "virtual reality" first became fashionable in the arts, business, and the armed forces.[9] Cyberspace at the time was another expression for a three-dimensional virtual reality. The Air Force had begun to fund research on virtual realities in the 1960s. Early cyberspace engineers were driven by the vision to incorporate a "virtual environment" with 3-D simulation into a piece of headgear or a "super-cockpit" for pilots or astronauts, first for flight simulation but then also for actual flights under conditions of limited visibility. The Army joined in with hopes to train and war game on virtual battlefields. The understanding of cyberspace, however, has changed considerably since the early 1990s.

American officials since have warned of the malicious effects of computer warfare. "Cyber warfare is already here," Gordon England said on 3 March 2008. As he described the new battlefield, the Deputy Secretary of Defense drew a historical parallel: "I think cyber attacks are probably analogous to the first time, way back when people had bows and arrows and spears, and somebody showed up with gunpowder and everybody said, 'Wow. What was that?'" He went on to describe cyber warfare as "one of our major challenges."[8] Yet a major challenge is also a major opportunity for the organization that tackles it first—promising funds, responsibility, and influence. Early on, the Air Force, the service in charge of outer space, saw itself as predisposed to deal with cyberspace as well. As the Air Force was under pressure to show its added value in two land-based counterinsurgency campaigns, it was all too keen to embrace a new frontier of warfighting to increase both its perceived importance and its sources of money. In December 2005, the Air Force Secretary, Michael W. Wynne, and T. Michael Moseley, the Chief of Staff, disseminated a letter to the entire Air Force in which they had "re-written" the mission statement for the nation's youngest service, sixty years after it was founded as a separate entity. "Our adversaries will contest us across all of the domains: Land, Sea, Air, Space, and Cyberspace," they wrote, with reference to the entire operational spectrum of the U.S. military. "As Airmen, it is our calling to dominate Air, Space, and Cyberspace."[10] In early 2006 the Air Force set up a "Cyber Task Force" to investigate cyberspace as a new kind of battlespace in and through which the Air Force "flies and fights." Dr. Lani Kass, Special Assistant to the Chief of Staff of the U.S. Air Force, led the Cyberspace Task Force. "Cyberspace is a domain where the Air Force conducts operations," she said. The task force defined the new warfighting domain as bounded by the electromagnetic spectrum, or the "maneuver space of the electromagnetic spectrum." The Pentagon's *National Military Strategy for Cyberspace Operations*, published in 2006, officially defined cyberspace as a "domain characterized by the use of electronics and the electromagnetic spectrum to store, modify, and exchange data via networked systems and associated physical infrastructures." Then, at the end of 2006, the Air Force officially announced the creation of a provisional 8,000-man Cyberspace Command, made up of the 8th Air Force, commanded by Lieutenant General Robert J. Elder. Many of the deliberations remained classified, and the grandiose but controversial project was suspended when the Air Force leadership was replaced in 2008.[11]

Gibson's fictional idea, however, had made a stellar career in the past two decades. Cyberspace, seen in 1990 as the space in which war games could be played was seen in 2008 as a space in which real battalions are supposed to fight. "Like space, cyberspace is a unique global domain in which the U.S. must maintain freedom of action," said General Kevin Chilton, Commander of the United States Strategic Command, one of nine unified commands, to the House Armed Services Committee on 27 February 2008. "As we continue to develop our cyberspace capabilities," Chilton said, "we look forward to the day when we have trained and equipped Service organizations (e.g., brigades, battalions, wings, groups, and squadrons) assigned to [the United States Strategic Command] conduct network warfare."[12] It is not surprising that large organizations are tempted to respond to unstructured problems through traditional structures. What is surprising, however, is the lack of precision illustrated by an abundance of metaphors such as "maneuvering," "flying," and "squadrons" in cyberspace.[13] In his testimony, Chilton even compared cyberspace to a worldwide "neural" network that links human activity and facilitates the exchange of information. The United States government, the general argued, should be prepared for operations in "this emerging war-fighting domain." Elder, the general in charge of implementing these metaphors, not surprisingly said that the Air Force first had to develop a more concrete idea of what it means to fly and fight in cyberspace.

The Information Operations doctrine, Joint Publication 3-13, provides only some guidance. It removes the term "information warfare" from the official doctrine and redefines the entire spectrum of information operations:

> The information environment is the aggregate of individuals, organizations, and systems that collect, process, disseminate, or act on information. The information environment is made up of three interrelated dimensions: physical, informational, and cognitive.[14]

This classification into physical and cognitive dimensions is remarkable. Transnational terrorist movements, jihadi groups, and local or regional insurgencies do not run their own computer networks: they do not have data centers, secure servers in their headquarters' data centers, or an infrastructure of fiber-optic cables, satellites, and wireless transponders that could be disrupted. Instead they run their telecommunication, both internal and external, on commercially available platforms—the Internet, cellphones, the commercial media, none of which can be attacked by conventional means without causing serious difficulties. The Air Force's offensive options, therefore, are very limited. The physical dimension is largely off limits, as American F16s will hardly be ordered to strafe Google's data centers. Instead, the military is forced to engage the adversary in the informational and cognitive dimensions of cyberspace. "Al-Qaeda and other terrorists' center of gravity lies in the information domain, and it is there that we must engage it," said Dell L. Dailey, the State Department's head of counterterrorism.[15] Some of the U.S. government's operations in the cyber-domain remain highly classified and secretive. Brigadier General Mark O. Schissler is director for cyber operations for the Air Force at national headquarters in Washington, DC. His responsibilities include electronic warfare operations, network warfare operations, and what is called influence operations. When U.S. forces recovered data storage devices in raids in Iraq, Afghanistan, and Pakistan, the Air Force officer commented that, "if you can learn something about whatever is on those hard drives, whatever that information might be, you could instill doubt on their part by just counter messaging whatever it is they said they wanted to do or planned to do."[16] Counterterrorism experts have understood that insurgents and globally operating terrorists use the Internet to spread their ideology, to finance their operations, and to recruit activists. "These adversaries can communicate globally with their agents, spread propaganda, mobilize support worldwide, conduct training, detonate improvised explosive devices and empty or create bank accounts to fund their causes," Wynne told an Air Force conference.[17] Proponents of the war of ideas think that the United States needs to offer a brighter future to Muslims as an alternative to extremism. "We've got to break the chain, and that's . . . the ideology. We really need to show the errors in Islamist extremist thinking," Schissler demanded.[18] Elder, the designated head of the former Cyberspace Command, had echoed this focus on influence operations, or psychological warfare.

Cyberspace, in short, has acquired a public dimension. Cyber-operators hope to be able to counter jihadi ideology, not technically by shutting down Web sites or denying their service, but culturally by influencing the thinking and the behavior of those who read and contribute on extremist Internet-based forums and platforms. Past operations involved the release of material that discredits al-Qaeda operations. Other operations allegedly involve the setup of fake Web sites and deceiving e-mails in order to sow confusion and distrust among jihadists and their sympathizers. But Western security services—even those with more experience with radical jihadism than the CIA, for instance France's DGSE—find it hugely difficult to infiltrate al-Qaeda training camps and jihadist organizations offline; it would be surprising if the U.S. Air Force, an organization better known for its technical prowess than for its cultural sensitivity, would be more successful online.[19]

Information engagement, the third mindset, a new concept, is for human targets. "Commanders use information engagement to shape the operational environment," the Army's recently republished *Operations* manual, FM 3-0, explained. The document's authors understood information engagement as one of several distinct "information tasks," next to such tasks as command-and-control, operations security, and military deception. The umbrella concept was not information operations any more, but "information superiority." Information engagement—the only of the Army's so-called information tasks that is exclusively concerned with the human, as opposed to technical, side of information—was also seen as the most important task, effectively elevating the human dimension over the technical dimension of information warfare. The Army's objective, the document is to inform, educate, and influence, first and foremost with respect to the local population in theater, and only then said, international and domestic audiences. It should be stressed that the truthfulness and the credibility of messages was seen as one of the military's most important assets. The recent handbook left no room for interpretation:

> When communicating, speed is critical—minutes and hours matter—and we should remember to communicate to local (Arabic/Iraqi) audiences first—U.S./global audience can follow. Tell the truth, stay in your lane, and get the message out fast.[20]

In this sense the *Operations* manual reflected the Army's current focus on coun-terinsurgency operations, and its inherent concern for the perceptions, the trust, and the legitimacy among the local population. "Land operations occur among populations," the section opens.[21]

The Army's novel concept could more accurately, and more simply, be described as public affairs, but then it would lack the neologism's excitement and attractiveness. "Information engagement," the Army writes, "is the integrated employment of public affairs to inform U.S. and friendly audiences." Several formats are supposed to be employed for that purpose: psychological operations, combat camera, strategic communication (including programs by other gov-ernment agencies), and defense support to public diplomacy. Yet information activities in counterinsurgency environments may have very little to do with command-and-control, the Internet, and cyberspace. Cyberspace and the public space are not identical, particularly in a social environment where newspapers and the Internet are rare or absent and where rumors and the word-of-mouth are the prevalent mass medium. Some thinkers in the Army and the Marine Corps have understood this essentially tactical problem. The land forces see the actions of individual soldiers and marines as "the most powerful component of informa-tion engagement." Personal interaction, without any information technology— over a cup of tea, and with hand-shake—is critical, a lesson that was painfully learned in several costly years in Afghanistan and Iraq. "Face-to-face interaction by leaders and soldiers strongly influences the perception of the local populace," FM 3-0 says. Such meetings may be "critical to mission success."[22]

In theory and in doctrine, therefore, public affairs has become a mission-critical part of counterinsurgency warfare. It also illustrates how the local population has begun to eclipse the weight of regional and global audiences. To understand the significance of this trend, and the difficulty of reaching that stage of doctrinal thinking on public affairs for any conventional force—historically focused on War 1.0—it is necessary to take a step back and to understand the historical back-ground of public affairs in the U.S. armed forces.

THE EVOLUTION OF PUBLIC AFFAIRS

Public affairs is a separate career track and specialization in all modern armies. Public affairs officers, often abbreviated as "PAOs," are trained to work with jour-nalists and representatives of the press and the public. In most armies this spe-cialization, however, does not attract the best and most ambitious officers. Careers are made by commanding companies, regiments, battalions, and brigades in combat, not by haggling with reporters.

The discipline of public affairs in the United States military performed a veri-table revolution in its own right between the Vietnam War, with its traumatic aftershock, and the invasion of Iraq. Media affairs in the American armed forces went through four overall phases: disastrous public affairs in Vietnam, restrictive public affairs from Vietnam to the Persian Gulf War, experimental public affairs through to the Afghanistan War, and eventually operational public affairs in Iraq, first conventional and then unconventional. The media coverage of the Vietnam War was seen by many as a disaster. Open press coverage of armed conflict used to be considered a mission-critical security risk by the American military. Undermined support at the home front, many feared, ultimately would lose the war. This was the lesson the U.S. military distilled from its traumatic experience in Vietnam. "Today's officer corps carries as part of its cultural baggage a loathing for the press," wrote Bernard Trainor, a former Marine Corps general and *New York Times* correspondent. "The credo of the military seems to have become 'duty, honor, country, and hate the media.'"[23] The U.S. military came to perceive the domestic media coverage of Vietnam, particularly on TV, as a stab-in-the-back. General William C. Westmoreland, commander in Vietnam, saw the reason for defeat in the "sensational media coverage" that was "piped for the first time into the homes of America."[24] Therefore military planners and political decision makers concluded after the American rout in Vietnam to ban the press from the battlefield in the next operation. The rationale was to control the coverage at the home front by limiting access to the war front. The American electorate's support of the military effort was considered essential, and allowing reporters freedom of movement and open access, as it was done in Vietnam, was considered an effective way to undermine that support. Keeping journalists out in the future, therefore, would keep out the problems they inevitably would cause.

That lesson, "keep the press out," resulted in the second phase, a phase of *restrictive public affairs*. It would last for nearly three decades. During the operations in Grenada, Panama, and the Persian Gulf the U.S. Army exerted a high level of control over the media coverage in these operations. A strict denial-of-access policy dominated Operation Urgent Fury in Grenada, a badly planned pool system and unforeseen incidents with public affairs implications beset Operation Restore Hope, and a stark contrast in media savvy between the Army and the Marine Corps characterized Operation Desert Storm. In these operations reporters were either shut out completely, or they were corralled by a restrictive pool system that set narrow limits to journalists' physical mobility. The idea behind the pool was that a small group of reporters on the ground would produce news stories, which would be subject to a "security review," and then "pooled" and distributed to all interested news organizations. The military's philosophy was not to control what the press could print—security reviews were hardly used to vet articles in the Persian Gulf War—but to control what the press could see, a method officially called "security at the source."

A pertinent illustration is the U.S. Army's approach to the press during the Gulf War. The Army, in contrast to the Marine Corps, was closed-minded and gave news coverage a low priority. A good example is its main mechanized advance into Iraq, known as the "left hook." Four Army divisions of the VII Corps, the 1st and 3rd Armored Divisions, the 1st Infantry Division, and the 1st Cavalry Division, led the main flanking attack, a maneuver designed to encircle the Iraqi units from the west. The objective of the Army's famous left hook was to outflank and destroy the Republican Guard with its units and to block the Iraqi army's get-away routes. The attack included more than 100,000 U.S. troops confronting tank-heavy armored Iraqi divisions. What ensued was one of the largest tank battles in military history, and a unique success for the U.S. Army. But the thirty-two reporters who were carried into battle with the VII Corps were effectively prevented from reporting it. Not a single picture of the battle exists, not even from Combat Camera units.[25]

The Marines, in extreme contrast, were open-minded and treated the media as a high priority issue. General Walter Boomer was the first high-profile exception. As a one-star, he served as the Marines' Director of Public Affairs for nearly two years, from mid-1986 to 1988. Yet his career was far from over after that posting. He later went on to become the commanding general of the U.S. Marine Forces Central Command and the 1st Marine Expeditionary Force during Operations Desert Shield and Desert Storm, and eventually received a fourth start to become the assistant commandant of the Marine Corps. Boomer pioneered what amounted to his own private embedded media program—he personally invited a couple of journalists to join Marine Corps units and his mobile command post. Molly Moore, quoted earlier, was one of the journalists who accompanied the general. "The Marines, unlike the Army, had indeed advanced since the Civil War," she wrote in a book she published after the war.[26] Boomer and the Air Force got outstanding coverage in the media; their role in the war, as a consequence, was exaggerated in the press. But that taught the Army a key lesson: restriction is not only difficult to achieve; it is also not in your interest. Something else had to be done.

The third phase, the turbulent period at the turn of the century can be described as a phase of *experimental public affairs*. Several small-scale military operations were rich in lessons for public affairs officers and commanders. Somalia demonstrated that the media—and the enemy—could penetrate the American decision loop: eighteen soldiers killed in Mogadishu, some shown on CNN, prompted the president to abort the operation. In the wars in the Balkans various ways to react to the new information environment were experimented with. In Afghanistan the armed forces eventually tested the idea to embed the media with military units, even with Special Forces, albeit not in combat operations. Chiefly because of security concerns about Army Special Forces units operating in Afghanistan, the Pentagon was, at first, reluctant to open up. Colonel Jay DeFrank, Director of Press Operations, explained why defense officials were hesitant:

> The reason was, the operation didn't support it, it was mostly Special Forces, often operating with tribal or warlord type organizations, some of them wanted media, some of them didn't. And in some cases, they just couldn't do it because it would give away their TTPs [tactics, techniques, and procedures] and if it was ever covered then they wouldn't be able to use it again. So as long as it was mostly small scale and Special Forces operating with irregulars, media embedding didn't lend itself to that conflict.[27]

But after a couple of months the land forces opened up, particularly the Marine Corps. Shortly before operation Swift Freedom was about to be launched on the night of 25 November 2001, General James Mattis invited a group of reporters to join the *USS Peleliu*. The military benefited from the open access policy because the journalists helped them—wittingly or unwittingly—to counter rumors and the Taliban's version of the story. Lessons-learned reports and the assessments of officials began to lend appreciation this change. Colonel Melanie R. Reeder worked as a public affairs officer in Afghanistan during Operation Enduring Freedom. Later she participated in writing the public affairs chapter of a Center for Army Lessons Learned (Call) report which focuses on the Combined Force Land Component Command's performance in Afghanistan. In an interview she said that "when journalists were provided access, the accurate story was told. When they were not provided with information, the result was speculation, misinformation, and inaccuracy."[28] The Army Component's chief public affairs officer, Colonel Rick Thomas, agreed: "When the marines landed and went into Kandahar, they had around twenty journalists with them . . . it was mutually beneficial."[29]

This assessment was echoed on a joint level. "Afghanistan was the watershed event," said Navy Captain Terry McCreary, then the special assistant for public affairs to the Chairman of the Joint Chiefs of Staff. McCreary would later help initiate the Iraq War's embedding program. In an interview he described his frustration with the dynamics in Afghanistan's information battlespace:

> You raid a camp, there wouldn't be any press with you, you do an operation, you leave, the enemy comes back, the press come in, and everybody tells them you murdered innocent people, you slaughtered them, and that becomes a story for the next 48 hours until you can fix it.[30]

The enemy, the planners were certain, exploited the U.S. military's slow internal communication channels and cumbersome official reporting chain: "Reacting from Washington to the enemy in theater is painful," McCreary said.[31] Operation Enduring Freedom's main lesson was, consequently, that embedding could be used as an instrument to counter the enemy's information. Public affairs was on its way to becoming more than just a way to send home feedback: it became forward deployed.

The fourth phase thus was characterized by *operational public affairs*: only in 2003, the Pentagon's policy vis-à-vis the press finally deserved the term media operations. The public presentation of the war was, for the first time in the history of the United States armed forces, beginning to be integrated into the operational planning process. From the military's point of view, the ingredients of a dangerous mixture were an IO-savvy adversary, global media organizations working in real-time, a twelve-hour time difference, and a lack of credibility of military spokespersons if contradicted by a journalist. The importance of credibility became ever more apparent, and with it the utility of truthful and accurate reporting.

The only way you can counter deception was to have the truth told first. The only way to do that is have an independent truth-teller tell it first. The only way to have an independent teller tell it first, is to have them with us. And the only way to have them with us was to embed.[32]

At Central Command, during the fall of 2002, few planners gave much thought to public affairs and the press—a topic that traditionally ranges on the lower end of a commander's priority list, if it appears at all: "You gotta remember," the 3rd Infantry Division's chief public affairs officer, Mike Birmingham, explained, "at the point in time when I was making planning assumptions in the summer of 2002 media wasn't on the mind of the brigade commanders. What's on their mind is: they're warfighting. That's why they hire public affairs officers."[33] A conventional army's deep-seated cultural reflex was to banish PR from operational planning.

Franks's staff was under immense pressure to plan one of the largest invasions since the Second World War. Unlike in the Persian Gulf War in 1991, it was not mass and the number of troops on the ground that was considered a decisive factor, but rather the unprecedented speed of the units' movements and the equally unprecedented momentum of their joint precision firepower. "We would not apply overwhelming force," Franks said, referring to the so-called Powell doctrine of overwhelming force.[34] "Rather, we would apply the overwhelming 'mass of effect' of a smaller force." From an operational point of view, "speed and momentum" were paramount in this war, as Franks, who called himself a "speed freak," often emphasized. Rapid, decisive movements of ground units were built into the war plan from the earliest stages—a plan made possible by unprecedented command-and-control technologies, Blue Force Tracker, drones, and improved reconnaissance and visualization—all based on modern telecommunication technology.

While the initial idea to put the journalists close to the troops was not new, the way it was communicated internally was unprecedented. Colonel DeFrank, a public affairs officer by training, provides some insight into this internal persuasion of the relevant leaders:

What we did was we tied our communications objective to operational objectives, working on the Sun Tzu concept that the acme of skill is to win the battle without fighting it. So you could encourage them [the Iraqis] to defect to surrender before we came; it was better for us and we didn't have to kill as many of them. Because the object of war, of course, is not to kill people and destroy things, the object of conflict is to get in the decision makers head and persuade them to do what you want them to do. What we did is we applied military objectives to our communications objectives. We made them the same. This is how we presented it.[35]

The pragmatic and target-oriented argument secured the support of the top military and civilian leadership: "We presented our communications objectives in operational terms and showed very clearly how we intended to use communication to help accomplish operational objectives," DeFrank said.[36] The language the public affairs staff in the Pentagon used to promote the idea of embedding reporters with military units was plugged into the operational logic of winning the war, and fully integrated into the war plan. At first, however, the top commander was skeptical: "When I heard the term 'embedded media,' it sounded dangerous." Franks was troubled by two issues: logistics and security. "Assigning newspaper and magazine writers and broadcast correspondents to combat units could present problems: transportation, support, and liability. And there were concerns about operational security in this age of satellite phones and Internet video cameras." The commander was one of the few remaining Vietnam veterans in leading military positions, and his anti-press reflexes might well have been a leftover of the molding experience in South East Asia. The former artillery soldier at the head of Central Command, however, was willing to think twice: "When Victoria [Clarke] and Jim [Wilkinson] briefed me on the details of the program, I saw it as a winner." The argument that finally persuaded him was the media's access to the troops and the reporting from the soldier's perspective that was expected to come from the embeds, based on the lesson from earlier wars: "One of the reasons the press coverage in Afghanistan had been so error-ridden and mediocre—and often anti-military in its bias—was that the journalists had been kept away from combat operations," the general reasoned. This was just about to change. "If the media were actually living and marching with the troops . . . they would experience war from the perspective of the soldier or marine." The resulting intimacy, it was clear for the designers of the embedded media program, would result in a more knowledgeable and detailed coverage of the operation. The military has long been unnerved by the obvious lack of expertise on the side of the war correspondents they had to deal with. The press people, soldiers would often complain, were so badly informed that they confused an F16 with an M16. "At least they'll get their facts straight," the general said. "Besides, the American people deserve to see the professionalism of their sons and daughters in uniform," he reasoned.

The message, headed "Command Support of Public Affairs Activities in Potential Future Military Operations," was sent out to all commands on 14 November 2002, and retransmitted on 21 February 2003. It bore Rumsfeld's signature and was distributed by McCreary even before the political decision to go to war against Iraq was officially made. The message, aimed at the operators, attempted to link the media operation to their success on the battlefield:

> Media coverage of potential future military operations will, to a large extent, shape public perception of the national security environment now and in the years ahead. This holds true for the US public; the public in allied countries, whose opinion can affect the durability of our coalition; and publics in countries where we conduct operations, whose perceptions of us can affect the cost and duration of our involvement.[37]

The P4 demanded to organize and facilitate access of national and international media to U.S. forces, particularly for those units engaged in ground operations. The intention of this openness was "to get it right from the start, not days or weeks into an operation." Speed was seen as essential to achieve "information superiority".

Fifth came *unconventional media operations*—by far the most radical step. To understand this leap, its doctrinal and operational context needs to be appreciated. What was to be designed as a fast, high-tech blitzkrieg morphed into a slow, more low-tech guerrilla conflict. American forces, confronted with a rising insurgency, were forced to rethink their approach. In December 2006 the Army and the Marines jointly published a new field manual for Iraq, Field Manual 3-24, *Counterinsurgency*. More than a year later, at the end of February 2008, the U.S. Army reissued an operational document of higher order, Field Manual 3-0, *Operations*. Every Army commander, junior and senior, is supposed to "read, study, understand, and implement the doctrine in FM 3-0," General William Wallace, the head of the Army's Training and Doctrine Command, wrote in the foreword. He also highlighted that the document is "a revolutionary departure from past doctrine."[38] For the first time in the history of the U.S. Army, the document elevated stability and support operations to a core military mission, often as important as—"or more important than" (p. vii)—offensive and defensive operations. "Soldiers operate among populations, not adjacent to them or above them," the manual said. It recognized that the enemy may not sit in tanks and planes any more, or hide in mountainous terrain; soldiers face their adversaries among noncombatants and civilians, among the people. Winning battles by military means, therefore, was not sufficient any more. The public's perception may be vital. "Informing the public and influencing specific audiences is central to mission accomplishment," FM 3-0 stressed upfront in the introduction. "These tasks have evolved from specialized ancillary activities—civil–military operations—into a central element of operations equal in importance to the offense and defense."[39] Public affairs, as a result, is not an ornament any more—at least not in doctrine—but one of the central pillars of operations, both conventional and unconventional. The U.S. Army was beginning to move toward War 2.0.

The practical example given by the field handbook is telling. On 10 January 2007 the Taliban attempted an attack on a U.S. outpost near Margah in Afghanistan's Paktika province. The fighters crossed over the border from Pakistan in two large groups. Their target, a U.S. brigade, quickly identified and engaged the advancing Taliban fighters. American reconnaissance units had already spotted the group of Taliban paramilitaries in the mountainous terrain of North Waziristan as they dismounted from lorries before filing over the border at two crossings. As the Taliban entered the Bermal district on the Afghan side of the border at 19.00 that evening, Apache assault helicopters fired air-to-surface missiles and 30 mm machine gun rounds. Attack aircraft dropped heavy bombs of 500 to 1,000 lb on the paramilitaries. The coordinated air and ground strikes occurred just 1.2 miles inside Afghan territory and lasted for approximately nine hours as U.S. aircraft tracked the disintegrating columns into the mountains. An estimated 150 fighters were killed by American air strikes and artillery fire.[40] The Associated Press quoted from the text message of a spokesperson of the Taliban, Muhammad

Hanif (sometimes spelled Anif), that NATO's casualty figure was "a complete lie." The terrain made it more difficult for journalists to cover the operation and its aftermath. "Because the battle area was so remote," the *Washington Post* reported from Kabul, "it was not possible for journalists to gather information directly."[41] Trained, objective observers were not there to do their work. The Taliban attack was part of a trend. In September 2006 the Pakistani government had entered an agreement with local elders. Pakistani units would be pulled out from North Waziristan in return for a pledge from local elders not to shelter militants. In the six months before that agreement, there were forty cross-border attacks in the Khost and Paktika provinces. In the two months after the agreement the figure had risen to 140 attacks. "We're seeing evidence that the enemy is taking advantage of that agreement to launch attacks inside Afghanistan," said Colonel Thomas Collins, chief spokesmen for U.S. forces in Afghanistan.[42] These three factors, the absence of foreign media, audacious enemy propaganda, and, most importantly, the role of the local population, made it necessary to complement the successful operation with aggressive public affairs action. In the ensuing weeks, the operation's public affairs follow-up had four operational objectives: to persuade Afghan elders in the region to deny support to the Taliban in the future, to erode the moral support of the Taliban, to reassure the province's local population, and to persuade the Pakistani Army to be more proactive in disrupting the Taliban. And the joint commander, Lieutenant General Karl Eikenberry, wanted to use this battle to inform regional and global audiences about progress in this part of Afghanistan. FM 3-0 again:

> Soldiers gathered evidence and met with the local populace to ensure they under-
> stood the situation. The provincial reconstruction team helped the Afghan governor
> to organize a meeting with the Margah elders to pressure them into cutting ties with
> the Taliban. The attached psychological operations detachment developed and dis-
> seminated sophisticated products, targeting Taliban survivors of the battle. The
> public affairs officer then organized a press conference on-site in Margah to allow
> the Afghan governor to tell the story of the security success to local and regional
> audiences. The joint public affairs team organized a similar event for the interna-
> tional media. The joint commander met with senior commanders of the Pakistani
> and Afghan military. (7-4)

Information engagement, ideally and in doctrinal textbooks, as the story illustrates, is more and more integrated into operational thinking, planning, and execution. Yet in practice the armed forces often have difficulties living up to the doctrine's ideals.

AN ORGANIZATIONAL GAP

"Our enemies have skillfully adapted to fighting wars in today's media age, but for the most part we, our country, our government has not," former Secretary of Defense Donald Rumsfeld said. His successor, Robert Gates, is known to share this frustration. "It is just plain embarrassing that Al Qaeda is better at communicating its message on the Internet than America."[43] Given the significance of the Web at war, any new head of the Department of Defense is likely to ask, at an early point after getting settled in his new job: what are we doing about the Web? The reply the institution would be able to deliver is complicated. The conceptual and operational disorder, in short, is mirrored and enhanced institutionally. A range of agencies with overlapping responsibilities nominally deal with cyberspace and the new media's public role at war.

Yet it would be shortsighted to focus only on the agencies and commands under the department's or the single services' umbrella that were created to deal with public information in the media, new and old. The very nature of the new media, as we argued in chapter 1, is that it increases the number of participants in a public dialogue and that it empowers individuals. This, naturally, also applies within the armed forces. The most salient feature of the DoD's response to the new media therefore is a gap, a gap between the Department's institutional reaction on the one side and the reaction of its soldiers and marines on the other side (less so sailors and airmen). The former is top-down, controlled, command-driven, risk-averse, and well resourced; the latter is bottom-up, spontaneous, motivation-driven, audacious, and often with modest resources. To comprehend this tension, a tension both cultural and generational, the two approaches will be reviewed briefly.

The nature of large administrative bodies is to specialize. If a new challenge arises, such as waging a "war of ideas" in the Muslim world, new units are created to deal with it. The natural instinct of competing large bureaucracies, like military service branches serving the same defense department, is to promote their importance and to mirror structures successfully employed by their competitors. This logic helps to explain the emergence and the growth of several DoD agencies that compete to deal with the public side of information at war. If the challenge, however, is too broad or even revolutionary, a normally useful this organizational reflex to specialize can be counterproductive. Admiral Michael G. Mullen, Chairman of the Joint Chiefs of Staff since 1 October 2007, quickly recognized this problem. On 14 December 2007 he sent a memorandum on "strategic communications" to the Deputy Secretary of Defense, Gordon England. The admiral understood strategic communications as an "enabling function" that guided and informed all American actions. A separate organizational structure should only exist to facilitate the transition to more organic processes that should be firmly rooted and "imbedded within existing structures," not in newly created structures.

At closer view, the strategic level created a huge problem for the Department of Defense. The Army, as discussed, introduced "information engagement" on a tactical level to deal with the populace in the area of counterinsurgency operations; its capstone manual, quoted above, is limited to the operational and tactical levels of war. But internationally or globally the strategic equivalent of information engagement is more difficult to do. In the "war on terror," most experts and politicians seem to agree, the war of ideas among a global population becomes just as important as the local population in a counterinsurgency. Strategic communications, accordingly, have become a key objective of the Department of Defense. "Victory in the long war ultimately depends on strategic communication," stressed the Quadrennial Defense Review in 2006, the Pentagon's most important strategic planning document (pp. 91–92).

The QDR mentioned strategic communications only on its last page but acknowledged it as a "vital element of national power" and identified the need to "improve integration" across the federal government. To close the "capability gaps" in communication, and to make it "seamless" across the U.S. government, as the QDR demanded, the Pentagon created the office of Deputy Assistant Secretary of Defense for Joint Communications, abbreviated as DASD(JC). The Strategic Communication Execution Roadmap, a document intended to institutionalize a process to improve the Defense Department's fitness to fight the global war on terrorism, was signed into action by Deputy Secretary of Defense England in September 2006. Strategic Communication has been defined by the QDR Strategic Communication Working Group as:

> focused United States Government processes and efforts to understand and engage key audiences to create, strengthen or preserve conditions favorable to advance national interests and objectives through the use of coordinated information, themes, plans, programs, and actions synchronized with other elements of national power.[44]

To implement these abstract and bold ideas, the Strategic Communication Integration Group, SCIG, was created in December 2006. In January 2007 the Deputy Secretary of Defense appointed Rear Admiral Thorp as the Director of the SCIG Secretariat. Thorp initiated work on several issues approved by England, but due to bureaucratic quarrels and frictions between the members of the responsible executive committee, minimal progress had been achieved by early 2008. Despite the new organization's disappointing track record, Admiral Mullen, in his memo to England, recommended reauthorizing the Strategic Communication Integration Group for one more year, but emphasized that organization's temporary role in a transition process. That group is led by the Principal Deputy Undersecretary for Policy, Assistant Secretary for Public Affairs, the Joint Staff Director of Strategic Communication, and the Director, Joint Staff. "Think of it—and treat it—more a Task Force or an integrated process team than a permanent office," the nation's highest-ranking soldier counseled the deputy secretary on the group. "Give it a sundown clause, and hold to it. The SCIG should work itself out of a job."[45]

Mullen instead advocated better and more synchronized communication executed by existing agencies and structures. These structures already are so numerous as to be confusing for external observers and internal operators alike.[46] Traditionally the Pentagon's central communicator on a strategic level was the Assistant Secretary of Defense for Public Affairs, internally referred to as

ASD(PA). The office is the principal staff advisor and assistant to the Pentagon leadership in matters concerning public information, internal information, community relations, information training, and audiovisual matters, as outlined in DoD Directive 5122.5. The assistant secretary, simply referred to as "spokesperson" in the press, is often a civilian with a background in journalism. The working relationship and the experience in the nation's newsrooms he or she brings into the job can be an important asset for a spokesperson. But because of such a background and because of an institutionally weak position, the assistant secretary does not have much leverage vis-à-vis senior military commanders.[47]

The structure responsible for communication is easy to understand only at the top and at the very bottom, in other words, at the grand-strategic and at the tactical level. At the top are the secretary and his supporting press office; at the bottom are the platoon leader and enlisted troops. In between there is a multitude of specialized agencies with overlapping responsibilities. Strategic communication, in contrast to public affairs, has a nearly unlimited set of target audiences: not only domestic, also but international and local; not only friendly and neutral, but also adversarial. Historically the armed forces have developed a range of specializations for communication in a rather stovepiped fashion to cater to the different audiences. The Quadrennial Defense Review calls these somewhat euphemistically "primary supporting capabilities" of strategic communication. Each of these capabilities, it should be stressed, has its own career tracks, its own traditions, its own philosophy, its own culture, and its own organizational structures. The Joint Staff in the Pentagon has specialized departments: regional commands such as Pacific Command or Central Command replicated this structure; the regional headquarters in Central Command's area of responsibility, the most important ones being Multi-National Forces-Iraq and Combined Joint Task Force 82 in Afghanistan, again replicate these structures in their regional headquarters. Outside the operational chain of command, the services staffs, large formations, and large commands have their own specialized units. Then there are several additional specialized commands, with specific designators related to strategic communications.

Perhaps the overarching problem faced by the Pentagon's communication architecture is the requirement to be proactive, and not just reactive. What sounds easy at first glance is exceedingly difficult. Regular armies and their communication specialists are traditionally reacting to events, either to events such as particular operations, battles, or attacks that subsequently were covered in the press, or to media reports and requests for explanation or access. In a global war of ideas, by contrast, such a reactive mode is more difficult. If the "event" is the alleged radicalization of diverse groups of Muslims in many countries all over the globe, what is the reaction to be taken by communication specialists? This problem is, at closer inspection, closely connected to the relationship between tactics and strategy. A tactical event might be a suicide attack or an intimidation campaign by the Taliban in an Afghan provincial town—and it might or might not be part of a global trend. But in such situations it is tactically much easier to react—and even to be proactive—than it is strategically. Particularly in communication, tactical is synonymous with tactile, tangible, detailed, up-close—attributes that make a good press story or blog entry. The strategic level in communication or "the war of ideas," by contrast, lacks the concrete: it is abstract, about values, beliefs, motivations, and political views. Particularly in communication, as Mullen stressed in his memo, the tactical can rapidly become strategic—strategic now in a more military sense of potentially having broad impact on an entire operation. The entire concept of strategic communications, therefore, appears in a very problematic light. Again Mullen:

> I have grown increasingly concerned about the military's fixation on strategic communications. We get hung up on that word, *strategic*. If we've learned nothing else in this war, it should be that the lines between the strategic, operational and tactical are blurred almost beyond distinction. This is particularly true in the field of communication, where videos and images plastered on the Web—or even the *idea* of them being so posted—can and often do drive national security decision making. With the aggressive use of technology, the tactical becomes the strategic in the blink of an eye.[48]

Yet the armed forces and their governments, despite the host of agencies they employ, have very little control over what events, in the blink of an eye, may assume a much broader significance by being pushed into the media limelight.

An ongoing cultural change in society, and within Western armies, is exacerbating this loss of control. A very concrete, tactical form of communication unexpectedly has emerged, thanks to the new media environment. Two venues, military blogs and online communities-of-practice, stand out. Blogging, the publication of Web logs, or online journals, today is a widespread phenomenon in America and around the world. Early in 1999 only a few dozen blogs existed; by the end of the year the number had grown to thousands. At the end of 2003, two million blogs were online and the number doubled every five months. In early 2006 Technorati, a search engine that tracks blogs, counted 27 million. In late 2007 more than 100 million blogs were measured. Only about 15 percent of these journals, however, are actively maintained by their authors. In Japan, where blogging is particularly popular, such abandoned or neglected blogs are called *ishikoro*, or pebbles.[49] It is no surprise that this global phenomenon has a martial offshoot, "milblogging." Soldiers, airmen, sailors, and marines of all ranks, but particularly of junior rank, publish such journals online. These take many forms and colors. Blogs may have a short life span of days or weeks, or they may be active for many years. Some servicemen or women blog only during their deployment; others write only after their tours. The online journals reflect the entire spectrum of America's armed forces. Some are stand-alone blogs on well-known platforms such as Blogger (weblogs ending on blogspot.com are published through Blogger, owned by Google); others are integrated into social-networking sites, such as MySpace or Facebook, that offer blogging or microblogging functionalities.

In terms of content and style, the differences are even starker. A few examples will illustrate this diversity. Many blogs are angry and brute in their language, and often apolitical, such as TheAngryAmerican, published at roodawg.blogspot.com. On 27 March 2008, when fighting between Mahdi Army fighters and the Iraq Army escalated in the first Iraqi-led operation, he wrote:

> I got online to check out the news to maybe find out a little more about what the hell is going on here. I read an article about how the Green Zone is "Under Seige" [sic] . . . . Wow. That's it, that's all the fucking news that is going on about recent events here. Have all the reporters gone home or they are just holed up in the GZ drinking mocha frappies and shit and a couple of rounds hit in the GZ so suddenly its under seige? [sic] I might be speaking out of turn but hey around the whole AO shit has gone a little loopy. If you call getting rocketed a few times Under siege then I don't know what you would call ol' Rocketmiyah? Under-apocalypse???

Some blogs are professional, almost journalistic, such as Michael Yon's blog, popular among conservative-leaning readers who look for an alternative to what they see as the liberally biased mainstream media.[50] Yon's best-known dispatch is "Gates of Fire," the story of a firefight in Mosul in which a Lieutenant Colonel, Erik Kurilla, was wounded. Yon himself had to pick up a weapon in self-defense. The report was one of the most downloaded blog entries on the Web for days.

> When the bullet hit that canister, Prosser—who I thought might be dead because of all the blood on his leg—was actually fighting hand-to-hand on the ground. Wrapped in a ground fight, Prosser could not pull out his service pistol strapped on his right leg, or get to his knife on his left, because the terrorist—who turned out to be a serious terrorist—had grabbed Prosser's helmet and pulled it over his eyes and twisted it. Prosser had beaten the terrorist in the head three times with his fist and was gripping his throat, choking him. But Prosser's gloves were slippery with blood so he couldn't hold on well. At the same time, the terrorist was trying to bite Prosser's wrist, but instead he bit onto the face of Prosser's watch. (Prosser wears his watch with the face turned inward.) The terrorist had a mouthful of watch but he somehow also managed to punch Prosser in the face. When I shot the propane canister, Prosser had nearly strangled the guy, but my shots made Prosser think bad guys were coming, so he released the terrorist's throat and snatched out the pistol from his holster, just as SSG Konkol, Lewis, Devereaux and Muse swarmed the shop. But the shots and the propane fiasco also had brought the terrorist back to life, so Prosser quickly reholstered his pistol and subdued him by smashing his face into the concrete.[51]

Other entries are clever and bitterly sarcastic, such as Army of Dude, at armyofdude.blogspot.com. Many of his posts are on fallen soldiers and the human toll of the war in Iraq. On 10 March 2008 he commemorated the death of one of his friends, 22-year-old Brian Chevalier, a week before the anniversary of his death:

> The only solace I found was that Chevy was killed instantly when the IED exploded beneath him. He went like he lived: quietly. His impact on us was not as muted.

> Every single person that knew him cried at his memorial service. Our emotions were
> bottled up after he was killed; we had no time to grieve in between missions. For two
> hours, we reflected on his loss. And we went back out into the night. This Friday, the
> remaining members of second platoon will get together on the anniversary of his
> death to celebrate his life. [52]

Such emotional and graphic writing can appear online fresh and untarnished, only hours after the events took place.

But how significant are blogs? The vast majority of blogs is abandoned, but even among the active blogs only a tiny fraction reaches a wider audience. There are several ways for blogs to reach a broad readership. Having a large number of online readers, such as Michael Yon's journal, might be the least effective way. Military blogs can be picked up by the mainstream media and hosted on their Web sites: *The New York Times*, for instance, experimented with hosting milblogs on its Web site—but just as real blogs out in the wild, they were not maintained very long. Military blogs can be used as source material: Cami McCormick of CBS News, for instance, read the blog about the upcoming memorial meeting honoring Army Corporal Brian L. Chevalier of Tacoma, contacted the blogger, joined the get-together of more than a dozen veterans, and made a CBS news story about their meeting. [53] Yet others are republished as books: David Bellavia's *House to House* is an example of a bestselling milblog-turned-book. Staff Sergeant Bellavia was a decorated NCO who served with an infantry regiment, the Ramrods, in Fallujah in 2004. Because of the vivid and graphic style of blogs, such books may sell surprisingly well. Another example is Colby Buzzell's *My War.* In almost all cases, it is important to note, the stories published on blogs get wider visibility only when they are picked up and recycled by the "old" media, be it a publishing house or the press.

The institutional army's reaction to bloggers has been mixed. A 6 April 2005 memorandum from Headquarters, Multi-National Force-Iraq, ordered milbloggers to register their sites with their units. Not all have done this. Regulation 530-1, issued 19 April 2007, went a step further. It required bloggers to "consult with their immediate supervisor and their OPSEC Officer . . . prior to publishing or posting information in a public forum." Not only was this level of control unrealistic, it was, in effect, a step back from the trust-based treatment embedded journalists received. Army Public Affairs subsequently drafted a fact sheet, "Soldier Blogging Unchanged," to rectify the overambitious regulation. [54]

Another approach was taken by General William Caldwell, first as spokesman of MNF-Iraq and later as commander of the Combined Arms Center in Fort Leavenworth, Kansas. This career step to one of the Army's most important posts, including a promotion to lieutenant general reminiscent of the career step of General Boomer in the Marine Corps almost twenty years earlier, is symbolic of the increased stature of public affairs in the Army. In Iraq Caldwell became convinced of the necessity to change the organizational culture of the army in order to communicate more effectively. As head of MNF-I's public affairs unit, he "broke through the bureaucratic red-tape," the general recalled (coincidentally on a blog). The U.S. military in Iraq then officially started posting on YouTube and similar platforms. MNF-I videos from Iraq were among the top ten videos viewed on YouTube for weeks after their posting; its most popular video of a battle on Haifa Street in Baghdad had accumulated more than 2.7 million views by April 2008, but the majority of videos are viewed far less often.[55] "These videos included gun tape videos showing the awesome power the U.S. military can bring to bear," Caldwell wrote. "Using YouTube—part of the new media—proved to be an extremely effective tool in countering an adaptive enemy."[56] Caldwell, when he assumed command of the Combined Arms Center, continued to pioneer new approaches vis-à-vis the new media. To help the Army understand the cultural change it is part of, Caldwell took an unprecedented step and required graduates of the staff college in Fort Leavenworth to write an elaborate blog entry instead of graduation papers.

The second phenomenon is community blogs, or more accurately communities-of-practice. Such community sites may be public or restricted to registered members. One of the best-known public community sites of the U.S. land forces is smallwarsjournal.com; in early 2009 the site had a daily reach of several hundred thousand and a usage profile comparable with that of major international think tanks.[57] The Small Wars Journal's editors and founders launched the project to facilitate and support the exchange of information among practitioners, thought leaders, and students of irregular warfare, in order to advance knowledge and capabilities in the field. By 2008 the site had indeed become a hotbed of discussion and many of its postings have been quoted in the nation's largest newspapers. It sported a daily press clipping, a magazine with articles on irregular warfare and counterinsurgency, usually with an operational view of problems, and it reported on important publications and events pertinent to counterinsurgency. Among its frequent contributors were some of the military's most prominent officers and thinkers, for instance, John Nagl, Paul Yingling, Pete Mansoor, Bing West, Frank Hoffman, and David Kilcullen. In March 2009 the site facilitated a remarkable, and self-reflective, discussion about the impact of the new media.[58]

The two prime examples for restricted community sites are Company-Command.com, which caters to the Army's approximately 3,300 current company commanders, and PlatoonLeader.org, a highly successful learning platform for the land force's circa 12,000 platoon leaders. Both platforms are today integrated into the institutional army's communication architecture—and their .com and .org were replaced by the official .army.mil. The Web sites' purpose, originally, was to facilitate dialogue among junior leaders and optimize the organization's ability to adapt to an ephemeral operational environment. The conversation takes place on "on front porches, around HMMWV hoods, in CPs [Command Posts], mess halls, and FOBs [Forward Operating Bases] around the world," the welcome statement said. The front porch is a hint at the Web site's founding history. At the end of the 1990s, the two captains Nate Allen and Tony Burgess both commanded

companies in separate battalions of the same brigade, based in Hawaii. They happened to be next-door neighbors and spent many evenings on their Hawaiian
front porches comparing notes. "How are things going with your first sergeant?"
they would ask, or "How did your company live-fire work out?" Realizing the positive impact of their peer conversations, the two majors wrote a book and posted
it on a Web site. Through this initial publication they got in contact with another
captain who proposed to model a Web site on alloutdoors.com, an online switch-
board for hiking and survival advice, such as how to skin a squirrel. Allen and
Burgess, together with a dozen more captains, among them Pete Kilner and Steve
Schweitzer, decided to adapt the outdoor model and go ahead. "Such a site for
company commanders would replicate, in cyberspace, their front porch," as Dan
Baum observed in *The New Yorker*.[59] The active-duty entrepreneurs did not ask
the Army for permission, nor for financial support, and they registered their project with a .com address, not on the U.S. military's .mil Internet domain.

Soon the Army discovered the value of the sites, and included them in its official information network. Army Major General Peter Chiarelli, commander of the
1st Cavalry Division, started another site, CavNet initially, that ran on the U.S.
military's "Secret Internet Protocol Router Network," or SIPRNET. The secure
system was built on hardware that is separate from the civilian Internet, and only
accessible from special computers. SIPR's downside has been that it is not as widely
accessible as the Internet. In Iraq it is available at the battalion level, but not at the
company or even platoon level. CompanyCommand.com grew to 6,200 members
in 2006, when the site was viewed about a million times. "Today's army is changing
so fast, that people at the high end don't always know because they haven't lived it,"
said Schweitzer, one of the site's administrators. For the first four years the Internet site was entirely open to the public, and to the enemy. On 8 February 2004,
Pentagon correspondent Thomas Ricks published an article in the *Washington Post*
that prominently features the site. Overnight, the traffic skyrocketed. Its
founders—not the Army—then decided to limit access to the site to professional
U.S. soldiers, mostly captains. The closure, Kilner pointed out, made the online
community much more powerful and much more successful. "It's not just information; it's a personal story, and commanders are able to connect with their peers who
share their knowledge. The forum fosters a powerful sense of shared purpose
among members." It worked not unlike MySpace or Facebook: profiles were created with photos, bios, and mostly information on a soldier's professional background, all focused solely on being a more effective company commander. "The
commanders see that the forum really is by and for them. They see others who
share their challenges and experiences; they see their own face and those of their
comrades, and that deepens their sense of professional identity. The learning that
occurs in and through the online connections," Kilner said, "has a real impact on
the war."[60] The private initiative then partnered within the official Battle Command Knowledge System, the Army's institutionalized system of chat rooms and
Internet blackboards, and was supported by the United States Military Academy
and government grants. Yet the military establishment understood the site's logic

of a peer-to-peer culture that generates commitment and refrained from micro-managing it. "We don't want to over-control," said William Wallace, V Corps commander during the invasion of Iraq and now head of the Training and Doctrine Command, TRADOC. "There's a certain amount of pride in these communities in thinking that they operate outside the institution."[61] The institutional Army did not significantly interfere with the operations of the CompanyCommand and PlatoonLeader sites.

The Marines, this time, proved the Army right. In May 2006, 2nd Lieutenant Andrew Schilling published an article in the Marine Corps Gazette which scored in one of the magazine's essay contests. "It is hard for a Marine to admit when the Army does something better," he wrote, and went on chastising the Corps for not making better use of peer technology, such as Company-Command and PlatoonLeader. The sites, the junior officer argued, were "superior to anything the Marines have because they treat their users as peers."[62] This was not to say that the Marines did not use the Internet, but they did so outside the service's control and awareness. Schilling described how his platoon, just as many others in The Basic School (TBS), used an Internet site on a private server to keep track of each other, provide study assistance, post photos, and organize the platoon's activities. The young officers shared their gouge online—jargon for tips, templates, study guides, and the like. Navygouge.com was one of those sites.

The new media's use on the battlefield is not limited to the Internet. "Most value is not created online," said Kilner. "It's in the chow hall, it's on the Humvee." The online part merely amplifies the face-to-face interaction. The CompanyCommand team, for instance, installed a podcasting capability and planned to equip commanders on their way to Afghanistan with new iPods, fully loaded with video-podcasted interviews with fellow commanders on their way out. Cellphones and private digital cameras were used both for documentation and calling home. Commercial gadgets, sometimes superior to the Army's own equipment, were more and more used to gather and document intelligence. "Take pictures of everything and even, more importantly, everyone. The right photo in the right hands can absolutely make the difference," one captain recommended online.

Blogs, social-networking sites, and community platforms have one thing in common: they understand, and use, communication not as a monologue, but as a dialogue. Some people in the Department of Defense have understood this dynamic. "Communication is as a two-way street," wrote the chairman of the Joint Chiefs of Staff in underlined print. His memorandum quoted one moderate Muslim leader who stressed that the United States should communicate "not by transmitting, but by receiving." A second lesson the chairman highlighted is that credibility counts more than content. Messages and communication plans crafted by the United States government would never have the same impact on foreign audiences as the commentary on U.S. actions by "credible third parties"—a term that has gained traction in the DoD bureaucracy for some years—that is, external analysts, foreign leaders, and journalists. "I share SECDEF's frustration that we are not as nimble as Al Qaeda in communicating our message," Mullen wrote, referring to Secretary of Defense Robert Gates in a common abbreviation. Yet the chairman again highlighted his skepticism vis-à-vis a "static, separate" strategic communications organization—"or even SC at all." The task, he wrote, is better served by inculcating communication execution and assessment into existing areas and into the department's culture in general. Decentralization, a policy that runs counter to bureaucracy's proper specialization logic, would be the right way forward. "Only then can we hope to be nimble enough to reclaim the information battlespace Al Qaeda has appeared to master."[63]

In sum, the U.S. armed services, particularly the land forces, made a serious effort to understand war among the people and its non-traditional requirements: that the human terrain is the central battleground, that local public perceptions may be decisive, that trust matters, that military tasks become much broader and more political, and that local commanders have to be empowered to implement local solutions. The U.S. military, in short, attempted to adopt elements of War 2.0. But the traditional focus on War 1.0 was not abandoned: technological innovation, high-tech precision weaponry, networked communication grids, and a veritable robotics revolution have not and will not be replaced by population-centric ideals—instead the U.S. armed forces will more and more be confronted with a tension. A tension between increasingly complex weapons systems and military operations, requiring a maximum of military specialization and professionalization—and increasingly complex social dynamics and political operations, demanding a minimum of military specialization and the breakup of a narrowly understood ideal of professionalization. War 2.0 has the potential to push a regular force to the edge, and is far more problematic than often assumed.

4

The United Kingdom

Media Operations in the United Kingdom are somewhat insular. Four particularities set the coverage of British military operations apart from that in the United States, the rest of Europe, or Israel. The British Army, for one, has a rich experience in fighting counterinsurgency on its own territory in Northern Ireland. The conflict regularly spilled over into England and London, which heavily affected the relationship between the Army and the British public. To this day, for instance, one rarely sees a British soldier in uniform in public other than on festive occasions such as Remembrance Sunday. Other than in most counterinsurgencies, both sides in the Northern Ireland conflict predominantly spoke, and published, in English[1]; as a consequence the press played a pronounced role in escalating political violence from a very early stage.

Second, the UK armed forces historically were among the most proficient in expeditionary warfare, due to the geography of the British Isles and the empire's global ambitions. In fact, the chief of staff stressed in 2004 that "[a]ll operations will be expeditionary."[2] The British Army fought more than fifty major irregular campaigns in the nineteenth century, two of them in Afghanistan. In the interwar period British soldiers have confronted several insurgencies in their colonies or close to home: in Ireland, Somaliland, India, the Iraq Revolt in 1920, and the Arab Revolt from 1936 to 1939. The pace of operations further accelerated after the end of the Second World War. The armed forces of the United Kingdom were in active service overseas in every year except 1968, and often in more than one theater at once. The major irregular operations were in Palestine (1945–8), Malaya (1948–60), Kenya (1952–60), Cyprus (1955–59), Borneo (1962–66), Aden (1963–67), Dhofar in Oman (1970–75), Northern Ireland (1969–2007), Bosnia (1992–2007), Sierra Leone (1999–2001), and again Afghanistan (2001–present) as well as Iraq (2003–2009). If there was a British approach to irregular war, it stressed the primacy of policing with the military in a subordinate role, and the army's willingness to show restraint in the use of force—although this approach might be fading in Afghanistan.[3]

Third, the British press traditionally has some of the most aggressive news-hounds anywhere. *The Sun*, a rabid tabloid published in Britain and Ireland, has the highest circulation of any English-language paper in the world. It is known for pulling no punches when it comes to criticizing the government. Others such as the *Independent*, the *Daily Telegraph*, *The Times*, and the BBC have a long history of investigative journalism. The government has long tried to tame and "feed the beast," as one Air Force officer working in the Ministry of Defence's (MoD's) press office put it.[4] The British armed forces, particularly since the practice of embedding has become more established in the Balkans and then, from 2003 onward, has forged close relationships with the British press.

Finally the British government equally is among the shrewdest democracies in public relations, or "spin-doctoring," to use one of British journalism's favorite phrases. Traditionally in the United Kingdom, when the nation committed its sons and daughters to war, the political and military elites have made a point of a bipartisan support for the operation among the political parties as well as within the executive. Cracks and dissent inside the government were the exception after the Second World War, and overall the government's unifying approach worked well during times of national crisis. The bipartisan consensus, however, was damaged in recent years by the highly controversial nature of the war in Iraq. The most vivid and visible scandal was the Kelly Affair, an unhappy episode about an allegedly "sexed up" government dossier. It illustrated the tension that continues to put the triangle of media–military–government relations under severe pressure. The largely unexpected irregular nature of the wars in Iraq and Afghanistan, with its lack of progress and lack of measures of progress, has inserted friction between senior civilians and top officers in London, increasing the civil–military tensions and opening leaks—a situation that is easily exploited by Fleet Street (and sometimes by Britain's enemies in theater). Recent reforms in the Defence Ministry's press office have only exacerbated these problems.

This chapter will first review the evolution of the British MoD's current press operations and recapitulate three key incidents that set the stage for today's military–media relationship. Second, we will look at recent changes in the media coverage of defense issues in Britain. Third, the government's press operations and their institutional setup will be reviewed, particularly the MoD's predominantly civilian-staffed press office vis-à-vis the military services. We argue that the new media, and a new type of irregular war, have exacerbated a double tension: between civilians and officers, and between political and operational approaches to communication at war. The outcome negatively affects the British Army's ability to confront irregular enemies.

THE EVOLUTION OF MEDIA OPERATIONS

Britain's century-long, complex history of irregular warfare shaped the military's culture significantly. Yet the wars an officer corps experiences first-hand are always more vividly remembered than those of the distant past. Fresh events therefore have a stronger influence on ongoing operations, be it as models to follow or to avoid. Of the most significant recent conflicts with respect to media–military relations, four stand out, two conventional wars and two unconventional operations.

One conflict shaped the British Army's culture, its doctrine, and consequently also its media operations probably more than any other: Northern Ireland, code-named Operation Banner.[5] The operation was the longest campaign ever fought by the British Army, and the largest since the Second World War. In 1972, during Operation Motorman, approximately 28,000 troops were inserted into Northern Ireland, more than twice the peak strength of Afghanistan and Iraq combined.[6] In total more than 250,000 members of the regular army served in Ulster during the campaign; over 600 were killed, 102 in 1972 alone. During the course of the campaign—the word "war" was rarely used—more than 10,000 terrorist suspects were arrested, and more than 3,100 people lost their lives.

Early on, the mass media played an important role in that conflict. Six counties of the province of Ulster remained part of the United Kingdom when Ireland was given independence in 1922. The Nationalists, or Republicans, who are Catholic, saw themselves as part of the Republic of Ireland; the Unionists, or Loyalists, were almost entirely Protestant and wished to remain part of the UK. The level of violence began to rise at the end of the 1960s. An Orange Order March on 5 October 1968 escalated into large-scale riots in Londonderry—and became the first fully televised event of this kind in the United Kingdom. The cameras caught the Royal Ulster Constabulary using excessive force, thereby paving the way for an escalation of the conflict. "The Troubles," as the violent conflict between the two groups became known, erupted in the summer of 1969 during a march in Londonderry when the first deaths were caused, at a time when the province had 1.8 million inhabitants. British troops were deployed to Northern Ireland also at the request of the Catholic community.

The operation's most salient feature is its duration of about 37 years; indeed it is one of world's longest armed confrontations since the Second World War. The conflict in Northern Ireland has alternatively been described as a civil war, an insurrection, terrorism, a liberation movement, a colonial war, and even a peace-keeping mission. One feature that is not disputed is the conflict's unconventional nature. The Provisional IRA was "one of the most effective terrorist organizations in history," an official Army report said in 2006. "Professional, dedicated, highly skilled, and resilient."[7] It mimicked foreign guerrillas who had successfully fought the British empire and initially assumed that a few British casualties would drive the occupier out. On 6 February 1971 the first British soldier in nearly fifty years was killed in Northern Ireland. The Provisional IRA's Army Council had an initial target of thirty-six killed soldiers, the number of fatalities in the Aden Emergency, from where the Royal Anglian Regiment had retreated in November 1967. When this number was reached, and the British did not withdraw, Dave O'Connell, a militant and influential member of the Council, proclaimed that "we've got to get to eighty."[8] By June 1972 more than one hundred British soldiers had been killed, and the numbers would continue to rise. And indeed, the death of professional soldiers made the public's support for the war more volatile. In September 1971 a poll for the *Daily Mail* found that a majority of Britons, 59 percent, favored an immediate military withdrawal from Northern Ireland. But the conflict would drag on, with occasional spikes of violence. While there had been accusations that government authorities used excessive force, it is noteworthy that the British never used heavy weaponry let alone bombardments by the Royal Air Force in Northern Ireland.

At first the British didn't know how to handle the public affairs side of the Troubles and made a couple of noteworthy mistakes. The military introduced harsh interrogation techniques that were developed in colonial theaters during the 1950s and 1960s in Northern Ireland. Operation Demetrius was a large-scale internment policy that produced some tactical benefits. But "the information operations opportunity handed to the republican movement was enormous," a study for the Chief of the General Staff noted in 2006. The report had the aim of recording the operation's major lessons for today's commanders. And the lesson of Demetrius was clear: the internment of a large number of suspects, and their harsh treatment, had "a major impact on popular opinion across Ireland, in Europe and the US," the report stated: "it was a major mistake."[9] The insurgents, the British slowly understood, had their deep roots in the local culture, spoke the local patois—in a metaphorical as well as in an actual sense—and were better connected to the local population than the government forces. The IRA just as easily took advantage of the ensuing violent incidents, most prominently that fateful January Sunday 1972 in Londonderry, when thirteen civil rights protesters were fatally shot by the British security forces. That day subsequently entered Europe's collective memory as Bloody Sunday. The day's enduring notoriety perhaps illustrates the success of insurgent media operations, or at least that is the view of some in the British army: "The events of Bloody Sunday were immediately exploited by a Republican information operation," the Operation Banner report stated.[10]

The campaign in Northern Ireland is relevant in this context for three reasons: It explains the government and the military elites' insistence on bipartisanship, as fears of a populist takeover and loss of Ulster ran deep on both sides of the aisle. It explains the government's sensitivity to *domestic* media coverage, and its desire to control what is reported in the press. Particularly the Conservative Party accused the British press of defeatism and undermining morale: "we must try to find ways to starve the terrorist and the hijacker of the oxygen of publicity on which they depend," as Margaret Thatcher famously demanded in a speech in 1985. And finally it explains the Army's continued experience and appreciation of the intricacies of counterinsurgency operations. Nearly every senior officer in the army served multiple tours in Northern Ireland. Officer postings in public affairs functions, as a result, traditionally had a higher esteem in the British military than in most other Western armies.[11] Yet it is important not to overrate the significance of Northern Ireland. Operation Banner ended only in 2007, and the conflict has affected an entire generation of servicemen and women. But many a junior commander 2009 either never served in Northern Ireland, or served there long after the early 1970s, when the tough lessons were learned first-hand.

A second milestone event for media operations in the UK was the Falklands War of 1982. The war, although it happened in a rather unique setting, established new standards on how to manage the media in limited, quick wars. The war against Argentina for the Falkland/Malvinas Islands was remote, 8,000 miles from Britain; it was fought and won mainly at sea, far from any well-connected larger city, 400 miles from the nearest land mass. The Ministry of Defence, therefore, had a major advantage: it, and only it, controlled the access to the war. Journalists could report the war only from the Navy's vessels. The rules imposed on journalists by the ministry were tough: twenty-nine British journalists accompanied the Task Force, but no foreign press was allowed. The Ministry of Defence hand-picked some preferred journalists, such as Max Hastings, who then worked for the *Evening Standard*, while denying 160 organizations any access to theater.[12] The ministry issued an "official communiqué" once a day. Alternatives were difficult to conceive of at the time. ABC television, an American news organization, considered chartering a steamer together with several other U.S. news channels and newspapers. The costs eventually were deemed too high. So was the risk: the British Navy threatened to fire at any vessel in the total exclusion zone, a method the U.S. Navy would repeat one year later during the invasion of Grenada.[13] Philipp Knightley, one of Britain's best experts on war reporting, aptly assessed the ministry's work: "the MoD was brilliant—censoring, suppressing, and delaying dangerous news, releasing bad news in dribs and drabs so as to nullify its impact, and projecting its own image as the only real source of accurate information about what was happening."[14] Officers saw journalism as a genuinely untrustworthy profession, the workings of which needed to be controlled in order not to compromise the military mission. Rear Admiral John Woodward, the operational commander, summarized the instructions to the six MoD minders as "co-operation, yes; information, no."[15] The Falklands War is remarkable here for two reasons: it intensified the conflict between the military and the press, as both sides were disappointed in the other's behavior; and it is noteworthy for the lesson the military and the MoD took away from the war: control of the press is not only necessary but possible. Only a few years after the Vietnam War, which many officers at the time believed was lost because the unrestricted, sensationalist media coverage eroded American support, the Royal Navy won a war by restricting and limiting the press access. The Falklands War's unique conditions were turned into a model for future media–military relations. The Navy did not apply any of Northern Ireland's pertinent lessons for what seemed were solid reasons; after all the Falkland conflict was a regular war among navies at sea, not an irregular policing campaign among the people on land.

Third, in the 1991 Persian Gulf War the ministry would work under more adverse conditions, yet the Falkland model was implemented not only by the United Kingdom, but more importantly by the UK's senior partner, the American Department of Defense. The sheer number of media representatives in the Gulf was overwhelming. Approximately 1,600 journalists waited for the war to start in the countries adjacent to Iraq's southern tip, more than four times the number that reported from Vietnam after the Tet Offensive. The Persian Gulf War, after all, was one of the largest conventional military operations in the second half of the twentieth century, and it was one of the shortest as well. The ground war was concluded victoriously after a mere 100 hours. The speed of ground operations made it necessary, in the commanders' view, to vigorously guard operationally relevant information. The war's logistical conditions were remotely comparable with the Falklands conflict: the vast Saudi and Kuwaiti desert was nearly as hostile to unilateral journalists as the deep sea off Argentina's shores. In the early 1990s mobile phones were rare and Internet connections nonexistent, so reporters had to rely on the military's cumbersome logistics—dubbed the "pony express"—to get their product back to the rear and from there to their media organizations' headquarters. Although CNN's unwieldy live coverage from the roof of Baghdad's Al Rashid hotel heralded a new era of war reporting, the military took away one main lesson: control worked. Yet some officers sensed another sea change: the adversary was getting better at using the media against the West to his own benefit, undermining public support at home by shrewdly pointing the Western media to allied mistakes and blunders.

The fourth operation that had a strong impact on today's media–military relationship in the United Kingdom was the Sierra Leone hostage rescue operation. In May 2000 Britain had sent about 1,000 troops and a naval task force to the West African country after the insurgent movement Revolutionary United Front came close to seizing control of the country to evacuate foreigners and, as events unfolded, to shore up the UN and stop the rebels. Most troops were withdrawn in June, when the RUF was on the defensive but retained control of the country's diamond producing areas. A 300-strong British contingent was kept in West Africa to train the Sierra Leonean army. Then, on Friday, 25 August 2000, eleven members of the Royal Irish Regiment were kidnapped together with a soldier from Sierra Leone about sixty miles east of Freetown. A militia group known as the West Side Boys had seized the soldiers outside the country's capital while the soldiers were on a mission to train local security forces in the town of Benguema. The British government discarded the kidnappers' demands as politically unrealistic and negotiations broke down. Whitehall considered a military solution.

The Ministry of Defence, with Geoff Hoon at the helm, came to regard the capture of the British soldiers by a rag-tag band of irregulars as a national humiliation. During the last days of August, the press started to speculate publicly that a rescue mission would be imminent. Elite SAS troops "were understood to be on hand to mount a rescue operation," reported *The Irish Times* from Belfast on 29 August; ten of the kidnapped troops were from Ulster. The MoD later fueled those speculations by saying on background that "more provocative measures" were being considered.[16] On 6 September *The Times* of London and several other papers reported that paratroopers were flown to Dakar in Senegal "last night" to "stand by for a rescue attempt." The paper even specified the number of men, 150, and the regiment, the Army's 1st Battalion of the Parachute regiment. "Any rescue attempt," the paper said, "would be the most daring mounted by the British Army in decades."[17] Swamps and the impenetrable jungle environment would make it a very risky operation. Through clever investigations and well-placed sources the British press had a rather precise understanding of the impending operation; they had already printed the date of a probable attack and were stunningly precise in their predictions. Military planners began to be concerned about the detailed publicity of the upcoming operation. Commanders decided to confidentially brief press representatives in Freetown about the impending rescue operation in order to make them understand the risks of publishing information of value to the enemy. The reporters, realizing that the safety and potentially the survival of British servicemen were at stake, held back the information and did not publish operationally relevant details. During the rescue, Operation Barras, one British paratrooper, Trooper Brad Tinnion, was killed and twelve others were wounded. Twenty-five members of the West Side Boys were dead, and eighteen were captured. The six British hostages were freed. Sierra Leone is remarkable for one important reason: it demonstrated to the armed forces that journalists, if properly informed, can be trusted, even in tense situations with enormous news value. The episode heralded the beginning of a more cooperative relationship between Britain's armed services and defense correspondents, a relationship that was remarkable because it increasingly left the ministry's civilian defense staff outside the loop.

Since the invasion of Afghanistan and Iraq, several situations have shaped the defense–media relationship significantly and set the stage for reform of media access to MoD sources and conflict between the two institutions. Three incidents, although different in nature and scope, stand out: an affair about a sexed-up government dossier, the Iran hostage crisis involving fifteen British sailors and marines, and an unusually outspoken chief of the general staff. The Kelly affair was the most intense. Although it did not involve any uniformed officers—only civilians working in the Ministry of Defence, most prominently the affair's victim, Dr. David Kelly—it was of high significance for the military's subsequent relations regarding media access to sources to officials. On 24 September 2002 the British government published a dossier on Iraq's weapons of mass destruction. In chapter 3, that dossier stated that "The Iraqi military are able to deploy these weapons within forty five minutes of a decision to do so."[18] Shortly after the invasion of Iraq, on 29 May 2003, Andrew Gilligan reported in the BBC's *Today* program that "the government probably knew that the 45 minute figure was wrong," and that the dossier was "sexed up" at the behest of Alastair Campbell, the Prime Minister's communication advisor. Gilligan, then a hated figure in the Ministry of Defence, said that his source had been David Kelly, a biologist and former UN weapons inspector. Shortly after he was identified as the source of the story, Kelly was found dead, apparently having committed suicide. The Kelly affair triggered rumors, speculations, and above all a gargantuan media interest in Britain as well as internationally. The Hutton Inquiry, one of several commissions, was the most high-profile investigation into the circumstances surrounding Kelly's fatality. Lord Hutton concluded that no third person was involved in Dr. Kelly's death. Yet the affair highlighted in the most dramatic way the risks and costs of government leaks to the press and the public. Many civil servants working on defense and security matters concluded that leaking information or just talking to press representatives could involve dramatic costs and merited the highest prudence. The entire Kelly affair also heavily damaged the reputation of the government and the Ministry of Defence while it left that of the armed forces intact, thus increasing the potential for civil–military tensions in London.

A second event with lasting consequences was the Iran hostage crisis. On 23 March 2007, a seaborne Iranian border patrol detained fifteen sailors from the Royal Navy and the Royal Marines who were patrolling off the *HMS Cornwall* in disputed waters in the Iran/Iraq border region; the ship was part of the British contribution to multinational forces in Iraq. Iran insisted that the soldiers made an "illegal entry" into Iranian waters; Tony Blair denied that and called the detainment "unjustified and wrong." A major diplomatic crisis ensued, and the media interest in the story in the UK and worldwide soared. The crew was released on 4 April by Iranian president Ahmadinejad as a "gift" to Britain. As a reaction to the media frenzy—the detainees' families had to be protected from aggressive media requests by specially trained "media shielders"—four days later the MoD announced that the detainees would be allowed under "exceptional circumstances" to sell their stories to the press.[19] Leading Seaman Faye Turney, twenty-six years of age and the only detained woman, allegedly sold her story for more than £100,000 to news organizations.[20] The decision to allow the deal was highly controversial and was quickly redrawn. Defence Secretary Des Browne told the House of Commons on 16 April that he had started a review of media access to personnel. The Iranian hostage affair thus triggered a rethinking of the MoD's media management. Tony Hall, chief executive of the Royal Opera House and an influential former BBC editor, was appointed to head an inquiry. The intention of the investigation was "to be forward looking and to identify lessons and recommendations for any necessary changes for the future."[21] The authors believed "that the lessons we have identified have broad application."[22] Hall criticized the fact that the fleet headquarters had a dominant role in the media management during the crisis, not the ministry. One of the report's key lessons, accordingly, was that "[r]esponsibility must clearly lie with the MoD." The review also recommended strengthening the government's resources to deal with such cases in the future. The hostage crisis created a strong momentum for change. It highlighted how ill-equipped the ministry was to deal with a PR crisis of this magnitude.

Third, there is the Army's frustration with the wars in Iraq and Afghanistan. At the end of August 2006, General Sir Richard Dannatt came in as the new Chief of the General Staff, Britain's highest post in uniform. He took over from General Sir Mike Jackson, a rugged and tough soldier with a deep baritone voice dubbed "Macho Jacko" by the boulevard press. Sir Richard, by contrast, had the looks of "a barrister or a banker," commented the *Daily Mail*, Britain's oldest tabloid and second best-selling paper after *The Sun*. Yet the fifty-five-year-old general proved more combative than his predecessor. Within days after taking office, the general began to voice the Army's deep-seated frustration with the wars in Afghanistan and Iraq. Dannatt questioned whether the £1,150 take-home pay for a month's fighting in Helmand would be sufficient; the treasury eventually decided to give a bonus to troops serving in war zones. After a hospital ward scandal involving returned veterans, the new army chief with a tellingly un-British lack of understatement said that he had voiced his complaint to Des Browne, the Secretary of State for Defence since May 2006: "I said to the Defence Secretary that the Army won't let the nation down, but I won't want the nation to let the Army down."[23] And in an interview with the *Daily Mail* he went on to question the government's Iraq policy. Speaking about the recent invasion in Mesopotamia, which was supported by his political masters at the time, the general noted that history would show that the preparations for the occupation, phase IV in military jargon, were "poor" and "based more on optimism" than on sound military planning. With respect to the British military presence in Baghdad and Basra, the general contended that "[we should] get ourselves out sometime soon because our presence exacerbates the security problems."[24] For the British Army with its strong traditions of political noninvolvement these were rare and uncharacteristically strong views from the nation's top soldier: "I want an Army in five years time and ten years time. Don't let's break it on this one," the four-star general said.[25]

Dannatt's outspokenness looked as if he was at odds with Tony Blair's foreign policy and an Iraq policy of remaining steadfastly on America's side. The *Daily Mail* reported that the government was "stunned" and "aghast" by the general's remarks; the *Telegraph* told that Dannatt's words "shook Downing Street last night." Even Al-Jazeera carried reports that said the general had delivered "a painful blow" to Tony Blair's government. Yet the prime minister decided to signal continued "full support" for the general in public. Predictably, the press seized on the interview. The following Saturday, the *Independent* sprinkled its front page with quotes from an army community Web site where soldiers discuss defense issues under pseudonyms.[26] "At last, someone told the truth," was printed in large letters as the day's headline. Several servicemen referred to the prime minister as "B'liar." At least as significant as that diffuse support from the armed services was a speech given by Dannatt's predecessor two months later. In the BBC's thirty-first Richard Dimbleby lecture in December 2006, Sir Mike accused the Ministry of Defence of not giving proper support to troops risking their lives in Iraq and Afghanistan. His criticism was less bold than Dannatt's, both verbally, as Jackson did not comment on the government's decision to go into Iraq in the first place, and because he didn't hold the Army's top job any more. Yet the reaction of many in the military and among outside observers was not that soldiers shouldn't criticize the government in public, as a sound civil-military relationship would want them to do, but that Jackson came out with his indignation too late. *The Independent* captured the prevailing mood well by quoting one blogger: "Jackson has lost all credibility. Dannatt got in first and showed more courage by saying it while in office. And to think Jackson used to have a fearsome reputation. Oh how the mighty are fallen."[27] The *Daily Mail* picked up quotes from the same Web forum, elevating one to a punchy headline, "General Hypocrite."[28] The media, jointly with both old and new formats, increasingly highlighted—and thereby amplified—civil-military tensions.

THE DEFENSE–MILITARY–MEDIA RELATIONSHIP

The traditional mainstream media and their reporting on defense are affected by four recent developments: fiercer competition, irregular warfare, better contacts to soldiers, and the new media. First, the established media industry has become more competitive. New formats in the traditional media landscape have made competition for scoops and exclusive stories fiercer: there are now 24-hour news channels seamlessly setting the news agenda and developing stories; the number of TV stations both international and local has increased; online editions of many newspapers and even the Web sites of TV stations are permanently updated, pulling the permanent deadline over from radio into print journalism; widespread podcasting among commuters and Internet-based broadcasting are making radio news more accessible and quite unexpectedly raised that medium's profile, prompting even newspapers to venture out into the audio market; and the number of political talk shows has mushroomed and diversified in recent years, catering to emerging news-consumption patterns of a younger generation. That diversification is complemented by a regional expansion: information in the traditional media is not confined to a particular time or region; the any more internet makes it possible to listen to a radio newscast or watch a TV show at convenience, and local papers can be read and used as sources from everywhere. Although newspapers will unquestionably retain a local character, there is now an increased cross-reading beyond nations within regions defined by a common language, such as the Anglo-Saxon world, *la francophonie*, or *der deutschsprachige Raum*. In addition to that, the increased transparency brought about by the global media also sheds light on disparities and inequalities, potentially giving rise to grievances and conflict. Naturally the British military is concerned about such scenarios. The chief of staff:

> The 24-hour news media will ensure that the results of globalisation, including global inequality, are visible to most. This could also fuel hostile reaction, particularly among those who perceive themselves to be on the wrong side of the divide.[29]

Yet neither this effect nor the more general changes in the mass media should be exaggerated or overestimated: leading national news organizations, such as the *Guardian*, the *Times*, or the BBC, remain attention filters, trusted sources, and markers of credibility and significance—no matter whether they are read online or offline. Even the debates and the press coverage within the Anglo-Saxon world, where language barriers do not exist, remain national, regional, and even local. In fact the opposite of globalization may be the case: the Internet contributes to an increased specialization and fragmentalization of news-consumption, as specific groups and communities find and maintain outlets that cater to their particular views or tastes, confirming and even narrowing them down instead of broadening them.

Second, more competition has produced a ferocious appetite for human-interest stories, a trend that increasingly applies to defense reporting as well. "In order to secure market share, media outlets are having to seek more 'exclusive' stories and are having to go to greater lengths to get them," Tony Hall pointed out in his report.[30] Some in the ministry's public affairs office believe that the British press is among "the most combative, aggressive, and ill-tempered" anywhere. One of the most high-profile examples for this appetite is Prince Harry's deployment with his unit from the Household Cavalry Regiment Battlegroup to Helmand province in Southern Afghanistan. In late 2007 the twenty-three-year-old Royal had to have his deployment to Iraq canceled after the press had reported on the plans under way. Intelligence sources had warned that he and his unit would be under threat if deployed. Then a secret attempt to deploy the prince in Afghanistan was made. Military officers approached the British media in summer 2007, suggesting an agreement for a news blackout on the prince's deployment. The negotiations eventually included all major British broadcasters, newspapers, and regional publications, more than 100 organizations in total. Part of the agreement was that a small number of journalists could go to Helmand to film and prepare reports for a postponed release. Harry left for Helmand on 14 December. British media organizations stood to the deal and remained tight-lipped. But details of the prince's time in Afghanistan leaked and were initially published in an Australian magazine, *New Idea*, on 7 January 2008. Only several weeks later, on 28 February, the story was picked up by the Drudge Report, a U.S.-based news aggregation Web site that originated as an e-mail list. From there, the story rapidly escalated into one of the British Army's highest publicity events in recent years.

Third, irregular warfare changed the rules of war reporting in the field. The Iraqi and Afghan operations took an unexpectedly negative turn. John Reid, Defence Secretary from May 2005 to May 2006, famously said that the Army's initial 3,300 troops may return home from Afghanistan, their job of helping reconstruction finished, "without a shot being fired."[31] The statement, although taken out of context, came to symbolize the initial optimism of some NATO countries when they first went into Afghanistan. Instead British forces in the south were soon engaged in high-intensity operations with heavy weapons and air force support; eighty-one British soldiers had been killed in Afghanistan by October 2007. Soldier were not only paying a high price in these fights; they wanted the public to know that they were paying a high price. Expectations of key constituencies have changed, driven by a new media environment, new consumption patterns, and the increased transparency of Britain's most important ally in these operations, the U.S. military. To put it bluntly, politicians and civilians would prefer to see the news of successful reconstruction and development work; soldiers would prefer to see the news of successful combat operations.

One additional problem for traditional defense correspondents and media organizations is the dangerous nature of counterinsurgency warfare. Journalists are fair game for insurgents and the kidnapping industry in war-torn places: a kidnapped Western journalist may bring a publicity stunt, a juicy ransom, political impact, or any combination of the three. When the security situation in Iraq reached a low point in late 2007, *The Times* was the only British newspaper that still maintained a Baghdad office, led by one British journalist. The security risks associated with maintaining such an office were ballooning the costs and diminishing the journalistic return. The major problem for journalists was "complete unpredictability," said *The Times*' Michael Evans. The increased risk makes journalists more dependent on the security forces and their protection, the access and information they provide, but also food, transport, and company. As a result, it became more difficult to be nonpartisan for journalists, a problem that was already arising in the MoD's and the Pentagon's embedded media program. Journalists were used to balancing a story internally, that is by consulting different sides. This was no longer possible when a journalist was "embedded for life" with one unit. "Is it possible to be totally objective when you are sharing the same risks?" wondered Evans.[32] The balancing of stories was pushed up to the editorial rooms, or even to the consumer: one journalist might be embedded with the British forces, whereas another might visit the Taliban. It is therefore likely that some journalists will take considerable risks to balance the story. An example is the BBC's David Loyn. Loyn traveled to Helmand province to interview several Taliban commanders and spokespersons, among them Mullah Assad Akhond. "We will fight them to our death," the Taliban activist said about the British. "We will not let them into our country. They can't deceive us about their propaganda that they are here for reconstruction or rebuilding this country." The correspondent added that the British are fighting an uphill battle.[33] The news segment spurned a small debate. "Some believe it is disloyal to our armed forces to film the enemy," *Newsnight* editor Peter Barron wrote after the film was aired. "But if we agreed not to show them, isn't that just a small step away from censorship and pro-government propaganda?" The press was gradually drawn into the conflict by giving selective visibility to warring parties, a visibility that is very much in the interest of both warring parties, the insurgent and the counterinsurgent—an insight that increasingly became clear also to the armed forces, particularly in the United States with its more intense combat experience. The U.S. Army, as has been shown, opened up. Terri Judd, a well-connected and energetic journalist for *The Independent* who embedded with both U.S. and UK forces, said that the Americans were more risk-taking in their press relations, and more open as a consequence. The British Army, she said, generally got better as well as it began to realize that they cannot control the media anyway, so they might as well work with them more constructively.

Risk taking lead to the third change, the improved contact between reporters and soldiers. The so-called Green Book was originally developed as "a general guide to the procedures that the United Kingdom Ministry of Defence (MOD) will adopt in working with the media throughout the full spectrum of military operations."[34] The small booklet covers practical aspects of war reporting, such as accreditation, logistics, etc., but also general aspects, such as mutual expectations and limits of coverage.[35] The document was revived after the Falklands conflict, when the British government clashed with the media on how to report the remote war. The Green Book then was updated prior to the Gulf War of 1991 and maintained with the aim to learn from the past; it "takes account of lessons learned from subsequent operations the Green Book pointed out."[36] But for many journalists and officers the Green Book is not the default reference document any more, mainly because it does not account for the flexibility of new arrangements. The actual relations between soldiers and reporters have evolved in a way that is not reflected in official regularia. "Embedding is a fantastic learning opportunity," said Judd, and it established a working relationship. "Now you've got people's mobile numbers," she said of the army.[37] The same is true for soldiers, points out Major General Andrew Ritchie, former commander of the Royal Military Academy Sandhurst and one of Britain's most visible and adept public affairs officers: "They now have the mobile phone numbers," he said of the press.[38] When the Ministry of Defence tried to control all public statements coming out of the officer corps, the improved direct contacts between commanders and journalists kept the information flowing, often on a nonattributable basis. As a consequence, contacts between military units and journalists were pushed down to lower levels. Correspondents kept in touch even with battalion and company commanders. The initiative for embedding a particular reporter could well come from a regiment or even a smaller formation. As a result, there was not only competition between different services, but even between single units. Not only are the "old" media more competent, embedded, and plugged into the military, they can also plug into the "new" media to get instantaneous insights into the community of soldiers, sailors, and airmen in a way that was unimaginable only a couple of years ago. The writing profession now can have its fingers at Tommy's pulse.

The fourth area of drastic change is the new media. In February 2007 the DGMC finished an internal draft of the MoD's *Communications Strategy*, a simple sixteen-page document devoid of logos and signatures.[39] The paper contains some out-of-the-box thinking, particularly on the role of the new media: "the public places more trust in personal networks rather than 'traditional' methods of communication like news or advertising," it argued. The document was produced under the leadership of Nick Gurr, then DGMC's Director of Communications Planning. Its conclusions are quite bold and far-reaching: "The internet has replaced 'traditional' media as the preferred, most trusted information source after personal contact," the *Communications Strategy* claimed.[40] The document then pointed out "citizen reporting," that is, blogs, mobile phone imagery, and pictures taken by amateurs, that are becoming more important news sources, if not news outlets on their own right. The document put forward that "mobile phone/digital camera images taken by amateurs [are] becoming an increasingly important news source."[41] The MoD, accordingly, identified a need to adapt to these fundamental changes. "The way we communicate has to adapt, to better reflect audience culture, attitudes, and expectations."[42] One of the document's recommendations was that "we . . . need to get our messages direct to the public without going through potentially distorting media." Although the document was only the draft of an internal working paper, it showed the insecurity and the unease that gripped some more traditional institutions faced with the new media—in government and the traditional journalism alike.

While the MoD's public affairs planning staff was strategizing, the younger generation of soldiers and sailors was already well-steeped in using various new media platforms. One of these platforms is not only distinctly military but also distinctly British, and deserves to be mentioned in more detail. Like the United States, Britain has seen the emergence of several community-organized online forums in the armed forces. But while American forums, both password-protected ones and public forums, tended to be largely professional in nature, the British armed services have developed a distinct online culture that includes a raunchy side, perhaps reflecting the British boulevard press's more aggressive style. It would be a mistake, however, to underestimate the quality and impact of the professional debates on these forums. They have become a firmly established component of Britain's debate on defense and military issues. The best known of them is the "ARmy Rumour SErvice," arrse.co.uk. The forum is the UK's premier unofficial military community site. The site was founded in 2002 by two majors in search for a business model; it was a mere coincidence that Britain's military engagement at the side of its U.S. ally was stepped up at the same time in Afghanistan and then in Iraq. One of ARRSE's founders is a helicopter pilot, and he was inspired by the "Professional Pilots Rumours Network," pprune.org, a Web site for professional aviators. After merely half a year, the rumor service attracted a million hits per month. In May 2008 ARRSE had nearly 35,000 members and many more readers. Throughout the year 2007, the forum had a constant daily reach of between 5 and 10 million page views.

The site's two founders said they ran the ARRSE like a business, and actually make some money through ads. Thus, in February 2006, they decided to diversify to meet the huge demand and opened RumRation, a forum aimed at the British Royal Navy and Royal Marines.[43] Yet even for BadCo, a smart end-thirties Scot in a dark suit who chose to meet us in a posh central London pub, the community spirit is the key: it is "100 percent democratic," said BadCo, one of ARRSE's founders who had risen to be an active duty Army major by 2007. "It's one man, one vote." In 2007 ARRSE also owned an island in Second Life, a virtual reality world, and was set to grow. "I'm proud of it all. We've even had a couple of weddings following 'meetings' online. It's almost grown out of our hands. I don't think we'd be allowed to stop now."[44] The forum, although it is public, is not so much external communication but an open form of internal military communication, albeit unofficial. It perhaps resembles the kind of conversations that go on in mess halls and dorms in the offline world. The forum's "official" policy is to ask its members to use a pseudonym, such as "Hawk" or "AnglianGuard"; users are not allowed to use real names. The site serves as a window into the inner workings of the army for many journalists. "I constantly monitor that," said *The Independent's* Terri Judd, stressing that the chatter on ARRSE might prompt her to write a story. When the Army Chief of Staff, General Dannatt, criticized Tony Blair's Iraq policy, her paper—a mainstream newspaper yet known for its unconventional reporting—took the unprecedented step and spread ARRSE quotes by those who supported the general's views over its entire front page.

Yet some professionals inside the institutional army are critical of the community sites. Both the use of pseudonyms and the self-selection of contributors bias the site. The naysayers and the disgruntled, according to both journalists and the ministry, tend to dominate debates on the platform. The site has been in the media for various reasons, from sexism to organizing campaigns to get the Home Office to issue a visa to a former Ghurka, or Fox expressing strong opinions on the hostages' behavior during Iran's seizure of the fifteen sailors. The forum, for instance, was instrumental in creating the British Armed Forces Federation (BAFF). Most British defense correspondents browse ARRSE on a regular, sometimes daily, basis to be better informed about internal debates. Some newspapers are using quotes or insider information from the forum. On 30 October 2005 *The Sunday Times* commended the site to its readers: "I particularly recommend www.arrse.co.uk for a pungent sense of how it feels to be patrolling Basra right now in your unarmoured Land Rover, risking getting your . . . well, arrse blown off for Queen and country," quipped Christopher Hart in the paper's Features section.

Yet ARRSE is a professional community site, and it accepts and enforces professional ethics, particularly when it comes to operational security, a description that does not fit more popular and broader social-networking sites, such as Facebook or MySpace—a deficiency that may have severe security implications. On 17 October 2007 the British MoD distributed an internal note warning that al-Qaeda and its supporters would use the Internet to identify potential targets, abroad as well as in Britain, such as service personnel using social-networking platforms. The alert marked the first time that a British security service, either MI5 or the military, warned troops of the dangers of posting personal information and imagery online. Under the heading "personal security," the document warned soldiers not to reveal "your service connections on chatroom and dating sites." It adds: "Be particularly careful if you are on Facebook, MySpace or Friends Reunited."[45] The ministry's media office pointed out that even upcoming dates of deployments of entire units could be read out from social-networking sites, as the online contacts mirror entire platoons and companies.[46] When the ministry distributed its internal warning, journalists were able to find nearly 900 names on the Royal Marines network on Facebook. Seventy-two soldiers of The Royal Anglian Regiment could be identified, many revealing their full names, dates of birth, home towns, names of family members, girlfriends, wives, the locations where they served, and pictures including fellow soldiers, weapons, and other details that could be gleaned from backgrounds.[47]

Thanks to recent trends both in the traditional mainstream media as well as in new outlets that do not have an editorial department and journalistic training, the public has a much wider spectrum of news sources to choose from. "Today," Tony Hall wrote in his report, "the public knows far more about the details of military operations and the thought processes behind them than at any point in the past."[48] That could have several consequences for the armed forces. The new media's increased availability of human interest raw material has met the old media's increased demand for celebrity stories. A changed understanding of privacy means that individuals may be more inclined to appreciate the mass media's attention. The "all of one company" ethos of the armed forces, as the Hall report argued, may be becoming less a norm in wider society. But complex defense and security problems do not lend themselves to a style of reportage that focuses on gossip and juicy stories.

The Hall report outlined the need to adapt to that new environment. "All of this means that it is important that the MoD keeps thinking through, even more carefully, its relationship with the media. The media and societal environment in which our Service personnel are working is changing rapidly."[49] The government's rules and institutions for communications, as a result, are under pressure to adapt. If official regulations are not adapted, or are adapted in the wrong way, the likelihood increases that pragmatic informal arrangements will evolve in their stead. The next section will explore what the changes in the MoD's institutional communication architecture look like, and whether they work.

AN INSTITUTIONAL GAP

The public relations work done by the civilian leadership of the Ministry of Defence should be distinguished from that of its subordinate military commands. Additionally, the formal and the informal institutional setup may diverge significantly, particularly in the public affairs field. To understand these intricacies, the ministry's reaction to the changes in the media environment—even more so in the context of irregular warfare—need to be reviewed. The government's civilian leadership reacted by attempting to impose increased control—control of all three principal areas of defense public affairs: the information that was provided to the traditional media, through new media platforms, and even to military public affairs officers. The result was a widening institutional gap between the political and the military level.

First, the ministry tried to control the coverage of all military affairs in the news media. One approach was tightening the rules. "The Director-General, Media and Communication (DGMC) has ultimate official authority for internal and external communications including all matters related to contact with the news media and communication in public," reconfirmed the official *Defence Instructions and Notices* in August 2007, an important internal document concerning all official communication with the media or the public, by any MoD agency and its staff of approximately 300,000, "military and civilian."⁵⁰ The MoD's press office, a so-called directorate-general, is made up of three separate directorates: First, there is the directorate for communication and planning (DCP), responsible for the MoD's "strategic communication planning."⁵¹ Second comes the directorate for news (D News), which is responsible for news events and specific announcements. Third, there is Defence Public Relations (D Def PR), responsible for long-term engagement with print, broadcast, and Internet media, such as working with education institutions, feature writers, film-makers, and documentaries. The directorate's authority is significant.

The media office's management of public statements by the defense establishment is best illustrated by a new set of authorization procedures. The ministry came up with different procedures according to military rank. All one-star officials and officers, civilian or military, were required to consult the ministry's Director of News or Communication Plans directorates at least one week in advance, before talking to the media. That in effect meant that a civil servant of a one-star equivalent decided about any flag officers' public statements, even a brigadier's, a commodore's, or an air commodore's speech or article in a military journal. Any public statement of a two-star general or above even required ministerial approval. Everyone below the one-star level—those without star would be Army colonels, Navy captains, or Air Force group captains—had to consult his or her line management or chain of command for "clearance." Staff had to consult ministers if necessary. If in doubt about the need to obtain authorization and release information, the *Instructions* advised, personnel should seek advice from the directorate's section 9 before communicating with the media or speaking or writing in public. The "guiding principle" for all contact with all news media for all of Britain's military personnel was that contact "must be referred to the appropriate D News staff."⁵² It even required prior approval by the ministry's communication experts when "speaking at conferences and private engagements" where "the public may be present." For scholarly papers published by defense academies and think tanks, it took between eight and ten weeks to receive clearance. One motivation for the tighter rules was the outspokenness of top officers in the previous months and years, the Iranian hostage crisis, and previous leaks from civilians, the most high-profile case being that of David Kelly.

Restrictive regulations and threats of punishment contributed to a fearful atmosphere among junior and mid-level public affairs officers. If in doubt, they opted for restriction instead of release. Michael Evans is defense editor at *The Times* and one of Britain's most accomplished war correspondents. He reported from Bosnia, Kosovo, Sierra Leone, and Macedonia, and traveled to both Afghanistan and Iraq many times. The Ministry of Defence developed, he said, a "paranoia" that journalists would not report "according to their script." Evans illustrated this with an example: He went out on a foot patrol with the 3rd Regiment

Royal Horse Artillery. One soldier of that unit, Sergeant Andy Wilkinson, 32, had witnessed during a night-time patrol on 18 October how a fellow soldier, Sergeant Chris Hickey, had died in an IED attack. Two months later the sergeant was speaking with Evans about the incident while leading a midnight foot patrol in the same area of Basra. In the conversation Sergeant Wilkinson recalled that he did not realize that he had also been injured until he returned to base later that night. A piece of shrapnel had pierced his boot and embedded in his ankle. "I was sitting on the steps outside when I felt pain in my ankle and when I took my boot off, it was soaked in blood," he recollected in the spontaneous interview with Evans. The public affairs officer present during the patrol, "an Army minder," interrupted the conversation: "You can't do that," he told them, prompting Evans to stop the unauthorized conversation.[53] Many journalists echo Evans's assessment of paranoia and increased micromanagement by the civilian-dominated ministry extending into theater. One journalist deplored the ministry's "control-freakery."

Second, the ministry was trying to control the new media environment. Although the user-generated new media are not part of the ministry's traditional portfolio, ARRSE, blogs, wikis, and comparable projects are explicitly placed under the directorate's control and supervision. The August 2007 *Defence Instructions and Notices* make clear that the department's new regulation "includes contributing to online debates." The document's authors in the DGMC even specified the formats that required the ministry's approval: publishing books, articles, papers, images, audio, video, including self-published material on the Internet, for example, "through a blog, podcast or shared text," but also communication on "a bulletin board, newsgroup, wiki, on-line social network, multiplayer game" and other applications. Yet the ARRSE project illustrates how difficult it is to implement such ambitious regulations. The founders and administrators remained unknown in person to the MoD's press office.[54] The ministry's attitude was that it is easier to live with a military forum, to monitor it, and to engage in discussions when they know where it is. The genie was out of the bottle, and shutting the site down would result in new ones springing up elsewhere unknown to the authorities, MoD's Internet expert, Robin Riley, argued. (In marked contrast to BadCo, the smart-suited and business-minded ARRSE-blogger, the ministry's Web-expert sported a long heavy-metal mane.) Asked how these tight rules applied to ARRSE and similar sites, Riley came up with a conceptual workaround: the act of writing or speaking under disguise—under pseudonym—must not be seen as an act of "public" speech, as the speaker's or the author's identity is not public; hence the regulations, strictly speaking, would not fully apply to Internet forums.[55]

Third, an organizational reform in the ministry's press office was important. "The MoD cannot control the media: what it must do is to control its own narrative," the Hall report had recommended.[56] The ministry took this recommendation to heart even before the report was published. Press offices in ministries and Departments of Defense are a tough spot in any modern army. It is a place where loyalties clash, an observation that is particularly apt in Britain: civil servants work primarily for their civilian minister. DGMC's approximately one hundred thirty-strong staff is a diverse group of former journalists or other career civil servants, many of them young, who often see their future in other government departments with more prestige such as the Foreign and Commonwealth Office. The ministry does not attract and retain the best PR pros. Consequently the civil servants are kept in low regard by officers, who tend to see them as failed journalists or inexperienced bureaucrats out of touch with operational realities. "I never met anyone there who impressed me," said Andrew Ritchie, who as a brigadier worked as the Army's director for corporate communications in the ministry's press office. Until August 2004 each military service branch in the United Kingdom, the Army, the Navy, and the Air Force, had a one-star officer—a brigadier, commodore, or air commodore—serving as a senior public affairs officer in the Directorate General for Corporate Communications, or DGCC, as the ministry's press office was known until August 2004.[57] These positions were called Service Directors of Corporate Communications, or DCCs, each with a staff of approximately a dozen or more. The one-star positions were regarded as highly attractive postings for potential flag officers with a good career still in front of them. Ritchie, one of the last DCCs, saw it as "one of the top one-star jobs in the Army."[58]

In 1999–2000 a survey done by the MoD showed that the British military, all three services, had a respectable reputation among the British public. The ministry, by contrast, had a poor reputation: it was seen as the least relevant institution, bureaucratic and money-wasting. Among the services, the Navy had the least good reputation. The Navy leadership deemed to correct this problem, and instructed the Navy's one-star in the ministry's media office, Commodore Richard Leaman, to be more outgoing. "We were encouraged to be aggressive to get good PR," said one lieutenant-commander[59] who worked for Leaman. There was intense but good-natured competition among the three DCCs to get their service the best press coverage. It is important to understand the wider context of this decision. For many years already, the British armed services had been fighting above their weight, with what many senior officers perceived as inadequate sources of funds. The overstretch had put huge pressures on the existing equipment, such as armored vehicles, ships, and aircraft; the effect was that service rivalries for resources increased. Thus the one-star senior positions in the media office worked very well for the military services. The one-stars were up-front, courted journalists, and—thanks to their seniority and good contacts—were able to quickly get the requested information or contacts from inside the services. Admiral Sir Alan West, head of the Royal Navy from 2002 to 2006, went out of his way to raise the Navy's profile and regularly invited journalists to luncheons on ships residing in London's waters. The media liked to work with the senior officers: they answered questions competently, they were knowledgeable about arcane details, and they didn't spin. "We were doing very well indeed," said one Navy insider. "The Navy tended to be leakier than the others," said the Army's Andrew Ritchie.[60]

But the arrangement did not work so well for the ministry. Not only was its reputation already low, now the increased competition between the armed services gave even more visibility to the separate military services. Some of the public affairs officers, in addition, were more loyal to their service and their service chief than to the overall "purple" military, let alone to career civil servants in the ministry they held in low esteem. Service interests particularly came to the fore when questions of procurement were concerned. The problem of service rivalries interfering with the overall military's interest or even that of the civilian leadership was real. Eventually a number of unauthorized leaks, along with increased pressure in the wake of the Hutton Report, prompted Geoff Hoon to revamp his ministry's PR architecture. In August 2004 he decided to abolish the service DCCs, and disestablished many positions in the professional military staff. Ian Lee replaced Tony Pawson and became the new Director General of Media and Communications. The change was intended to have the ministry speak with one voice. It was also to increase the civilian leadership's control of the information emanating from the MoD. And indeed the influence of civil servants over the military's public relations was greatly increased. But the ministry's ability to provide high-quality information to the press decreased: "The media hated it," one insider said. For journalists it became more difficult to be referred to a military contact, and the civilians did not have the knowledge of military hardware and details. The ministry's attempt to make the British defense establishment speak with one voice, paradoxically, was thus counterproductive in terms of getting the message across. The public is less interested in the ministry; it likes to hear about tanks, fighter planes, and submarines, and, of course, ongoing operations. Any journalist writing on military affairs would prefer to talk to professional soldiers rather than to civil servants. In 2007 only one one-star flag officer was working in the DGMC, informally rotating between the services. One former Army director called the reform a "devastatingly bad decision."[61] What was intended as a move to empower the civilian side in the ministry was having the opposite effect: leaking and gossip increased; personal contacts between journalists and servicemen and women in the real army became more important; senior officers were now more inclined to speak *directly* with the media; and the public affairs posting became less attractive for the best and most enterprising officers.

In the context of this reform, the MoD also created the Defence Media Operations Centre (DMOC), predominantly located at a Royal Air Force base in Uxbridge, a good hour's drive from central London. In 2007 the center employed forty-seven staff members full time, composed of Navy, Army, and Air Force personnel; it reports to the Director General Media Communications at Whitehall. Two "rapidly deployable" Joint Media Operations Teams serve as the core of the center. The media center, in theory, is set up to "respond to directives from the MOD and also work to assist other government departments such as the FCO and DfiD." Yet in practice it is handling training and education of public affairs officers, not actual media operations. It was designed and created as a compensation for the DCCs, but it is not looking after the media in theater, and journalists are not supposed to get information from the center. "The media do not ring the DMOC," said one Navy officer who worked for the institution as an instructor.

In the operational commands, the media offices are staffed with other specialists, not media ops specialists. For them it is a routine deployment after getting some training in the media center at Uxbridge. Media requests and the information flow have to go through the bottleneck of the press office in Whitehall.

The head of the ministry's Media Directorate General is a high-flying two-star equivalent civil servant job, earning up to £160,000 (€200,000 or over $310,000 in 2007 exchange rates), plus bonuses. Yet a vacancy announcement for the directorate's top post in March 2008 by the ministry's Corporate Capability Directorate did not even require applicants to have any specific knowledge of defense issues: "[I]t is desirable, but not essential that you have some knowledge of defence issues and have an interest in the work of the Armed Forces," the ad read.[62] The directorate indeed is set up only with the UK domestic media in mind; international audiences play a minor role; local audiences in theater are largely ignored. Operational considerations—considerations about how the force is perceived by key audiences and decision makers in theater—hardly figure for civil servants, who have neither experience as commanders facing increasingly media-savvy irregular adversaries nor deep knowledge of strategic affairs. The internal MoD report drafted by Gurr's planning unit highlighted the diminished defense expertise in the public and the press: "there is less 'defence' experience among the public and key stakeholders," the MoD's internal communication strategy outlined.[63] The same assessment also applies to the ministry's media shop. PR for them means the routine coverage of events, policies, or contracts, such as the aircraft procurement, the closing of bases, etc. Media operations, the operational contextualization of public affairs at in a counterinsurgency environment, is nearly absent. The Arab media, such as Al-Jazeera, Al-Arabiya, or Abu-Dhabi TV, became frustrated with the MoD because they were treated as a low priority by the civil servants who answered the phone in London.[64]

On an operational level the picture was different. In March 2004 the Chief of the Defence Staff published Joint Doctrine 01, *Joint Operations*. The document is the highest order doctrine of the British armed forces. It identified eight core strategic effects: prevent, stabilize, contain, deter, coerce, disrupt, defeat, and destroy. Particularly the use of deterrence and coercion, the chiefs of staff argue, "requires the demonstration and communication of credible military capability and strategy, with the clear political will to use it."[65] The primary target group of such thinking and action, evidently, is not the home audience, but adversarial, neutral, and friendly audiences in theater. On a tactical level, the doctrine found that the context for communication was changing: "both the media and other civilian agencies will be in the JOA [joint operational area] before military forces have even deployed."[66] Under media operations, the MoD's doctrine writers recognized that the media have become so important that a commander cannot delegate media work entirely; "there will be moments where the importance of the message to be conveyed will require his personal lead."[67] Immediacy and speed may be critical in such situations. "Occasionally the issue may be of such a critical nature that he may have to compromise Operations Security (OPSEC)."[68]

One of the defense ministry's internal strategy papers recommends to "[c]ontinue with our 'embed' policy which has been successful both in demonstrating the tactical and operational success of our Armed Forces and in introducing media to the reconstruction and development line of activity."[69] Yet between these two lines of operations, tactical combat operations on the one hand and reconstruction activities on the other hand, potential for tension was slowly building up: military units do combat and civilian agencies do reconstruction, which does not have to be a contradiction. But the news value as well as the political damage of the former may be much larger than that of the latter. Soldiers will have a strong interest in getting out the story about their fight: "When people die, they become more honest," said one defense correspondent.[70] General Sir Richard Dannatt, Britain's top soldier, expressed concern along these lines in an interview. "I hope the British people never forget that our soldiers are doing what the Government requires them to do," he said.

> That is why it is important that the story of what is happening in Afghanistan is told. It is important that Paras back on leave can go down to the pub and people will know what they have been doing. It should get out how difficult it has been, how dangerous, how tragic at times, and that they have done well.[71]

The general regularly warned that a lack of public appreciation for the troops' hardship was in danger of "sapping" the soldiers' willingness to serve on dangerous missions.[72] Ironically, General Dannatt's remarks may have made it more difficult for soldiers to get that message out—both strategically to the UK public as well as tactically to the Afghans. Instead of raising the military's responsibility in media operations, he provided another reason for lowering it. The requirements of effective media operations are strikingly at odds with the ministry's restrictive guidelines and long-winded clearance procedures.

In sum, the British Ministry of Defence was torn between the two paradigms, between War 1.0 and War 2.0. On the one hand, the ministry implemented two problematic decisions in the public affairs field: it focused on more control at the top of the hierarchy, and not on *Auftragstaktik;* and it focused on the domestic audience, not on local perceptions in theater. Both steps, while in line with the imperatives of War 1.0, are hardly conducive for successful media operations under the conditions of twenty-first-century counterinsurgency warfare. On the other hand several characteristics of War 2.0 have evolved from the bottom up: the armed forces moved ahead of their civilian masters in understanding the social dimension of irregular warfare in the information age—in a new type of population-centric warfare as well as in the new media. Officers in the field have experienced that a strict demarcation of political and miliary tasks became more difficult to sustain in many operational activities, but specifically in public affairs. Facilitated by the military's evolved relationship to journalists and the Web, the British army's overstrech in its expeditionary counterinsurgency operations translated into civil-military tensions in London.

5

Israel

Since its creation in 1948, Israel has been in a condition of perpetual conflict with its neighbors. Occasionally this confrontation resulted in war, both regular war against Arab states and irregular war against militant groups, most importantly Hezbollah and Hamas. Israel's irregular wars differ in many important aspects from the American and British examples previously discussed.

Israel's exceptionalism affects the relationship of the country's armed forces and the press. In Israel the effects of the information revolution might be felt with even more intensity than elsewhere: the country is a high-tech hub; mobile phones are ubiquitous in the region even beyond Israel; Israel Defense Forces (IDF) soldiers usually fight within the range of their home networks; and the Jewish State is the subject of ferocious propaganda in the region, intensified by an Arab media landscape that is densely populated with satellite TV channels fiercely competing for viewers. Yet in some respects Israel's communication policy, at least in military affairs, is not exceptional: like the U.S. and the UK armed forces, its military forces have been exposed to a highly stressful operational pace over the past years, a tempo that coincided with rapid change in the media environment. Yet, despite its glorious reputation for being one of the most nimble and adaptive armies, and despite the unorthodox and innovative enemies it is facing, the IDF has long underperformed in its public communication activities.

The argument is presented in three steps. We will first explore Israel's exceptional situation and its effect on the press coverage. Second, the Israeli army's various attempts to manage a tense and unsteady relationship with the media leading up to the Lebanon War in 2006 will be outlined. Finally the PR challenges of that war will be reviewed in some detail and briefly contrasted with the media operation of the 2008/2009 war in Gaza.

ISRAEL'S EXCEPTIONALISM

The major difference lies in Israel's view of the perpetual conflict and its stakes: its wars are seen as existential.[1] The reasons for this are manifold, but three should suffice to illustrate the point. The concept of "survival" is rooted in Israeli culture—and, most importantly, in its strategic culture. The Second World War and the Holocaust formed the historical background for the establishment of the Jewish State in 1948. Since its very inception, the State of Israel was at war with its neighbors in regular intervals. In almost each of these wars defeat was an unthinkable option because it would have been synonymous with a flat-out destruction of the state or even the annihilation of its people.

The second reason is related to the first: the proximity to the theater of operations. American and British troops are usually deployed far from their home territory, like in Afghanistan and Iraq. Jenin, Nablus, Gaza, and Bint Jbeil, by contrast, are located only a few tens of kilometers from Jerusalem and Tel Aviv, literally at Israel's doorstep. But more than that: during the Second Intifada, Palestinian fighters have successfully carried the war into the Israeli heartland, causing a stream of civilian casualties and fatalities in the country's major cities.[2] Rocket barrages over extended periods of time have put Israeli democracy under pressure to act.

The small size of the country is the third element to consider. Israel is a small country both in terms of its surface area—about 20,000 square kilometers—and in terms of the numbers of its inhabitants. Israel's population crossed the threshold of 7 million in 2007, which is less than the population of greater New York or London. This means, first, that the concept of strategic depth has limited meaning for Israelis and, second, that armed attacks often take a personal dimension: it is not rare for Israelis to have witnessed a terrorist attack or to personally know victims. After four years of Intifada, the official Israeli record was more than 1,000 fatalities and 5,500 casualties.[3] The authorities have identified sixty suicide attacks just during the year 2002, the bloodiest year of the second Intifada for Israel.

These increased stakes affect Israel's approach to warfare. An asymmetry of political will to escalate the use of force, often seen as a given in Western military interventions against non-state actors, is less tangible in the case of Israel. As a result, Israeli policy makers and officers have access to a range of instruments that is potentially wider than that of their American and British counterparts. Conscription is a well-known example. Every Israeli is obliged to serve for three years (two years for females). Exemptions, for instance, those pertaining to the Haredim, continue to be fiercely criticized.[4] At the end of their military service, Israeli citizens keep regular contact with the institutional army, including through the reserve system, the *miluim*.[5] Another example is that the Israeli public more easily tolerates some controversial tactics, such as targeted killings, and the use of contentious weapon systems, such as mines or cluster bombs. To say that Israel is waging a total war would be false, but the corridor of action for the IDF is less limited than that for most Western military forces, particularly those in Western Europe.

The differences highlighted so far have consequences for communication to the three most important target audiences: national, international, and adversarial.

Compulsory military service and *miluim* mean that the Israeli public is by and large familiar with military matters. The army does not necessarily feel the need to teach the 101 of military action to the Israeli public to the extent that is required in most Western democracies where conscription is successively abolished, again particularly in Western Europe. *Tsahal*, as the Israelis call their defense forces, remains the "people's army,"[6] and Israel, as a democratic state, holds it accountable: its soldiers, airmen, and sailors must inform the public accordingly. In addition, defense correspondents tend to be former conscripts or even career officers and are obliged, like their fellow citizens, to *miluim*. The official army radio *Galei Tsahal* and the military weekly *Bamahane* are two important news sources for Israeli defense correspondents.[7] Ido Dissenchik, the editor of *Maariv*, one of the largest daily Hebrew newspapers, declared during the 1991 Gulf War: "I am first of all an Israeli and an IDF soldier, only then a newspaper editor."[8]

The communication vis-à-vis adversarial audiences, in the case of Israel, also comes with peculiarities. Unlike Americans and Britons, whose current doctrines maintain the importance of "hearts and minds," Israel has given up on appealing to the benevolent emotions of its opponents. For one, the majority of Israelis doesn't have any illusions about their ability to arouse benevolence and compassion among the Palestinians or among Hezbollah's numerous supporters after so many years of conflict. The policy of unilateral withdrawal and separation, applied in Gaza in 2005 and in the West Bank through the construction of the "security fence," considerably limits the need to "win" Palestinian hearts and minds. This statement must be qualified, however: the Israeli military makes an important distinction between Palestinian moderates and extremists. The former must be allowed to prevent them from becoming more radical. Regarding the latter, it is better to try to dissuade them from switching to the act of trying, unsuccessfully, to "win their hearts and minds."[9] Informants also appreciate incentives to cooperate that go beyond personal gain.

Regarding the third key target audience, the international public, a widespread idea in Israel is that the communication efforts would be futile because Israel's image is already negative and tenacious. Apart from the United States and, according to some, in certain Arab countries,[10] it is worthless to engage in costly media battles. Specialists in Israeli public relations, who work hard to improve the image of their country, of course, contest this notion.[11]

The view that press operations are irrelevant or hopeless has been increasingly questioned. Some consider the year 1991 pivotal. For one, Nachman Shai, a former journalist, demonstrated during the Persian Gulf War that even someone who did not previously work in military intelligence could be an effective spokesperson for the IDF. And, also in 1991, General Eitan Ben Eliahu, later the chief of the Israeli Air Force from 1996 to 2000, published an article in the military journal *Ma'arachot* in which he highlighted the essential role of the media at war.[12] But in sum, whether with respect to domestic, international, or opposing target groups, communication policies have long been regarded as secondary, both by military commanders and by political leaders. An adage summed up the general idea, attributed to Shimon Peres, a former prime minister and later president of Israel: "Good policies are good P.R.; they speak for themselves."[13] But that widely held formula is making the task of shaping a coherent message more difficult for the country's public affairs professionals. Peres's maxim may even be reversed: a minor political mistake can turn into a major media disaster, especially in a country—and this is another distinctive feature of Israel—where the number of foreign correspondents per square kilometer is higher than anywhere else. At the beginning of the first Intifada in 1987, 942 foreign journalists were registered with the Government Press Office (GPO).[14] The number was set to grow rapidly. In the first seven months of 2002, the GPO granted 3,500 three-month press cards and reissued 1,000 long-term cards.[15]

The relationship between the Israeli press and the defense establishment can be divided into four main periods that were leading up to the Second Intifada.[16] From the country's independence in the Yom Kippur War in 1973, soldiers were largely suspicious of journalists and reluctant to grant access to information. Military censorship was ubiquitous and supervised all defense-related publications. With few exceptions, such as the highly controversial weekly paper *Haolam Hazeh*, the press largely accepted the restrictions imposed by the military.[17]

That consensus was broken during the Yom Kippur War. Israelis widely held the view that they stood at the brink of the abyss in that fateful October 1973. The conflict was the most modern and conventional war fought anywhere since 1945.[18] The conflict shook up the country, and the government appointed the later controversial Agranat Commission, led by Shimon Agranat, chief justice of Israel's supreme court, to investigate the circumstances leading to the outbreak of the war. As a result of the report, the IDF chief of staff David Elazar resigned. In a patriotic spirit, Arganat also encouraged journalists to be more critical of the military establishment. Abba Eban, at the time foreign minister and a tantalizing orator often seen as the "father" of professional Israeli public relations,[19] even went so far as to name the docility of most journalists as a reason for the partial failure of 1973.[20]

The second period extends from the Yom Kippur War to the 1982 Lebanon War, also known as Operation Peace for Galilee. The press indeed became more alert and the journalists' new attitude pushed the military to gradually change their ways and slowly open up. Even military publications started occasionally to publish civilian authors. For instance, before the Yom Kippur War the majority of authors writing in the IDF journal *Ma'arachot* were regular officers. After the 1973 War, the number of reservists and civilians contributing to this publication rose dramatically.[21] Yet some themes remain strictly off-limits, such as the country's nuclear weapons. In 1980, the military censorship banned the journalist Ami Dor-on and the lawyer Eli Teicher from publishing their book *None Will Survive Us, the Story of the Israeli A-Bomb*, and threatened them with fifteen years in prison.[22]

The third period stretches from 1982 to the Oslo Accords in 1993, most visibly marked by the outbreak of the First Intifada in 1987. The military became aware that it would be hard to strictly control information emanating from the occupied Palestinian territories. Some news organizations, somewhat foreshadowing a development that took off only two decades later, came up with the idea to equip Palestinians in the territories with cameras and recorders.[23] As a result of the situation on the ground, the Israeli defense forces slowly became more cooperative vis-à-vis the press. The "closed military zones" in the West Bank and in the Gaza Strip were well respected by journalists during the first days of the Intifada. When the zones were accessed by journalists, the army refrained from severe sanctions against the trespassing reporters.[24] Then, in 1988, the Israeli Supreme Court made an important decision in the so-called Schnitzer Affair, named after the journalist Meir Schnitzer. The court ruled that "censorship is entitled to stop or amend news reports only when there is in them 'near certainty of a real harming of state security.'"[25] The vagueness of the formula opened the door to a gradual decline of military censorship in Israel. The Supreme Court's decision was still in force in 2008, although some voices—especially within the Winograd Commission appointed to investigate the failures of the 2006 Lebanon War—were in favor of reversing it.[26]

The fourth period, finally, encompasses the seven years from Oslo to 2000. By and large the Israeli press encourages the peace process and is critical of the army and its harsh tactics in the Palestinian territories. Yehiel Limor and Hillel Nossek, two Israeli scholars of communication, have linked the harsher tone adopted by the press to a changing profile among journalists: the Israeli-Palestinian conflict is increasingly covered by generalists, less so by defense correspondents, who were more likely to share the army's perspective on the conflict.[27]

ISRAEL'S MILITARY–MEDIA RELATIONSHIP

Right after the turn of the century, Israel was swiftly confronted with three events that powerfully demonstrated that the press possessed an increased explosive potential and needed to be handled with care. At the beginning of the Second Intifada, the Israeli army found itself embroiled in its first major public relations emergency. The episode was marked by a characteristic imbalance: a tactically minor event caused massive news coverage and a bitter debate that soon spun out of control. On 30 September 2000, Muhammad al-Durrah, twelve years of age, was killed by gunfire at the Netzarim junction in the Gaza Strip. The images of the last moments before the boy's death, picturing a screaming child clutched behind his father's back, hiding behind a barrel, were front-page and prime-time news around the world. A bitter debate ensued about who killed the child, and whether the event was staged.[28] The episode was the subject of hundreds of articles, several books, and investigative journalism research. The consequences and lessons for the Israeli army were significant, especially with respect to media access to combat zones.

The footage of Muhammad al-Durrah's death was originally broadcast by France 2, a leading French news channel. The channel's Israel correspondent, Charles Enderlin, was not on scene during the tragedy. The images were delivered by a Palestinian cameraman on France 2's payroll, Talal Abu Rahma. For Israeli officials, Muhammad al-Durrah was caught in crossfire between Palestinian fighters and IDF soldiers; he was simply in the wrong place at the wrong time. Israeli authorities maintained that the Abu Rahma's images could not prove that Israeli bullets killed the child. But neither does the coverage confirm Palestinian fighters accidentally shot al-Durrah. Israeli officials at first reacted cautiously, and referred to an investigation under way to determine the origin of the deadly bullets. From the outset, the Israeli commission of inquiry was criticized for its partisanship—Major-General Yom Tov Samia was both the head of the investigation and the head of the IDF's southern command, responsible for Gaza.[29] The investigation concluded that the bullets which killed Mohammed al-Durrah could not have come from IDF soldiers. In terms of communication, Israelis have drawn two conclusions from the affair: first, Palestinian technicians and journalists are likely to manipulate public opinion, and their work should therefore not be facilitated by giving them accreditation; the second conclusion was that having only Palestinian journalists in theater was the worst of all solutions. Consequently two principal options were possible: either deny access to anyone equipped with a camera, or allow the presence of Israeli and foreign journalists.

The Israeli army oscillated between these two possibilities until the Battle of Jenin in April 2002. Israel had been hit by sixteen suicide bombings between 16 February and 1 April 2002. In response the IDF undertook several incursions into Palestinian refugee camps, from where the attacks emanated. The army's primary communication policy was a blackout. Journalists were simply kept on the sidelines, and duly protested. In response to pressure and lobbying by various media organizations, the IDF relented slightly. The commanders reasoned that the coverage could have a positive effect if the journalists' access would be controlled and limited through a press pool. The deal with the reporters looked as follows: the IDF agreed to "embed" a few journalists into the operation and in turn these journalists would share their material with colleagues who were not selected for the pool for logistical reasons. With memories of the al-Durrah affair still fresh, the distribution of all images was to be approved by the IDF spokesperson.[30]

Eventually dozens of hours of raw footage were produced and the influx of material quickly overwhelmed public affairs officers as well as journalists. In mid-March, the fear of all press officers became real: an unfiltered report was released in the evening news on Channel 2, Israel's most popular TV channel. The story was rather violent: it showed an Israeli incursion into a civilian house in the refugee camp of Al-Ayida. The door was forced open with the use of explosives, a mother mortally wounded in the blast, her daughter choking back tears and begging the soldiers not to tear down the wall to enter the next row house. In vain. To round it off, a soldier, lounging in a living room at the camp, looked into the camera and offered his comment: "I don't know what we're doing here. Purification? Apparently it's dirty here. It's not clear to me what a Hebrew soldier is doing so far from home."[31] The report provoked an outcry in the military—particularly the army—and some senior officers turned to the IDF's press office, *Dover Tsahal,* to be held accountable.[32] The result was prompt: Defense minister Binyamin Ben Eliezer immediately suspended the pools. His spokesperson, Yarden Vatikay, confirmed that the minister banned TV crews from accompanying IDF missions. "If you have soldiers inside houses, even though it is the reality, it doesn't always look good. And if it doesn't look good, why should you invite reporters?" Vatikay added.[33]

The return to a policy of restriction meant that journalists, like all civilians, were officially banned from entering the closed areas. But in practice reporters tried to bypass the checkpoints and often managed to enter banned areas, then at their own risk and peril. On 2 April 2002, Ann Cooper, executive director of the Committee to Protect Journalists (CPJ), addressed a letter to Prime Minister Ariel Sharon.[34] The letter denounced the extension of prohibited zones for journalists, criticizing the fact that two journalists from Abu Dhabi TV had their press cards withdrawn and that CNN and NBC had been threatened with prosecution for having filmed inside a sealed-off area. Cooper also insisted that two journalists had suffered wounds from gunshots. Then, on 3 April, the Battle of Jenin started. The blackout was total. Fighting raged in other West Bank towns, including Nablus. On 8 April, Aviv Lavie, a journalist, wrote an article in *Haaretz* denouncing the lack of any notable public affairs policy on the side of the army. In response to a growing discontent in the Israeli press and public, the IDF press office organized a tour for a select group of reporters with a specialization in military affairs. But instead of taking the group to the hotspots of Jenin or Nablus, *Dover Tsahal* led the journalists to the region of Tulkarem, a camp of lesser interest in the north of the West Bank, thus increasing the media's frustration and dissatisfaction.[35]

It soon became evident that the blackout imposed on Jenin was entirely counterproductive. Rumors started to spread. High numbers of civilian fatalities were claimed, from 500 to 3,000. Israelis, it was reported, would commit atrocities. The term "genocide" made its appearance. To counter these rumors, the IDF organized a tour for experts in military affairs. However, it took the unusual step of giving access not to journalists, but to a group of foreign defense attachés stationed in Israel. The move failed to appease public opinion, although the defense attachés could at least wire more realistic combat assessment to their home governments.[36] The first journalists accompanied by a *Dover Tsahal* team entered Jenin on 14 April—far too late according to Jacob Dalal, who had worked for four years as army spokesman and was part of that team. "Israel learned a valuable PR lesson from Jenin: during a low-intensity conflict, give the press maximal access."[37] Yet this was the conclusion of a public affairs officer, not the conclusion of a commander in charge.

A third episode in that time frame demonstrated, furthermore, that the media coverage of military action could have a negative impact even if no journalists were present at all. In late 2001, Israeli intelligence learned of a Palestinian freighter, "Karine A," that was carrying a fifty-ton load of advanced weapons bound for the Palestinian Authority. The Israeli Navy's interception, Operation Noah's Ark, began in the early morning hours of 3 January 2002 in the Red Sea, 300 miles south of Eilat at Israel's southern tip. Israeli commandos surprised the ship's crew and took control of the vessel without firing a shot. The ship was then confiscated and taken back to Eilat. It was an extraordinary catch: the 4,000-ton vessel carried Katyusha rockets, mortars, high-tech explosives, sniper rifles, and munitions. But the timing was unfortunate. Lieutenant General Shaul Mofaz, then the chief of staff, announced the operation in a news conference in Tel Aviv on 4 January. At the same time a U.S. special envoy, General Anthony Zinni, was meeting with Yasser Arafat to promote negotiations between Israel and the Palestinian Authority, also a highly publicized and potentially significant event. Palestinian officials first denied any link to the shipping. The operation, they argued, was a propaganda hoax to undermine Arafat and to avoid peace talks, which could lead to painful political or territorial concessions for Israel. "We insist that the Palestinian Authority has nothing to do with this ship," said Yasir Abed Rabbo, then the Palestinian Authority's minister of information. And he added: "We wonder why they chose this particular time, when Zinni was meeting with President Arafat, to make such a declaration."[38]

The IDF succeeded in seizing the ship, but not in seizing the opportunity to get the news story right. The information about the vessel's capture was largely made public by the IDF without coordinating with the Foreign Ministry. Even the head of the Government Press Office (GPO) heard for the first time about Noah's Ark on the radio, and the prime minister's office was not involved in disseminating the news. A defense attaché who worked in Tel Aviv during the episode explained that the communication was so clumsy that some international observers began to doubt Israel's official version.[39] Some European newspapers also were skeptical.[40] On 7 October 2002, after the events in Jenin, a report of the State Comptroller Eliezer Goldberg heavily condemned the institutional architecture and Israel's public relations efforts. Never since Israel's establishment in 1948 had its government succeeded to successfully respond to "the broad-based propaganda and incitement by the Arab world."[41] The report specifically pinpointed a lack of a strategic plan, redundancies, insufficient coordination, ill-defined responsibilities, and a waste of resources. Goldberg singled out the "Karine A" incident and its mismanaged press coverage.

The Israeli–Palestinian conflict was covered worldwide. Up to 2002 the GPO, part of the prime minister's office and the body responsible, among other things, to grant press accreditations, did not display a real desire to curb the numbers of reporters. Accreditation was so easy to get that even the pro-Palestinian International Solidarity Movement was able to register. Israeli left-wing activists such as ISM, an organization that advocated stopping IDF operations in the Palestinian territories, used fake assignments from local newspapers as a means of entering the territories just to reassume their activism, such as acting as human shields in front of Palestinian buildings targeted for destruction.[42] During 2002, the GPO's policy hardened. The allocation of press cards became stricter and, more importantly, the PR operatives decided to discontinue their collaboration with journalists deemed anti-Israeli.[43]

In October 2002, GPO director Danny Seaman gave an interview to *Kol Ha'Ir*, a weekly owned by the same publisher as *Haaretz*.[44] Seaman came down hard on the foreign press, questioning its objectivity and denouncing its partiality. Some foreign media outlets, he claimed—and he cited AP, Reuters, CNN, BBC, ABC, and CBS—would hire Palestinian journalists and technicians with a political agenda. "At the direct instruction of the Palestinian Authority," explained the GPO director, "the offices of the foreign networks in Jerusalem are compelled to hire Palestinian directors and producers. Those people determine what is broadcast. The journalists will certainly deny that, but that is reality." Israel's nominal chief public affairs official even accused three senior producers, without naming names, of having cooperated with Marwan Barghouti, a prominent Palestinian leader of the Second Intifada. Seaman put forward that the media had been informed in advance of certain attacks and went on to explain, in considerable detail, that Palestinian photographers were willing to provoke incidents and to rig photographs, for which they were then paid 300 dollars by foreign news agencies. These photographers "have degraded photography to prostitution," he contended. As a consequence, in early 2002 the GPO refused to renew the accreditations of most Palestinian journalists.[45] Yet this measure did not, in fact, prevent foreign news organizations from working with Palestinian reporters. By that time mobile phones had become more widespread, and offered an easy way to circumvent military restrictions.[46] Before the restrictions were in place, Palestinian journalists could travel easily from the West Bank to Jerusalem, so many news agencies saw no need to establish offices in the West Bank. With tighter restrictions, it became much harder to travel from the West Bank to Jerusalem and even to move around within the West Bank. News organizations, as a result, had to open several offices in the Palestinian territories. *Agence France Presse*, for example, opened branches in Gaza, Ramallah, Tulkarem, Hebron, and Qalqilya.[47]

In the interview with *Kol Ha'Ir*, Danny Seaman also argued that the European press would have a responsibility for the rising anti-Semitism then plaguing the European continent. Then he singled out four journalists with what the Israelis saw as a specifically pronounced bias for special treatment: Suzanne Goldberg of

The Guardian, Lee Hockstader of the *Washington Post*, Sandro Contenta of the *Toronto Star*, and ABC's Gillian Findlay. "We simply boycotted them," recounted Seaman:

> We didn't revoke their press cards, because this is a democratic country. But in the
> name of that same value I also have the right not to work with them. The editorial
> boards got the message and replaced their people. When the *Washington Post* saw
> that a smaller newspaper, such as the *Baltimore Sun*, was getting exclusive material,
> they understood that they had a problem.[48]

The government's remarks shocked the foreign press. Newspapers and news channels rejected the accusations, including the *Guardian*, which published an editorial on the *Kol Ha'Ir* interview.[49] In the months that followed, relations between foreign journalists and the Israeli government did not improve. In 2003, the Foreign Press Association called on foreign journalists in Israel to voice their complaints. In only a few days, some thirty responses were sent in. One of the critical issues for reporters was border crossings; some protested what they called officially sanctioned harassment.[50] The confrontation between the foreign press and the government also became the subject of court proceedings; several cases were even brought before the Supreme Court.[51]

Supporting good "objective" journalists and obstructing those considered biased might not result in positive media coverage. Some military actions inevitably will result in stressful and violent situations and consequently in stressful and violent footage and reporting. Particularly if taken out of context, such media coverage will have negative effects on Israel's image. The case of tunnels connecting Gaza to Egypt, crossing the so-called Philadelphi Route, is illustrative in this regard.

Elaborate tunnel systems were used to traffic arms and explosives into the Gaza Strip, but also to import consumer goods from Egypt. To stop the weapons supply for terrorist attacks against Israel, the IDF began a veritable hunt for tunnels in 2002. As soon as the entrance of such a tunnel was located, the army went in and detonated it. When the tunnel entrance was outdoors, such operations posed not much of a problem. The task became much more complicated when the traffickers camouflaged the tunnels by putting them inside civilian houses. The army's response, initially, varied little. When the intelligence services designated a building supposed to house a tunnel, the army went there to confirm. If a tunnel was discovered, the soldiers would evacuate the inhabitants and other civilians and detonate not only the tunnel entrance but the entire house. For security reasons, reporters were not present during those operations, particularly not inside the houses where the tunnel entrance would be visible. Such operations consequently produced dreadful scenes without visualizing the reasons: often the only footage showed sobbing Palestinian civilians digging in the rubble of their crushed homes to salvage their remaining personal belongings.

To counter the negative impact of such images, *Dover Tsahal* sent military photographers and cameramen to accompany enforcement units to carry out these missions. In times of crisis, the IDF's public affairs command is staffed by about 300 persons,[52] the vast majority of them conscripts. At the end of April 2003, one of these conscripted cameramen, Lior Ziv, nineteen years of age, was shot dead by a sniper in the Gaza Strip as his unit was preparing to take out a tunnel on the Philadelphi Route. The ministry and the army subsequently were criticized for subjecting their conscripts to unnecessary risks. General Ruth Yaron, who then headed *Dover Tsahal*, summed up the prevailing sentiment at that time with a question: "What price are we willing to pay for an image?"[53]

To avoid such incidents in the future, the army adopted two measures: first, it strengthened the training and the protection of soldiers specialized in communication; second, it adopted a new technique for particularly dangerous operations, what was called "combating camera." The idea was to equip special operations forces with a mounted mini-camera and have them film their missions. These soldiers were not public affairs officers, but elite forces. Initially, the footage gained in such operations was not always usable. The public affairs command therefore lobbied to have improved training procedures for combat troops with more emphasis on the basics of filming and public affairs, and thus raise the troops' awareness for the PR aspect of their operations. In early 2008 approximately forty soldiers had done such training.[54]

In September 2004 a survey by an Israeli pollster found that merely 19 percent of the population trusted the army's press releases.[55] Soon thereafter, operation Days of Penitence in the Gaza Strip was launched, a ground incursion by the Israeli army in the region of Beit Hanun and the refugee camp of Jabalya, used as launching sites for Qassam rockets against Sderot. The operation is remembered for two episodes that hardly helped improve the popularity rating of the IDF's media department.

The first could be called stretcher case. It illustrates the danger of releasing unconfirmed information. Israel accused UNRWA, the United Nations Relief and Works Agency for Palestine Refugees in the Near East, of allowing Palestinians to use ambulances for militant purposes. The international aid organization had long been criticized by Israel for its unconcealed pro-Palestinian viewpoint. It was not the first time that such allegations had been made, yet this time the military claimed to be in possession of a video showing that a Qassam rocket had been loaded into an ambulance. Peter Hansen, UNRWA's Commissioner-General, was not convinced after he viewed the video in question. The pictures, filmed by a drone, were of poor quality and it seemed impossible to identify the object that the rescue workers loaded into their vehicle. But for Hansen it seemed likely that the object was simply a stretcher. On 2 October, his agency released an outraged press release: "I should like to emphasize in closing that I am concerned that such false allegations can lead to increased aggressive behaviour by Israelis towards the United Nations in general and UN humanitarian staff in particular, and therefore seriously increase the risks which UN personnel face in this zone of violent conflict."[56] Two days later Hansen sent a protest note to Israeli Foreign Minister Silvan Shalom, denouncing Israel's "malicious propaganda," and demanded an apology.[57] At first Israeli weapons experts insisted, after a review of the material, that the men in the picture may not have carried a stretcher but a rocket—if not a Qassam then at least an anti-tank missile. That same evening Israeli officials acknowledged for the first time that the filmed object perhaps might not have been a Qassam rocket. Later, facing mounting political pressure, the army reassessed the situation. Although officers maintained that the object in the ambulance was a weapon, "it's impossible to swear" that it wasn't a stretcher, the IDF announced.[58] The video, which was posted on an IDF Web site, was finally removed.[59] Aluf Benn, a *Haaretz* journalist, wrote: "After this mistake, who will ever believe Israel's 'photographic evidence' against the Palestinians—or the Syrians or Iranians?"[60]

The second episode took place several weeks later. It illustrates the potential impact of leaks at the highest military level. Thanks to the ubiquity of cellphones and close social ties in Israel, reporters today have easy access to soldiers on the ground even when at war. This way even senior officers and generals can be contacted directly by journalists—or they can contact trusted reporters—without any press officers being even aware of the information flow. This is what probably happened during operation Days of Penitence. Several days before the operation officially ceased, the press quoted anonymous military sources from inside the Gaza Strip criticizing the IDF Chief of Staff and the Prime Minister for not aborting the operation earlier.[61]

Furious, Chief of Staff Moshe Yaalon ordered an investigation to identify the leak. Fifteen officers were heard and forced to take a polygraph test.[62] A promising general and the former commander of the Golani Brigade, one of the IDF's oldest and most highly decorated infantry units, Shmuel Zakai, failed the test. To make an example, Zakai, then the commander of the Gaza Division, was forcibly discharged by Yaalon after twenty-four years of service.[63] But the witch hunt and the discharge of the popular general caused a huge stir. Alex Fishman, a journalist for *Yediot Aharonot*, commented: "If senior officers had to resign for every leak about disputes, half the high command of the IDF over the years would have had to leave."[64] On the newspaper's Web site numerous contributors identified themselves as having served under Zakai and deplored the ugly departure of their former leader. "The IDF doesn't deserve officers like you," wrote one.[65] Defense Minister Shaul Mofaz, himself a former chief of staff of the armed forces, concluded the episode by altogether suspending polygraph tests in the armed forces.[66] Polygraph tests were indeed suspended but resumed later, when a new regulation was adopted.

Some were convinced that only personal enmities could explain Yaalon's treatment of the Zakai case. Others insisted that the chief of staff had to make a deterring example in order to end the leakage problem. But it soon became evident that the Zakai example failed to halt the chatter between officers and journalists. According to Or Heller, a defense correspondent of a major Israeli TV channel, it would be illusory to ziplock the IDF: "Everyone has a brother or a cousin in the army. It is impossible to prevent a journalist talking to his brother or his cousin."[67]

Soon General Moshe Yaalon's term was over and his successor, Dan Halutz, took over. Halutz, an air force general, was not known to be a particularly gifted communicator. In July 2002 the Israeli Air Force, IAF, under Halutz's overall command, bombed the house of Salah Shehadeh, a military leader of Hamas. Fourteen people were killed in the attack, including several children. Naturally the IAF faced criticism for causing unnecessary civilian casualties. In an interview, Halutz, himself a highly decorated combat pilot with four air-to-air kills in the Yom Kippur War, was asked by a *Haaretz* journalist how a pilot feels when he drops a bomb. "I feel a light bump to the plane as a result of the bomb's release. A second later it's gone, and that's all," the air force chief of staff replied.[68] Predictably his statements did not help deflect criticism but caused a public outcry in Israel. Several demanded an apology and, two years later, human rights organizations tried to block his promotion to chief of staff.[69] In addition, smooth cooperation between Dan Halutz and Ruth Yaron, then the IDF spokesperson and widely considered highly competent, seemed hardly possible. Yaron later admitted that she had considered resigning in October 2003 after several Palestinian civilians had been killed in an Israeli targeted assassination from the air in the Nuseirat refugee camp in Gaza.[70] At the time Halutz, then still the air force chief of staff, allegedly passed on false information on the details of the attack to the IDF spokeswoman.

In the spring of 2005, just months before Israel's unilateral withdrawal from the Gaza Strip, Miri Regev replaced Ruth Yaron as the top military spokesperson. Yaron's professional education before joining the team of the National Security College and then *Dover Tsahal* was that of a career diplomat[71]; Regev's previous job had been the chief military censor.[72] True to form, reporters and editors feared the worst: that the IDF would curb press freedoms and try to manage its media coverage. But these concerns soon evaporated.[73]

At the time, in the summer of 2005, the unilateral disengagement plan from the Gaza Strip, the *hitnatkut*, was controversially discussed in Israel. The government faced massive public opposition to its plan. As the IDF prepared to execute Ariel Sharon's decision to remove all Israelis from the Gaza Strip, many feared that the forced abandonment of twenty-one Jewish settlements, where Israeli armed forces would be used against Israeli citizens, would turn into a PR fiasco.[74] But the pullout went surprisingly well, both operationally and in terms of its communication to the public. Miri Regev apparently opted, from the outset, for a policy of relative openness.

The general staff, the southern command in charge of Gaza, and the institutional army were not in favor of open access. The event that tilted the army toward more openness occurred on 30 June 2005, with the decision to evacuate hard-line settler activists from the hotel in Neve Dekalim, then the largest settlement in the Gaza Strip. The army considered the operation dangerous and predicted violent confrontations. Cameras, they reasoned, might even incite the settlers to act more violently. Consequently the media representatives on scene were kept about ten kilometers from the hotel, at the Kissufim checkpoint; only when the situation was under control would they be driven there by public affairs officers. When *Dover Tsahal* received the green light to come in with the press, protesting settlers blocked the way for the buses. When reporters finally arrived on the spot the evacuation had been completed. Yet some unilateral journalists who circumvented the IDF's embargo and managed to get to the hotel illegally were able to document the evacuation. Yet again, two journalists had been caught and handcuffed by the security forces—which was captured on tape by other cameramen present without permission. The evening television news did not spotlight the successful evacuation of the hotel, but focused instead on tensions between the media and the military. Regev drew "a fundamental conclusion" from this episode, she said in a lecture delivered on the Army Radio's Open University program several months later: angry and frustrated media are bad media.[75]

The rest of the Gaza disengagement took place without similar incidents. Police and military personnel were briefed to raise their awareness for the public affairs impact that even minor actions could have. A press center was established, transport was facilitated, and correspondents were given the opportunity to report from both the point of view of the law enforcement agencies as well as from the perspective of the evacuated families, provided the latter agreed to the coverage. Some restrictions, however, were imposed on the mobility of journalists in particularly high-risk zones.[76] Yet eventually both the military and the media saw their refurbished relationship during the disengagement in a positive light. Regev enthused that "the IDF didn't have such media coverage since 1967."[77] The press was equally impressed. "The IDF spokesperson's organization operated better than I've ever seen," concluded Enderlin, the Franco-Israeli anchorman. "If someone planned it in order to change the IDF's image in the international media, it was a success."[78] Yet it is important to keep the operation and its PR in perspective. One Israeli journalist who was experienced in defense reporting tempered such enthusiasm: "It is true that the disengagement was a success. But it was a large-scale operation and not war. The baptism of fire is war."[79] Less than a year after the well-managed Gaza pullout, the IDF faced such a baptism of fire.

THE LEBANON WAR AND ITS LESSONS

The 2006 Lebanon War is known in Israel as the Second Lebanon War and in Lebanon as the July War. For Israel, the conflict started out as a two-front war. A fortnight before the outbreak of hostilities, the IDF launched operation Summer Rains in the Gaza Strip. Its objective was to suppress Qassam rocket fire and the release of an abducted corporal, Gilad Shalit. Palestinian militants captured the soldier in a bold cross-border raid in Kerem Shalom on 25 June 2006. But another event, which happened two weeks prior, helps shed light on the media aspect of what was to follow. On 9 June, one noteworthy incident took place on a beach in Gaza. That day a Palestinian family of seven, including several children, was killed under controversial circumstances. First reports blamed the Israeli army: an artillery shell had caused the tragedy. Twenty-four hours later—too late according to some observers[80]—Israeli officials denied this version and argued that the deadly explosion could have been caused by a mine deployed against potential seaborne Israeli attacks, adding that an investigation was underway. On 12 June Amir Peretz, the defense minister, announced the results of the investigation at a press conference: Israel would not be responsible for the family's death. Peretz's version was called into question by NGOs[81] and journalists[82] that had done their own investigations.

The episode is exemplary. It illustrates the difficulty of being an objective and accurate observer in a conflict where the different parties put forward conflicting versions of the same events. Journalists face huge difficulties in playing their role as guarantors of objectivity because they inevitably support one version rather than another. Their neutrality will therefore be contested by the opposing side. Often the press does not have the necessary resources, time, expertise, and political clout to get to the truth. The Gaza beach incident was one of those cases in which probably only an international expert commission could have made a difference. But such a commission never emerged, although the idea of its creation was floated.[83] For reporters it was, not surprisingly, difficult to adhere to their professional standards. "Both the Israelis and the Palestinians lie. So it is very difficult to find out the truth," said a French journalist with more than a decade of experience in Israel and the Palestinian territories.[84] This assessment was shared by Mitch Potter, a former head of the *Toronto Star*'s Middle East office: "Take the example of the explosion on the beach. The Israelis have every interest to create doubt on the real origin of the explosion. If the banner of breaking news on CNN said: '7 killed in an explosion in Gaza; Hamas and Israel rejected responsibility' and not '7 civilians killed by Israeli shells in Gaza'—that is a PR victory for Israel."[85] After the unfortunate beach incident and the ensuing controversy the Qassam attacks continued and militants on both fronts started acting more aggressively: after Hamas had abducted Shalit in the south, Hezbollah kidnapped two more and killed eight soldiers in a bold cross-border raid in the north. Israel's leaders decided to respond fast and with force.

If conducting an unplanned military operation is a difficult task, then communicating an unplanned military operation to the public is even more intricate. Some staffing problems added friction to the Israeli government's media staff: Ra'anan Gissin, the foreign press advisor to the prime minister had just left and his replacement hadn't been announced yet. Gideon Meir, the deputy director-general for media and public affairs in the Israeli foreign ministry had been appointed ambassador to Italy just days before the war began, although he helped out. And the head of the international PR department at *Dover Tsahal*, Major

Sharon Feingold, had just left her job. Her successor, Avital Leibovitz, was on maternity leave so that a relatively junior officer, Captain Noa Meir, found herself in a preeminent position.[86] Perhaps as the result of a bureaucratic machine that wasn't running smoothly, some foreign journalists complained that it would be easier to reach Lebanese and Palestinian spokespersons than get comments from Israeli officials.

But staffing issues should not distract from a larger problem. For the reasons discussed above, all military operations are PR challenges for Israel. But the thirty-four-day war was more than that; it was a huge strategic challenge for Israel. And as the days went by it became increasingly questionable if Olmert and Halutz had made the right strategic and operational decisions. The more the war was seen as going badly, the more convoluted it became for public affairs staffs to turn operational mistakes into media successes, to "put lipstick on the pig," as that kind of problem is known in Washington. The statements about the objectives of the operation began to vary from person to person and from day to day: the goal could be the release of the abducted soldiers, to stop the rain of Katyusha rockets, or even the outright eradication of the Party of God.[87] Overwhelmed by the operation, Olmert's office waited until two weeks into the war to hold a coordination meeting between the spokespersons of the office of the prime minister, the ministry of foreign affairs, and the armed forces.[88] These offices had already tried to coordinate among themselves but, lacking leadership, had found it difficult to allocate tasks and resources, and thus to conduct the official cacophony.[89] Meron Medzini, a former head of the GPO, pointed out that it is futile to put makeup on disagreements inside the government and inside the military leadership when these are discussed publicly. From the fourth day of the war onward such disagreements began to leak out: political discrepancies between Tzipi Livni and Ehud Olmert, and military disputes between Chief of Staff Dan Halutz and the general commanding the northern zone, Udi Adam.[90]

The Israeli government's communication architecture was complicated and the lines of authority unclear. Several agencies were involved at different levels: the press office of the prime minister, GPO; the department in charge of *hasbara*[91] within the foreign office; the office of the spokesperson of the defense minister, *Dover Tsahal*; and the press operations of the various commands.[92] The responsibilities and the actual power of these administrative bodies often were not clearly defined, and hugely depended on the persons in charge. One Israeli defense and security correspondent, when asked about the government's setup he was dealing with, just frowned. "It's a shambles, a large glorious mess," but he added: "At war it's easier—the army commands."[93]

Indeed *Dover Tsahal* played an important role during the thirty-four days of war, even too important for some. During the ongoing operations the presenter of Channel 2, Amnon Abramovitch, admonished Miri Regev for assuming political prerogatives and for engaging in *hasbara*, a Hebrew concept that literally means "explanation" and can roughly be translated as advocacy or public diplomacy. Regev retorted that viewers are reassured when they see senior officers explain their missions on television. Yet Abramovitch hit the nail on the head with his question of civil–military relations in the press coverage of an unfinished operation. Anshel Pfeffer of the *Jerusalem Post* added: "What Regev didn't say was that the army feels there is a vacuum, with the politicians, especially Prime Minister Ehud Olmert and Defense Minister Amir Peretz, deserting the PR front by refusing to give interviews or even conduct a press conference."[94] The inverse accusation has also been brought against Regev, that she had not been present enough in the media. Especially after the bombing of Qana, the Israeli government and Regev were not visible and aggressive enough in getting out the word to the international media. One reason was that the head of the army's public relations office did not speak English well enough to feel comfortable in front of CNN's cameras.[95]

In addition to the army's media staff, it is worth considering the role of the GPO, the Government Press Office. Most people interviewed in Israel tended to dismiss the office as unimportant, noting that its director is not a proper spokesperson but only an administrator. Yet the agency's function should not be discredited so easily. When foreign journalists arrive in Israel, the GPO manages more than their accreditation. A press card alone does not turn foreign journalists into well-equipped correspondents ready to report from Israel. In fact local journalists claim that a mere press card is not that useful. To pass a check point, for instance, it is more effective to speak colloquial Hebrew and show off some military slang with the troops. Potter, of the *Toronto Star*, put it succinctly: "speaking fluent Hebrew trumps ten press cards."[96] Being a foreign journalist in a culturally, historically, politically, and linguistically highly diverse country can be challenging. The GPO's responsibility is therefore to help foreign correspondents to do their job. During the Second Lebanon War the agency actually did well in its role as a facilitator. At the time of their registration with the GPO, special envoys had to provide their e-mail addresses and phone numbers. Throughout the operation, the government public affair specialists offered daily assistance. Such assistance could take the form of a telephone call announcing that a Katyusha rocket has hit a certain area and that there would be witnesses ready to be interviewed in the language of the reporter's country of origin, even providing the mobile phone numbers of such eyewitnesses directly to the journalists. Another example were the GPO's daily e-mails to journalists proposing new storylines and events to cover. The office also established a bus to transport journalists to the scene of those reports. According to a *Spiegel* journalist who participated in one of the group tours to meet the parents of an abducted soldier, such jaunts were often popular with foreign correspondents.[97] Seasoned correspondents, by contrast, preferred to work with the army's public affairs command in order to get access to potentially breaking news, according to one veteran foreign correspondent in Jerusalem. During the war, officers from *Dover Tsahal* even took the initiative and visited the offices of the largest media organizations at regular intervals to personally answer questions from the journalists who were present.[98]

The government's communication professionals are not the only ones facing criticism for their action (or lack thereof). Defense correspondents, especially in Israel, also stand accused of a number of issues. The most serious accusations are related to security—not operational security in a strict sense, because very few journalists are embedded in combat units during the combat operations. The security at issue is that of Israeli civilians targeted by Hezbollah's and Hamas's rockets. The fear was that reports broadcast live from the target areas would in effect allow Hezbollah operatives to adjust the accuracy of their weapons, although several military experts argued that such fears were unfounded and unrealistic—for instance, Ze'ev Schiff, one of Israel's most authoritative defense correspondents, wrote on the subject just a few months before his death.[99]

Israeli journalists were also accused of opportunism. First, the press rallied around the government in the early days of the war just to turn around and pounce on their political leaders and rant at their army. Not unlike what happened in the United States after the Iraq War, when some of America's top journalists regretted their uncritical coverage, the country's top newspapers indulged in a *mea culpa* about their unsatisfactory performance during the war. An editorial in *Haaretz* deplored the reluctance to ask the hard questions: "If there was any media failure at all, it was a failure to be sufficiently critical in the first week of the war."[100] Amnon Levy, of *Yediot Aharonot*, was more colorful in his assessment:

> Like sheep blindly following their shepherd, the Israeli press trotted along our bedazzled politicians. The columnists who dared to speak up against the war could be counted on the fingers of one hand. The overwhelming majority of Israeli journalists preferred to renounce their watchdog role. Instead of barking, they begged for sugar.[101]

The third group that was criticized was the military. A large number of officers were speaking with journalists without any authorization to do so. The Zakai episode is a minor escapade compared to what happened during the Lebanon War. Daniel Ben-Simon, a *Haaretz* journalist, summed up the extent of leaking during the conflict in the summer of 2006 with a pithy remark: "each defense correspondent had his generals."[102] For many defense correspondents the war was the most transparent major military event they had ever experienced. Battalion and brigade commanders would take the initiative and call journalists in the midst of an ongoing operation.[103] There were different reasons for the military's unofficial openness. Initially it was confidence in the operation and later irritation about the war's management that pushed many officers to be more open than in the past: "in the beginning it was optimism, towards the end it was frustration," said one senior defense correspondent.[104] As a result, the IDF public affairs staff often learned from the press about operational developments. General Halutz, dismayed and curious about the extent of leaking, ordered an investigation after the war. Telephone records were sifted through and the polygraph was again put to use.[105] The results were startling: it was uncovered that approximately 460 officers had, without authorization, passed on information to their press contacts during the thirty-four days of war.[106]

Not only were the leaks probably more numerous than in any previous operation, they were also faster thanks to the wonders of modern communication technology and more numerous thanks to a rising frustration with the IDF's bad management of the war. Nothing could be a better illustration of the staggering speed of such leaks than the attack against the corvette *INS Hanit* in the night of 14 July. That night a Hezbollah projectile, probably a C-802 Noor anti-ship missile, hit the Israeli Sa'ar 5-class corvette as it was patrolling in Lebanese waters approximately ten nautical miles off the coast of Beirut. Four sailors were killed, but the vessel stayed afloat. Hezbollah's leader instantly exploited the successful strike in a veritable PR blitz. The IDF's leadership, by contrast, first learned about the strike through a journalist—although in a quite unusual way. At the time of the attack Chief of Staff Dan Halutz was in a live press conference with Regev, his spokesperson. Suddenly she received a text message on her cellphone from Alon Ben-David, a television reporter of Channel 10, asking her to call back. Regev replied saying that she was in an important meeting. The journalist insisted on the urgency, so Regev eventually returned the call. What had happened off the coast of Beirut? he quizzed her. The official reporting chain had not yet conveyed the news to the IDF's top general. But many sailors, it turned out, had their mobile phones with them, and called their families and friends to tell them they were unharmed. Only minutes after the ship was hit by the Hezbollah rocket, some crew members made calls on their mobile phones. A Navy contact tipped off Ben-David about the incident—without providing precise information—only minutes after it happened.[107] To find out what was going on, Regev then called the Navy chief, who was in the midst of assembling a picture of what happened. It would take the Navy about ninety minutes to establish a full operational picture of what happened; it took Hezbollah fifteen minutes to broadcast a video of the attack and dominate the Israeli media coverage.

By 2006 the mobile phone coverage in Israel was impressive; nearly everybody had a phone and nearly everywhere those phones had good reception. But more than that: nearly every phone also came equipped with a camera. For soldiers, being at war is either dramatic or boring, and either is conducive to lots of picture taking. So it does not come as a surprise that hundreds of images were indeed taken during the war by professional soldiers, conscripts, and reservists, and less so by public affairs officers whose professional mission it is to bring back images of operations, such as combat camera units. Instead ordinary soldiers often brought digital cameras or camera-equipped mobile phones, even some 3G mobile phones with video capability, sometimes violating the restrictions banning the use of such gadgetry. *Sometimes* is an important qualifier: in normal times Israeli soldiers are not banned from taking pictures or shooting videos. A former trooper explains that young soldiers, especially conscripts, are used to taking many photos as souvenirs of their military service, often a phase in a young Israeli's life that is associated with positive memories.

The institutional army therefore tolerates the picture taking. The awareness of the potentially negative consequences is rather low. For one interviewed conscript—a tank soldier—it was limited to one rule: don't take pictures of a Merkava 4's interior. And young conscripts tend to relax these rules limiting photographs in their hunt for memorable snapshots toward the end of their service. Thus, posters on military bases warn of the perils of taking pictures. One of them shows soldiers posing arm in arm, as eighteen-year-olds do, but in the background a detailed map is pictured. The legend reads: "Warning! A photograph can help the enemy—even if you do not realize it."[108]

Many photos and videos shot during the war in 2006 went online rather quickly. Either these images were uploaded directly by soldiers returning from theater, or the material was sent by cellphone or e-mail to relatives who then made it available on the Web. The most popular video platform in Israel during the war was YouTube. Several of such videos that depicted mistakes or equipment malfunctions—such as ill-equipped or unsupplied soldiers, or units receiving contradictory orders—were then used by the mainstream media in Israel and abroad. Still photos were distributed on other sites. Facebook opened to the public—it used to be limited to students—only after the war, in September 2006. But the site quickly gained popularity in Israel, and conscript-age people were the early adopters. It soon became clear that the spread of social networks such as Facebook would create a security problem for the IDF. By connecting to the "Israel" network on Facebook, a self-organized subset of the site's members, each user was able to access the pages of hundreds of soldiers and thousands of photos. Soon almost every IDF unit had a specific "group" on Facebook. Even elite units, the Sayeret Matkal or Sayeret Golani, for instance, were represented with their own groups. In an interview with a former twenty-three-year-old soldier, he insisted on a demonstration of Facebook. He swiftly opened the group page of his tank unit with around sixty people. The online tank group brought together former troopers as well as those on active duty—in his case forty-three members. The tank-soldier estimated that 30 to 50 percent of all enlisted men and women who belonged to this unit during the last five years were part of the Facebook group.

The photos posted online by the active-duty soldiers are most often photos of family and friends, but also military life, training, and even operations. Many pictures of operational or propaganda value are taken but never become public. In 2000, however, several photographs of Israeli soldiers posing with dead Hezbollah fighters were disseminated on the Web, including on the Web site idf2000.co.il, an unofficial site formerly maintained by Israeli soldiers and activists.[109] The affair triggered a very moderate response in the press. But cameras have become smaller, resolutions have become better, the connectivity of mobile devices has become faster, picture- and video-sharing have become more popular, and social news consumption has hugely increased dissemination speed.

The institutional army's reaction was slow. Neither commanders nor public affairs officers in key positions fully grasped the significance of the new trends or understood the risks. Consequently conscripts were not briefed on what to do and what not to do in their all-too-familiar world of online social networking. For those in charge, "The Internet" was still a catchall phrase that could be used with universal qualifiers. For the IDF's censorship the Web was clearly not a priority. Rather than looking at the new sources from a journalist's point of view, Colonel Sima Vaknin-Gil, the chief military censor during the war, took the perspective of an intelligence officer:

> In a big way, it doesn't interest me what is in the blogs. The main advantage of the Internet is also its main disadvantage, and your ability as an intelligence officer to clarify the huge amount of info on the net what is irrelevant, is very difficult. Therefore also I, as a censor, focus more on the media which have higher credibility.[110]

That view was indeed mirrored by the IDF's media arm, *Dover Tsahal*, whose role it is not to censor but to promote the army's image. Regev, the IDF spokesperson during the 2006 war, dismissed the Web on the same grounds. Information published on the Web, in her view, was less troublesome than information published in the press because Web-only sources could not be trusted. Therefore, if you don't know what is true and what is not true, the information does not have credibility—and therefore no intelligence value or operational risk. "The Internet is not a problem," Regev brushed away the question.[111]

The Second Lebanon War was widely—although prematurely—seen as a failure on the part of the IDF. Israel's aggressive response to the kidnapping of two soldiers and continued rocket attacks achieved none of the three declared objectives: it did not liberate the two soldiers, it did not destroy Hezbollah, and it did not completely stop the missile attacks. The week after the war ended, *The Economist* memorably opened with "Nasrallah Wins the War" spilled over its front page, spreading this interpretation of events across the world's newsstands, airport terminals, and the desks of many executives. After the Lebanon War several investigations were undertaken and various reports assessed Israel's shortcomings in various fields. The Winograd Commission with its interim and final report was only the most publicized panel of experts. One could add the report by the State Comptroller Micha Lindenstrauss or—specifically on the treatment of the press—a report compiled by the Israeli Press Council, a body chaired a former Supreme Court justice, Dalia Dorner. All of these reports were dealing, to a varying degree, with public relations. And they all arrived at a similar conclusion, condensed in a *Jerusalem Post* article headed by Paul Newman's punch line in "Cool Hand Luke": "What we have here is a failure to communicate."[112] The two main problems identified by these reports were, first, the absence of a clear message on the part of the political and military leaders, and, second, a lack of coordination between the various agencies responsible for getting out that message. Defense Minister Amir Peretz and Chief of Staff Dan Halutz, who anticipated heavy criticism, preempted the publications of the reports by resigning their posts.

One other aspect of the military's public perception cannot be ignored. Because of Israel's exceptional situation, that aspect perhaps eclipses the significance of institutionalized public affairs and spokespersons: deterrence. Deterrence is the prevention of action by fear of the consequences: a state of the adversary's mind brought about by the existence of a credible threat of unacceptable counteraction.[113] Israeli politicians and senior military leaders understand that their country's potential to deter any attack, from large-scale conventional assaults to small-scale irregular attacks, is crucial. They also understand that deterrence is an act of communication that does not necessarily need the media, but it does need military action or the credible threat of it. The IDF doesn't do hearts and minds, but instead it tries to set the "rules of the game." If militant groups such as Hamas or Hezbollah deviate from these rules, they have to understand the consequences.[114] Deterrence had to educate the recipient about the consequences of certain actions.

One example is Operation Grapes of Wrath, a sixteen-day military raid against Hezbollah in 1996. It was a reaction against increased Hezbollah shelling of Israeli towns in the north. The operation, the name of which was inspired by a John Steinbeck novel, had the objective to "establish new rules of the game" and to draw new red lines for Hezbollah. A related example involves the threat of military action: Hezbollah again changed its behavior in 2002 and started to use air defense weapons not to shoot down airplanes, but to attack Israeli villages. Yaalon, the chief of staff at the time, flew F16s over Beirut at an altitude of approximately 10,000 feet and had the pilots perform supersonic flight operations, even breaking windows in the Lebanese capital. The rationale was to make the Lebanese question why they have to pay the price for what Hezbollah does in the country's south. Deterring suicide bombers is more complex than deterring missile operators. Someone who has decided to die soon cannot be deterred as an individual. But one has to take a broader perspective. "The leadership can be deterred," Yaalon argued. Targeted killings were one option. One memorable assassination used a mobile phone in a rather innovative way: in January 1996 Yahya Ayyash, aka "the engineer," was assassinated with a booby-trapped mobile phone. Ayyash was held responsible for devising the tactic of suicide bombing and allegedly planned attacks that killed dozens of Israelis. The Shin Bet operation that killed the terrorist leader with a rigged cellphone was celebrated in Israel and had an intended psychological effect on the wider Palestinian population.[115] Even the press may be used in such deterrence operations in unforeseen ways: One example is that of a militant who tried to escape Israeli units one night in Jenin, so claimed his family, and who was then assassinated in cold blood. The story was not true, said Yaalon. "We denied it, but we did not explain." The attempt was to create confusion and to leave the impression that the IDF is willing to redefine the rules of the game.

"I didn't want to be interviewed," Yaalon said. In an attempt to create the impression that the IDF was ready to escalate: "I used the media as a tool by not responding."[116] The media may also serve as a force-multiplier in deterrence when no military force is used. Ruth Yaron, a former IDF spokeswoman, organized a VIP tour for Arab journalists to attend an Israeli maneuver. For the first time, a helicopter full of Arab journalists was allowed to film the use of Israel's overpowering military force. "For them it was a scoop, for me it was a reassurance of Israel's deterrence potential."[117]

The 2008/2009 war in Gaza illustrated how far the IDF had come, and that the organization had made an effort to implement the lessons learned from the war in 2006 both with respect to its public affairs and the way public affairs can be harnessed to deter. In contrast to 2006, the objectives of operation "Cast Lead," which started on 27 December 2008 against Hamas in the Gaza Strip, were deliberately kept vague from the outset. Israeli political and military leaders initially mentioned several aims: to pummel and de-arm Hamas, to stop the permanent Qassam attacks on Israeli cities, and to again redefine the "rules of the game." But operationally, the IDF in many ways did the opposite of what it had done in the war against Hezbollah two-and-a-half years earlier. It seriously banned the use of cellphones among the troops; it restricted access to the battlefield for Israeli and foreign journalists; and it prevented information leaking out from the army to the press—at the same time the army made a large effort to have both military and civilian spokespersons on message, even those not on the payroll of the government.

Most remarkably, the new IDF leadership seems to have reversed its attitude toward the Internet: the army embraced Web 2.0 platforms as a venue for its public affairs operations, effectively using a YouTube channel, idfnadesk, to substitute for its comprehensive press ban in the field. The channel opened on 29 December, immediately after the operation was launched. Two weeks later the IDF had uploaded more than forty video clips and registered approximately 1.7 million views. The footage showed, for instance, video-feeds from drones that document the use of precision weaponry against Hamas targets, interviews with individual soldiers about their experiences, evidence recorded by combat-camera personnel that anti-aircraft cannons were used by Hamas inside mosques, and even a clip in which an army spokesman explains in Arabic-only why Israel is acting forcefully against Hamas and that it will not back down.[118] At the same time the army successfully limited leaking on interactive platforms.

Two aspects of this new approach should be highlighted. First it satisfied the public's demand for information from the battle. Professional journalists continued to complain fiercely about the near-total press ban and still generated political pressure to allow more access. But that pressure was limited by the IDF using the Web to directly reach out to key target audiences: first and foremost the Israeli public, but also the international public, Arab audiences, and adversaries, as well as important multipliers such as bloggers and journalists. Many journalists used the YouTube channel as a source even if they did not explicitly reference it. Second, the IDF's public affairs policy was geared toward highlighting military strength, not weaknesses. Particularly against the background of inevitable Palestinian civilian casualties and mounting international pressures to stop the violence, the IDF's innovative public affairs policy visualized the IDF's resilience and power, and thus fortified its deterrence. Israel's army demonstrated that War 1.0 could be effectively combined with some elements of War 2.0.

6

War 2.0

The classic literature on revolutionary war has one *Leitmotiv*: the inferiority of non-state militants vis-à-vis established state authority. The world's most successful and famous insurgents essentially considered two ways to deal with this key weakness: mass support and tactical innovation. Marx and Lenin tried to rally the support of the working masses against the state, to counter the opponent's quality with quantity. Mao Tse-Tung then applied their theory to China's "semi-colonial and semi-feudal" conditions: the peasant masses would be the "true bastion of iron," the chairman wrote.[1] Mao's tracts became probably the most influential pages ever written on irregular warfare, but they needed to be heavily adapted to the peculiar conditions of each theater. For instance, Vo Nguyen Giap adjusted Mao's concepts to Indochina's anti-colonial war and Amilcar Cabral further remodeled it to Africa's colonial situation.[2] More creative modifications, deviating significantly from Mao's ideas and far less successful in practice, were attempted by Che Guevara in Bolivia[3] and by Carlos Marighella in densely populated urban settings in Brazil.[4] More recently Abu Musab al-Suri, one of al-Qaeda's strategic masterminds, explicitly quoted Mao, Che, and Giap as "the greatest theoreticians in military art" and attempted yet another scheme, more of which later.[5]

The support of the masses is not a necessary condition to start an insurgency. It becomes an important enabler only if the political objective of the insurgent is to seize power and then to stay in power. Tactical innovation is, however, a necessary condition for all irregulars, whatever their objective. Without tactical innovation, insurrectionists are doomed to be defeated by regular armies. Mobility, harassment, and the willingness to improvise in order to achieve temporary and relative superiority are the basis of tactical innovation. Simple designs may benefit the insurgents in unexpected ways: T. E. Lawrence operated in a vast empty desert and saw canned food as a way to gain mobility: "The invention of bully beef had profited us more than the invention of gunpowder," Lawrence wrote from Arabia, and, referring to the desert environment: "but [canned beef] gave us strategic, rather than tactical strength, since in Arabia range was more than force, space was greater than the power of armies."[6] Such logistical and tactical innovations could make a difference, for instance, the use of bicycles as vehicles to transport large quantities of supplies and ammunition (in the Indochina war in the 1950s[7]) or as improvised explosive devices (in the Afghan war in the 1980s[8]).

Mao had well recognized "that the important thing is to be good at learning."[9] And being good at learning first and foremost means being good at understanding the environment in which the uprising is to take place. "We must study not only the laws of war in general, but the specific laws of revolutionary war, and the even more specific laws of revolutionary war in China," Mao wrote in December 1936.[10] What was true in Beijing in December 1936, in other words—and the chairman would surely have agreed—might not be true any more elsewhere seventy years later.

This chapter argues that insurgency in the twenty-first century is again in flux: consumer electronics, the Web, and a changing culture of consumption and production of information have an impact on irregular warfare. But the impact is lopsided: on balance, sociotechnological trends affect the insurgent more than they affect the counterinsurgent. Throughout the history of revolutionary Europe, the colonial era, the Cold War, and into the twenty-first century, insurgency has been a highly politicized kind of warfare. Revolutionary war was focused on the population and aimed to establish alternative political systems. Such wars could last a long time and often they did not end with clear victory. Initiatives in these conflicts often came from the bottom up, with decentralized structures of authority. In many of these struggles, the public sphere has been the central battleground. All of these features are historically stable and by no means a product of the information age or any other recent development. Yet information technology does have an enhancing effect in irregular war, we argue: it makes political violence more violent and more complex, it draws it out, it opens up a broader spectrum of militant and political action, and it stabilizes some militant groups. At the same time it opens up a new range of vulnerabilities, costs, and perhaps insurmountable problems for both sides, the irregular and the regular.

The argument is organized in four steps. We will first outline the relationship between military force and communication, whether mediated or not. Second, when a non-state group is battling against government forces, several asymmetries bias this relationship heavily in favor of the insurgent. Third, as a result, information operations on the public domain assume a broader utility for the insurgent. This utility of public information is, eventually, enhanced in unprecedented ways by modern information technology. The most significant aspect of this change is that the traditional and classic role of the population in irregular violent conflict is altered.

THE MESSAGE OF FORCE

Almost any use of military force is, first and foremost, an act of communication. "War is an act of force to compel the enemy to do our will," wrote Carl von Clausewitz. The philosopher of war was writing about the collective use of force, of clashing political entities. War, Clausewitz argued, is always permeated by politics. "How could it be otherwise?" he asked. The political motivations of the warring parties remain unaffected even when the diplomatic communiqués fall silent and the weapons speak, Clausewitz wrote. War remains an instrument for a political purpose, a continuation of political intercourse by other means. Yet it is the form of the interaction that fundamentally changes as missiles take the place of missives. "Isn't war just another way of writing and speaking their [the people's and the government's] thoughts?" Clausewitz rhetorically asked. He then continued with a widely quoted aphorism: "War has its own grammar, but not its own logic."[11] The language metaphor was aptly chosen: armed conflict is not a realm of its own, it remains a form of politics—and therefore political communication.

Perhaps no author grasped war better than Clausewitz did. Given the spirit of *On War* and the author's treatment of politics and occasionally communication, Clausewitz would certainly have dedicated a significant section of his work to the mass media and the Web, had he not written in the Germany of the 1820s, even before the invention of the telegraph, let alone television, personal computers, and cellphones. Yet *On War* is an excellent starting point to understand the role of communication in war, and by extension that of the media and the Web. Clausewitz starts his discussion of war with the image of a competition, a struggle between two opponents; he actually uses the analogy of two wrestlers. Each side's overarching *purpose* is to impose its will on the other one. Both therefore have the same *objective*: to render the other one "defenseless." Both use the same *means*, physical force. He proceeded from these three basic but abstract elements of war: purpose, objective, and means. If both adversaries would relentlessly focus on their objective and increase the use of force, they would "give the other side the law [of action]." Each side would, as a necessary consequence, be forced to react to the other's reaction, back and forth, without bounds and without limitations. Clausewitz then identified three escalations (*Wechselwirkungen*): first, the mutual increase of the physical means, an escalation of force; second, the mutual increase of the psychological impetus, or objective, to succeed before the other side does, an escalation of will; and third, the combination of both force and will, "a couple that cannot be divided," an escalation of effort (*Anstrengung der Kräfte*). Clausewitz makes it very clear that such a concept of war is possible only in "the abstract realm of pure notions," pushed to the extremes by man's "restless reason," artificially isolated from actual political influences and logistical difficulties. Such an abstract theory, he wrote, would be "a mere book law, and nothing for the real world."[12] Absolute war, he unequivocally makes clear, does not exist in reality.[13] The war that we observe in reality is tamed and "moderated" by time, by friction, by decisions, by human error, by logistics, by chance, even by the weather. And most important, it is never isolated from political motivations and influences. Clausewitz calls this real war, in a merely descriptive sense. Real war can nevertheless approximate absolute war, although it can never be reached entirely.[14] That would be physically and politically impossible: war cannot be isolated either from friction or from politics. In *On War*, the Prussian philosopher of war was writing only about conventional state-on-state war. He was not writing about irregular war, or small war, where the military capabilities of one side are very limited in the first place; the potential for the first mutual escalation, the escalation of force, is therefore limited as well.[15] The insurgent does not have the military capabilities and means to push his adversary to the extremes.

Communication, now, is tightly connected to this distinction between absolute war and real war. Absolute war would not only be isolated from politics, but also from communication. The first escalation, the escalation of force, presupposes that a collective military actor—composed of an army, navy, air force, many layers of hierarchy scattered across large areas of operation, all in sync with the political leadership in a nation's capital—is working smoothly and efficiently. It presupposes a robust command-and-control setup. In any modern force for the past 200 years, this setup is more and more reliant on telecommunications. The second escalation, the escalation of will, presupposes that a political body, a nation or state, backs up the use of military force morally, economically, and politically—a rule that applies in any political system, but with particular urgency in any democratic system. The second escalation, in other words, presupposes a supportive public opinion, continually informed about the war by the government and the mass media. It follows that the use of force and the media narrative about the use of force are two sides of the same coin, a coin that is spent with only one objective, to undermine the adversary's will.

The more escalated and powerful the use of force, for instance, the aerial bombardment of an entire country, the less need there is for a separate channel to amplify the use of force through its reportage and dissemination in the news. Perhaps the most extreme example is the maximum use of force through nuclear weapons: if a country's industrial centers and the majority of its cities would be wiped out, it would be nearly irrelevant how the few remaining survivors of that country interpret the news. On the other end of the spectrum is a minimal use of force by irregulars, such as kidnappings or the killing of a single person, often selected for no other reason than ethnic affiliation or by pure chance, for instance Nicholas Berg's beheading. Such acts of force have a negligible or no physical impact on the opponent the perpetrators are intending to attack. These operations gain their moral and psychological force only through their representation and their widespread coverage in the news media. A general rule can be derived from this observation: the smaller the physical power of force, the larger the need for psychological amplification. Insurgents, by definition non-state actors, do not dispose of the same resources as the governments or occupying forces they are struggling against. Insurgencies do not have air forces, navies, regular army units, highly sophisticated weapons systems, or other powerful and expensive means to project physical power. They cannot escalate the use of force. It follows that insurgents have to compensate in the psychological dimension for a lack of force in the physical domain.

Three imperatives for insurgent movements can be derived from this: First is to attack the regular army's capability to escalate force, its command-and-control network. Second is to attack the state's capability to escalate its political will, its public opinion. The third imperative is to build, maintain, and protect friendly capabilities to escalate both force and will. This is what irregular movements have done and what they continue to do, as we argued in chapter 1: in the nineteenth century they attacked their adversary's command-and-control network; in the twentieth century they attacked public opinion; and in the twenty-first century they are using commoditized telecommunications to build up and protect their own will and their own capabilities with more sophistication than ever before. Irregulars can no longer physically target command-and-control systems because they are too sophisticated and too protected (very rare exceptions might be possible). But they continue to target public opinion. It follows that the pressure to be effective in what modern armies divide up into public affairs, psychological operations, public diplomacy, and information operations—media operations, in short[16]—is higher for the insurgent than it is for the counterinsurgent. For the irregular fighter the psychological war is unlimited, is existential, and if lost would likely mean the end of the militant movement. It is almost everything he has. The counterinsurgent, by contrast, is inclined to operate under the assumption that the utility of superior hardware and firepower is more important and decisive than the benefits of merely getting "good press." The psychological dimension therefore is seen as limited, as an annex to the physical counterinsurgency campaign.

ASYMMETRIC MEDIA OPERATIONS

Communication and media operations in conventional war cannot be seen as an area distinct and isolated from military operations narrowly understood. This was one of the most fundamental insights that, for the first time in modern American military history, guided the operational planners in Central Command as well as the public affairs planners in the Pentagon and elsewhere in the months leading up to the invasion of Iraq in March 2003. The Pentagon accommodated journalists with military units under its innovative embedded media program. One of the Pentagon's and Central Command's planning assumptions was that Saddam Hussein and the Iraqi regime would be skilled at using the commercial media to amplify mistakes the coalition might make or to construe false stories. Based on the experiences of Operation Desert Storm in 1991, the assumption was that Iraq has learned its lessons in propaganda and information operations on the public domain. The remedy, or the major counterpropaganda operation, was "to put independent objective observers throughout the battlefield" in order to refute the enemy's false or exaggerated claims. U.S. officers held the firm belief that truth was on their side; "truth can be propaganda," as one lieutenant colonel involved in the planning summed up the policy.[17] But Operation Iraqi Freedom was designed and planned as a conventional operation. Iraq's regular military formations were considered inferior in terms of equipment, training, planning, and operational capabilities. So the rules of the game, U.S. planners assumed, were by and large those of regular, conventional, interstate war. That assumption would not hold very long. Already on the march to Baghdad it became clear to troops on the ground that they were facing an unconventional enemy who was not playing according to these rules: paramilitary Fedayeen fighters without uniform caused the first U.S. fatality in a drive-by shooting from a civilian vehicle; guerrilla fighters executed suicidal missions; the enemy evaded battles and harassed supply lines instead; adversaries and civilians were difficult to distinguish. The war quickly mutated into an irregular campaign that pitched insurgents against counterinsurgents. This shift immediately affected the media operation, and the "asymmetry" that defines the very character of counterinsurgency soon extended into the field of communication.

The image of "asymmetry" between the insurgent and the counterinsurgent was probably first used by David Galula, a French veteran of the War in Algeria, in 1964.[18] Opponents in irregular war were characterized by a differential in assets and liabilities, Galula argued. On the one hand, the counterinsurgent has, whether it is a domestic government or a foreign authority, both assets and liabilities. He controls financial resources, industrial resources, agriculture, energy, and the transport and communication infrastructure. The authorities are usually in command of a government bureaucracy and the security forces. But the counterinsurgent also has a heavy liability: to maintain order and a functioning social and economic system, and to maintain legitimacy. If order breaks down, the government is held responsible for a failure to maintain social coherence, stability, and peace. If chaos continues over an extended period of time, the counterinsurgent's legitimacy is damaged and undermined.

The insurgent, on the other hand, has few assets and no liabilities. The assets in weapons and organization are, at the beginning of an insurgency, difficult to establish. An insurgency starts from almost zero while its adversary has the full spectrum of means and capabilities at his disposal. During its embryonic phase any resistance movement is "as vulnerable as a new-born baby," Galula wrote.[19] The few assets the insurgent has are intangible: one of the insurgent's most important assets is strategic initiative, since it is he who starts the conflict (not necessarily the use of force). Another essential asset, equally intangible, is his cause. The cause mobilizes resistance and ideological as well as political power. The insurgent's goal is to turn his intangible assets into tangible ones. The insurgent, initially, has no liabilities. Even the most blatant acts of terror and aggression help his initial goal: to undermine the government's legitimacy. Resistance fighters and rebels are not responsible for public goods and basic services. That only comes later if the insurgency is successful and assumes political power. It is the insurgent's aim in war to grow from small to large, from weak to strong; the counterinsurgent has the inverse objective: to prevent the insurgent from degrading him from strong to weak, from large to small, Galula outlined. "The peculiarities that make the revolutionary war so different from the conventional one derive from this initial asymmetry."[20]

Galula's initial asymmetry of assets and liabilities extends into the field of communications. Technological change and a change in news consumption patterns have amplified the differential of asymmetric media operations. The rules of conventional media operations are distinctly different from the rules of irregular media operations. At least six such asymmetries should be considered.

1. The counterinsurgent is bound by the truth; the insurgent is not. Propaganda is a "one sided weapon," wrote Galula. The insurgent, having no responsibility and accountability, is free to use every trick; "he is judged by what he promises, not by what he does." For the counterinsurgent, by contrast, facts speak louder than words; "he is judged on what he does, not on what he says." Media operations, Galula reasoned, cannot be more than a "secondary weapon" for the police or military forces of a legitimate government, particularly so for a democratically legitimized one.[21]

2. The show of violence tends to benefit the insurgent; it damages the counterinsurgent. Any demonstration that militants are able to inflict violence, even extreme violence against innocent civilians, demonstrates that the government and the counterinsurgent's security forces are not in control, that they are not keeping their pledge to provide security, and that they do not have the power to protect the population. There are, however, limits: it is a delicate balance between undermining government legitimacy and alienating the population irreversibly. Excessive violence committed by militants may tip that balance back in favor of the government forces. Galula grasped this aspect of violence, but his analysis of what he calls "propaganda" is very quickly exhausted. Several more aspects should be added.

3. In the media sphere, the insurgent has the initiative while the counterinsurgent reacts. This is often true even if an event, such as civilian casualties or a military operation, was launched by regular forces. The public and journalists want information fast. But before the counterinsurgent can react to an event, the information needs to be gathered, analyzed, verified, often declassified, and disseminated to the right spokespersons. Only then can a situation report be briefed or communicated to the public and the press. The mass media's appetite for breaking news therefore helps the insurgent and hinders the counterinsurgent.

4. Anonymity benefits the insurgent while it harms the counterinsurgent. Government authorities as well as journalists are forced to substantiate any information they release to the public by reliable and credible sources. Anonymous government or military sources are therefore under pressure from journalists to be named, because the press in turn would damage its own reputation and credibility if it didn't keep a healthy distance from officials. Names and affiliations provide such reliability and credibility. The same expectation is strongly reduced vis-à-vis insurgents, where close access to sources is more appreciated because it is more difficult. For irregulars the use of aliases and noms-de-guerre is permissible and increasingly

accepted by the press. Shaping the mass media coverage with high speed and low risk therefore becomes easier for anonymous militants.

5. The costs for media operations rise for the counterinsurgent while falling for the insurgent. Technology, competition, and diversification have accelerated news cycles. Spokespersons need to act faster, their products have to be more sophisticated, and the spectrum of media channels is broader—pushing up costs for human resources, education, expertise, technological prowess, adaptability, and speed in large regular military forces. The opposite is true for militant movements: prices for consumer electronics have fallen, the technology is widely available, and dissemination platforms such as blogs, forums, video-sharing sites, and CMS-freeware have become freely available global public goods. Cellphones and satellite phones allow insurgent spokespersons to comment on military operations in real time even from remote mountain ranges in Afghanistan.

6. Modern information technology—by and large—increases risk for the counterinsurgent; it decreases risk for the insurgent. Tactical mistakes, for instance, bombs that went astray, accidental shootings at check points, misbehavior of individual low-ranking troops, can instantly have strategic effects when picked up through new media and amplified in the mass media. For the insurgent, the risk of producing videotapes, posters, or audio recordings—and getting caught with fresh evidence—has been greatly diminished. This asymmetry in media operations has important effects on how information can be used by insurgents and irregular militant groups. The functional spectrum of irregular media operations has become broader than that of regular armies.

INCREASED UTILITY

The utility of irregular media operations cannot be understood as "propaganda." The term is prejudiced, pejorative, and imprecise. A sober analysis of the use of communication by any militant organization needs to carefully isolate the different strains of what is commonly referred to as propaganda. The U.S. military uses "propaganda" mostly to refer to the information campaigns of its adversaries and sometimes to describe information activities by U.S. agencies. The official definition of propaganda is "any form of communication in support of national objectives designed to influence the opinions, emotions, attitudes, or behavior of any group in order to benefit the sponsor, either directly or indirectly," the U.S. Department of Defense Dictionary of Military and Associated Terms says. This definition is not useful. It would make it impossible, for instance, to distinguish between propaganda and politics.

Because information and communication pervade most policies, it is indeed rather difficult to analyze media operations and to write consistently about a rather complex set of activities. There are six principal ways to structure information and, by extension, information policies: by source, content, form, channel, destination, and purpose. Governments, for simple historical reasons, usually employ the first possibility, structure by source. The system evolved this way along with modern communication technology. Yet it is of little help: the official setup is too input-oriented. It is designed to reflect a slowly evolving set of offices and suborganizations, complete with separate career tracks and competing views. Perhaps more important, it creates competition for money. The U.S. military's and NATO's terminology illustrates this: information operations, psychological operations, public affairs, and public diplomacy reflect a bureaucratic division of labor, not an output-oriented approach. A second way to structure information is by content, or by the type of messages that are communicated. Yet the extent and the fluidity of the mass media market make it impossible (at least for the purposes of this study) to structure information according to content. A third possibility would be to distinguish media operations by their form: whether they employ the spoken word, images, audio messages, videos, or other means such as acts of violence or community support programs. Communication can entail an interaction and dialogue, with feedback, or it can be a monologue without feedback. Yet form is too abstract a criterion to be of much help here. A fourth way to structure an insurgency's information operations is to look at the channels that are being used, such as word-of-mouth, newsletters, radio, television interviews, or Internet videos. Yet such an approach would be far too static and heuristically unimaginative.

An insurgency's communication could, fifth, be structured by a target group (or in the alternative terminology of communication theory, by destination, receiver, decoder, or recipient). Targets can be friendly, neutral, or adversarial. The target audience of information policies can be broad, such as the ummah or the American public, or it can be narrow, such as the Shia in Baghdad or members of the U.S. Congress in Washington. The target groups can be local, regional, and global. The geographical way of distinguishing the media operations of insurgents and militant extremist organizations has a good value-added: it highlights the differences between the various organizations, their constituencies, and their political ambitions, whether they are regional or global.

Yet the most precise and most insightful way to classify any militant actor's information operations, whether state or non-state, is to dissect the different purposes of messages and media products—their function, or in other words, their utility. This approach has several distinct benefits: the impact and the effect of a message comes into focus. It becomes easier to assess success (success is if the intended impact, and not a side effect, has been achieved). It is possible to distinguish multiple utilities of one message; a very common phenomenon as the mass media cannot be targeted to specific audiences, and stories spiral out of control very quickly. And finally it becomes easier to understand the full significance of modern information technology.

Insurgent groups and non-state actors are far more reliant on public information than governments and regular military organizations. The reason is simple: states and armies can afford to build and maintain an expensive information infrastructure, protect it, classify files, and create a sphere that is firewalled from the public domain and vigilantly defended against foreign intelligence agencies; for non-state actors that is much more difficult. Yet an increasingly sophisticated public information infrastructure—commercially available mobile phones and Web services—allows such groups a more elaborate and efficient use of information than ever before. As a consequence, an insurgent movement's spectrum of functions serviced by public information products today is likely to be broader than that of a modern state and its security agencies. Subversive militant groups and movements, in other words, are forced into the public domain, albeit into its more shady and dodgy corners. Irregular media operations consequently have manifold functions. They fall into broad conceptual categories—political, organizational, and operational—and will be outlined in the following paragraphs. The next three chapters will then identify some of these utilities in Hezbollah's, the Taliban's, and al-Qaeda's media operations.

1. Irregular movements may use public information to legitimize their actions ideologically. Engaging in subversive activities means taking considerable personal risk. If operatives are caught, they might face deportation, prison sentences, possibly harsh treatment, and, depending on their country of residence, torture and even consequences for families and friends. Perpetrating violent acts outside the moral conventions of symmetric classical warfare—acts that often are executed in a way that contradicts broadly accepted ethical codes—requires strong spiritual and moral orientation, particularly so if the killing of innocent civilians and bystanders is involved. Providing ideological orientation, stability, and defensive arguments against moderate voices is a critical enabler of insurgent or terrorist activity. Closed and self-referential ideological systems, such as radical Islam, act as enablers.

2. Irregular media operations may be used to justify action. The demand for ideological and quasi-juridical justification of violent action is great, particularly so if an insurgent movement is conservative at heart and appreciates authority. One of the best known examples is the use of fatwas and the concept of *takfir,* or excommunication, to justify the killing of civilians and, even more problematic for Muslims, the killing of fellow Muslim civilians. Fatwas may even substitute, albeit diffusely and imperfectly, for command-and-control.

3. Media operations may be used to build a political base. Insurgencies have constituencies. The local population is any revolt's prize: the people's trust, their support, and the legitimacy of popular consent is what makes an insurgency eventually successful. Without popular support, most armed struggles are doomed to fail, both from the insurgent's point of view as well as from the counterinsurgent's. The mobilization, maintenance, and enlargement of political support is therefore one of the most essential functions of any public information campaign, even if accompanied by terror tactics that may undermine that support at the same time.

4. Media products open up a variety of *organizational* functions for radical groups as well. Doctrinal debates have been moved into the semi-public

space. The armed forces in most NATO countries have an extensive body of military journals and doctrine covering issues on various levels of war, the strategic, the operational, down to the tactical and technical level. Land forces usually are more sophisticated in their doctrine than navies or air forces. Depending on national or service culture as well as the topic covered, doctrinal publications, or "field manuals" as the documents are often called, are sometimes public, sometimes for official use only, and sometimes classified. Irregular forces do not have this level of organizational sophistication. As it has become more difficult to disseminate doctrine covertly for insurgents, it is increasingly spread with the help of the Internet. The equivalent to doctrinal debates is therefore not only happening on the public domain; these debates may also be more sophisticated and yield more useful outcomes.

5. Media products may be used for training. Subversive action requires a broad set of skills on how to gather intelligence, prepare attacks, recruit operatives, use all kinds of weapons, build explosives, administer poisons, resist interrogation, etc. All such training has two sides, a theoretical side and a practical side. Theoretical manuals and instructions are widely available electronically. One of the most comprehensive jihadist manuals is the *Mawsu'at al-I'dad,* or Encyclopedia of Preparation, compiled and updated during the Afghan Jihad from 1979 to 1989. This material often comes with Web links to videos, or directly in the form of CDs, and may include how-to videos. Some handbooks are designed for experts and require a background in chemistry or electronics; others are written for the novice. In the absence of physical training camps, visual illustration material facilitates the transition to practical training and execution, and thus the transition from passive sympathizer to active militant—although, of course, the best videos cannot replace personal expert training and rehearsals. Even interactive technology and personal online training sessions cannot overcome certain limits.

6. Media operations may be used to recruit operatives. Many products and channels can be used to advance the recruitment of activists, any violent movement's most essential resource: pamphlets, press articles, videos, memoirs, sermons, Internet forums, and social networks both offline and online. The logistical challenge of joining a training camp or a combat zone may also be facilitated. Skilled recruiters may even be in a position to spot talented potential recruits online and get in touch with them both through interactive formats and ultimately face-to-face.[22]

7. Public affairs may be used to raise funds. As in political campaigning, violent movements rely on targeted fundraising efforts. Loyal groups can be tapped for smaller and mid-sized donations or wealthy individuals through trusted personal networks for larger donations. The newsletters or Web sites used for fundraising can be public, semipublic, or secret.

8. The interactive media facilitate networking. Anonymous and encryptable Web-based applications such as discussion forums, instant messaging, VoIP,

or e-mail enable a semipublic dialogue and even a near risk-free establishment of personal contact. This significantly facilitates the outreach of militant groups to sympathetic individuals and organizations such as suppliers,
other radical groups, potential supporters and recruits, or journalists.

9. The Web enables militant peer-production. Well-known examples of benevolent peer-production are open-source software or Wikipedia. Peer-production is an alternative model to firm-production or market-production. Its
production mode is open, nonproprietary, non-hierarchical, incremental, and
asynchronous, and the "peers" may be anonymous. The requirements are that
the product must be composed of modules, ideally of various size and of low
cost.[23] Two aspects of the violent acts committed by insurgent groups and
militant extremists lend themselves to peer-production: the innovative development and transfer of necessary expertise (for instance, know-how to build
and deploy IEDs), and the production, editing, translation, adding subtitles
or audio, marketing, and dissemination of media products of all sorts. The
Web enables breaking a media production process into modules that can be
edited by individuals ("peers") unknown to each other, on their own initiative.

10. Media technology is not limited to political, organizational, and technical use.
It also enhances *operational* action, by serving as a force multiplier. Irregular
conflict is a competition for legitimacy among the neutral local population
where two other perceptions have to be considered: the morale of the troops
and the support of external constituencies, which can be of critical importance
for both the counterinsurgent and the insurgent. In all three cases the objective is to maximize friendly support and erode adversarial strength. Civilian
casualties and minor tactical events, as we shall see in the following case studies, are often magnified by their media coverage.

TECHNOLOGY'S IMPACT

Information technology affects the communication efforts of subversive movements in multiple ways. Some of technology's most significant aspects are unsur-
prising and quite obvious, as they apply not only to subversive activities but modern
societies in general: technology has reduced costs for creating and disseminating
media products. Technology has also increased the volume and the quantity of
information products available—huge amounts of information were found by U.S.
units in Iraq and Afghanistan. The quality of these data has improved, thanks to
inexpensive recording devices, better software, better Internet access, and more
highly skilled users. But technology has four effects on irregular media operations
that are less evident, and therefore deserve to be highlighted in more detail.

First, and perhaps most significant, technology reduces the tactical risk of
using media products in the first place. Omar Nasiri, a former al-Qaeda operative
of Moroccan origin with ties to Algeria's GIA, described an instructive anecdote
in his memoirs. During the mid-1990s he smuggled a car with Belgian-produced

weapons and explosives to Morocco for shipment to the GIA in Algeria. In Tangiers he was supposed to pick up a videotape that featured jihadi operations in Algeria for recruitment and ideological rallying and take it back to Europe. The relative who was supposed to keep the tape had made a mistake and it ended up in a pawnshop, where the owner had showed it to friends. It was highly dangerous to be caught red-handed with extremist material in Morocco at that time, and the secret police would find people who talk. Although Nasiri wrote that he was able to recover it, he had to destroy it: "I began to pull the black tape out from the spool—meters and meters of tape. I ripped it into small pieces," he wrote. "This tape was far too dangerous for all of us."[24] Modern technology has not eliminated the risk of radicals being associated with propaganda material. Blog entries and video-uploads can still be traced to IP-addresses and sometimes to individuals. Internet content can be filtered by government agencies. Yet it is possible through simple anonymization techniques or with easily available more sophisticated software to reduce the remaining risk significantly.

Second, participation in media work is facilitated. The culture and ease of participating in illicit activities has been increased by technology. Technology also affects what is public and what is private, or secret. This observation applies across the Web: most users of MySpace, YouTube, Flickr, Wikipedia, and most Web 2.0 applications do not use their real names. There are exceptions such as Facebook, where a majority of users registers with their real names. Yet the Web has fostered a culture of anonymity or, to be more precise, a culture of pseudonyms. Yet it would be naive to assume that online anonymity and offline action are incompatible. eBay and Craigslist.org are two of America's and the world's most successful and highly trafficked Web sites. The two platforms perfectly illustrate the ease with which anonymous and "virtual" Internet users establish "real" contact and thus enable transactions of significant proportions. Very few users, including sellers and buyers, use their real name in the public section of those Web sites. A comparable transition—although more sophisticated and still with more risk—can be observed in radical Web forums. Anonymous online participation leads to offline action.

Third, the recruitment pool for insurgent and radical movements is growing fast. The world's Internet penetration is uneven, and as a consequence growing unevenly. European countries on average have an Internet penetration of almost 50 percent; North America's is approaching 75 percent. From 2000 to 2007, Europe's market roughly tripled and America's doubled. Both the Middle East and Africa have, by comparison, a very low penetration rate (21 and 5 percent, respectively). But as Europe's and North America's markets approach a saturation point, both of these regions now lead the world's statistics with more than 1,000 percent growth in the same period.[25] As a consequence, a larger number of conservative disenfranchised Muslims with a potential for radicalization will have access to the World Wide Web in the coming years and decades. Support for jihad, tacit and outspoken, passive and active, is bound to increase in absolute numbers merely as a result of this trend.

Another feature, equally a result of the Web's uneven penetration, is that offensive information operations have been strengthened. The role of modern communication technology is more relevant to attack the remote adversary population than to attract or impress the local population. This is because technology's significance is ultimately a function of the recipient audience's sophistication or developmental level. SMS-messages only work if the recipient audience has mobile phone coverage. In rural Afghanistan, for instance, Internet and even mobile phone penetration, although it is spreading, remains low or even absent. The most efficient form of mass communication may be word-of-mouth, posters, night letters, or old-fashioned radio. Highly developed democratic information societies are more vulnerable and prone to attack by irregular media operations staged by insurgents in developing countries than vice versa.

Finally, as the most significant consequence of many of the aforementioned trends, modern communication technology affects the role of the local popular support for militant groups. To understand the significance of this development, some conceptual background is required. Two classic paradigms are available to grasp the population's role in war: Carl von Clausewitz's "trinity" and Hubert Lyautey's "terrain." The first attempts to grasp the population's role in conventional war; the latter is an attempt to understand the population's role in unconventional war. Both are essentially political concepts, and both are necessary to understand the population's role—in fact several populations' roles—in today's counterinsurgency operations.

One paradigm, the trinity, sees the population as a key pillar. Outlined by Clausewitz at the end of *On War's* first chapter, the famous section on the "trinity" of war is probably one of the most-read passages on strategy ever written. He isolated the three basic elements of war: first, passion, hate, enmity, and a "blind natural force [blinder Naturtrieb]," which is predominantly borne by the population, *dem Volke*. Second, there is the game of courage, talent, probability, and chance, which is the commander's task. Then, third, there is war's ever-present nature as a political instrument, the realm of reason, which is in the government's hands. Passion, probability, and politics are understood as three "tendencies" of war. Any theory that attempted to fix and determine the ratio of the three elements would be doomed, Clausewitz wrote. War is a "true chameleon" as its final character is determined by the specific blend of its three basic elements. This view essentially sees the population as a source of support, both psychological and material. In a clash of two states, the population therefore becomes part of the contest: two opposing popular wills clash, pushing their growing armies to more forceful confrontations. After the advent of industrial war, the population became the fighting army's industrial production base, churning out weapons, munitions, and hardware; ferrying the materiel to the front lines in order to feed the war machine; and all that in competition with the adversary's population which was doing the same for its army on the other side. The classic way of thinking about war is limited to force-on-force wars. Force-on-population contact or "war among the people," is essentially not foreseen in the classic theory of war. An alternative

paradigm is to see the population as the insurgent's "terrain," as French counterinsurgents did—or as the "sea" in which the insurgent, the "fish," is swimming,
to use Mao's better-known image. Mao wrote about the "relationship that should
exist between the people and the troops." He referred to his irregular units as
troops. Then the chairman introduced his famous analogy: "The former may be
likened to water and the latter to the fish who inhabit it."[26] There are still groups
that have a firm local popular base and rely heavily on various forms of support;
Hezbollah and to an extent the Taliban are examples.

But technology's perhaps most vexing effect on irregular war is that it calls the
validity of both paradigms into question: neither Clausewitz's concept of the trinity nor Galliéni's and Mao's paradigm of the "fertile terrain" or the "fish in the
water" reflect the altered role of the population for some groups. Throughout its
history, even before the rise of the Web, al-Qaeda was an insurgent group in exile
without a popular support base. It attracted a pan-Islamic global crop of fighters,
it was financed by radical sympathizers from across the world, graduates of training camps operated worldwide, and the al-Qaeda leadership planned attacks without geographical limitation. The utility of communication technology has
amplified this development. Some violent movements are able to survive and
even to continue operations without popular support in the classic sense. The
next question is whether they would even be able to thrive without a territorial
base in one of the world's ungoverned spaces, or in a state that tolerates and
harbors radical militant activities—a theory that can hardly be tested, because
large parts of Afghanistan, Pakistan's tribal areas, portions of Iraq, and many
other places across the Middle East, Central Asia, and Africa can and do serve
this purpose. It is unlikely that physical sanctuaries for violent movements with a
global agenda can be eliminated entirely in the foreseeable future. What is
evident, however, is that the Web has added a third "terrain" to the equation.
That virtual platform may divorce the "moral terrain" from the "physical terrain."
Technology, in short, has made some irregular wars less population-centric. The
following case studies will explore how.

Hezbollah

Hezbollah is a Lebanon-based Islamic political and paramilitary organization. Since it first appeared as an independent entity in the early 1980s, the group's communication skills have evolved notably in both substance and form. The Party of God has reached a level of sophistication in its dealings with the press that is truly surprising for a movement whose only messages, merely two decades ago, were bursts of gunfire. To fully grasp the magnitude of these changes, a few key elements of Hezbollah's history of media management will be outlined in the following pages.

HEZBOLLAH AND THE PUBLIC

To understand the militant group's public relations strategy, it is first in order to understand its overall political and military strategy. The date of Hezbollah's creation is contested. The movement rose from the violence and the confusion in the months and years after Israel's invasion of Lebanon in 1982. The Shia movement's leaders were initially inspired by the new Iranian leader Ayatollah Khomeini. In the early 1980s, during the Lebanese Civil War, a number of attacks and kidnappings were attributed to various smaller militant groups difficult to identify. When responsibility for a militant action was claimed by Hezbollah, it was done well after the fact; in the case of Ahmed Qassir, who died in a suicide attack carried out against the Israeli army in Tyre on 11 November 1982, Hezbollah claimed responsibility only in 1985.[1] Other attacks widely attributed to Hezbollah, such as a devastating twin suicide attack of 23 October 1983 that killed 241 American soldiers and 58 French servicemen, have never been endorsed by the group. Senior Hezbollah leaders have, to the contrary, maintained that their group was not involved in the attack on the Beirut barracks.[2]

Two points are nevertheless clear: Hezbollah has its deep roots in the political mobilization of Lebanon's Shia in the 1960s and 1970s and eventually took off after Operation Peace for Galilee was launched by the Israelis in 1982. At that time the Shia minority in Lebanon was not organized as a political force. The ethnic group was among the poorest of Lebanon's minority groups, and large segments of its members voted for parties on the far left, such as the Lebanese Communist Party or the Syrian Social Nationalist Party.[3] But slowly two new elements of political ideology were introduced, resistance and faith. In 1974, the Iranian-born cleric Sayyid Musa al-Sadr founded the Shia group "Movement of the Disinherited"—Harakat al-Mahrumim—and eventually, in 1975, the Lebanese Resistance Detachments, Afwaj al-Muqawmat al-Lubnaniyya, better known by their eloquent acronym Amal, which means "hope" in Arabic.[4]

The budding radicalization process is best illustrated in a speech delivered by Musa al-Sadr, in February 1974:

> Our name is "those who revolt" (rafezun), those of vengeance, and those who revolt against all tyranny. . . . Though we may have to pay in blood and with our lives . . . we do not want rhetoric, but action. We are fed up with words, sentiments and talk. I have given more speeches than anyone. And I am the one who has called for calm, more than anyone else. And I have called for calm long enough. From today forward, I will not be silent. You may wish to do nothing, but I do not.[5]

In the 1970s, several future cadres of Hezbollah were involved with the Movement of the Disinherited, including Sheikh Naim Qassem, Ibrahim al-Amin al-Sayyed, Husayn al-Musawi, and Hassan Nasrallah, Hezbollah's secretary general since 1992 and the movement's most visible leader to date. In August 1978, the founder of the Movement of the Disinherited and Amal, al-Sadr, disappeared mysteriously during a trip to Libya. Nabih Berri eventually replaced him as the movement's leader. In 1982, Nasrallah became a member of political bureau of the organization and assumed responsibility for the Beqaa Valley area, Lebanon's most fertile region. But under Berri's leadership and pragmatic and secular influence, Amal moved into a new strategic direction. After the Civil War Berri joined a National Unity government and Amal largely abandoned resistance operations against the Israeli occupiers and eventually evolved into one of Lebanon's most powerful political parties. Berri's decision increased the tensions within Amal, which had been split for many years between its secular wing and a religious faction led by Husayn al-Musawi, who formed a new organization by the name of Islamic Amal for an interim period. This split eventually gave rise to Hezbollah.

Even before 1985 Hezbollah had been a significant actor in Lebanon's political landscape, but it was not known as such. In order to be recognized as a coherent organization an act of communication is necessary. Although the date of the formal inauguration of the Party of God remains unclear, the date of Hezbollah's first major act of communication is well known: 16 February 1985. That day an "open letter to all the downtrodden in Lebanon and the world" was read at an anniversary ceremony honoring the death of Sheikh Ragheb Harb, a young imam who had been killed by Israeli fire a year prior. The twenty-page letter, which was also sent to the Lebanese newspaper *As-Safir*, first put the name Hezbollah into the international spotlight. In 1986 the letter was published in French in the *Cahiers de l'Orient*. In 1987 Augustus Richard Norton reproduced an English copy of it in the annex of a book dedicated to Amal in Lebanon, and in 1988 excerpts of Hezbollah's pamphlet were published in the *The Jerusalem Quarterly*.

The letter started out by praising the Ayatollah Khomeini as a leader and by highlighting the Iranian cleric's juridical, religious, and ultimately his political authority.[6] Referring to Khomeini, the open letter saw Hezbollah not as a regional and "closed" party in Lebanon, but as a movement connected to the "ummah" and concerned with "the Muslims in Afghanistan, Iraq, the Philippines and elsewhere," the document said. The early Hezbollah identified its enemy in an order that was, in hindsight, quite prescient: "America, its Atlantic Pact allies, and the Zionist entity." But the document was also marked by a tension between a lofty global rhetoric and Hezbollah's first and very concrete regional objective: "to expel the Americans, the French and their allies definitely from Lebanon, putting an end to any colonialist entity on our land."[7] From its very outset, Hezbollah was thus torn between its local roots and its global aspirations, what Judith Palmer Harik called "ideological ambiguity."[8] Another aspect of this ambiguity is the early movement's expressed tolerance of Christians. An entire chapter of the open letter—probably inspired by the more liberal views of Sayyed Muhammad Hussein Fadlallah, an important Lebanese Shia cleric who would later rise to become Grand Ayatollah—is devoted to the Maronites, a Christian minority. After the authors state their preference for a system governed by Islam, the activists stress that they do not wish to impose their religion by force, and call for an end of all "hateful confessionalism," all fanaticism, and all parochialism, "which are rejected by our religion [Islam]." The people of Lebanon should "freely" adopt the political regime of their choosing. Hezbollah, the authors wrote, was ready to respect Christians if they refrained from violence against Muslims. With respect to Muslim believers, the document calls for unity. The pamphlet has a strong anti-imperialist undertone in its rejection of both superpowers at the time, the United States and the Soviet Union. Both would not be able to lay the foundations for a "just society." Yet, for all its ideological confusion and ambiguity, in one aspect the letter is everything but ambiguous, the definition of Hezbollah's enemy: Israel. The United States and France are described as enemies of Lebanon that must be expelled, and even the UN gets its portion of spite. But it is the "Zionist entity" that must necessarily be destroyed and eliminated ("our struggle will end only when this entity is obliterated.") The open letter truly marked the arrival of Hezbollah as a political organization with public visibility. Naim Qassem, the deputy secretary general of the Party of God, highlighted the open letter's significance in a much-quoted book published in 2005. He pointed out that his organization had a spokesperson only since 1985.[9] That spokesperson was Sheikh Ibrahim al-Amin who first read the pamphlet, before it was published, at the al-Ouzai Mosque in west Beirut.

Lebanon's Shia are the first constituency of Hezbollah. They are the "oppressed" the movement strives to defend. To improve their living conditions, Hezbollah over many years has developed a vast network of social institutions serving predominantly, but not exclusively, the Shia in the south. This institutional support network could be seen from an instrumental point of view: any guerrilla movement is competing for legitimacy and public support, and providing services to its core constituency is perhaps the best way to this end. But such a view would be too narrow. Hezbollah's social institutions make a real difference and actually improve the living conditions in the region south of Beirut, in southern Lebanon and the Beqaa Valley, where it fills a niche left open by failed policies of the Lebanese State. Even the government in Beirut acknowledged the constructive role played by Hezbollah's social organizations: the charitable organization al-Imdad (the resource) was created by the Party of God in 1987 and was officially recognized with charitable status in 1994.[10]

But Hezbollah's charitable institutions and NGOs arose in the context of the Lebanese civil war and reflect the movement's origin in that conflict. In 1982 it created al-Shahid (the martyr) and al-Jarih (the injured). Al-Shahid provided financial and material support to the families of combatants killed in guerrilla operations as well as to the victims of political violence; Al-Jarih cared for the wounded and promoted their reintegration into society and the labor market.[11] In the mid-1980s, it formed the association Jihad al-Binaa (reconstruction effort), whose mission was to provide assistance for the reconstruction of damaged houses.[12] This association was inspired by an Iranian organization of the same name, but there was no organic link between the two.[13] In addition to helping individuals to rebuild their houses, Jihad al-Binah repaired and maintained public infrastructure, such as sewers.[14] In 1990, to cope with recurring shortages in water and electricity in the southern suburbs of Beirut, the association installed generators and water tanks that were refilled several times a day by tanker trucks.[15] Other public and social activities included the creation of agricultural cooperatives in the Beqaa Valley, lending microcredits to farmers, managing infirmaries, or maintaining village schools. Naim Qassem's objective was an "educational mobilization."[16] Twelve schools, known as al-Mahdi, served nearly five thousand pupils.[17] Even a stipend scheme was put in place for needy students. The Hezbollah-sponsored education put a particular emphasis on history of the Shia, but also on learning Arabic and English. In addition to the al-Mahdi schools the Party also ran religious schools (*hawzas*) where the curriculum reflected Hezbollah's Islamic ideology.[18]

Hezbollah delivered not just an impressive military performance during the Second Lebanon War. Its efforts continued after the war ended: the Shia group was quick in dispatching engineers and architects to assess the damage Israeli bombs had inflicted. Within a week, Jihad al-Binaa, Hezbollah's construction arm, identified about 20,000 homes that were destroyed or damaged, and its charitable foundations gave out $10,000 to each family that had lost a home, so they could rent an apartment for a year.[19] The Party is not shy to put out word about its social and charitable achievements, particularly when Israeli attacks have harmed civilians or public infrastructure. Al-Manar regularly carries reports on the subject. In 1996 already, after the Israeli operation Grapes of Wrath, Jihad al-Binaa had distributed press releases highlighting the effectiveness of its reconstruction work.[20] Hezbollah's social work has been a constant in the organization's history since its emergence in the 1980s. Yet the Party of God has changed its original positions in other areas, particularly in its relationship to Iran.

LEBANONIZATION

Hezbollah is controlled by Iran, it is often assumed. Indeed the Iranian ambassador to Damascus one day claimed that he was directly involved in the creation of Hezbollah, the British reporter Robert Fisk pointed out.[21] Its founding document bows to Iran's Grand Ayatollah in the first paragraph. During funerals of fighters from the "Islamic Resistance" throughout the 1980s—at least until the Taif Agreement in 1989—Iranian banners, not Lebanese flags, were an omnipresent optical marker at demonstrations and public gatherings. Today Iran's green-white-red striped banderoles are far less visible in Shia areas, even if the portraits of Khomeini and Khamenei remain pervasive. Ruhollah Khomeini, for instance, glares down from the top margin of *al-'Ahd,* a newspaper linked to Hezbollah. And Hassan Nasrallah regularly spoke at the anniversary of the death of the great leader of the Islamic revolution of 1979, pronouncing Khomeini one of the most important figures of Shia Islam.

Yet, as Hezbollah itself approached the proud age of a quarter century, its celebrations can be drowned in a sea of Lebanon's red-white cedar flags alongside the yellow Hezbollah banners with Allah's green AK-47-wielding fist. The Party of God even published leaflets in Lebanese colors with slogans such as "the whole nation is resistance."[22] The symbolism indeed indicates a shift in the organization's orientation, what some experts have called "Lebanonization." Hezbollah's exclusive focus on Lebanon began after the Taif Agreements in 1989 and was consolidated in 1992 when the movement's leaders decided to participate in Lebanon's parliamentary elections. Now not only the Party of God but also increasingly a party of the people, Hezbollah's program stated two central goals, to "liberate Lebanon from Zionist occupation" and to "abolish political confessionalism."[23] Hezbollah attempted to "create a society of resistance" and to set up a "Lebanese nation transcending religious denominations and political favoritism." The program also called for religious freedom and for a policy of "opening" (infitah) to other faiths, particularly Christianity, favored by the party throughout the 1990s.[24] The expression "Islamic resistance," omnipresent in the 1980s, was increasingly replaced by the more neutral, stand-alone "resistance" (muqawama) in the 1990s, abandoning the religious epithet. In order to prevail against an opponent as powerful as the Israeli army, Hezbollah guerrillas needed all the support they could get, even if it was Christian. Hezbollah's integration into Lebanon's political process proved to be a payoff. A large number of Hezbollah representatives have been elected in every election since 1992. Of the 128 seats in parliament, Hezbollah obtained eight seats in the legislative elections of 1992, seven in 1996, twelve in 2000, and fourteen in 2005, when the Party of God first entered government. After a violent crisis in 2008, Hezbollah was granted veto power in parliament and control over eleven of thirty seats in the cabinet.[25]

The evolution and political consolidation of a militant group just north of Israel was a troubling development. Israeli leaders, in an attempt to solve a simmering crisis, withdrew troops from southern Lebanon in 2000. The situation presented the increasingly Lebanon-centric Hezbollah with a paradox: it got what it wanted, the liberation of Lebanon as a consequence of its hard-fought resistance. But the Israeli withdrawal also raised an existential question for Hezbollah: what would be Hezbollah's raison d'être if it got what it wanted? Hezbollah's answer was that Israel's withdrawal from southern Lebanon all but eliminated the reason for "resistance." Lebanese territory has not been fully liberated because Shebaa Farms, a twenty-two-square-kilometer patch of land bordering the Golan Heights, remained under occupation by the Israeli army. But that was not all. Hassan Nasrallah, in an interview he gave shortly after the Israeli withdrawal, did not hesitate to portray his organization as a guarantor of Lebanon's national interest. The problem would not only be the liberation of the remaining occupied territories, but also the defense the "Lebanese people" in case of any Israeli attack. When asked if that wasn't the responsibility of Lebanon's army, Nasrallah retorted that if Lebanon was facing an army as powerful as the IDF, "the margin of maneuver of a resistance movement—especially when it is a popular movement [. . .]—is infinitely greater than that of a regular army."[26]

The Nasrallah interview demonstrates that Hezbollah has come a long way in the past fifteen years, at least judging from its pronouncements. The secretary general's reasoning contrasts sharply with the open letter of 1985: the declared objective of the "destruction of the Zionist entity" had not been highlighted any more in the interview; no longer did Hezbollah call to liberate Jerusalem; and UNIFIL was no longer seen as a hostile force but as a potential cooperation partner. It remains unclear how much Nasrallah's conciliatory tone might have been the result of the mayhem Israel had inflicted on his country or if the old leader, now in need of external support, simply said what European leaders wanted to hear. Hezbollah's headmen, beyond doubt, have developed a high level of sophistication in navigating their country's diverse political landscape and finding the right words that strike a chord with the intended listenership. Judith Palmer Harik distinguished four such audiences: facing a Shia audience, for instance at rallies in the southern suburbs of Beirut, jihad is presented as a religious obligation; in front of a general and multi-confessional Lebanese audience, the need to "resist" is outlined in patriotic terms; to a pan-Arab audience, more emphasis will be put on the injustices inflicted by the West on the Arab world, along with punch lines on "American-Zionist imperialism"; and a Western audience is best satisfied with references to the number of UN resolutions not respected by Israel, the illegal occupation of contested territories, and a nation's right to self-defense.[27]

In September 2000, four months after the Israeli withdrawal from south Lebanon, the Second Intifada started. Hezbollah cadres concluded that it was their duty to come to the help of their Palestinian brethren. Various ways of assistance were possible. One was to open a second front in northern Israel. In October 2000 Israeli soldiers were duly ambushed by Hezbollah fighters in the Shebaa Farms area. Between this opening salvo and the Second Lebanon War of 2006, seventeen Israeli soldiers were killed by Hezbollah fighters and twenty-one more were wounded.[28] A second way to help the embattled Palestinians was to provide technical and material assistance to the combatants. Hezbollah's assistance was limited to the transfer of know-how rather than the transfer of weapons, although evidence suggests that Hezbollah was involved in the Karine-A arms shipment to Gaza, a shipload of arms that was intercepted by the Israeli Navy.[29] The third way to support the Intifada was by spreading the message: Hezbollah's television channel, al-Manar, openly and vigorously supported the Palestinian fighters. Programming times, for instance, were listed in "Jerusalem Standard Time" instead of Beirut time, which would be identical. In December 2001, when the IDF had destroyed the building and transmitter of the Voice of Palestine in Ramallah with bombs and bulldozers, al-Manar replaced its own logo with the Palestinian one for two days. Al-Manar officials acted out of "solidarity with an Arab media organ," they said.[30]

Hezbollah, it is clear, has evolved considerably. Its raison d'être, since the early 1980s, the resistance against Israel, remains one of its defining characteristics. Gradually, however, the organization has become more complex and Hezbollah is no longer a mere guerrilla movement. The Party of God has become an important element in Lebanon's political and social landscape. The evolution of the movement's communication skills illustrates and reflects this journey: in 1985 a makeshift spokesman read an open letter in a suburban mosque; less than two decades later Hezbollah's TV channel al-Manar, the station of resistance (*qanat al-muqawama*), is run professionally and has a truly global reach.

Organizational evolution generally involves increased specialization and a more sophisticated division of labor. Hezbollah's communication activities are marked by an impressive diversity, including newspapers, radio, television, Web sites, and even a branded video game in two editions, Special Force. The intention behind this broad information campaign was rather shrewd. Sheikh Ali Daher, a Hezbollah spokesman, outlined the rationale of Special Force 2: "This game presents the culture of the resistance to children: that occupation must be resisted and that land and the nation must be guarded."[31] But the sophisticated media operation should not obscure the more immediate and direct low-tech side of Hezbollah's public campaign.

Direct communication can be defined as a form of communication that reaches its recipient without an interlocutor, be it a printed medium (newspaper, magazine, journal, leaflets) or telecommunications (radio, TV, SMS, the Web). Direct forms of communication generally have several distinctive features; two of the most important ones are that they are pervasive while they tend not to be recognized as explicit political messaging, and they are markers and drivers of identification. Perhaps the best examples are the paraphernalia of popular sports teams, such as shawls, baseball caps, T-shirts, or bumper stickers. The border between fashion item and political statement can become very difficult to draw. Hezbollah examples can be found in the notorious old prison of Khiam, a place that for many became a symbol for the cruelty of the Israeli occupation. After a failed assassination attempt, Souha Bechara, a twenty-one-year-old woman, was famously tortured in the Khiam interrogation center run by the South Lebanon Army, a proxy of Israel. Human rights groups repeatedly alerted the world to the harsh methods used in the detention center. After the Israeli retreat in 2000, the old French fort was transformed into a "museum of torture," and the shop in the former prison yard offered Hezbollah's yellow items, such as baseball caps.[32] Hezbollah offers various objects bearing the organization's insignia and colors for free or for sale: flags, bracelets, pins, posters, stickers, T-shirts, lighters, key fobs, toys, and other fashion or everyday items.[33] Omnipresent in market stalls or on display in windows or cars, these objects make the party more visible in everyday life.

Hezbollah's iconography is ubiquitous in the urban and rural landscapes of Lebanon, predominantly Shiite areas. The organization even established an office for art and design, with three regional branches, one in Beirut, one in the Beqaa Valley, and one in southern Lebanon.[34] The office is in charge of designing and marketing Hezbollah paraphernalia, photos, and paintings—in coordination with the movement's political arm. It also caters to specific historic or cultural events, such as Ashura, Yom Al-Quds, and the day of the martyr. The day after the Israeli withdrawal from southern Lebanon, for example, specially designed posters were distributed to celebrate the event. Some of them were marked "1742," in reference to the number of "martyrs" who died for Hezbollah. Indeed the martyr (*shaheed*) is a particularly dominant feature in the iconography of resistance. The only living member of Hezbollah who is prominently displayed is the secretary general, Hassan Nasrallah since 1992. The only other portraits of party members are those of martyrs, such as the former secretary general Abbas al-Musawi, killed during an Israeli operation in February 1992, or simple combatants killed in action. Kinda Chaib, who studied the theme of the martyr, was granted access to the photographic archives of Hezbollah's al-Shaheed foundation. Her research indicates that the dominant pictorial themes of the martyrdom imagery are soil, flowers, and blood. The soil and the land, in 41 percent of the images, symbolize both the nation in a religious sense—that is, the Muslim nation—and the nation in a secular sense, the homeland. This double meaning is reflected in the wills of the martyrs, where the fighters refer not only to the ummah, but also mention "watan"—the homeland—literally in each testament.[35] In the iconography of martyrdom, dry soil is usually cracked open, an allegorical representation of drained and suffering land waiting for the martyr's reinvigorating blood. In 40 percent of the imagery flowers are shown on the cracked ground. These flowers, often in red, embody the martyr. They symbolize the fighters killed in combat and the fruits of their sacrifice, nourishing and reviving the land. Blood, depicted in 38 percent of the images, in rare cases is shown as flowing from the wounds of a martyr's body, more frequently as dripping from a flower. The landscapes in the portraits' background reflect the attachment to their country, showing Lebanese landscapes of mountains and rivers, sometimes highlighted by the columns of Baalbek or the country's signature cedars. Jerusalem's Al-Aqsa Mosque is shown in more than two-thirds of the images, a sign that the fight transcends strictly national motivations.

But the Lebanese resistance movement's communication campaign outside the media should be put into perspective. The Party of God has no monopoly over flags and pins. Even in Lebanon's southern Shiite areas, green flags and portraits of Musa al-Sadr with Amal's insignia are widely on display. Another aspect is that this highly symbolic and vague form of messaging leaves a lot of room for misunderstandings. Some less-educated Lebanese evidently mistook the Al-Aqsa Mosque on Hezbollah posters for other local buildings, such as the city's former *husayniyya* or the Bir 'Abed Mosque in the suburbs of Beirut.[36] Finally such direct forms of communication are always geographically rangebound, and therefore limited to local audiences. If a resistance movement wants to address a wider audience, it has to use the mass media.

AL-MANAR

Before launching its own TV channel, Hezbollah already had its own radio station. The first station, The Voice of the Oppressed (sawt al-mustad'afin), began broadcasting in the Beqaa Valley in 1986; The Voice of Faith (sawt al-imam) started service in Beirut one year later. A third station, Al-Nour, began broadcasting in May 1988. Al-Nour quickly established itself as a professional radio station and helped Hezbollah to become a household name throughout the Arab world. The station won several awards, including at the eighth festival of radio and television in Cairo in 2002 where it won nine prizes.[37] But Hezbollah's leaders understood that the power of images was superior to that of the spoken word. The party duly launched a TV channel in July 1991, al-Manar, "lighthouse" in Arabic. "It's a political weapon, social weapon, and cultural weapon,"[38] said Nayef Krayem, a former chairman of al-Manar's board. He envisioned al-Manar as a "channel of resistance." The station has grown rapidly. Initially it broadcast four hours a day; then seven hours by 1993, the year it became technically possible for the inhabitants of the Beqaa Valley to receive the channel; and in 1998 the programs were again extended, now to twelve hours daily. In 2000, when al-Manar also became a satellite channel that could be received by a worldwide audience, its programming was racked up to eighteen hours a day. The transition to satellite had originally been planned for the second half of 2000 but was then hastily rescheduled to start a few months sooner in order to cover the Israeli withdrawal. In early 2001, finally, the channel began broadcasting continuously, 24/7.[39]

The Hezbollah station expanded not only its broadcasting time per day, but also its geographic reach. The most critical statistic for a TV station is the number of its viewers. Al-Manar's viewing statistics vary, according to different sources, between 10 million viewers per day to 200 million casual viewers.[40] In 2000 one-fifth of Lebanon's population watched al-Manar.[41] Five years later, at the eve of the thirty-four-day war, the channel had become one of the four most popular stations throughout the Arab world; some sources even ranked it number two, only surpassed by Al-Jazeera.[42] Al-Manar's budget is difficult to gauge, but it is safe to say that it increased constantly, from an estimated $10 million in 2001— already a huge increase over the past ten years—to $15 million in 2002.[43] It is probable that the station received and continues to receive vastly larger sums of money from Iran and other oil-flush benefactors. Another telling figure for the channel's development is the number of employees. Its staff grew from 250 in 2000 (150 full-time and 100 part-time) to 350 in 2006.[44]

Initially, al-Manar produced only an Arabic-language program. The decision to produce and broadcast segments in Hebrew was made in 1996 during the Israeli operation Grapes of Wrath.[45] The station's Hebrew program developed fast. A special office was created to monitor the Israeli news coverage and to create short programs likely to affect Israeli morale. One such clip, for instance, showed the slaying of Israeli soldiers in combat with Hebrew subtitles: "who will be next?" A Hezbollah veteran, who was imprisoned by the Israelis in 1986, first headed the office responsible for producing programs; he had learned Hebrew in order to be able to speak with his captors.[46] It was probably the first time ever that an Arab-language media outlet tried to influence Israeli public opinion with direct broadcasts in Hebrew. The impact of Hezbollah's psychological operations campaign, however, remained limited. Few Israelis directly received al-Manar's broadcasts. Residents of the Israeli–Lebanese border region could technically receive Hezbollah's channel with simple antennas. Others would have to subscribe to a satellite service that carries al-Manar. But neither "Yes," Israel's only satellite provider, whose main shareholder is the telecommunications company Bezeq, nor cable networks carried the channel. In addition to programs in Hebrew, Hezbollah also started broadcasting news segments in English in 2001 and, in 2002, even a newscast in French. Until December 2004, the twenty-five-minute news show could be received in France through the satellite Hot Bird 4, managed by Eutelsat, a French satellite provider.[47]

Al-Manar first established its name through the coverage of the conflict with Israel. The purpose of its reports was not to give a balanced view, but to show the guerrilla operations against Israel from the viewpoint of Hezbollah's fighters. Some journalists and cameramen were veteran militants themselves. To get close to the action, al-Manar journalists took significant risks. Two of them, Bakr Haidar Ahmed and Behjet Dakroub, were killed in action in July 1993; their portraits subsequently were on display in the marble-floored lobby of al-Manar's headquarters until the destruction of the building during the summer of 2006 by the Israeli Air Force.[48] Reports usually highlighted successful attacks against the Israelis. To amplify the psychological effects, Hezbollah began impressively early and with great skill to embed cameramen into its operations. In late 1994, for instance, a Hezbollah unit briefly infiltrated the Israeli *Dla'at* military compound in Lebanon. The fighters brought a cameraman with them and managed, at one point, to raise the organization's flag inside the Israeli base.[49] They were quickly driven out, but the symbolic images of the attack, filmed with the immediacy of a hand-held camera, were broadcast on al-Manar in a loop and picked up by Israeli media. Another memorable videotaped Hezbollah operation took place in February 1997, when a naval Israeli special forces commando penetrated Lebanon in a covert operation. When they moved forward inland near Sidon, Hezbollah fighters ambushed the Israeli commando from a hideout in a grove of banana trees.[50] The skirmish was captured on film by a Hezbollah camera crew, televised in Lebanon, and picked up by Israeli media. Other spectacular operations carried out by fighters of the Party of God were filmed and broadcast on al-Manar, such as the deadly IED attack against General Erez Gerstein in February 1999 or the bombing that killed Colonel Akel Hashem, deputy commander of the Israel's proxy militia, the South Lebanon Army, in January 2000.[51]

Shortly after the outbreak of the Second Intifada, al-Manar put its experience in war reporting to work in the Palestinian territories. Again its objective was not to be objective but to turn its newsrooms into a weapon of psychological warfare. On several occasions Hassan Nasrallah spoke in person on the media's role in asymmetrical conflict. On 17 November 2000, in an interview with Syrian TV, he explained:

> Through al-Manar, we are offering moral and communication support dedicated entirely to the Palestinian issue. Hizbullah understands how important television is to the resistance in Lebanon as it is for the Intifada, and so there are broadcasts in al-Manar from the morning till midnight, all of them on the Palestinian issue.[52]

At the second international conference of Arab and Islamic media to support the Palestinian people, which took place on 22 September 2003, Nasrallah expanded on the role of the media:

> The relationship between the media and the resistance, I can assure you from experience, is very strong and close. It is said that the media aspect represents half of the battle, or three quarters or two thirds. These calculations are inaccurate, but without doubt the media are one of the most important weapons of combat and resistance; it has considerable effects on the enemy, on allies, and the morale of the resistance. We lived this experience ourselves and we found that, in certain cases, the media performance affects the cause of battle, the course of the confrontation, by

moving the combatants in the field from a state of frustration, despair, and gloom to a state of vigor, hope, and ardor.[53]

After these general remarks, Hezbollah's secretary general spoke specifically about the Second Intifada and advised the Arab media representatives in the room on how to cover the events in the Palestinian territories. His first recommendation was to adapt the message to specific audiences. For a Western audience, images of oppression should dominate and arguments that Palestinians' rights are violated. For viewers in the Arab world, Nasrallah cautioned, a permanent stream of images of oppression could lead to discouragement, and should therefore be balanced by displays of heroism. The secretary general's second recommendation pointed to the Intifada's military and political significance. Nasrallah again:

> It is important that we support the resistance in Palestine, not by slogans and zealous speeches, but with concise figures, without exaggeration. What the Palestinian resistance has managed to accomplish in just three years, with its materially and military modest means, but with its extraordinary human capacity and faith, that is far more important than what Arabs and Muslims have done in fifty years of conflict with "Israel."[54]

The Arab media, he recommended, should carefully choose the language of its coverage. He criticized journalists who used expressions such as "a Palestinian was killed" rather than "a Palestinian was killed as a martyr." The press should also insist on Palestinian national unity and not to allow the Palestinians to fight among themselves and to dismember their cause on Arab media platforms. Arab media should be advocates of press freedom, but keep in mind the stakes. "We value freedom of information, but there must also be responsibility in the media." The Arab media, Nasrallah counseled, should put aside political differences and adopt a unified front with respect to the Palestinian question.

Al-Manar's coverage of the Palestinian resistance made the channel extraordinarily popular in the Palestinian territories, even more popular than al-Jazeera.[55] Some even criticized the Qatari channel for broadcasting a message from Osama bin Laden during ongoing Israeli operations in Jenin in April 2002, thus diverting the viewers' attention from the Israeli–Palestinian conflict.[56]

Al-Manar is not just a news channel. The station also carries documentaries, religious programs, sitcoms, sports, and music. But all types of broadcasts can be, and often are, used for political purposes. During the Intifada, live reporting and music videos of so-called resistance songs, many especially composed for the occasion, were stacked between quiz shows, documentaries, and sermons, tailored to the millions of Palestinian viewers and their sympathizers across the Arab world. One such quiz, broadcast on Saturday night, was al-Muhemma (the mission). Participants had to answer questions about the history of Hezbollah, such as the dates of particular operations against the IDF and names of martyrs, but also about the Arab world, Islam, and other general themes. Whoever knew the answer to the most questions won a sum of money, 20 percent of which was dedicated to resistance in Palestine. Even documentaries were used with a clever political subtext. During Ramadan 2001—during the month of fasting and waiting for nightfall, TV ratings are phenomenally high—al-Manar broadcast a historical drama about Ezzedine al-Qassem, a guerrilla leader who fought against the British and the French in the 1920s and 1930s. With a budget of $100,000, the documentary, "A story of Jihad and Resistance," was the channel's most ambitious program to date. The miniseries had a symbolic context: Qassem also was the namesake of Hamas's military wing. The story of one man in a struggle against colonial occupiers resonated powerfully with Palestinians as well as Hezbollah's Lebanese supporters. But the raging Palestinian Intifada perhaps pushed al-Manar too far in its unconditional and—by journalistic standards—rather unprofessional and emotional support for the Arab side. Two cases illustrate that the media battle could also backfire.

The first case was an internal affair that showed the fragility of Hezbollah's media operation. It involved one of al-Manar's most skilled communicators, Nayef Krayem. An agricultural engineer by training, Krayem became a journalist in the early 1990s. He quickly rose in Hezbollah's and al-Manar's hierarchy and held high positions such as president of the governing council of the Lebanese Media Group, the parent company of both al-Nour and al-Manar. Krayem also acted as director general of al-Manar and was a member of Hezbollah's politburo. Krayem became one of the most-quoted Hezbollah spokespersons in the international press.

But Krayem's star in Hezbollah's sky was about to sink. On 5 March 2003 he triggered a scandal that shook the Party of God by publishing an opinion piece in *as-Safir* magazine, the headline of which demanded to "Boycott the Legend-Makers" *(Qâti'ou Sonnâ al Asâtîr)*. The text contained excerpts from a book by the late Sheikh Moqtada al-Motahari, *The Epic Journey of the Husseinite Dynasty.* Krayem's article caused an outcry among many Hezbollah clerics because he used the highly controversial al-Motahari, an author notorious for having called into question the group's interpretation of the story that underlies the traditional Shia celebrations of Ashura. Krayem's views on celebrating the Ashura were seen as unconventional. What is more, he had implicitly questioned the doctrine of *wilayat al-faqih.*[57] Suspected of being a supporter of Fadlallah and Mohammad Khatami, a liberal reformer, Krayem was suspended from his duties for one year. But the spokesman and writer considered the politburo's punishment disproportionate and again published an article in *an-Nahar,* protesting his dismissal, on 12 May 2003, the day of the visit of President Khatami in Beirut.[58] The letter is worth quoting at length:

> Bearing in mind all the efforts I have made during 16 years to develop and improve the efficiency of some institutions within the Party have been brushed aside. Only because I have published a critical vision of some general cultural phenomena which are not exclusively linked to the Party and which are based on opinions from enlightened clerics. Bearing in mind the scale of the intellectual and cultural repression

reflected by that decision and its humiliating generalization, I regret to inform you of my resignation from Hizbullah. Yet I pray to Allah to protect it from Shi'ite Salafism, and from American and Zionist aggression. I also hope that the leaders will continue to move towards political open-mindedness and progressive militancy in a spirit of tolerance and cultural uplift, reinstating religion as a means to "exult the treasures buried in the soul," as the Imam Ali Ibn Abi Tâleb put it. Peace be on Him, instead of restraining and repressing him.[59]

The Krayem affair illustrated that even well-reputed and influential Hezbollah members would be punished when they deviated even marginally from the Party's zealous and rigid philosophy. For a movement that aspired to be a political force with wide popular appeal, such a development could spell trouble. The incident also illustrated that even a disciplined, hierarchical, and well-led organization like Hezbollah is not monolithic and exhibits cracks that can be exploited.

But it was another episode that spelled real trouble for Hezbollah's media activities, not internal but from the outside, from the international arena. It involved a highly controversial program broadcast in 2003 during Ramadan, when religious sentiment runs high. *Al-Shatat,* diaspora in Arabic, was a twenty-six-episode series aired nightly by al-Manar. The series traced the history of the Jewish people from an unequivocally anti-Semitic viewpoint. In what was essentially a modern version of the Protocols of the Elders of Zion—the series indeed embraced the fake document as fact—Jews were accused of a world conspiracy and it was purported that Christian children would be slaughtered for Passover in order to make unleavened bread. In one episode, an STD-infected prostitute, working in a European brothel run by a Jewish madam, principally refuses Jewish customers, as she did not want to infect them with her disease, thus implying that she's paid by her Jewish boss to infect non-Jews. The series predictably caused an outcry in the United States, Europe, and Israel.[60] First Hezbollah tried to defend the story. Foreign criticism was dismissed as interfering with another state's sovereignty. The anchor of the chain, Mohammad Haidar, was on thin ice when he attempted to justify the broadcast. Those responsible at al-Manar, he said, had bought and broadcast the series without having reviewed its content; they would regret the dissemination of certain "unacceptable sequences."[61]

But the al-Shatat affair played into the hands of the channel's critics, who had been looking for some time to alert the international public to the true nature of al-Manar's agenda. The campaign against the channel had already gained momentum in the United States several months prior, in October 2002, when an article in the *Los Angeles Times* pointed the finger at American companies. Avi Jorisch, an expert on Hezbollah, argued in an op-ed, "Hezbollah Hate with a U.S. Link," that big U.S. companies, such as PepsiCo, Procter & Gamble, and Western Union, were advertising on al-Manar and thereby helping to finance an organization that systematically "glorifies suicide bombers, exhorts Palestinians to kill Jews and revels in the carnage of terrorist attacks on civilians."[62] Jorisch claimed that this form of financing was not only likely to offend shareholders of the companies in question, but that such advertising could also be illegal. According to Executive Order 13224, Hezbollah—although not al-Manar—was officially named as a "specially designated terrorist group." The document empowered the U.S. government to impose financial sanctions against individuals and organizations "that support or otherwise associate" with such terrorist groups. Over the next months public pressure to act against Hezbollah's hateful propaganda was building up, not only in the United States but also in Europe. In France, on 31 January 2004, at the annual dinner of the Jewish Council of France, Crif, the group's chairman, Roger Cukierman, pinpointed al-Manar and al-Shatat in his speech. France's prime minister was sitting in the audience. The French government, Cukierman demanded, has to "understand the barbarity of these enemies of democracy" and act to prevent the spread of such "heinous lies." Jean-Pierre Raffarin, then the prime minister, promised the government would move to curb the spread of anti-Semitic material. Several months later France officially banned al-Manar, as did many other countries, among them the Netherlands and Spain, which also suspended the channel in Latin America via its satellite Hispasat. Even years after the series was broadcast, U.S. pressure groups and media outlets were able to use the al-Shatat episode to put the heat on companies seen as cooperating with Hezbollah's channel even if it only concerned broadcasts in Lebanon and the Arab world.[63] Taking advertisers off al-Manar or taking al-Manar off satellites were only two ways of limiting the station's reach. Jamming or overriding its frequencies was another possibility, occasionally practiced by Israel without durable success. So, of course, was military force.

AN ASYMMETRIC MEDIA WAR

The Lebanon War in 2006 stretched Hezbollah's press operation to the extreme. Even before hostilities started, al-Manar had a key role in the standoff that led up to outright war. The station first reported the kidnapping of the two Israeli soldiers on 12 July 2006, only an hour after their abduction. That abduction eventually triggered the Second Lebanon War. On the second day of hostilities, the Israeli Air Force opted for a more drastic approach to stop the channel's broadcastings: it blasted its headquarters. Israeli warplanes bombed and entirely destroyed the al-Manar five-story building in Haret Hreik, injuring five staff members. The IDF also attacked the al-Nour radio headquarters. But the core team operating al-Manar's newsroom that night apparently knew the evacuation drill; the program was back on air ten minutes after the attack from an alternative location. "We knew this day was coming, so we took suitable precautions across all of Lebanon," said Ibrahim Farhat, al-Manar's public relations director.[64] The channel continued to broadcast throughout the war, despite repeated Israeli efforts to silence it. Israeli experts had various assumptions about the channel's alternative installations; some officers even suspected a relocation of its facilities beyond Lebanon's borders. In retrospect it appears that production continued in the southern suburbs of Beirut, according to statements by Marwan Abd Assater, a journalist with al-Manar, in an interview aired on al-Jazeera in July 2007.[65] To avoid being spotted by the Israelis, Hezbollah's journalists and technicians developed a number of precautions: they traveled by motorcycle or with rented cars, they used pre-paid mobile phones which are more difficult to track, and they changed their style of dress, shaved beards, and the like.[66] Batul Ayyub, an al-Manar news presenter during the war, said she was forced to live in different hotels throughout the conflict, and that she—deviating from her normal practice—went to work covered by a niqab, the full-body veil leaving only the eyes uncovered, in order not to be recognized.[67] As Hezbollah's journalists were forced to operate clandestinely and go underground, so did al-Manar's broadcasting operation. As it became more difficult to operate under normal conditions, Webcasting—largely immune against legislation, jamming, and bombs—became a more attractive option. Yusuf Wehbe, the head of al-Manar's Internet unit, explained the site's evolution. "The site has been operating since 1996, but back then, it was just a site for Al-Manar." By 2005, Wehbe said, almanar.com.lb had become a news platform because the satellite channel was blocked in several countries and continents. After the Israeli attack, the Web site was upgraded into an alternative venue to receive programs: "in 2006, the live streaming service was activated and since then al-Manar can be watched and read anywhere and anytime."[68] Evasion tactics such as live-streaming and full-body veils were surely an important enabler for al-Manar's success during the war, but its true breakthrough was more traditional.

During the Second Lebanon War of 2006 Hezbollah accomplished a previously unthinkable tactical success, and al-Manar played an essential role in turning a singular tactical event into a strategic and even highly political affair that resonated in the region in ways that even Hezbollah did not anticipate. On 14 July 2006, on the third day of the war, Hezbollah fired an Iranian-supplied Noor anti-ship cruise missile at the Israeli corvette *INS Hanit*. The attack killed four crew members and caused heavy damage to the ship's flight deck and steering system. The military significance of the attack for Israel's naval operations during the war was negligible. But its psychological effect can hardly be exaggerated. On the same night the ship was struck (see the chapter on Israel for the IDF's side of the story), al-Manar went on the air with a clip that allegedly displayed the attack complete with a commentary by the organization's leader, Hassan Nasrallah. As his voice spoke triumphantly but calmly, the screen showed Beirut at night, some lights lit, with occasional tracers and rockets illuminating the sky. The camera zoomed into the center to show one larger rocket being fired from the lit areas out into the dark background, the sea, and then a larger explosion. "Now, in the middle of the sea, opposite to Beirut, the Israeli military war ship which assaulted our infrastructure and the houses of the people and civilians," Nasrallah paused for effect. "Look at it . . . burning." To furnish the viewers' imagination of what just happened in the dark, archival pictures of an Israeli corvette operating at daylight were cut in.

The *Hanit* video was Hezbollah's opening salvo of the media war. And it contained one of the central features of the ensuing campaign: it was built around one person, the secretary general of the Party of God, Nasrallah. Three elements of his biographical background should be recalled to understand the weight the cleric carries and the legitimacy he enjoyed among supporters. The first is the extent of Nasrallah's political engagement. Since a very early age, he engaged in political activities and acquired a range of skills, particularly as an orator, that allowed him to quickly climb the ranks of Amal and then Hezbollah. When he was fifteen years old, the young Nasrallah was appointed head of Amal in Bazouriyeh, a small town located some sixty kilometers south of Beirut where his family had settled after the outbreak of civil war. The second is Nasrallah's standing as an accomplished cleric. He visited Najaf in Iraq from 1976 to 1978 where he studied in the Baqir al-Sadr's *hawza*, a highly reputed seminary of traditional Shia Islamic studies. By 1986 he also received the personal support of Imam Khomeini.[69] The third element was his image as a man ready to sacrifice for the good cause. This selfless image was reinforced by the death of his eighteen-year-old son Hadi Nasrallah, who was killed in a military operation against Israel on 13 September 1997. Nasrallah's media appearances gained considerable momentum after 1987 when he joined Hezbollah's majlis al-shura al-qarar, or executive council, and then became secretary-general in 1992, following the assassination of Abbas al-Musawi. Since then he has given hundreds of speeches.[70] In the approximately 120 speeches Nasrallah gave since May 2000, he positioned himself as commander-in-chief, political leader, and religious authority. His theme of choice is "resistance." He used the reference to muqawama nearly 2,470 times in the speeches during the six years leading up to the thirty-four-day war. Other recurring themes were "martyr" (shaheed) 900 times, "confrontation" (muajaha) 689 times, jihad 476 times, mujahideen 423 times, and "battle" (ma'raka) 374 times. The second most popular reference in his speeches is religion. The word "Islam" is used 1,700 times. Nasrallah specifically stressed the dangers that threaten Islam, especially America's nefarious influence. The line between religion and politics is often difficult to draw in Nasrallah's speeches, particularly when he blames "confessionalism," a problem he referred to 340 times in 120 speeches (the term "ummah" was used nearly 900 times).

During the war of 2006, Nasrallah gave eight speeches, with a duration ranging from fourteen to forty-six minutes. He gave one interview to al-Jazeera. With the exception of two, these speeches start with remarks on ongoing military operations and then move on to more political issues. Nasrallah's first speech was broadcast on 16 July. The words "victory," "patience," "resistance," "tenacity," "humiliation," prominent references in other presentations as well, dominated the address. Facing relentless bombing by the IDF, the secretary general wanted to be encouraging. He recalled the painful experiences of 1982 and 1996 and claimed that Hezbollah now was stronger than ever before. Clearly aware that the Israeli government and public would be keenly watching his pronouncements, he opted for fearsome religious rhetoric and aimed directly at his opponents:

> You do not know who you fight today. You fight the descendants of Mohammed, Ali, Hassan, Hussein, the Prophet's relatives and the Prophet's companions. You are fighting a nation of faith unmatched on this earth.[71]

As the war ground on, the world was watching closely. And one of dominant themes in the war's coverage were competing claims by the two sides, about the number of civilian casualties and tactical military successes. In the third speech, two weeks after the outbreak of hostilities, the secretary general emphasized the role of "psychological warfare" and the distortion of facts. Hezbollah's claims would be "transparent and clear" while the Israeli side would put forward misinformation and lies.

In his fourth speech, Nasrallah attempted to rally Lebanon's various political factions to unity and solidarity, "so that all these sacrifices are not in vain." He asked the Lebanese "not to fear the victory of the resistance but its defeat." The speech also marked a change of tone with respect to other Arab countries, which Hezbollah previously had criticized for their inaction. Nasrallah: "we will have great affection, gratitude and respect for any Arab country moving in the right direction toward Lebanon and offering the necessary assistance to stop the war." Syria and Iran were singled out as positive examples as they were already "making every effort [. . .] to stop the Zionist aggression on Lebanon." The statement might reflect Hezbollah's increased popularity, and hence power, across the Muslim world at that point in time during the conflict. Widespread and intense popular support for the resistance was increasingly making Arab governments uncomfortable. If their own populations so ecstatically embraced the resistance in Lebanon, what would that mean for the simmering resistance movements in their own countries, where the anger was not conveniently funneled against Israel but often directed against the very governments Nasrallah was now asking for help. One event soon offered at least a symbolic opportunity to "help" Hezbollah.

On 30 July 2006 the Israeli Air Force carried out a fateful airstrike in al-Khuraybah, a small hamlet near the South Lebanese village of Qana. A large number of civilians perished in the rubble of a three-story building, half of them children. Initial accounts put the number of fatalities at sixty people, but as bodies were pulled from the debris, the toll was lowered to twenty-eight, fourteen of them children. The Israeli government, in an attempt to defend its actions, claimed that rockets had been launched from the site and that Hezbollah had been using human shields. But the Red Cross and residents of Qana claimed that no Hezbollah rockets were launched from the village prior to the airstrike. Bahia Hariri, who represented south Lebanese charities, claimed that "there were 15 physically or mentally handicapped children among the children killed in Qana."[72] Russia demanded an "immediate cease fire." European countries condemned the bombing. UN Secretary General Kofi Annan surmised that Qana could be part of a "pattern of violations of international law." Arab leaders, both those friendly and hostile toward Israel, predictably leapt on the incident: Jordanian King Abdullah II denounced the Qana bombing as a "criminal aggression" and "a strong violation of the international law." Egyptian President Hosni Mubarak said the action operation was "irresponsible." Arab League Secretary General Amr Moussa saw the raid as "barbaric." Syrian President Bashar al-Assad spoke of Israeli "state terrorism," and the Kuwaiti parliament speaker Jassem al Kharafi chastised the Israelis as "savage and barbaric." A "war crime," offered Palestinian President Mahmoud Abbas, and a "heinous massacre," blasted Hamas leader Ismail Haniyeh. The Qana raid, fumed Munshir al-Masri, a Hamas spokesman, "has crossed all red lines"; he added that "all options are open for the Palestinian and Lebanese resistance to respond to this terrorist crime." Public demonstrations in a number of countries ensued. Following the international outcry over the bombing, Israeli Prime Minister Ehud Olmert expressed "deep regret" for the bombing and declared a forty-eight-hour cessation of airstrikes in order to carry out a military probe into the Qana killings, although 61 percent of Israelis, according to a poll, continued to back the airstrikes.[73] Israel's air strikes, in short, provided ample grounds for international pressure to build up and ultimately backfire politically against Israel.

Nasrallah reacted to Qana in his fifth speech. Less calm than in previous speeches, he accused Israeli leadership of lying, hurled insults, and chided their "stupidity," "senility," "arrogance," and "ignorance." For the first time since the war began, Nasrallah referred to Afghanistan and Iraq and spoke of "fighters who are defending Lebanon and the ummah, the ummah that the United States and Israel again seek to divide in Lebanon, in Iraq, in Afghanistan, and elsewhere." Nasrallah gave his sixth speech on 9 August, when it already became clear that Israel would not be able to achieve its stated goals: retrieve its two kidnapped soldiers, destroy the military capability of Hezbollah, and end the constant stream of missile attacks. Hezbollah's leadership was surprised both by the intensity of the Israeli attack, which considerably damaged Lebanon's infrastructure and parts of Beirut, and by its own resilience in the face of such overwhelming force. Nasrallah spoke of "miracles"—a term already used in some previous speeches—and about the amazing success of the resistance. He employed twice the expression "divine victory" (nasr min allah), thereby coining a theme in Hezbollah's rhetoric on the war. Visibly encouraged by the conflict's development, he now warned the Israelis by quoting his predecessor Abbas al-Musawi: "I say to the enemy—borrowing a phrase from the father our martyrs and our grand leader Sayyed Abbas al-Musawi—'until now, you have only seen a part of our power.' So welcome to the large-scale ground operation and you will see, God willing, the full extent of our power."

In his last two speeches, on 12 and 14 August, Nasrallah followed his own methodological script laid out at the conference in Cairo and carefully catered his words to different audiences. He was already preparing the ground for the post-war phase. The leader thanked not only Hezbollah fighters but the Lebanese people as a whole, appealing to the country's unity and "national solidarity." For the international community he highlighted UN Security Council Resolution 1701 and deemed it "unfair and unjust," but conceded that "the resolution could have been much worse" and directed conciliatory words at UNIFIL.

Hezbollah has managed the transition from the intense 2006 war to the post-conflict phase with astonishing ease, particularly in the field of communication. Two examples illustrate how the Party of God has exploited the war's outcome. Nasrallah, for one, skillfully branded the end of the Israeli's counterattack as a "divine victory" already in mid-August. That expression partly reflected the disbelief of many Muslims, including many Hezbollah sympathizers, that a small resistance force could indeed prevail—or rather avoid being totally crushed—against a force as powerful and as invincible as the IDF; a supernatural power must have helped Hezbollah's young men. "We feel that we won," the secretary general said to a massive crowd waving his organization's yellow-green flags, on 22 September in a southern suburb of Beirut: "Lebanon won; Palestine won; the entire Arab nation won."[74] Indeed the entire Arab nation was enthusiastic about the success of the resistance in Lebanon. An outpouring of highly emotional support for Hezbollah ensued across most Arab countries. Countless ordinary people called and wrote to newspapers and talk shows on the major satellite channels, reciting poetry and praising the resistance. To help get the message across, Hezbollah organized bus tours of bombed areas for Lebanese and foreign journalists.

Another example is more creative and original: Hezbollah organizers set up a vast, free exhibition presenting the main victors of the war, Hezbollah's fighters, and the alleged weakness of their opponent. The museum was cleverly named the House of the Spider. In 2000, on the occasion of a victory celebration in Bint Jbeil, Nasrallah gave a speech in which he compared Israel to a "house of a spider." The expression was a shrewd reference to the Quran, Sura 29, The Spider, specifically to verse 41: "The parable of those who take protectors other than Allah is that of the Spider, who builds (to itself) a house; but the flimsiest of houses is the Spider's house." The House of the Spider since became the title of a talk show on al-Manar that had the objective of showing the vulnerabilities and weaknesses of Israel, to shatter the myth that its army is invincible.[75] The exhibition, installed after the "divine victory" had delivered the proof, shared this objective. It is organized in glass cases sunk into the ground, displaying Israeli items captured in the war: helmets, boots, guns, radio equipment, oxygen tanks, and even personal objects such as iPods or *tefillin,* Jewish prayer straps. "Watch it burn," boasts a poster of a capsized warship in reference to Hezbollah's infamous *Hanit* video of the night of 14 July.[76] The museum shop has a range of items to offer, from Hezbollah DVDs to a Raad-1 cologne, a perfume named after an Iranian missile.[77] This unusual PR measure should not be underrated. It is estimated that one million visitors physically came to see the exhibition; that would be a number roughly equivalent to one-fifth of Lebanon's population.

Like the Taliban and like al-Qaeda, as we will see in the following two chapters, Hezbollah has understood the significance of media operations for their cause and for the resistance. Already in 2001, even before the Second Intifada started and helped Palestinian resistance fighters to appreciate the power of the media, Nayef Krayem illustrated Hezbollah's grasp of the information environment:

> Sometimes the media is a more important weapon than the real weapon. Without the camera, without the TV, the resistance operations would not have had as great an impact and influence in the conflict.[78]

The Party's leaders and its ground troops have, by and large, skillfully implemented the lessons in media and perception management in the 2006 war against Israel. But at the same time Hezbollah has performed a transformation that is in many ways inverse to that of al-Qaeda and to an extent that of the Taliban: it became less global in its militant ambition and more local by consolidating its political constituency. It does not so much rely on the new electronic media to recruit activists and to reach its most important local audiences. Instead it uses very traditional means, sometimes even without the use of any media, either traditional or electronic. Hezbollah pins and caps and toys, moreover, illustrate that the movement has a popular appeal that compares more to the appeal of major European or American political parties or trade unions than to a terrorist group. In terms of popular appeal, discipline, and professionalism in public affairs the Party of God outperforms almost all other militant movements across the Muslim world.

8

Taliban

At the end of 2006 the press and experts reported the Taliban's resurgence. The Taliban's numbers grew to a level unseen since 2001, to an estimated 12,000 to 17,000 militants. The purists favored a literalist interpretation of the Sharia on the Wahhabi pattern and an absolutist Islamic state. Huge numbers of radical volunteers streamed in from Pakistan. Suicide bombings, a previously unknown tactic in Afghanistan, rose to more than 130 that year. As a consequence, "civilian deaths from insurgent attacks skyrocketed,"[1] Human Rights Watch reported, bringing the organization's count to 669 killed Afghan civilians in 2006. The number of military casualties equally rose. That fifth year after the U.S.-led invasion of Afghanistan had been the deadliest years for NATO troops ever, with 191 coalition fatalities.[2] Opium production hit an all-time high, with 6,100 tons produced on 165,000 hectares, an increase of 59 percent over 2005.[3] Then 2007 broke all of these records: more Taliban, more Afghan civilian casualties, more attacks, more NATO air strikes, more coalition casualties, and more opium. The opium cultivation area increased by 17 percent to 193,000 hectares, and the land was put to more efficient use: 8,200 tons of opium were harvested, 34 percent more than in 2006, increasing the share of opium in the country's GDP to 53 percent.[4] The drug revenue in turn fed the insurgency.

As NATO defense ministers gathered for a summit in Vilnius in early 2008, the predictions were accordingly gloomy. "The Taliban in Afghanistan now control more of the country than at any time since 2001, and their confederates in the tribal areas of Pakistan are expanding their operations almost day by day," said Senate Foreign Relations Committee Chairman Joseph Biden.[5] "Make no mistake, NATO is not winning in Afghanistan," wrote Marine Corps General James Jones, the former Supreme Allied Commander Europe, in a report.[6] Stern numbers, grim trends, and ghastly assessments dominated the Western media coverage, threatening to further undermine shaky public support, particularly in European

NATO countries. General Dan McNeill, Commander of the International Security Assistance Force, traveled to Washington to counter what he maintained was overly pessimistic news. The general maintained that progress in the reconstruction effort was made, that the coalition is in good shape, and that more troops would be on the way. Yet he acknowledged that ISAF was "under-resourced" and that progress in Afghanistan as well as in NATO countries ran into political obstacles.

It was therefore not surprising that Western leaders pointed to the Taliban's propaganda operations as one explanation for the high perceived impact of the militants' operations. Des Browne, the British defense secretary, alerted the press in 2006 to the Taliban's "impressive information operation" in an interview with the BBC.[7] This assessment was echoed by General McNeill in early 2008: "They did very little on the battlefield. They were very successful in staying in the press, and they continue to be."[8] The Islamist movement has ratcheted up its media operations vis-à-vis the international media, toward sympathizers across the Muslim world, and the local Afghan population. But the Taliban have long had to deal with an internal tension: between being a local political force or a more globally oriented Islamic militant group, or even a local branch of al-Qaeda. The group's media operations reflect this tension.

THE TALIBAN'S RISE

The Taliban is a fundamentalist Sunni movement: ethnically the radicals tend to be Pashtun. The movement's name is derived from "talib," Arabic for student. The Taliban originally drew its membership from Afghan and Pakistani madrassas, conservative Islamic schools.[9] The Taliban started as a classical insurgency in the sense that it had popular support and a cause—but in a very unclassical sense it did not fight to topple the authority of an existing and established government. Its opponents were bands and warlords who themselves had little legitimacy and popular support. That made the Taliban's initial success appear more significant than it actually was, and as a consequence led to the movement's bloated self-esteem today.

Mullah Mohammed Omar, the Taliban's top leader from the beginnings to today, had fought against the Soviet Union and, between 1989 and 1992, against the communist Najibullah regime. The years following the Soviet withdrawal were characterized by chaos and anarchy in Afghanistan; the population was exploited and abused by competing mujahideen-turned-warlords and their voracious militias. In 1994, two Singesar neighbors allegedly came to Mullah Omar and told him that a paramilitary commander had abducted two teenage girls. Their hair had been shaved, they were taken to the military camp, and they were repeatedly raped. Omar decided to act. He gathered thirty Talibs, armed with only sixteen rifles, it is said, and attacked the base. The girls were freed and the commander was hung from the main gun of a tank. Another story involved a young boy, captured by two mujahideen commanders in Kandahar, both of whom wanted to sodomize him and so started a firefight over their booty. The Mullah's new group of fighters reportedly freed the boy. Soon public calls for help in other disputes came in, and Omar "emerged as a Robin Hood figure, helping the poor against the rapacious commanders," Ahmed Rashid wrote.[10] Yet, given the absence of archives and documentation, it remains unclear whether these very stories are not myths and the result of early Taliban propaganda.

Another reading suggests that the emerging Taliban movement was at least partially organized and supported by Pakistan's Inter-Service Intelligence (ISI). The triggering event was the "liberation" by Pakistani volunteers of a convoy of goods held up by Afghan bandits. These madrassa-educated fighters formed the core group of the Taliban. What is undisputed is that the movement was helped by the population's frustration with a continued state of chaos and war under the mujahideen warlords. The Taliban captured Kandahar, Afghanistan's second largest city, merely weeks after Omar had started the movement. By the end of 1994, some 12,000 students from Afghanistan and Pakistan had joined the Taliban movement in Kandahar. During the next three months, the Taliban captured twelve of Afghanistan's thirty-one provinces. Its advances stopped only at the outskirts of two of the country's most important cities, Herat and Kabul, the capital. On 2 February 1994 the Taliban seized the city of Wardak, only fifty-five kilometers south of Kabul, and continued their advance on the city. Kabul at the time of the Taliban advance was under the political control of then President Burhanuddin Rabbani, and under the military command of Ahmad Shah Massoud, at the time one of Afghanistan's most revered and skilled militia leaders. In early January 1995 several opposition groups, including the Taliban, advanced on Kabul and against each other: in the north Hikmatyar had joined forces with the Uzbek warlord General Rashid Dostum who held a part of Kabul; in the south Abdul Ali Mazari, a leader of the Hazaras of central Afghanistan, held a portion of the city. Both tried to capture the city from Rabbani themselves. The provinces of Nimroz and Farah as well as the Persian-speaking city of Herat were under the control of the more liberal-minded Ismael Khan, all former mujahideen leaders who had gritted their teeth in the jihad against the Soviets. To complicate matters the Pakistani government and security services supported various parties to the war with the ISI: for instance, brokering an agreement between the Taliban and Dostum to join forces against Ismael Khan. All were surprised by the Taliban's successes.

These successes, however, were not unchecked. Initial advances on Kabul in February were successful, and the Talibs captured Hikmatyar's headquarters, sending his troops into panic. In March Khan launched a ferocious attack on Taliban positions in Kabul, pushing their new and inexperienced forces out of the city in bloody street fights. By March the Taliban had also been pushed out of Shindand, a former Soviet base close to Herat, and lost all previously captured territory. The movement suffered thousands of casualties. Mullah Omar's fighters, however, were numerous and determined, and were well supported and equipped by outside powerful and resourceful supporters such as Pakistan's ISI and Saudi Arabia. The Taliban pushed back on Ismael Khan's troops in September 1995, and Herat fell just before the winter would make the continuation of operations much more difficult. Herat's downfall heralded that of the Rabbani government in Kabul. Massoud ordered a retreat from Kabul on 7 April 1996, after the Taliban had bombarded Kabul. By the end of the year the Taliban controlled two-thirds of the country.

Mullah Omar's organization clearly had a regional focus, although it hosted al-Qaeda cadres, which focused on the "far enemy." For the Taliban, the exceptional situation was that there was no "near enemy:"[11] after the mujahideen had chased out the Russians, Afghanistan just did not have a well-established home government that could be opposed. The radical Taliban's victory in 1996 was precisely what other radical organizations such as Zawahiri's al-Jihad tried in Egypt or Bin Laden's al-Qaeda had tried in Saudi Arabia: seize government authority and establish an Islamic Caliphate. Mullah Omar, although without any connection to al-Qaeda at the time, did so in Afghanistan. Omar originally joined Hizb-e-Islami, a group founded by Younis Khalis, a former anti-Soviet commander who died in 2006, and from 1989 to 1992 fought under the commander Nek Mohammed against the Najibullah regime.[12] The regime's political ambition seemingly was exhausted by an orthodox application of the Sharia, following a rigid and strict interpretation of the Sunna.

The old Taliban and the Northern Alliance very rarely used suicide bombings as a tactic. Open martyrdom operations were never planned and used by Afghan mujahideen against the Russians. The first known suicide attack in Afghanistan was executed in 1992, when the Salafi warlord Maulvi Jamil-ur Rehman was assassinated in Kunar province by an Egyptian fighter for Gulbuddin Hekmatyar. But it was not until the fateful assassination of Ahmad Shah Massoud on 9 September 2001 by al-Qaeda operatives posing as journalists that the notion of suicidal attacks slowly became more common in Afghanistan.[13] There were no suicide attacks in 2002, two in 2003, and three in 2004.

In March 2001 the UN had reported that the Taliban had enforced a ban on poppy cultivation and that Afghanistan produced virtually zero opium in that year. But the Taliban's drug policy was far from unambiguous. The United Nations Office on Drugs and Crime (UNDCP) reported that Afghanistan's opium production in 1999 doubled to 4,600 tons. At least 97 percent of the narcotics were produced in Taliban-controlled areas. Mullah Omar banned opium cultivation only on 1 August 2000. After the battle of Tora Bora, in Operation Anaconda, an engagement over several days that played out in early March 2002 in the remote Shah-i-Kot valley, U.S. commanders thought they had delivered the final blow to all military resistance by the Taliban and al-Qaeda.[14]

But Afghanistan is a huge country. It is the size of France and the Benelux countries combined. More than four in five Afghans live in rural areas and only a dozen cities have more than 70,000 inhabitants. Moreover, Afghanistan is ethnically, culturally, linguistically, and geographically diverse. Afghanistan's tribal structure and the country's socioeconomic setup gives the central government—and that even applies to the Taliban—only a small corridor to maneuver. At the same time Afghanistan's ethnically diverse society, with its long-standing grievances and conflicts, offers a rich pool of potential recruits to insurgents, particularly if these insurgents, such as the Taliban, offer an ideologically unifying alternative and claim to stand above tribal and ethnic fault lines. It is therefore to be expected that any insurgent movement would reflect this diversity, especially if it faces a formidable opponent that monitors and exploits communication linking a center to its various parts.

Experts agree that in the years since the Taliban regime's fall in October 2001, Afghanistan and the world witnessed the rise of a "next generation" of Taliban or "Neo-Taliban."[15] The second-generation Taliban began to rise in 2002, following their predecessors' removal from power. Many of the top cadres were identical. The most powerful groups are Mullah Omar's generic Taliban. Distinct from his movements is Gulbuddin Hekmatyar's *Hezb-i-Islami,* a group that became an ally of the Taliban (and al-Qaeda), yet never merged with them. So is Maulavi Jalaluddin Haqqani's so-called *Haqqani Network;* Haqqani's precise relationship to the Taliban leadership is not known. All three leaders are old mujahideen who bitterly fought the Soviets in the 1980s, and now continue their struggle against U.S. occupation. Then there are additional factions that have some form of allegiance to Mullah Omar's core Taliban. A large number of Taliban fighters come from Pakistan and specifically the area around Quetta and the South Waziristan agency, where the *Pakistani Taliban* are led by Baitullah Mehsud, the "unofficial amir" of Waziristan.[16] Another group that is still active is *Hizb-i-Islami Khalis,* founded by Younis Khalis. Yet another group is *Jaish-e-Muslimeen* (alternatively spelled Jaish-ul Muslim), which allegedly split off from the main organization in August 2004 under the leadership of Akbar Agha, a former commander. Then there is *Jamiat-i-Khudamul Furqan* (or Koran), a breakaway faction with allegedly close contacts to Pakistan's ISI as well as U.S. intelligence services. These groups significantly differ in some of their policies, and so does their reputation among their various constituencies.[17]

The second-generation Taliban have a more pragmatic approach than their ideologically more purist first-generation forbearers: they exploit the opium business, they avidly use suicide operations, they embrace the media for their own propaganda, and they use new technologies, even digital films and music. During their five years in power, the Taliban showed some flexibility, and allowed the filming of some of their fighters, but never the leaders. The movement's political aims are part of what might have changed with the Taliban's maturation. After an initial period of surprising calm in which American special forces met less resistance than expected, several thousand fighters re-emerged around Gardez, in Paktia province. The current crop of fighters has, for instance, adapted a less purist but more pragmatic attitude toward new technologies and methods. They produce relatively sophisticated media products, such as documentaries, interviews, videotaped operations, and speeches by Taliban leaders. They use a much more market-based approach for operations and support, from fundraising campaigns, exploiting the opium business to their advantage, to paying mercenaries for specific operations. Suicide attacks, one of the insurgency's signature weapons, started to appear with regularity only in mid-2005. In 2006 came a surge, with 123 suicide attacks, and in 2007 that number rose to more than 140 bombings.

The Taliban's leadership structure is not known in detail. Given Afghanistan's geography and cultural setup, it is likely that Taliban units operate without detailed guidance from top commanders. The leadership operates under a high risk of being executed from the air. Mullah Akhtar Osmani, one of the Taliban's more moderate leaders, was killed by a NATO air strike in December 2006. In August 2007 the U.S. Air Force liquidated Mullah Berader, a senior Taliban command. Mullah Dadullah, the first Taliban commander to give interviews to print and electronic media after the fall of the regime and perhaps the movement's most feared leader, was killed by ground forces in May 2007. All three allegedly had been members of the Taliban's ten-member Shura Majlis. As a result, the second-generation Taliban have fewer rigid leadership structures and a larger, more diverse, yet more pragmatic, base of cadres and fighters; the movement thus has more cohesion and it is less vulnerable to both internal divisions and external attacks than their predecessors were.

The most salient difference between the old and the new Taliban is their enemy: the movement again faces a "near enemy." But this time, as in Iraq, the near enemy becomes identical with the far enemy—the United States. As a result, it is more difficult to distinguish between the new Taliban's regional and global ambitions. If the second-generation Taliban are indeed, as some experts argue, predisposed to turn the Afghan cause into a global jihad, the consequences for the movement's political aim would be far-reaching. The leadership's majority would then want to keep foreigners in the country and wear them down slowly—as originally envisioned by Osama Bin Laden when he planned the attack on the USS Cole in 2000 and eventually on the World Trade Center in 2001. These attacks were intended to "lure America into the same trap the Soviets had fallen into: Afghanistan," writes Lawrence Wright in *The Looming Tower*. The mujahideen would swarm upon the foreign invaders and "bleed them until the entire American empire fell from its wounds."[18] This had happened to Great Britain, and it had happened to the Soviet Union. Bin Laden was convinced it would happen to America.

THE TALIBAN'S INFORMATION OPERATIONS

The Taliban's approach to public information, perhaps more than any other feature, reflects the movement's two-tiered evolution. Despite the fact that many of the Taliban's top leaders remain in place, the movement's first- and second-generation media ops stand in the starkest contrast to each other.

The Taliban's reign began with a gesture that couldn't have been more symbolic. After the Taliban's first attempt to storm north to Kabul was blocked, Mullah Mohammad Omar returned to Kandahar, the old royal capital and rival of Kabul. There he appropriated the title *Amir ul-Momineen,* or commander of the faithful, in an exalting gathering in Kandahar. On 4 April 1996 he appeared on a roof above thousands of cheering Taliban who had gathered in a shrine's courtyard, wrapping himself in the *Khirqa.* In 1761 the *Khirqa,* a piece of the Cloak of the Prophet Mohammad, was carried with full pomp and ceremony from Turkistan to Kabul and Kandahar, along streets lined by the masses who wanted to see and touch the religious relic. The cloak, which had not been removed from its Kandahar shrine in sixty years, had for centuries symbolized the prophet's blessings of the new rulers, and the transfer of power from Kabul to Kandahar.[19] Omar was harking back to the Fourth Caliph, a nephew of Prophet Mohammad, by publicly accepting the title, a ranking in Islam nearly second to the Prophet.[20] The public display of the *Khirqa* was an ingenuous propaganda stroke of epic proportions.

This skill and sophistication in dealing with the public, however, was not carried over into the modern media. Ahmed Rashid, one of the region's most renowned chroniclers, recalled how different the Taliban's approach to public attention was. "I persuaded an ABC television journalist to come with me to Kandahar, and I was shocked they wouldn't allow us to take pictures," he said of the newly installed Taliban regime in Kandahar. "I'd been living with the mujahedeen, who loved publicity. When these guys in Kandahar wouldn't be photographed, I suddenly realized this was a completely new thing."[21] They cut most contact to the outside world and internally installed a purist reign. "Thieves will have their hands and feet amputated, adulterers will be stoned to death and those taking liquor will be lashed," Radio Kabul announced on 28 September 1996.[22] Radio Kabul was soon renamed Radio Shariat, and music entertainment was banned, along with kite flying, dancing, and films. For the remaining time of the Taliban's reign these draconic regulations were kept in place. The Taliban used the media as an extended muezzin, to lecture the population. Mullah Mohammad Ishaq Nizami, the former head of the Voice of Sharia, "Afghan people have to be told that we are good for them, that is our job and that is what we will continue to do."[23] The Taliban's broadcast media operations were blunt and unsophisticated. "When the Taliban were in power, they were not focused on this important thing," said Abdul Salam Zaeef, the Taliban's former ambassador to Pakistan. "[B]ut they have learned from al Qaeda the importance of media in their operations."[24]

But the Taliban face a problem in their media work that is more pronounced than in other insurgencies today: their two most important audiences couldn't be more different. The publics of ISAF countries engaged in the fight offer a stark contrast to local Afghans: the first are among the world's most educated and technologically sophisticated media and news consumers; the latter have a low literacy rate and still a low penetration of television, internet access, and—compared to the developed world—mobile phones. Satellite phones in large numbers were reportedly in use by the Taliban as early as 2003. That year the Taliban began using satellite phones imported from the Arabian Gulf, serviced by Thuraya, a regional satellite phone provider based in the Emirates. Thuraya phones bought in Pakistan, it was assumed, were bugged by the CIA.[25] The phones were initially used in combination with small motorcycles, mainly 125ccm Hondas, fitted with phone chargers. The vehicles were likely used by spotters and reconnaissance teams. But satellite phones are ill suited to coordinate tactical movements of larger units. Field radios first appeared during the summer of 2005. It took the insurgents until 2006 to put the new technology to proficient use on the battle-field to coordinate company-sized groups of fighters. As the Taliban grew in num-ber, and battles grew larger, it became more difficult to control them in battle. The limits of shouted verbal communication were quickly reached. The use of radio communications significantly improved the Taliban's ability to amass larger numbers of men and even to scatter and regroup when attacked. But both the phones and the radio systems were commercial, with a fixed frequency. Military radios, by contrast, permanently change their frequency to make it more difficult for the enemy to listen in.

But the local commanders were increasingly open to using their newly acquired telecommunication equipment to get the message out to others. Taliban spokespersons residing in Quetta pretended to be in Afghanistan, briefed Pakistani journalists, and threatened them if their papers did not run the appro-priate storyline. Increasingly they even saw the benefit of talking to the interna-tional media. The Taliban movement belatedly recognized the utility of public relations. Sami Yousafzai, a *Newsweek* journalist, reported in December 2006 how the Taliban's attitude to the media had changed. Earlier in the year, the Taliban were hiding in the mountains, living in the shadows, and shy vis-à-vis the press. He was able to communicate with commanders only through satellite phone. "When I could arrange a clandestine meeting, the journey to the rendezvous site was haz-ardous, and once there, commanders and fighters were reluctant to talk or show their faces for security reasons." That attitude, allegedly, has changed radically. "I'm dealing with a different insurgent movement," Yousafzai wrote. "I can contact com-manders easily on their cellular phones. They are more confident, are eager to talk and have started inviting 'trusted' journalists to visit their newly secured zones."[26] Many commanders and fighters would even freely pose for photos.

"The Taliban Islamic movement has recognized the extraordinary importance of the news media in deciding [the outcome of] conflicts, particularly ideological conflicts." Such opens an article of *Al-Somood* magazine, the Taliban's glossy online magazine that had published twenty-four issues in Arabic by January 2008. The U.S. State Department agreed with this assessment. In 2007 it found that "Taliban information operations have grown increasingly sophisticated."[27] Aggressive prop-aganda allegedly helped bolster the Taliban's financial sources, the recruitment of rural Pashtuns, and their technological capabilities and military power. The new generation of Taliban has come a long way after the first movement had banned most media products, films, and music. After their ouster, and after al-Qaeda demonstrated what successful media operations can look like, the Taliban are now "convinced" that the media are among the most powerful tools to wage psychological warfare. The "Taliban has been able (with God's Help) to take the battle to the heart of the enemy." The broadcast media specifically are mentioned, world as well as local outlets, and the "pictures of jihadi operations against crusader soldiers."[28]

The information environment for the NATO coalition as well as for the Taliban is evolving fast in Afghanistan. The country's cellular phone industry in particular is growing rapidly; in fact Afghanistan's is one of the world's fastest-growing mobile phone markets. This is partly because the country launched mobile phone services only in 2002. Two large companies dominate the market, Afghan Wireless Communications and Roshan; both operators have each hit 2 million subscribers in June 2008.[29] Yet this impressive growth took place, and continues to do so, against the backdrop of an ongoing and increasingly violent insurgency.

Afghan Wireless was the first company allowed to set up a GSM wireless network in a deal signed in April 2002. Less than three months later, the company had 41,000 wireless subscribers in four cities. In mid-2008 its network covered 300 towns in all thirty-four Afghan provinces. Roshan, which entered the market in July 2003, has even more staggering growth rates. The company's first business plan had predicted 12,000 mobile phone subscribers in the first half year. It reached that goal in three days, reported Canada's *Globe and Mail,* with thousands of people waving application forms besieging its offices. In June 2007 it had become the biggest private business in the country, with a staff of 900 at reasonable wages. Roshan, which means "light" or "hope," had invested $300 million in Afghanistan by 2007 and was planning to continue this investment with approximately $75 million per year. Roshan's taxes alone supplied 6 percent of the Afghan government's revenue in 2007.[30] With a penetration of approximately 12 percent and falling prices for cellphones and subscriptions, there is a lot of space for expansion in the future. Approximately 42 percent of all Afghans had access to a mobile phone in 2007 (only 37 percent to a TV set).[31]

It is unclear how this growth will affect the insurgency and the conditions for insurgency. Yet some initial trends are revealing themselves. In early 2008 the Taliban demanded that the country's booming telecom providers shut down their mobile phone networks between 5 p.m. and 7 a.m. each night. The Taliban, who often move at night—for instance, to post night letters—most likely were concerned that local Afghans reported the physical movements and whereabouts of militants to coalition forces with the help of their mobile phones. Mobile phone technology has hugely reduced the risks for informants to be exposed as "spies" by the insurgents. At the same time it has increased the value of intelligence that can be passed on, mostly because it can be used as real time targeting information if it is sufficiently robust. On 25 February 2008, two spokesmen, Qari Yousuf Ahmadi and Zabiullah Mujahid, threatened Afghanistan's four mobile phone providers through the international media. "The council has decided to give a three-day deadline to all mobile telephone companies to stop their signals in order to prevent the enemy obtaining intelligence through cellphones and to prevent Taliban and civilian casualties," Mujahid announced.[32] When none of the telecom companies heeded the ultimatum, a new one was set and again not met. Ultimately the Taliban destroyed at least three wireless transmitters.

Another example is the use of mobile phones in prisons. In December 2007 *The Gazette* in Montreal reported that the use of cellular phones is widespread among the about 3,000 inmates in Pul-e-Charkhi prison. The phones create a dangerous link from within the prison to outside activities. "With the phones," said the prison's commander Haji Dolath, "they [prisoners] can guide other Taliban members on the outside—and the outside members can give them guidance."[33] After 100 phones were turned in voluntarily, thirty-five were seized by prison officials, the report said. Yet the prison management knew that about 400 more prisoners, through bribes, managed to keep their phones. The criminals used the phones to threaten wards, coordinate outside action, and lobby politicians.

The two examples illustrate that the more widespread use of mobile phones in Afghanistan's volatile environment will have unforeseen effects, both positive and negative. Threats that are presently posted as night letters are already substituted by targeted anonymous telephone calls and text messages. In an illiterate society rumors are more easily regarded as fact, and therefore turn into reality more easily: SMS are likely to increase the speed and reach of rumors; demonstrations will be easier to coordinate; and the ways news is consumed will change. Incentives to learn to read and write will increase as text messaging becomes ubiquitous. In other developing countries where, for instance, market information for local farmers is distributed by SMS, illiterate sellers ask their literate children to read out the information for them. Eyewitnesses may be easier to contact for journalists. In five to ten years, when smartphones might enter the mass cellphone market even in lower-tier countries such as Afghanistan, the new technology will dramatically increase the Internet penetration in remote areas.

A LOCAL CAMPAIGN

The diverse set of mujahideen movements that fought against the Soviets did so for nationalistic reasons, not for the global jihad. The Taliban under Mullah Omar, an old anti-Soviet resistance fighter, retained this local focus. Consequently, one of the main target audiences for Taliban information operations is illiterate villagers and farmers, a large and important group of Afghanistan's population. The Taliban portray the Western coalition as foreign invaders, infidels, who want to impose Western liberalism on a Muslim country.

Cheaply produced videos and images, distributed on markets and bazaars in Afghanistan and Pakistan, depicted the Taliban's humiliation: soldiers of the

Afghan National Army poking their guns into the corpses of Mujaheed; U.S. Special Forces troopers as they burn killed Muslims. In 2006, it was possible to find video discs on local markets in Kabul, Kandahar, and Quetta that invoked nostalgia for the anti-Soviet jihad. Elizabeth Rubin concisely described some of the videos for *The New York Times Magazine:*

> One begins with clattering Chinooks disgorging American soldiers into the desert. Then we see the new Afghan government onstage, focusing in on the Northern Alliance warlords—Abdul Rashid Dostum, Burhanuddin Rabbani, Karim Khalili, Muhammad Fahim, Ismail Khan, Abdul Sayyaf. It cuts to American soldiers doing push-ups and pinpointing targets on maps; next it shows bombs the size of bathtubs dropping from planes and missiles emblazoned with "Royal Navy" rocketing through the sky; then it moves to hospital beds and wounded children. Message: America and Britain brought back the warlords and bombed your children.[34]

The nature of these videos makes one thing clear: even if some Taliban have aspirations for global jihad, the movement remains locally rooted. And the Taliban's local character is reflected in their relationship to the local population. *Weltwoche,* a Swiss weekly, interviewed Mullah Mohammed Sabir, the Taliban's governor of Ghazni province and a member of the Shura. The journalists asked him whether Karzai's free election wasn't a popular gaffe for the Taliban: "Let me say one thing very clearly," Sabir said. "We wouldn't be here if the population wouldn't support us. As the Afghan saying goes: 'you can't be part of the village, if the village doesn't want you.'"[35] It is a much contested question whether the Taliban have success in getting the trust of the local population. Yet for many the choice is not between Taliban rule or a democratic central government and the rule of law; the choice often is Taliban rule or local warlords supported by a corrupt central government. Even in Kabul in 2007, most Afghans, whether illiterate or educated civil servants, think it is only a question of time until Taliban will return to power.[36] This raises the question why the Taliban—although they lose all conventional military operations against NATO—have such success in their local information campaign.

Night letters, or *shabanamah,* played a critical role in the Taliban's effort to bolster their popular support base in their attempt to undermine Karzai's central regime in Kabul.[37] A variety of written communications have been called night letters in Afghanistan's wars: pamphlets, underground journals, communal messages, and threats against individuals. The concept emerged during the anti-Soviet jihad in the 1980s, when various mujahideen factions covertly distributed their subversive messages. Even during the Taliban's reign, dissidents inside Afghanistan distributed night letters in support of the former King and even the United States. When the Taliban were removed from power and pushed back into a subversive mode of operation, they again took up the practice. "It is now the duty of all Afghans to begin the struggle against the USA and its allies," demanded a pamphlet distributed in March 2002 in a refugee camp in Peshawar. "We think that the days are very near when Afghanistan shall prove worse than Vietnam or Somalia for U.S. forces."[38]

In the absence of more sophisticated media, communal letters are a traditional way of spreading information in rural Afghanistan, not only at times of war but also for propaganda purposes. The *shabanamah* are a cost-effective and proven method of informing the public about communal and political events—but also of intimidation and instruction. The Taliban probably assume that the educated literate members of a community pass on the *shabanamah*'s messages to illiterate villagers. The letters are posted to trees, on public walls of official buildings, and in mosques, visible to all. Pro-Taliban elders hire or order youth to distribute the pamphlets. In some instances the night letters were bulk-produced and printed in Pakistani border cities, and then distributed across several Afghan districts.[39]

The best illustration is an example from Ghazni province, the province of Mullah Sabir, who emphasized the significance of the local population:

> Greetings toward the respected director [of education] of Ghazni province, Fatima Moshtaq. I have one request, that you step aside from your duties. Otherwise, if you don't resign your position and continue your work, something will happen that will transform your family and you to grief. I am telling you this as a brother, that I consider you a godless person. I am telling you to leave your post and if you continue your work, I will do something that doesn't have a good ending. It should not be left unsaid that one day in the Jan Malika school I heard Wali Sahib praise Ahmad Shah Massoud, I wanted to transform your life to death and with much regret Wali Assadullah was present there and I didn't do anything to cause your death. But if you don't resign your work, I will attack you and take you to death.
>
> With respects,
> 27 Meezan 1384
>
> Look dear Fatima consider your poor employee who will suffer. He was in front of the house look at how many body guards you have for instance the one who was there but if you have them it doesn't matter to us. I was following you from four in the afternoon until seven at night.
> With respects.[40]

Such letters are not limited to local recipients. In 2005 in Paktia province, Gardez was the location of the first and one of the largest Provincial Reconstruction Teams established in Afghanistan. Even Western aid workers were specifically named in threat letters they received in Zurmat district, a restive region in Paktia.[41] In August 2004 insurgents shot and killed a worker for a Catholic German nongovernmental organization (NGO), Malteser Hilfsdienst, in Zurmat.[42] One of the district's tribal elders put it succinctly: "At night, the government is the Taliban. They rule by their night letters."[43] The letters also warn locals to avoid dangerous areas or targeted individuals that might be attacked in the future. It is, however, difficult to identify the source of night letters. Criminal groups might use the posters to spread fear in the name of the Taliban if it is in their interest.[44]

And not all night letters are brutal and blatant threats. Some night letters are remarkably sophisticated and speak to the patriotic spirit of Afghans by tracing their struggle back to ancient times, using references that might seem arcane to the outsider, but are full of emotion and destiny for some Afghan readers.

Message to the 'Mujahed' (freedom fighter) Afghan Nation!
     You have served Islam a great deal throughout history and have defeated the non-Muslims of the world. Your ancestors such as Ahmad Shah Abdaali, Mahmood Ghaznawi, Shahaabuddin Ghori and other heroes have recorded a great history in fighting against non-Muslims, but it is a pity that today some America-trained servants under the name of bright-minded have destroyed the honoured history of Afghanistan. Today once again your sons, clerics and Taliban and the faithful people in these circumstances are fighting against non-Muslims and are serving Islam. If you don't do anything else, at least support your Mujahedeen sons and do not be impressed by the false propaganda of non-Muslim enemies. God forbid one and half million martyrs of Jihad (religious Islamic fight) against Russians and one hundred thousand of martyrs of Islamic Emirates of Afghanistan (martyr Taliban) will ask you for the cost of their martyrdom, so we hope that you meet our expectations. They're stopping the Islamic education and instead are teaching Christianity to your children. Taliban never want to kill common civilians, but unfortunately some so-called Afghanis have become the supporters of our enemies. Non-Muslims want to kill and pit Afghan against Afghan and in the name of Talib they are attacking everybody and they are killing Afghans and destroying your houses and they are destroying Islamic madrasahs (Islamic schools) in Afghanistan. They burn their Afghan arms and ammunitions. They want to make Afghanistan as helpless as Palestine. You have seen that in all madrasahs nowadays they teach Christianity to your children. Once again, we request you not to support non-Muslims, otherwise you will have the whole responsibility here and hereafter.
     Be happy[45]

In more urban areas the Taliban adopted both the narrative and the format of the night letters. Approximately 37 percent of Afghan households have access to a TV set; many of these probably have DVD functionality.[46] Alcohol consumption, pornography, and prostitution were more prevalent in modern and more advanced urban environments than in remote rural areas. Yet this also presented an opportunity to the purists. In 2006 the Taliban began to use DVDs as night letters, an old tactic to deliver letters or other threats to inhabitants to scare them. The insurgents started to target residents with digital videos, delivered to their doorstep at night. A young doctor, NPR reported, awoke one October morning to find a DVD deposited in the courtyard of his family's home.[47] Messengers had scattered hundreds of DVDs around Niyazi, a small town less than three miles from Kabul. The video on the CD showed how Taliban fighters beheaded a teacher and another man, wearing a national army uniform, blowing himself up on a motorbike. Attacks against soldiers and representatives of the state seem to be prominent in these propaganda videos. They tend to depict attacks on NATO forces more often than attacks on the Afghan National Army, although in reality the ratio is inverse.[48] On a DVD circulating in Dera Ismail Khan in the North-West Frontier Province in late 2007, a teenager sawed the head off a soldier while three young bystanders chanted "Allahu akbar" in the background.[49] The narrative of foreign occupation tied these activities together: foreigners occupy Afghanistan, kill civilians, and install a puppet regime that has to be opposed. One such DVD documented how Uruzgan's governor, Jan Mohammed, used sexual insults and filthy language against a young detainee, seemingly supported by a group of NATO soldiers. The subtitles read: "The Americans want to strengthen human rights in Afghanistan? You should judge."[50] But the Taliban also realized that an overly brutal approach—they beheaded about 100 people on spying allegations in eleven months before February 2008, often recording the action—could backfire. The DVD production of beheadings seems to have abruptly stopped that month.[51]

These nightly threats have to be put into context. As for all serious insurgent movements, the Taliban have well understood that threats have to be supported by action. In an internally distributed guidebook the movement's leaders define what is tolerable and what is not tolerable. These guidelines were allegedly part of the movement's command-and-control, not an external propaganda operation. "Those non-governmental organizations that came to the country under the government of the infidels have to be treated in the same way as the government," the guidebook, or Layeha, demands. The foreigners came under the pretense of helping the people, but in reality they would be part of the regime. "Therefore we do not tolerate their activities, be it the constructions of roads, bridges, hospitals, schools, madrassas, or other things."[52] The Layeha was distributed by Hadschi Obaidullah, allegedly the Taliban's "minister" of defense, to the thirty-three members of the Shura, the Taliban's highest leadership council, during a Ramadan meeting in 2006. Section 24 of the guidebook specifically calls for action against the educational institutions:

> It is forbidden to work as a teacher under the current regime, because this strengthens the system of the infidels. True Muslims should apply to study with a religiously trained teacher and study in a Mosque or similar institution. Textbooks must come from the period of the Jihad or from the Taliban regime.[53]

The execution of these rules is much condoned. On the morning of 14 December 2005, in the village of Zarghon in Helmand's Nad Ali district, two men on a motorbike assassinated thirty-eight-year-old Arif Laghmani, a teacher of a boys' school, in front of his pupils. "I saw these two men," one eye-witness told Human Rights Watch:

> One of them fired a full magazine in Laghmani's chest. . . . I was afraid for my life and hid around a corner. I did not know who the victim was. After the killers fled, I went to the gate and saw Laghmani laying dead. . . . It was awful. . . . We have been receiving night letters, but no one thought they would really kill a teacher![54]

Eighteen schools in the Helmand province had been burned down. By January 2006 a total of 165 schools had closed as the result of such assassinations and the accompanying night letters.[55] In another southern Afghan province, Zabul, Malim Abdu Habib, the headmaster of Shaikh Mathi Baba high school, a coeducational secondary school with 1,300 pupils, was assassinated in January 2006. In Qalat, the province capital, armed men burst into his home at night. They dragged him into a courtyard and forced his family to watch his beheading. Such operations did not fail to achieve the intended effect. At least 100 of Zabul province's 170 registered schools, mostly in remote rural areas, were closed between 2004 and 2006 because of security concerns. Only 8 percent of the pupils were girls.[56] Other ways of intimidation are leaving notes on the bodies of assassinated victims, warning other collaborators that they will meet the same fate. The methods the Taliban use, however, remain crude and only partially effective.[57]

The Taliban and their sympathizers and supporters flirted with several formats that reach a broader audience than night letters and local deterrence operations. One is radio. "Voice of Sharia" broadcasts could be received in Kandahar for a brief period in 2005. The broadcasts carried *tarana* chanting, known as *nashid* in Arabic, instead of instrumental music, which is considered un-Islamic by purists.[58]

Another channel is Web sites. The Taliban maintain Web sites, some with the help of foreign supporters. One of the best-known pages often referred to as run by the Taliban is *al-Emarah*, the emirate, which has been published under various domain names.[59] The site is also known as "Voice of Jihad"—like several other Taliban publications, including DVDs and its former radio station. It started publishing in 2006 and offers information about Taliban operations, communications, and their spokesmen's statements in Pashtu, Dari, Urdu, Arabic, and English, often in poor quality.[60] The Web site is rather different from the al-Qaeda Web site; it does not include military manuals, discussion forums, links to other jihadi groups, or an archive of leadership statements. Some statements, moreover, are not necessarily accurate and tend to exaggerate the insurgency's effectiveness. Unlike night letters, this Web site is not made for local audiences. Its multiple languages are intended for a regional or even global audience. The Internet penetration in Afghanistan remains low, at 1.8 percent, but connectivity is significantly higher in Pakistan, where more than 10 percent and a huge number of people in absolute terms—more than 17.5 million families and individuals—have Internet access.[61] Pakistani youths are enthusiastic consumers of the Taliban's multimedia products. Yet the primary audience, Jane's reported in 2007, may actually be "foreign donors who want reassurance that their money is being spent on armed operations."[62]

The Taliban also started to publish magazines and periodicals in September 2002. One of the first magazines was the monthly *Sirk* (or *Srak*), which stands for "Beam of Light," published in Pashto and some material in Dari. Its editor was identified as Lutfullah Momand.[63] A quarterly magazine, *Murshal*, "the trench," had a military focus. Initially a weekly newspaper, *ad-Damir*, "the conscience," was published in Pashtu and Dari. In early 2006 the Taliban's media center began to publish "al-Somood" magazine, which means "standing firm."[64] The magazine was founded by Sa'ada Nusayru'ddin, who goes by the nom de guerre of "Herawi," one of the movement's most influential and pre-eminent members in early 2008.[65] *Al-Somood* itself published a detailed article on the history of the Taliban's publication efforts. The magazine's issues came complete with a press clipping, interviews with Taliban leaders, reports on the resistance, and detailed news on Afghanistan. It was of higher standard than comparable publications but written in simple Arabic, probably because it was the editors' second language. It was available as PDF and hard-copy.[66] *Al-Somood* was probably intended as a fundraising magazine for a non-Afghan Muslim audience willing to support the Islamists' cause.

A GLOBAL CAMPAIGN

The Taliban's global information campaign appeals to two entirely different audiences: their supporters and their enemy's supporters, that is, global jihadis and the publics of the countries engaged in Afghanistan. To impress the latter, the mujahideen have dedicated spokesmen who try to focus the international media on civilian casualties; to impress the former, some Taliban leaders team up with al-Qaeda.

Mullah Sayed Ghiasuddin Agha was acting Minister of Information from 1994 to 1997. Mullah Ahmadullah Muti was in charge of communications during the Kabul Shura of acting ministers in 2000. Mullah Omar also released statements to the media, in the form of press communiqués, for instance, on an impending spring offensive. Initially Omar had an official spokesman and trusted confidant, Mullah Wakil Ahmad. Wakil was a former student of Omar's, and had begun to work for his teacher as driver, food taster, note-taker and interpreter. His master was happy with Wakil's performance and promoted him to more important tasks such as interacting with visiting diplomats and representatives of development agencies. Eventually Wakil had the job of managing the contact with the foreign press, supervising the Taliban's coverage, and criticizing the journalists harshly when he felt the Taliban were covered unfavorably.[67]

The Taliban have used numerous spokespersons, sometimes anonymous and difficult to verify. The large number of self-proclaimed spokesmen makes it quite onerous to steer clear and assign credibility to any specific one of them. Initially the media unit operated under the direction of Sa'ada Qudratu'llah Jamal, the Taliban's former minister of media and culture. In 2004, Sheikh Ustaz Muhammad Yasir succeeded him. Abdul Latif Hakimi spoke to international news organizations in 2004 and 2005 about Taliban attacks against U.S. targets and Afghan troops. He was captured on 4 October that year by Pakistani commando units in Balochistan province. Hakimi's contacts to the Taliban dated back to the time when Mullah Omar's regime controlled Afghanistan. In 1999 and 2000, Taliban-run media outlets referred to him as the head of the information and culture department in the city of Herat. Other self-proclaimed spokesmen were

Mohammad Mokhtar Mojahed. One of the best-known spokesmen is Qari Mohammad Yousef (sometimes spelled Yousuf or Yousaf, sometimes with the additional nom de plume "Ahmadi"). He was appointed in the fall of 2005 by Mullah Omar as part of a campaign to revive the Taliban's media profile. Interviews with Qari Yousef are conducted by satellite phone, arranged through an intermediary or directly, and sometimes translated simultaneously by an interpreter if necessary.

For some commanders the media cooperation worked well. On 27 December 2005, for instance, NBC's Lisa Myers broke an exclusive story about the alleged Taliban "Commander Ismail." Myers reported that Ismail was "behind some of the most deadly attacks against U.S. troops."[68] The reporter had interviewed the alleged commander in August and again in December 2005, both times at unknown locations. NBC's television report was illustrated with various Internet videos showing scenes of Taliban training sessions, weapons, and U.S. forces operating in the region. Ismail claimed to have lured U.S. forces into an ambush in June. A tape obtained by NBC News allegedly showed that battle, and the Taliban's unsuccessful attempt to coax a Navy Seal to surrender. The U.S. military then sent in a rescue team, which was attacked by Ismail's men with rocket-propelled grenades, downing a Chinook helicopter and allegedly killing another sixteen Americans. NBC showed the Taliban video with images of American weapons and hi-tech equipment displayed as trophies. But for Taliban celebrities fame comes with risk. One spokesman, Mohammed Hanif, was particularly agile and articulate. In an equally criticized interview in 2006, the twenty-six-year old media activist eloquently told the BBC that "[d]emocracy set up under the shadow of B52 bombers and elections held under the shadow of F16s is not acceptable for the Afghan nation."[69] Hanif had moved closer and closer to being caught. For months, he used his mobile phone to call up journalists in order to correct what he saw as "misreporting" in their stories.

By far the most important focus of Taliban media operations is the number of civilian casualties caused by NATO. Both the correctness and the sophistication of insurgent media operations are regularly downplayed by Western military organizations. "The insurgents continue to follow their pattern of falsely reporting civilian casualties and continuing to put civilians in harm's way in a vain attempt to stop the advance of the (Islamic Republic of Afghanistan) forces toward their support areas," said Vanessa R. Bowman, a Combined Joint Task Force 82 spokesperson.[70] The insistence that the Taliban's messages and swift reactions are factually wrong is a constant theme in the coalition's press releases. Sometimes the Taliban spokespersons call the international media in Kabul within minutes of a NATO air strike, exploiting the time lag between the event and an official coalition statement, and thereby maximizing the news value of the information on offer. Colonel Edward Reeder, who commanded the 7th Special Forces Group for eight months in 2007, reckons that coalition forces have a time window of approximately ninety minutes before Taliban spokespersons will contact the international press after the start of a noteworthy military operation or strike. Reeder's Special Forces troops realized the need to be the first-out with information, and started to videotape their air strikes to prove that they took care not to endanger civilians.

But the Taliban's press statements, whether accurate or not, are generally out faster than those of coalition forces. Elias Wahdat served as a stinger working for Reuters and the BBC in Khost province in 2007. Every time the Taliban attacked on coalition forces, or when U.S. troops called in Close Air Support, Taliban spokesmen sent him a text message. The Taliban then told their version of the story, reported damage, and often claimed that U.S. bombs killed civilians. That NATO accidentally does hit civilian targets every now and then is giving the Taliban a credibility advance even if they have a track record of overstating civilian deaths. NATO spokespersons have to verify information and possibly get clearance before they can make a statement to representatives of the press. This takes time. Lieutenant Colonel David A. Accetta was the public affairs officer of the 82nd Airborne Division, the U.S. Army's largest formation operating in Afghanistan, and general spokesperson of all American forces in the country. "They do not have to tell the truth and are more likely to use propaganda than they are to put out true, verifiable, factual information."[71] The Taliban also threaten journalists to ensure the reported stories or numbers are in their interest: "the Taliban exaggerates, the government reduces the numbers of casualties," said one local journalist in an interview with the Crisis Group in Kabul. "So if we say the Taliban numbers, the government threatens us; if we say the government numbers, then the Taliban threatens us."[72] The journalist has moved to the capital out of security concerns. Two pupils he had interviewed at a government school had been assassinated because they spoke with the media. Schools are often the only government-run institutions in the countryside.

Civilian casualties, or the mere possibility of civilian casualties, it should be noted, are not only beneficial for the Taliban in that they put NATO publics under pressure strategically. Mistaken attacks against civilians, and even unverified reports of such attacks, put local political pressure on tactical operations, too. The Afghan government has to react to domestic criticism of NATO in order not to lose even more credibility and legitimacy. "During 2007, the Taliban has mastered their ability to quickly capitalize on any 'perceived' civilian casualties," a special operations report stated in August 2007. The Taliban had succeeded in forcing the ISAF commander, through pressure administered by Afghan President Hamid Karzai, to "impose operational pauses or restrict operational areas." In more detail:

> These operational pauses brought about by local public pressure, statements by district and provincial leaders or the Kabul Administration have allowed the Taliban to withdraw when engaged with United States Special Forces (USSF) at critical junctures in major combat operations. [73]

The Taliban's improved media work is best illustrated with an example. On Thursday, 2 August 2007, in the evening, a U.S.-led task force attacked an alleged meeting of Taliban leaders in Baghni Valley, in the Baghran district of Helmand. According to an unpublished CJSOTF-A report, intelligence sources had indicated that a senior Taliban commander, Mullah Ihklas Ahkundzada, and his deputy had gathered a large number of fighters, possibly as many as 200, and convened a court "to convict three suspected spies among their ranks." U.S. Special Forces, with approval from NATO, called in a B-1 bomber to drop six GBU-31 precision-guided bombs along a tree line where the two "high value individuals" were suspected, the report stated. A subsequent review concluded that the bombing killed 154 Taliban fighters, "including six operational commanders and 29 tactical commanders."[74]

The press reports of this event reflect that both sides wanted to get their spin on the story. "Nearly 200 civilians were killed and injured as foreign troops pounded an area in the remote Baghran District of the southern Helmand Province," Pajhwok Afghan News, an independent news agency, reported on Friday, 3 August, from Lashkargah. The Pajhwok report stated that a "large number of civilians" had gathered at a shrine to attend a fair on the afternoon "when coalition aircraft dropped bombs on them." The agency report was widely disseminated by the Associated Press, Agence France Presse, Xinhua, and the BBC, and picked up the next day by many newspapers world wide. An alternative version of the story, also quoted in the initial report, was put forward by the coalition. The U.S.-led force put out the statement that a Taliban "leadership meeting" was held at the time of the attack. "Coalition forces gained actionable intelligence on the location of two Helmand-area Taliban commanders and monitored their movements near the village of Qala-i-Chah," Pajhwok reported.[75] Several eyewitnesses had reported that Taliban militants had executed two locals for alleged spying for the government when the bombs hit the crowd of bystanders. Enayatullah Ghafari, head of the health department for Helmand province was quoted as saying that the youngest victim would be an eight-year-old boy and the oldest a fifty-year-old man. "The rest are aged between 22 and 40," AP reported. On 5 August, al-Jazeera released a three-minute report on the bombing that said the air strike killed 350 people and wounded 200, the intelligence report states. The al-Jazeera story allegedly claimed that the raid "hit a mosque and a nearby market" and that "the people killed included women and children [who] go on a picnic here every week," according to the U.S. armed forces.[76]

The Afghan Defense Ministry tried to counter the reports of civilian dead. It put out a statement pronouncing that "a number of senior Taliban commanders and scores of hardened fighters" had been killed in a coalition air strike. The ministry's spokesperson, Major General Zaher Azimi, even named names and told Pajhwok Afghan News that Mullah Dadollah Mansur, Mullah Bolbol, Mullah Rahim, and his brother Mullah Najib had been killed, among others. NATO equally tried to counter the storyline of the civilian casualties as quickly as possible. "During a sizable meeting of senior Taliban commanders, coalition forces employed precision-guided munitions on their location after ensuring there were no innocent Afghans in the surrounding area," a coalition statement was cited by

AP the next day, 3 August.[77] The coalition, however, did not provide any details on casualties, giving the press little to report on. "This operation shows that there is no safe haven for the insurgents," Major Chris Belcher, a spokesman for United States forces in Afghanistan, was quoted in *The New York Times*. But he qualified his statement by saying that "[i]t will take some time to determine if both targets were killed."[78] In any case the civilian casualties, whether merely reported or real, caused public outrage in Afghanistan and forced the President Hamid Karzai to react with emotional criticism.

A subsequent intelligence report sheds some light on how the Taliban worked to get their story out. "Mullah Ihklas coordinated the movement of media personnel to this remote valley . . . and ensured they filmed what the Taliban wanted them to film," the CJSOTF-A report said.[79] The U.S. special forces learned that Ihklas not only survived the attack but "issued orders to his subordinates the day after the strike on how to manipulate the media." The Taliban commander allegedly directed his men to get a group of 50 to 100 locals and instructed them to tell the media representatives that the bombs had hit a civilian picnic area. The U.S. report describes the incident as "the best manipulation of the international media using video of the 'locals' telling the pre-fabricated Taliban story in a multimedia interview."

The Taliban allegedly merged their media operation with al-Qaeda. "The Taliban have changed immensely in the last year due to the mentoring they are getting from leading Arab jihadists in Pakistan with al Qaeda, both in the realm of battlefield tactics and media operations," Lutfullah Mashal, a senior official in Kabul's National Security Council responsible for strategic communications, said in May 2007. Some insiders and former insiders agree. "When the Taliban were in power, they were not focused on this important thing, but they have learned from al Qaeda the importance of media in their operations," said Abdul Salam Zaeef, the Taliban's former ambassador to Pakistan. Zaeef, who spent four years in Guantánamo Bay, did not believe that the Taliban "in their hearts" had global jihadist ambitions. Afghans would not strive to attack the U.S. homeland as long as America's military abandoned Afghanistan. It remains unclear how closely integrated the Taliban's more conventional operations, such as suicide bombings, kidnappings, and IED attacks, are with al-Qaeda's. Before Taliban military commander Mulla Dadullah was killed by coalition troops in May 2007, he had claimed that al-Qaeda and Taliban planning were one and the same. "The Taliban is now an integral part of an internationalized jihad," argued Waheed Mujda, an Afghan writer and former deputy minister in the Taliban government between 1997 and 2001. "The Taliban's war has now moved outside the boundaries of Afghanistan and is part of a global struggle."[80] Indeed the Afghan insurgents' slick media operation, with videotaped attacks and training exercises, is reminiscent of al-Qaeda. Indeed on many major operations a cameraman allegedly travels with Taliban fighters—a steep and rather pragmatic learning curve for purists who earlier had banned television.

Yet cooperation with al-Qaeda is a double-edged sword for the Taliban. When the United States launched an attack after 9/11, some Taliban pointed to the Arab jihadis as provocateurs of the devastating strike that ended the Islamic Emirate of Afghanistan. In the following years the Taliban continued to be supported by Pakistan's ISI. Yet Pakistan, at the same time, cooperated with the United States to find al-Qaeda leaders, and Pakistani intelligence cooperated with the United Kingdom to identify jihadis among the many British citizens who traveled to Pakistan each year. At the same time the Taliban were not seen as the most important enemy by the United States and NATO—after all they never planned or attempted attacking America or Europe at home. Abdullah Abdullah, the Afghan foreign minister, went to Washington in 2002 to try to get the American government to put more pressure on President Musharraf to stop supporting the Taliban. His trip was not successful. "The CIA wanted Arabs, not Afghans," he concluded.[81] The closer the Afghan Taliban movement associated itself with Arab-dominated al-Qaeda, the more difficult it would be for the U.S. and Pakistan's intelligence and military services to maintain that distinction; it is therefore highly likely that the Taliban leadership is torn between aligning itself with bin Laden and keeping themselves separate. This undecided position is reflected in the Taliban's information operations. The Taliban's communiqués show that there are actors with different agendas within the movement.[82]

9

Al-Qaeda

The Taliban rose in the turmoil of Afghanistan's civil war that followed the Soviet withdrawal from Afghanistan in the early 1990s. Al-Qaeda, already well established as an organization with global goals in the mid-1990s, saw the newcomers as innovators. The Afghan purists were regarded as overreaching in their application of the Sharia—as overly zealous, uneducated, and provincial. "They were innovators, the worst thing of all," Omar Nasiri recalled, a European-educated graduate of two al-Qaeda training camps in Afghanistan in the mid-1990s. "There is no innovation in Islam": there is only the Quran, the eternally valid word of God.[1]

Yet the more impressive innovators were doubtlessly al-Qaeda, in both spiritual and operational terms. The group's ideological justification of terrorism, its actual operations, and specifically its use of telecommunication is characterized by a level of creativity and sophistication that is unrivaled by any other militant organization in the early twenty-first century. The methods developed by—or *for,* in some cases—al-Qaeda cannot be left out in any study of insurgents' use of an evolving information environment. Their media operations cover the entire spectrum of utilities outlined above. To understand why al-Qaeda became so nimble, it is necessary to take a closer look at the organization's rise and its metamorphosis into a movement. It will then become evident how closely al-Qaeda's resilience and the new media are interlinked.

AL-QAEDA'S RISE

Al-Qaeda has its ideological origins in Egypt's prisons of the 1960s and 1970s. Its military roots lie in Afghanistan's mountains and the jihad against the Soviet Union in the 1980s. Its determination was wielded in brutal campaigns in Syria, Chechnya, Bosnia, and Algeria, where the Muslims often suffered heavily. Its self-perceived humiliation stems from Israel's occupation of Arab lands and American bases established on holy ground in Saudi Arabia after the Persian Gulf War. The most central figures in the movement's constitution were Osama bin Laden, a wealthy Saudi; Ayman al-Zawahiri and Sayyed Imam Al-Sharif (aka Dr Fadl), both Egyptian radicals and founders of the Egyptian terrorist organization al-Jihad; and Abdullah Yusuf Azzam, a militant Palestinian cleric and fundraiser for the Afghan jihad. From its outset, the jihadi vanguard was a multinational organization with global ambitions and aspirations.[2]

The organization with the name "al-Qaeda," or *The Base,* was formed on 11 August 1988 in Peshawar by bin Laden, Abdullah Azzam, and several senior leaders of the Egyptian organization al-Jihad, among them Zawahiri and al-Sharif.[3] In May, the defeated Russian Army had begun its withdrawal from the war-ravaged country. The new and, in its own view, victorious organization—not unlike NATO on the other side of the crumbling Soviet empire—had to find a new raison d'être, a new enemy. Initially there were two currents: Azzam, who was born in the British Mandate of Palestine, was educated in Islamic jurisprudence at Al-Azhar University, and had helped create Hamas, was opposed to *fitna,* or discord, the killing of Muslims and innocent civilians, particularly women and children. He wanted to focus the jihad on Palestine, Kashmir, Central Asia, and other occupied territories. The second current, represented by the Egyptians Zawahiri and al-Sharif, propagated revolution against Muslim "apostate" authoritarian regimes, such as in Egypt and Syria. *Takfir,* the excommunication of Muslims in order to justify violent action against them, was a necessary component of their thinking. The two sides disagreed strongly over al-Qaeda's future direction. The dispute ended when Azzam, together with two of his sons, was blown up by a car bomb on 24 November 1989. Two weeks earlier the Berlin Wall had fallen, and ushered in the collapse of the Soviet Union; the infidel communist empire, the Afghan jihadis believed, crumbled because they had administered the decisive blow.[4]

Postwar Afghanistan was plagued by infighting between warring Mujahideen groups and slowly descended into a fierce civil war. Frustrated with the Mujahideen's internal bickering, Osama bin Laden returned to Saudi Arabia in 1990 to continue work for his family's business. Then one of the key events of modern global jihad occurred: Iraq invaded Kuwait. Bin Laden, confident to be ready to fight against Saddam, began to lobby the Royal Family to organize a popular defense of the peninsula. He even offered to help organize a force based on veterans from the Afghan jihad to defend the kingdom against an impending Iraqi attack. But King Fahd called the Americans for help, a move that deeply shocked and disappointed bin Laden and with him a sizeable number of conservative clerics. When, during operation Desert Shield, 540,000 U.S. troops arrived on the Islamic land of the two holy places, a country with perhaps 10 million citizens in 1990, bin Laden openly criticized the Saudi royal family. When 20,000 troops remained in Saudi Arabia after the war, bin Laden clashed with the country's rulers. After a confrontation with Prince Naif, the Saudi minister of the interior, King Fahd declared Osama, the son of the kingdom's most revered builder of roads and mosques, a persona non grata. In 1992 bin Laden left for Sudan.

While in Africa, the al-Qaeda founder set up the "Advice and Reform Committee," a London-based organization. The committee distributed newsletters by e-mail and sent them to Saudi clerics, scholars, and judges who shared his Islamic views. Bin Laden and the senior leadership of his still young and fragile organization moved back to Afghanistan in May 1996. Then, in August, bin Laden issued his first fatwa, the "Declaration of War against the Americans Occupying the Land of the Two Holy Places," and published it in *Al Quds Al Arabi,* a London-based newspaper. "The horrifying pictures of the massacre of Qana, in Lebanon are still fresh in our memory," bin Laden wrote, referring to an Israeli operation in Lebanon. He then named a series of "massacres," including Cashmere, Chechnya, and Bosnia-Herzegovina. "The latest and the greatest of these aggressions, incurred by the Muslims since the death of the Prophet . . . is the occupation of the land of the two Holy Places"[5]—a reference to the continued U.S. military presence on the Arabian peninsula after the 1991 Persian Gulf War.

The publication of the *fatwa* constituted a turning point in al-Qaeda's media operation, both in terms of form and content. First, the message's content would now be more sophisticated. Before 1996 the jihadi message was somewhat crude and blunt, primarily graphic attention grabbers and simple injunctions to follow the path of god. The declaration, by contrast, contained new objectives and new themes. America was now considered the enemy of all Muslims, and the supporter of those who oppressed the Muslim masses, particularly the hated "apostate" Arab regimes, the "near enemies": the House of Saud in Saudi Arabia for bin Laden, the government of Egypt for Ayman al-Zawahiri, the governments of Syria, Libya, and Jordan for others. The regional focus on the country at the Hindu Kush and the juxtaposition of the strong Soviets versus weak Afghans was extended to the global struggle. Now al-Qaeda pitched the world's Muslims against their various repressors and occupiers: Israel, China, India, the United States, and, of course, still Russia in Central Asia. The focus shifted from the near enemy to the far enemy. On 23 February 1998 another fatwa was issued and published in *Al Quds Al Arabi,* "Jihad against Jews and Crusaders." It stated that "for over seven years the United States has been occupying the most sacred of the Islamic Lands," the Arabian Peninsula.[6] Therefore it was the duty of all Muslims to kill U.S. citizens and their allies everywhere, civilians and soldiers alike. Part of this new global perspective was the reference to the *ummah,* the larger global Muslim community, which suffered constant oppression and humiliation at the hands of various infidel perpetrators. Al-Qaeda reframed what used to be seen as many conflicts of local oppressors against local resistance organizations, such as in Egypt and Syria and Palestine, into one overarching jihad of one global oppressor against one global victim, an American–Jewish conspiracy against the *ummah,* a powerful cause for many Muslims.[7]

In addition to these changes in message, al-Qaeda was quick to embrace new technologies, particularly the Internet. Early on, al-Qaeda faced the challenge of communicating with a global audience from one of the world's most remote spots. From al-Qaeda's beginning, Osama bin Laden had established a media department as part of the organization's setup, the Maktab al-Khidamat. When bin Laden was in Sudan from 1991 to 1995, his London-based public affairs office regularly transmitted subversive electronic newsletters in Saudi Arabia. The "Declaration of War on the United States," was accessible on the Web site http://www.yaislah.org on 1 September 1996.[8] Electronic journals started to appear. *Al-Ansar*, *al-Neda*, and *Sawt al-Jihad* were among the first.

Simultaneously a series of increasingly successful terrorist operations applied these violent principles in practice: in December 1992, al-Qaeda allegedly and unsuccessfully bombed U.S. troops in Aden on their way to Somalia. Bin Laden's organization is thought to have been involved in Ramzi Yousef's attack on the World Trade Center in New York with a massive truck bomb.[9] Al-Qaeda claimed responsibility for arming Somali fighters for the Battle of Mogadishu in October 1993. It attacked the Saudi National Guard Training Center in Riyadh in November 1995, killing five Americans.[10] On June 25, 1996, a truck bomb detonated outside the northern perimeter of the U.S. portion of the Khobar Towers housing complex in Dhahran, Saudi Arabia, killing nineteen servicemen and wounding hundreds more.[11] In August 1998, the U.S. Embassies in Nairobi, Kenya, and Dar es-Salaam, Tanzania, were struck; more than 300 individuals died. On 12 October 2000, the USS Cole in the port of Aden, Yemen, was attacked by a sea-borne suicide commando, killing seventeen U.S. Navy members and injuring another thirty-nine. Then 11 September 2001 irreversibly altered the environment of international terrorism.

AL-QAEDA'S TRANSFORMATION

After the 9/11 attacks, the America's intelligence services and the military trained their sights on al-Qaeda. Less than one month after the events in New York and Washington, America invaded Afghanistan, toppled the Taliban, and started to cripple the terror organization with swift and fierce military strikes. The world's best-known and most powerful terrorist organization thus was forced into a metamorphosis by its enemies. Large physical training camps in Afghanistan and elsewhere were easy targets and became nonviable. For the organization's surviving leadership it became exceedingly dangerous to communicate, be it face-to-face, by messenger, by mail, by telephone, or by electronic means. Command-and-control became impractical.

Al-Qaeda's reaction, in essence, was to change its organizational form. One person in particular epitomizes the organization's transformation: Mustafa bin Abd al-Qadir Setmariam Nasar, better known as Umar Abd al-Hakim or Abu Musab al-Suri, one of the most important and most impressive strategic minds of global jihad.[12] Al-Suri is credited as being the primary intellectual architect for al-Qaeda's metamorphosis from a hierarchical group to a movement with mostly flat decentralized structures, composed of organizationally independent cells. Al-Suri is pivotal for two reasons: his career epitomizes how jihad and media operations have effectively merged, and his writings on the guerrilla theory of modern jihad both describe and continue to shape the movement. Al-Suri's book has one of the major traits of a classic of strategic theory, as it persistently oscillates between the descriptive and the normative.[13] From the point of view of conventional armies, al-Suri's writings demonstrate the narrow limits and even the blindfolding effects of the standard Western terminology of "information operations" or the notorious "battle for the hearts and minds."

Al-Suri's biography epitomizes the rise of the jihadi movement. He was a Syrian activist with Spanish citizenship who spent his most productive years in the London suburb of Neasden.[14] Born in Aleppo in 1958, al-Suri studied engineering and was engaged in the Muslim Brotherhood's revolt against Syria's Hafez al-Assad in the late 1970s and early 1980s. Many of his coconspirators were slaughtered when Assad cracked down on the insurgency in the old city of Hama in Northwestern Syria in February 1982. Between 10,000 and 25,000 people died when government forces crushed resistance in the city that had been proclaimed "liberated" by insurgents. At the time, al-Suri, who supported the opposition of a country that stood on Iran's side in an ongoing war, went through military training in Iraq. Al-Suri returned to Spain in 1985, and went to Pakistan two years later to take part in the Afghan Jihad, where he trained at camps and met Osama bin Laden. In July 1987 he met with Sheikh Abdallah Azzam, who would one year later be one of al-Qaeda's founding members. Al-Suri became the Syrian representative on the Shura Council. He returned to Spain in 1992, where he set up a cell. In 1995 he moved to the London suburb of Neasden, where he wrote for the GIA's *al-Ansar* journal, edited by Abu Qatada, a Palestinian cleric known at the time for his uncompromising views and justifications of gruesome massacres in Algeria. But al-Suri's media work extended to other bulletins, such as the Libyan Islamic Fighting Group's *al-Fajr,* and *al-Mujahidun,* published by the Egyptian Islamic Jihad. Sheikh Qari al-Jazaeri, the founder of the GIA, personally had sent him to help with the group's media operation.[15] The Syrian jihadi also helped al-Qaeda pioneer interviews with the world's mainstream media. From 1996 to 1998, al-Suri arranged for several journalists to interview the al-Qaeda leadership, among them *The Independent's* Robert Fisk and CNN's Peter Bergen, who spent several days in al-Suri's company. The resulting publicity, particularly after the embassy bombings in Africa, created problems for the Taliban. Al-Suri, who had close contacts to Taliban leader Mullah Omar, wrote an e-mail to bin Laden on 19 July 1999 criticizing him for his thirst for publicity and for putting his Afghan hosts at risk.[16] He referred to him by his *nom de guerre,* Abu Abdullah:

> The strangest thing I have heard so far is Abu Abdullah's saying that he wouldn't listen to the Leader of the Faithful when he asked him to stop giving interviews. . . . I think our brother [bin Laden] has caught the disease of screens, flashes, fans, and applause.[17]

At that time, from 1998 to 2001, al-Suri worked at the al-Ghuraba camp and at the Derunta training complex near Jalalabad in Afghanistan, sat in al-Qaeda's Shura Council, and even worked for Mullah Omar's Defense Ministry. After the

fall of the Taliban he fled first to Iran and later to Pakistan, where he was in hiding for more than three years. During that time al-Suri completed a 1,604-page
book, *Da'wat al-muqawamah al-islamiyyah al-'alamiyyah*, or *The Call for Global
Islamic Resistance*. A first sketch had been completed already in 1990. Then, in
November 2004, the U.S. Department of State put a bounty of $5 million on
al-Suri. Probably sensing that the net around him might be closing, his reaction
was to end his self-imposed period of isolation, and make his ideas immortal
before he could be caught or killed. "As a result of the U.S. government's declaration about me, the lies it contained and the new security requirements forced
upon us, I have taken the decision to end my period of isolation," al-Suri wrote.
"I will also resume my ideological, media-related operational activities. I wish
God that America will regret bitterly that she provoked me and others to combat
her with pen and sword."[18] Two months later, in January 2005, al-Suri published
his book and twenty-nine audiofiles of lectures recorded in al-Ghuraba; the
material was soon copied and republished many times. Later that year, in
November 2005, al-Suri was indeed captured by Pakistan police in a raid in
Quetta. But it was too late. Files continue to be found by police in various
European countries. Some of his ideas can only be described as brilliant. Bergen
recalled al-Suri as "tough and really smart" and, he claims, more impressive than
bin Laden. Jamal Khashoggi, a Saudi journalist who also met al-Suri and Qatada,
went so far as to say that bin Laden merely provided an organization for the two
men's ideas; "[h]is organization became the vehicle for their thinking."[19]

One key to al-Suri's strategic thinking was the power of governments, particularly in the form of brute military force and airpower. When some of the Afghan
training camps were attacked by U.S. cruise missiles in 1998, it dawned on al-Suri
that not even Afghanistan's inaccessible massive mountains could provide protection from modern precision-guided munitions. In only two years following 9/11,
when America employed "her stunning technological superiority," al-Suri wrote,
80 percent of the mujahideen were eliminated. Fixed bases were not feasible any
more and American determination ruled out the establishment of sanctuaries in
friendly states. His conclusion was that the "'Tora Bora-mentality' has to end."[20]

This is the point of departure for al-Suri's own military theory. U.S. superiority
in firepower and any conventional confrontation was only the latest incarnation of
a problem the Muslim Brotherhood had encountered twenty years earlier in Syria,
most brutally when the Syrian Air Force and artillery leveled the old city in Hama:
as soon as the state's superior power was unleashed, the insurgency was in trouble.
His challenge was to find a way to level the playing field, to deny the enemy the
benefits of superior conventional power:

> In short, I was searching for a method which the enemy has no way of aborting, even
> when he understands the method and its procedures, and arrests two thirds of its
> operators. A method, which is susceptible to self-renewal and to self-perpetuation
> as a phenomenon after all its conditions and causes are present and visible to the
> enemy himself.[21]

The jihadi strategist started out by distinguishing three different ways of waging holy war. First comes what he calls a *tanzim,* Arabic for organization. The *tanzimat* (plural) are hierarchical and often secretive subversive organizations, set up locally or regionally. Examples are the Egyptian group al-Jihad, the Shabiba movement in Morocco, or the Asbat al-Ansar group in Lebanon. Al-Suri himself was a member of one typical *tanzim,* the Combatant Vanguard Organization in Syria. *Tanzimat,* as a consequence of superior conventional armies and intelligence services, became much more difficult to run. The organizations' hierarchical structure, in addition, made them easy targets for intelligence organizations who were not only able to gather intelligence from one or a few captured members, or through infiltration, but could also then paralyze or take out an entire organization in one piece, for instance, through the use of the enemy's "unimaginable technological superiority, [. . .] especially in the air, in their control over space, and the enormous abilities of taking satellite photos and directing air and missile strikes."[22] The tanzim also failed to operate over large areas and did not successfully incorporate the Muslim youth.

Second, there are "open fronts" or large-scale insurgencies against an occupying power on Muslim lands. A precondition for open-front jihad is a cause. That cause, al-Suri argues, must be local as well as global; it must mobilize locals to take up arms and it must unite the *ummah,* or the "Islamic nation," behind their cause to send fighters, money, material, and moral support. If a cause doesn't meet those criteria, it is weak. The "most suitable cause" is resistance against foreign aggression. Al-Suri's three prime examples for open-front jihad are Chechnya, Bosnia, and Afghanistan against the Soviets.[23] He also thought that the demographic, religious, economic, strategic, and geographical conditions for open confrontations are good in Yemen, Turkey, Central Asia, and North Africa. Open-front jihad would create several benefits: it enabled the fighters to strengthen their military skills, to improve their training, and to recruit and select capable operatives to work in their home countries, while avoiding the vulnerabilities of *tanzim,* the secret organization.

Al-Suri's third type of subversive war is the "jihad of individualized terrorism,"[24] single acts of terrorism organized and executed by small cells, acting autonomously, without central leadership or the hierarchical setup of larger organizations. Al-Suri starts his extensive discussion of "individual terrorism" over more than 100 pages with a definition of terrorism. One of the largest successes of the "American Jewish Crusader" is on the media field. He then refuses "to understand this term according to the American description" and distinguishes between blameworthy and praiseworthy terrorism, the latter being a religious duty. He then proceeds to quote, as he does several times, the sura al-Anfal 8:60, "Against them make ready strength and the utmost of your power, including steeds of war, to strike terror into (the hearts of) the enemies, of Allah and your enemies." Another sura apparently inspired the entrepreneurial approach at the core of al-Suri's theory, an-Nisa 4:84, "Then fight in Allah's cause—thou art held responsible only for thyself—and rouse the Believers."

Only the second and the third organizational form of fighting was feasible at all in a "post-September world."[25] Compared to the first classical insurgent organization, the "common goal" and the cause of individual jihad is reduced in ambition. For a traditional classic insurgency, the goal used to be to topple the government, al-Suri writes, and to establish a legitimate government in a geographical area. For his resistance units, by contrast, the common goal is much less ambitious, "to repel the invading and occupying assailants and combat those who collaborate with the invaders."[26] Financing is not provided by a clandestine organization, but by the single units; sources are war booty and donations.

From this perspective, the individualized terrorists constitute a "long arm" that is able to fight jihad for the open front's causes, through "deterrence" and operations "behind enemy lines," both in cooperation with the emirs and leaders in the open fronts, or in a covert and "programmatic way."[27] Al-Suri summed up his alternative idea as *"nizam, la tanzim"*: system, not organization. His vision for jihad was to have an "operative system" instead of an "organization for operations." He advocated templates, available for self-recruited activists and entrepreneurs with a desire to take part in the global jihad, either on their own or with a group of trusted accomplices. Connections and organizational links between the leadership and units were thus avoided. General guidance replaced specific orders. The glue was "a common aim, a common doctrinal program and a comprehensive (self-)educational program."[28] Such collectively motivated individual action would open up the possibility for thousands and hundreds of thousands of Muslims to participate. An important component for individual jihad is the community of Muslims, the Islamic nation. Al-Suri's aim was it to create a method

> for transforming excellent individual initiatives, performed over the past decades, from emotional pulse beats and scattered reactions, into a phenomenon which is guided and utilized, and whereby the project of jihad is advanced so that it becomes the Islamic Nation's battle, and not a struggle of an elite.[29]

These individual actions, he argues, need to be glued together by a common program, by spreading the culture and the ideology of resistance, the legal, political, and military sciences that the Mujahidun need to fight. These units, al-Suri says, "base themselves on individual action, action by small cells completely separated from each other and on complete decentralization, in the sense that nothing connects them apart from *the common aim, the common name, a program of beliefs and a method of education*."[30] America's response forced the organization to focus on two main venues: the "guidance center," which supervises and distributes ideological material, a doctrinal program, educational items, and communiqués. The second component of this more resilient setup, al-Suri hoped, will be the "resistance call units," which will be established spontaneously without central command-and-control.

One noteworthy feature of al-Suri's militant organizational teachings is that the Internet does not figure prominently. He traces individualized jihad throughout Islamic history, quoting, for instance, the case of Suleyman al-Halabi, a student from Aleppo who, in Cairo on 14 June 1800, stabbed and killed Jean Baptiste Kléber, Napoleon's top general in Egypt and commander of all French forces there.[31] Other examples he gives predate the Web, for instance, Ramzi Yousuf's World Trade Center bombing in 1993, or Sayyid Nusayr's assassination of Rabbi Meir Kahane in 1990. Al-Suri himself had developed his military theory "into its final forms," as he said, in the summer of 2000, before the Web's interactive revolution.[32] He also borrowed heavily from literature on insurgency from the period of decolonization, most importantly from Robert Taber's *The War of the Flea,* on which he gave a series of lectures in August.[33] But he also used Mao, Giap, Guevara, and Castro for inspiration[34]—and, of course, the Quran.

When his theory was married with the Web, an explosive composite was created. This potential may have been beyond al-Suri's imagination; in his writings he does not come across as a particularly tech-savvy jihadist, and there is no evidence that he ever participated in Web forums himself. Yet the Web is important for his writings on two entirely different levels: philosophical and practical. Had al-Suri spent some time in the late 1990s not in Shah-i-Kot valley but in Silicon Valley, he might have recognized the philosophical and metaphorical similarities between the organizational form he propagated for Islamic resistance and the new organizational logic propagated by Web 2.0 aficionados: both assumed entrepreneurial individuals as part of a global community of like-minded activists, self-motivated participation, decentralized networks, self-administration, a common purpose, and global collaboration; both tolerated anonymity and the use of pseudonyms, heterogeneous levels of participation, and fuzzy membership; both were created not out of necessity or in a top-down fashion, but evolved imbued with a pragmatic spirit, from the bottom up; and both combine proven organizational patterns and necessary components of authority and command with leaderless initiatives.

Yet the second level might be more significant. Partly thanks to these similarities, the Web was one important driver in bringing al-Suri's vision to practical fruition. But before this aspect will be outlined in some detail, a disclaimer is necessary: the Web's significance should not be overestimated, but it should also not be underrated. It would be shortsighted to assume that a high density of Internet penetration is necessary for it to have a significant impact. The Web, first and foremost, reduces risk for jihadis: no longer is it necessary to smuggle videotapes from jihad's open fronts across borders to disseminate them; no longer is it necessary to send treacherously large quantities of newsletters by mail, and to store information material in private homes; and no longer is it necessary to carry or mail notebooks back from training camps to conserve the precious lessons learned. The new media have become a platform on which both will and force can be forged, maintained, and escalated.

AN ESCALATION OF WILL

Telecommunication technologies are used with sophistication to maintain and escalate al-Qaeda's collective motivation and political will. Its vehicle is Salafi ideology, its fuel is the perceived oppression of Muslims on many fronts, and its highway is the susceptible subset of the Muslim youth in the Islamic world and mainly in Europe. By tapping into existing grievances and frustrations, ideology offers a cause for *why* to wage jihad; the Web merely spreads the message more effectively and more widely, in line with what al-Suri had called guidance centers. "All military schools agree that a will to fight and moral strength of the fighter is the basis for victory and good performance," he wrote.[35] For conventional armed forces with the powerful group dynamic of battle, morale is an important element; but for insurgents the will to fight is essential, "the fundament for the guerrilla fighter in general and the jihadi resistance fighter in particular."[36] Radical thinkers therefore saw the strong need to equip activists not only with tactical training, but more importantly with ideological and doctrinal training.

Entire libraries full of books and journals argue the jihadists' cause. Topics range wide, from the humiliation and disgrace of Muslims, the relationship between jihad and the acquisition of knowledge, to the role of women and children and religion from a Salafi point of view. The formats include glossy books authored by recognized authorities, shorter articles often published in established periodicals, stand-alone working papers, debates, video-documentaries, audio-recorded lectures, and many more. The frequency of publications, taken in total, is impressive: in July 2007 alone, al-Qaeda-affiliated entities published approximately 450 items, 90 percent of them text, 9 percent videos, the remaining one percent audio and image files. Operational or topical messages made up the vast majority of media products. Only about 4 percent were in-depth materials focusing on more social, political, or religious issues—ten books, four essays, and five periodicals—estimated Daniel Kimmage.[37] The spiritual and political guidance, discussed in these books, is of the highest importance for the movement.

One of the movement's most popular and widely disseminated publications is the book *39 Ways to Serve and Participate in Jihad*. Its original author is Mohammad bin Ahmad al-Salem. The text first appeared on forums in 2003, and the download links are updated from time to time. The book outlines how anybody can participate in the global jihad without leaving home: by praying honestly, giving money, helping to outfit a fighter or support his family, praising and encouraging the mujahideen, exposing hypocrites and defeatists, abandoning luxury, raising children to love jihad, and boycotting American and British goods, but also through physical training, weapons training, marksmanship, and other preparation. One chapter deals with "electronic jihad." The Internet would be "a blessed medium," al-Salem wrote, "that benefits us greatly by making it possible for people to distribute and follow the news" and "publicize ideas and goals."[38] The *39 Ways*—the document's popularity itself is a case in point—hints at the wide span of utility of information.

A prominent case involves Sayed Imam Abdulaziz al-Sharif, a founder of Zawahiri's al-Jihad organization in Egypt that later merged with al-Qaeda. A prominent Salafi thinker, al-Sharif was known under the nom de guerre "Doctor Fadl" when working with Zawahiri in Afghanistan. He was one of the guiding forces behind both the violent Islamist insurgency in Egypt during the 1990s as well as the evolution of al-Qaeda's doctrine in later years. In Peshawar in 1988, Al-Sharif wrote *Al-omda fi eddad al-edda,* or "The Master in Making Preparation [for Jihad]," then under the name Abdul Qadir bin Abdulaziz. His *Master in Making Preparation* is a jihadi classic that has been translated into English, French, Turkish, Farsi, Urdu, Kurdish, Spanish, Malay, and Indonesian. It covers in detail, among other things, the religious justification for political violence under the banner of jihad. In the spirit of *takfir,* or excommunication, the book called for the killing of Islamic autocratic rulers, and everybody who works for them, as infidels if they fail to implement Sharia law. Anybody who registered to vote disrespected god's authority by laying it onto the hands of the people and was thus eligible for *takfir,* and hence execution.[39]

More than a decade later Sharif made an ideological U-turn. In November 2007 he published a ten-volume document called *Tarshid al-amal al-jihadi fi misr wa al-alam* [Rationalizing the jihadi action in Egypt and the world] in the Egyptian daily *al-Masry al-Youm.* In this work, Sharif criticizes the use of violence with the aim of overthrowing governments on spiritual grounds: nonviolence would be religiously lawful and in accordance with the Sharia; the potential harm of taking violent action, and the escalation thereof, should be considered against the benefits of peaceful action. Leaders from both major Egyptian terrorist groups, al-Gama'a al-Islamiya and al-Jihad, had previously renounced violence in a series of debates that took place largely among radicals jailed in Egypt.[40] At the end of the 1990s several leaders of Gama'a al-Islamiya indeed renounced violence and declared a cease in operations, in turn causing doubt among imprisoned al-Jihad loyalists as well. The Egyptian government, in a permanent struggle to quell radicalism at home, was keen to highlight that the most influential jihadi cleric behind bars had renounced violence.

Sharif's former comrades-in-arms all had reason to take the threat seriously, and reacted quickly. Predictably, the self-styled resistance fighters leaped on the fact that the publications came out of prison. A press release of Sharif's upcoming book was faxed to the London-based *al-Sharq al-Awsat.* Zawahiri, who himself was tortured brutally in Egyptian prisons, replied on 5 July 2007 with a video message spread on the Web:

> I read a ridiculous bit of humor in *al-Sharq al-Awsat* newspaper, which claimed that it received a communiqué from one of the backtrackers, who faxed it from prison. [. . .] I laughed inside and asked myself "Do the prison cells of Egypt now have fax machines? And I wonder, are these fax machines connected to the same line as the electric shock machines, or do they have a separate line?"[41]

The tone should not be misleading. Sharif commands considerable authority among radicals, and the fact that he wrote from prison might give him not less but more street credibility in the eyes of many radicals—certainly more credibility than somebody who never was jailed or in battle.[42] Al-Qaeda was only preparing a more substantial response. In March 2008 as-Sahab published a 188-page document as a more formal and authoritative defense; its unwieldy title is *A Treatise Exonerating the Nation of the Pen and the Sword from the Blemish of the Accusation of Weakness and Fatigue,* authored by al-Zawahiri. In it he questions the publication's timing and Dr Fadl's motivation, and he points out that the text is lacking context, that it is biased, incomplete, inconsistent, unscientific, and that it benefits the Crusaders, Zionists, and apostate Arab regimes.[43] The U.S. government soon proved him right by endorsing al-Sharif's new writings.[44] At the time of writing it was still too early to say whether the "unraveling" or the "rebellion" within the global jihadi movement and its wider support base is a significant trend or just a flare.[45]

Al-Qaeda is clearly using the Web to spread its messages. Two new features are remarkable: the extent to which al-Qaeda is using the Web to reach out interactively to its supporters, and new formats that circumvent the egalitarianism that is built into anonymous forums. One part of al-Qaeda's reply to the authoritative attacks on Salafi doctrine demonstrates both. As-Sahab announced in December 2007 that Ayman al-Zawahiri would answer questions from the public posted on the password-protected Al-Ekhlass and Al-Hesbah forums. The move was motivated by Dr Fadl's publications. Both "individuals and the media" were invited to participate in the public interview. Al-Qaeda would respond "as soon as possible." By the deadline of 16 January 2008, a total 1,888 entries were posted, often multiple questions.[46] Zawahiri, in his response to open questions, thanked the "unknown soldiers" who are "garrisoned on our frontlines in jihadi media."[47]

The Web's significance for the jihadi brand of terrorism can be observed elsewhere. The radicalization of young Muslims is a problem not only in the Middle East, but also in the EU. Europe's 15 million Muslims, representing approximately 3 percent of the continent's total population, are the world's biggest Islamic diaspora and the continent's largest religious minority.[48] France, Germany, Belgium, the UK, and the Netherlands have the largest Muslim populations. Most of Europe's Muslims have national citizenships and identities, and value the political participation in European democracies; many are active in European Political Islam.[49] Only a small minority sympathizes with political violence; the German Ministry of the Interior estimates that 6 percent of Germany's Muslims see politically and religiously motivated violence as justified.[50] But even when only a small subset of this group subscribes to Salafism's revolutionary streak, a large pool of potential recruits remains. In 2007 the Algemene Inlichtingen- en Veiligheidsdienst (AIVD), the Dutch general intelligence and security service, estimated that only in the Netherlands 25,000 to 30,000 individuals were susceptible to Salafist radicalization.[51] In other European countries the picture is comparable. On 11 September 2001, approximately 250 Islamists were investigated on terrorism-related charges in the United Kingdom. By July 2004, that number had grown to 500; by the end of 2006 there were 1,600; by the end of 2007 more than 2,000 individuals posed a "direct threat" to national security only in Britain.[52] The ratio of European citizens among the radicalized is on the rise, so is the number of EU nationals who went through militant training in Pakistan and other countries.

It is difficult to precisely determine the role of the Internet in the process of radicalization and self-radicalization of jihadis. The German Federal Office for the Protection of the Constitution, the Bundesamt Für Verfassungsschutz, finds that "Web-disseminated propaganda guarantees that activists and sympathizers of global 'jihad' perceive themselves as part of one coherent movement, even if the participants' lifestyles and motivations may be highly variant."[53] The report sees the Internet as the "most important" medium of jihadis. Other intelligence services also assume that the Internet's significance is growing. The AIVD found in 2007 that the number of individuals who are radicalized via the Internet increased; "in the Netherlands that mostly affects of young Muslims, particularly susceptible to this medium, who take advantage of the opportunities the Internet offers them."[54] The set of recruits in Europe is not only more diverse than in the past, but also younger. The average age of terrorist suspects apprehended in Europe has decreased after 2005. Before December 2003, the average age of jihadi activists arrested was approximately twenty-six years; the average age of those detained after 2006 was only twenty years.[55] The Austrian Ministry of the Interior found that, thanks to the Web, "radicalization and recruitment become a dynamic two-way process, in which engagement can originate either from the user and/or from terrorist organizations."[56]

Most European security agencies come to a similar set of conclusions—and so does the al-Qaeda leadership. They seem convinced that the media in general and the Web in particular are crucial to their cause. At the height of Zarqawi's violent campaigns in Iraq, Zawahiri reminded his lieutenant to exercise restraint, "more than half of this battle is taking place in the battlefield of the media."[57] The movement's leaders decided to do a virtual public affairs blitz in 2007. In September, Osama bin Laden appeared in a fresh video, for the first time since 2004. Then several audio messages followed. Simultaneously Ayman al-Zawahiri stepped up his visibility in speeches and tapes that were distributed through al-Sahab, an extremist news outlet. To make it easier for second- and third-generation immigrants in Europe, who often speak only shoddy Arabic, al-Sahab started to use European languages, such as German, French, Italian, and Dutch—but also Turkish, Pashtu, Urdu, and Russian—in order to target other diaspora communities.[58]

One the most illustrative recent episodes that highlights the dynamic two-way process between wannabe activists and seasoned terrorists occurred in the United Kingdom. Waseem Mughal, Tariq al-Daour, and Younis Tsouli, better know as Irhabi007, were attracted to the jihadi cause and felt it necessary to take action.

Tsouli was an IT-student at a London college, who arrived in the United Kingdom in 2001. He was outraged by images he found on the Internet depicting the brutality of the Iraq War. The twenty-two-year-old son of a diplomat lived in a top-floor flat in W12 Shepherd's Bush in west London. He joined Web forums but found their technological sophistication not satisfactory. Soon Tsouli pioneered fresh and rather effective propaganda methods and started a career that made him a ubiquitous figure in al-Qaeda's online activity.[59] Zarqawi saw Tsouli's work online and decided to "recruit" him—although that recruitment did not result in Tsouli physically training in Pakistan or joining an open front in Iraq or Afghanistan or elsewhere.

Tsouli, of course, knew well that his online activism was not the same thing as joining the brick-and-mortar jihad in Iraq or elsewhere. Being only virtually connected to the brothers who fought and died was a problem for the young activist. In one encrypted chat conversation he openly struggled with the dilemma of matching words with deeds. "Dude," Tsouli complained to another online jihadist, who chose the pseudonym Abuthaabit, "my heart is in Iraq."[60] The ensuing chat dialogue, already quoted in the introduction, illustrates the link between online organization and offline action. Tsouli was far away from the battlefield in London, and, like many, badly wanted to have an impact on what is happening in Iraq. Yet his was a struggle to inspire other potential extremists to fight, mounted from Europe and targeting the Middle East. In 2005, he became an official administrator of one of the most influential and widely read extremist forums at the time, Al-Ansat. Tsouli was the quintessential example of a self-recruited member of a globally active "elite" of radicals, with little in common—beyond rage and spiritual disorientation—that could be the basis for a veritable political movement with a territorial agenda.

Tsouli was sentenced to sixteen years in prison by the British Woolwich crown court in December 2007. The evidence for Tsouli's trial was gathered from a "hugely gigantic" amount of material found in his home: computers, DVDs, memory chips. The trials produced no evidence that the British jihadists ever met any of their foreign associates face-to-face. There is even no evidence that Tsouli ever encountered Mughal or Daour in person.[61] Deputy Assistant Commissioner Peter Clarke, head of Scotland Yard's antiterrorist branch, said that it was the first time the British police encountered a criminal gang preparing a crime without ever having met in person. "It was the first virtual conspiracy to murder that we have seen."[62] Europol's annual status report on terrorism is unequivocal on the Web's role:

> The [Tsouli] investigation revealed a large international network of people who jointly provided support to jihadist movements on a global scale without ever having met in person. Videos and films calling on Muslims to take part in the global jihad continue to play a significant role in the recruitment process. . . . The increasingly sophisticated methods of promoting this agenda, in particular using the Internet and other electronic media, have been identified as factors contributing to the increasing number of Islamic terrorists.[63]

Such Web-enabled work goes beyond the mere dissemination of ideological material. Activists, (self-)radicalized and (self-)recruited without ever having been exposed to practical boot camps in Central Asia or elsewhere, may be entrepreneurial and decide to take practical action on their own, by trying to join a training camp, setting up a cell, traveling to Muslim land under occupation to fight, and even planning and executing terrorist attacks in non-Muslim countries.

AN ESCALATION OF FORCE

Telecommunication technology serves to maintain and escalate al-Qaeda's ability to use force. The Web has a critical enabling role in the spread not only of motivation and will, but also in the distribution of doctrinal and operational knowledge on *how* to wage jihad.

Tsouli, although a highly useful operative for al-Qaeda, never received physical training and never decided to actually engage in violence. But he facilitated the training of others by getting them in touch with the right people and the right material. Michael Scheuer, chief of the bin Laden unit in the CIA's Counterterrorist Center from 1996 to 1999 and a leading expert on al-Qaeda, points out that the organization "has developed what can only be judged as a spectacularly successful online university of strategy, tactics and training for guerrilla warfare and terrorist operations."[64] Detailed manuals and videotaped instructions teach a broad variety of skills, down to a very detailed level: how-to videos explaining the production of acetone peroxide, how to set up a TNT detonator, ambush techniques, the use of military electronics, how to launch surface-to-air missiles, methods for concealing IEDs, how to prepare the "rotten meat poison," alternate methods for suicide bombings, flight simulator training, how to maintain physical fitness, and how to use secure encryption software.

Terrorism experts and intelligence analysts have debated if physical training, particularly for complex operations that involve the use of explosives, can be substituted by virtual training material that explains these complex tasks.[65] Some of the debate's most contentious questions are whether there is bottom-up self-recruitment, or top-down planning and some form of command-and-control; whether the wars in Iraq and Afghanistan help to combat or fuel terrorism in non-Muslim countries; and how significant the ideological coherence is for the movement's continued existence and its continuity of performance. Skeptics point to the fact that almost all successful attackers had some form of physical training in Afghanistan, Pakistan, or elsewhere. Some strategists among the radical Islamists, by contrast, seem to hope that do-it-yourself startup operations are possible. For instance, training, al-Suri writes, should be moved to "every house, every quarter and every village."[66] As fixed training camps became hard to run, he recommends mobile ones.

The areas of chaos are on the verge of coming under American control and being closed . . . the only [training] methods which remain possible for us now, in the world of American aggression and international coordination to combat terrorism, are the methods of secret training in houses and mobile training camps.[67]

In absence of professional drill instructors and trainers, "one needs to spread the culture of preparation and training . . . by all methods, especially the Internet."[68]

Since around 2004, global jihad's insurgency doctrine is extensively discussed and developed in widespread Internet journals, such as *al-Ansar, al-Neda,* or *Mu'askar al-Battar,* or in books published online. Among the movement's most prolific and creative writers were Abu-Hajer Abd-al-Aziz al-Muqrin, Abu Ubayd al-Qurashi, Abu-Ayman al-Hilali, Abd-al-Hadi, and Sayf-al-Din al-Ansari. One of their core tenets is to orchestrate the political and the military side of the insurgency in sync. "[W]orking in an organization dedicated to jihad," al-Hilali argued,

requires a fundamental working knowledge of planning, administration, security, psychology, sociology, history, geography, politics, strategy, law, education, preaching, and military science, not to mention religious knowledge.

Muqrin, the former leader of al-Qaeda in the Arabian Peninsula, specifically referring to the war against the allies in Iraq and Afghanistan, wrote that Islamist forces must be ready to fight a "long war of attrition." The insurgency's leadership must "know the enemy it is fighting," he advised. He proposed the "1000-wound" tactic of harassing the enemy to prolong the war. The goal is to "exhaust" the patience and the resources of the enemies. "We can exhaust him without fighting any real battles with him," Abd-al-Hadi was convinced. Americans love "fixed bases," al-Qurashi wrote, referring to a century-old mistake by counterinsurgents of amassing too many troops in a secured parameter. Their troops would be "highly paid and overloaded with comfort facilities that often restrict their movements." American bases were "known and immovable"; those of the mujahideen are "light and movable." Such journals and manuals cover the entire spectrum of conflict, from strategic guidance, and operational guidelines, to tactical and technical nuts-and-bolts knowledge, illustrated by video instructions with different formats, styles, and practicability. Thomas Fingar, the U.S. Deputy Director of National Intelligence for Analysis, said in a congressional testimony:

[T]he growing use of the Internet to identify and comment with networks throughout the world offers opportunities to build relationships and gain expertise that previously were available only in overseas training camps. It is likely that such independent groups will use information on destructive tactics available on the internet to boost their own capabilities.[69]

Tactical and technical manuals accessed online played an enabling role in the Khan al-Khalili bombing at a Cairo tourist bazaar in April 2005, and in the failed attempt to bomb passenger trains in Cologne in July 2006. These cases raise the question of the Web's role in operational planning. The German domestic intelligence service thinks the Web is used not only for ideological and doctrinal preparation, but also for operational planning. "Restricted chat-rooms, encrypted emails, and voice-over-Internet-telephony can be used for the exchange of sensible information, and therefore to plan attacks," the ministry of the interior wrote in its annual report in 2007.[70]

Many examples show that the use of Internet-distributed tactical knowledge—TTPs in military jargon, tactics, techniques, and procedures—is a widespread phenomenon. If conventional armies are beginning to use the Web as a platform for tactical exchange of information during operations, it would be surprising if young and tech-savvy jihadi operatives did not. In 2007 Europe's police and security services foiled three major terrorist attacks. Some operatives had personal training experience and even contact with al-Qaeda leaders in the Pakistan-Afghanistan region; all of them used the Web for purposes related to operations.

On 29 June 2007 two car bombs were discovered in London. The first improvised explosive device was deposited near the Tiger Tiger nightclub in Haymarket, the second in Cockspur Street. Here the operatives had training experience in an al-Qaeda training camp in Pakistan. And again the Internet played an enabling role—for both the plotters and the police. The suspects were trailed by the police to Internet cafés, and the ring allegedly communicated by e-mail, by mobile phone, and in chat rooms on hardcore porn Web sites to evade intelligence agencies, who might be less inclined to search for Islamic purists there.[71] Salahuddin Amin, a thirty-one-year-old part-time taxi driver from Luton, testified that he provided a formula for explosives to a conspirator through a public Internet forum.[72] Only hours before the bombs were discovered, a message was posted in the al-Hesbah forum: "Today I say: rejoice, by Allah, London shall be bombed."[73] The attack was eventually foiled by intercepted chat room conversations on Internet forums, through surveillance, and by the discovery of the fertilizer in a storage depot.[74]

On 4 September, the Danish police arrested eight people who were suspected of plotting an attack. All were between nineteen and twenty-nine years old. The case became known as the Glasvej case; a Danish citizen of Pakistani descent was the ringleader.[75] One of the perpetrators had received training in a Pakistani training camp on surveillance, close combat, and the use of explosives; after his return he manufactured and tested tricycloacetone triperoxide (TATP). But he also made "extensive use of the Internet for various operational purposes," reported the Politiets Efterretningstjeneste, the Danish security and intelligence services abbreviated as PET.[76]

One day later—yet unrelated—three men were arrested in Germany. Fritz Gelowicz, twenty-eight, and Daniel Schneider, twenty-one, were German converts to Islam and had attended training camps run by the Islamic Jihad Union in Pakistan. The third operative, Adem Yilmaz, was born in Anatolia but had lived in Germany for more than fourteen years. Gelowicz spoke neither Turkish nor Arabic. The operatives learned to build the bombs mainly in explosives training courses they attended in training camps in Pakistan, run by the Islamic Jihad Union (IJU).[77] Eventually it was the e-mail communication—in English— between Internet cafés in Stuttgart and counterparts in Pakistan that led to the arrests in the first place. The suspects even ordered canisters of a hydrogen peroxide-based mixture of chemicals, the equivalent of more than 550 kilograms of TNT, from an online vendor in Hanover. A day after the arrests, Jörg Ziercke, the president of the German Federal Crime Office, BKA, pointed out that bomb-making manuals had been readily available on the Internet.[78]

MEDIA OPERATIONS

For almost all irregular violent movements, communication on the public domain permeates almost all ideological and operational activities. The wider public's view of the resistance ultimately will decide about its long-term success and survival. Al-Qaeda's use of telecommunications is probably more sophisticated than that of any other terrorist organization in recent history. That is mainly the case because it can use the Web's interactive elements, a luxury that even twentieth-century terrorist organizations and insurgents did not enjoy, a novelty that any serious statistical and historical comparison of insurgencies should take into account.[79]

The use of the media in military operations can be traced back to the Afghan jihad against the Soviet Union. Some Afghan insurgent groups, such as Gulbuddin Hekmatyar's Hezb-e-Islami and Ahmad Shah Masoud's Jamiat-e-Islami, aimed for a media presence in their fight against the Russians: magazines, posters, local radio programs, newsletters, films, and audiotapes. The foreign mujahideen who joined the war against the communists used these media outlets as a template, translated the texts into Arabic, and distributed these media products across the Arab world. From there Arab NGOs copied and disseminated these items, translating them into yet more languages to reach the entire Muslim world, including Europe, the Far East, Africa, Central Asia, and North America.[80] Sheikh Abdullah Azzam, the founder of the Afghan Services Bureau, the Maktab al-Khidamat, played an important role in marketing jihad's propaganda world wide, but particularly to the developed world. With respect to neutral target audiences, he added that the mujahideen's continued military activity will broadcast a warning "through the language of blood or fire" to the people of nations allied with America that "their governments are getting them involved in wars and conflicts with which they have nothing to do."[81] Initially the target audience was limited to supporters and would-be supporters. The productions were graphic, designed to evoke sympathy for the suffering of the Afghans and to trigger and amplify outrage against the Russian occupation.

Al-Qaeda's first spokesman, perhaps with some irony, used the nom de guerre of Abu Reuters. Bin Laden spoke with Western journalists for the first time in Sudan. His first television interview with a Western news organization was with CNN in Afghanistan in 1997, with the journalist Peter Bergen. "He asked us to submit a list of questions in advance. He only wanted to answer the questions he wanted to answer, and not personal questions."[82] More and more, al-Qaeda came to see media operations as an integral part of the military fight. Among those who most thoroughly discussed the integration of military and media activities was Abu-Hajer Abd-al-Aziz al-Muqrin, the former leader of al-Qaeda in the Arabian Peninsula. He advised the planning and conducting of political and military operations in sync. "[There must be] no trace of doubt left on anybody's mind that they [the mujahideen] are present all over the land," Muqrin explained. "This will prove the mujahideen's power, rub the nose of the enemies in the dirt, and encourage young men to take up arms and face the enemy—Jews, Christians, and their collaborators."[83] The strategist also had donors and financial supporters in mind; "jihad eats up enormous funds," he added.

Today al-Qaeda's best-known media office is the as-Sahab Foundation for Islamic Media Publication, or just as-Sahab. The word means "the clouds" in Arabic, allegedly a reference to Afghanistan's skyscraping peaks—but quite ironically the name also describes as-Sahab's new platform, "the cloud," as the global network of commercial datacenters is referred to in the IT-industry.[84] It is possible to identify at least thirteen established "media production and distribution entities," virtual groups that share a radical Salafist ideology but have developed separate logos and brands. The three most important ones are al-Fajr Media Center, the Global Islamic Media Front, and the al-Sahab Institute for Media Production. As-Sahab's activity is on a steady upward trajectory since its inception, and skyrocketed in 2006. In 2002 it published six videos, then eleven in 2003, thirteen in 2004, sixteen in 2005, fifty-eight in 2006, and ninety-seven in 2007.[85] The distribution entities collect and distribute material that originates from multiple armed groups. Other well-known entities are the Echo of Jihad Media Center, the al-Boraq forum, the Jihadist Media Brigade, and the Taliban's Sawt al-Jihad as well as the Media Front of the Islamic Emirate of Afghanistan. These entities only connect various armed groups into the wider al-Qaeda movement. The vast majority of these products focus on conflict zones, particularly Iraq and Afghanistan, but also North Africa and Somalia.[86]

Although this performance is impressive, it comes with its own set of problems. For reasons outlined by al-Suri, no centralized distribution for jihadist media exists, a fact that creates costs and risks for the jihadist movement. Some strategic thinkers have well recognized this problem. Kimmage does a great service by quoting extensively from a twenty-three-page paper published by the "al-Boraq Media Institute" in September 2006, entitled *Media Exuberance*. The paper confronts the problem of credible attribution from a jihadist point of view. Its authors warn against exuberance, which they see as efforts undertaken "without official authority or prior study," such as unsolicited and unsanctioned postings by individuals without endorsement by a recognized distribution entity. The al-Boraq publication warns against the

> distribution of jihadist audio and video products without official sanction or per-
> mission from the producer, the distribution of statements by jihadist groups under
> personal names and user IDs, [and] the release of personal [audio and video] prod-
> ucts and works under the names of jihad groups.[87]

Such actions, the authors maintain, undermine the integrity and credibility of the jihadist media. What then follows is a highly impressive analysis and conclusion: Western media organizations, such as ABC and CNN, were able to maintain their "credibility" in the face of the ongoing "information revolution." As an illustration of the continued dominance of these outlets, the authors point out, information still leaks from other sources *to* such outlets, rather than *from* them. The movement's virtual media organizations, the document argues, face two problems when compared to traditional, industrial age TV stations or newspapers. First, they are "not alone." The users of forums are reminded that "intelligence services of the tyrant, members of media institutes opposed to 'electronic terrorism,' and jour-nalists and correspondents from various stations and news agencies" are scouring their conversations for actionable hints. Second, while they attempt to create alternative media organizations, jihadist outlets lack the professional standards of high-quality journalism; "it is regrettable that Western media institutes treat jihadist forums with care, attention, and rigor that we do not find among the sup-porters of such forums."[88] The view that Western media organizations offer a time-tested model to create credibility is more widespread. *The New York Times* interviewed a young activist and computer shop owner who went by the nickname of Abu Omar in Amman. He helped speed as-Sahab's jihadi messages among trusted online networks. "We are typically observers, but when we see something on the net, our job is to share it," Abu Omar said. The activist told the journalist that he no longer trusts the news on television, including al-Jazeera which would still be tied to Arab governments. "We become like journalists ourselves."[89]

Ayman al-Zawahiri repeatedly emphasized the need for improved media opera-tions in his communiqués. It is therefore not surprising that the organization as well as the movement are struggling to find the right methods of public affairs; they operate, after all, under very adverse conditions in the media field. The organiza-tion's experiments included attempts to work with the Web's most successful inter-active platforms. On 1 October 2007, Al-Qaeda's Islamic State of Iraq even opened a YouTube channel, a Web site on the video-sharing platform that serves as the online equivalent to a TV channel. It has trouble establishing itself, however, and its statistics are hardly impressive.[90] The movement was far more successful with its own various media outlets. But al-Qaeda's appropriation of the new media has, to an extent, taken control out of its leadership's hands. The Web has proliferated ide-ologues and commoditized militant ideas. The resulting decentralization of author-ity is making it much more difficult for any would-be leader to control the debate.

Al-Qaeda's writings should not be overestimated in their prescriptive authority. Many operational visions and requirements were not new, but had already developed into trends. The label "Al-Qaeda" has developed into the "common name" some jihadi commentators wished for. Bin Laden's own conceptual shift of main enemies, away from local apostate regimes toward global oppressors of Islam, to an extent foreshadowed the call for a common cause, a common program, and a common name. Several local terrorist groups had renamed their secret organizations to "al-Qaeda"—and analogously adopted the pen names based on their nationality, such as al-Suri, "the Syrian," or al-Libi, "the Libyan." The terrorist offshoots assumed the names of their native region: jihadis in Iraq chose the name of "al-Qaeda of Mesopotamia": Algeria's former *Groupe Salafiste pour la Prédication et le Combat,* or GSPC, in September 2006 chose the new name "al-Qaeda in the Islamic Maghreb." Most recently, Al-Jama'a al-Islamiyyah al-Muqatilah fi-Libya, or Libyan Islamic Fighting Group (LIFG), merged with al-Qaeda. As-Sahab released a video interview with a bearded man identified as Abu Laith al-Libi in spring 2007. In the clip Libi accused Shia Muslims of fighting alongside American forces in Iraq. He also assured that the mujahideen would crush NATO troops in Afghanistan. In November 2007, after thus adopting the views and rhetoric of global jihad, the Libyan appeared together with Ayman al-Zawahri in a video to announce that a Libyan Islamist group had joined the global terror organization. Zawahiri called for the overthrow of the Qadhafi regime:

> Islamic nation of resistance and jihad in the Maghreb, see how your children are uniting under the banner of Islam and jihad against the United States, France and Spain. . . . Support . . . your children in fighting our enemies and cleansing our lands of their slaves Kadhafi, Zine El Abidine, Bouteflika and Mohammed VI.[91]

In a 1999 interview, LIFG spokesman Omar Rashed lamented that the Libyan people had not "passed beyond the stage of sentiments to the stage of action." Then he referred to the organization's shift from the near to the far enemy. "The United States no longer relies on its agents to constrict the Islamic tide; it has taken this role upon itself," Rashed said. Yet the significance of these local branches should not be overrated. There is significant disharmony between local groups and the global leadership of al-Qaeda, and insignificant central authority to muzzle this disagreement.

An assessment of the costs and benefits of al-Qaeda's transformation has to be nuanced. Both extremes, entirely leaderless jihad on the one hand and top-heavy command-and-control on the other, are caricatures; the accurate description of global jihad lies in between. So does the prescriptive vision of how to wage it put forward by the most serious radical strategists. It is equally difficult to write a premature obituary on al-Qaeda, even if more leading ideologues would jump ship. Al-Qaeda is alive and has regrouped in the tribal areas between Pakistan and Afghanistan, according to the 2007 U.S. National Intelligence Estimate (NIE), a report authorized by all sixteen official U.S. intelligence agencies. The terrorist organization may be planning an attack on the American continent, the NIE stated. Both sides, those who see the beginning of the end of al-Qaeda and those who fear that the movement is alive and well and ready to strike big, would do well to keep a balanced view. Because al-Qaeda and the global jihad were forced to abandon most characteristics of War 1.0—and instead had to assume many of the principles of War 2.0—they confront unprecedented challenges, as we will outline in the conclusion: the mix of refurbished ideologies and new technologies enabled the movement to become tactically more nimble but has created strategic inertia and loss of control; some operational risks have decreased but political risks have increased; the insurgency may be less dependent on local support but more dependent on global grievances; and ultimately terrorist violence may be more resilient but also less dangerous than assumed.

Conclusion

The first part of this book analyzed the media operations of the world's three most active and battle-hardened militaries. The Israel Defense Forces, the British Army, and America's land forces are difficult to compare in many ways: each organization has its own history, its own political leadership, its own professional culture, its own preferred approaches to the use of force, and its own set of challenges in vastly different operational theaters. The same applies to the media operations of these armies: the press landscape, journalistic traditions, and attitudes vis-à-vis the use of military force in those three democracies differ widely. Most importantly, their political masters represent electorates with starkly different political cultures, threat perceptions, and attitudes towards the use of force. Yet generalizations are possible. All modern conventional armed forces have in common that they used to see public affairs not as an essential operational task; instead the press was treated as a nuisance and as a low priority for much of the second half of the twentieth century. The newest information technology was employed not to communicate more efficiently to civilians and journalists either at home or in the field, but to enhance military power.

This old perspective on the public seems to be changing in the cases studied for this book—albeit rather slowly. America's, Israel's, and Britain's armed forces have learned in their own ways that the media both old and new are a permanent feature of the battlespace in the twenty-first century. Leading strategic thinkers have realized that wars are likely to be fought "among the people," where the competition is for legitimacy, not lethality, thus highlighting the public dimension of the use of force.[1] This change in the nature of war coincides with a change in media technology and its role in society. Journalists, citizens, and soldiers come equipped with gadgets that often are superior to the IT equipment of institutional armed forces. This creates risks as well as opportunities.

The second part of this book dealt with the other side: with the world's most powerful and adept irregular violent movements and insurgencies, particularly in the fight against a conventionally far superior enemy. Hezbollah, the Taliban, and the al-Qaeda movement are also hard to compare and differ fundamentally on several accounts: each militant group has its own support base, its own political vision, its own brand of Islamic radicalism, its own enemies, specific territorial ambitions, and its own preferred methods and tactics. Yet, with respect to the media, similar generalizations are possible. Militant groups also learned that the media are part of their operating environment. Historically, as we argued in the first chapter, insurgents and resistance movements were more inclined than their governmental adversaries to use publicity for operational purposes, as a weapon to undermine their opponent's support. The power of public opinion and perceptions, after all, have always been at the heart of any terrorist strategy. But the information age has brought radical change also for irregular fighters. The world's most powerful insurgents, Hezbollah, the Taliban, and al-Qaeda, have realized that the public use of telecommunication comes with huge benefits, both internally and externally. Enabled by the Web and mobile phones and their new dynamics of social interaction and production, militants were able to use telecommunication technologies for a broader spectrum of operational functions.

The effects are counterintuitive. Quite ironically, the described adaptations have resulted in a reversal of historic trends: regular armies engaged in counterinsurgency operations are increasingly refining the use of modern information technology for *external* purposes, to reach the local population in the theater of operations; irregulars, by contrast, are more and more using the Internet for *internal* purposes, to communicate with fellow radicals and like-minded extremists, thereby increasing the risk of losing touch with the general population in their area of operations and elsewhere. This latter trend, we conclude on the following pages, diminishes the significance of the first.

The concluding remarks are organized in three brief sections: the first will outline some general trends that are beginning to influence the conduct of irregular war in the twenty-first century, then the strengths and weaknesses of counterinsurgent media operations will be analyzed, and finally we will argue that the public dimension drives a wedge between modern terrorism and modern insurgency. We end with some recommendations.

GENERAL TRENDS

Several trends that shape the media environment of future wars are not under the control of governments and armies. Some of these ongoing developments are still fresh, and more research into their likely trajectories and their potential effects is needed. Yet on a general level, five changes with enduring effects can be identified.

First, the costs of global communication continue to decrease. Internet penetration in the poorest countries and across the developing world—the most likely theaters of future war—are growing rapidly, driven by lower costs for personal computers, notebooks, and mobile devices. Intel, the world's largest chip maker, estimated that more than 50 million low-end laptops will be sold per year world wide by 2011 (annual computer sales were at approximately 150 million in 2008). The Middle East's average Internet penetration in early 2009 was about 22 percent, with a growth rate of more than 1,000 percent.[2] The picture of the mobile phone market is even more dynamic. Mobile phone companies rapidly expand into the low-saturation markets of Africa, the Middle East, and Central Asia. In late 2008, the world's more than 700 mobile operators were adding new connections at the rate of 15 per second, or 1.3 million per day.[3] Emerging markets are responsible for 85 percent of that growth. In the fourth quarter of 2007, the top five countries with the largest mobile phone growth rates were Uzbekistan with 96 percent, Iran with 94.5 percent, Afghanistan with 92.9 percent, Sierra Leone with 89 percent, and Tajikistan with 83 percent. Pakistan alone added more than 5.5 million subscribers in those three months, nearly twice as many as Germany.[4] Two previously distinct spheres, Internet and mobile phones, are not so distinct any more. The number of people who use their mobile phones to access the Web is growing at a phenomenal rate, especially in the developing world. In June 2008, 73 million people in China, for instance, accessed the Internet only with cellphones, after an increase of 45 percent in six months.[5] As prices for smartphones come down, these numbers will go up. Ultimately, it should be noted, all phones will be smart. The Web's future will be mobile.

Second, information will become more social and more local. Although globalization is a word often employed in connection with the, alas, global telecommunication market, an opposite trend can be observed. Social technologies are leaping forward: among younger generations instant messaging, or IM, the use of instant text or video messages on personal computers, is becoming a more popular communication channel than e-mail. Two out of three American teens and young adults between age thirteen and twenty-one say they send more IMs than e-mails; and 87 percent of these messages are between family and friends.[6] Text messaging—the use of instant messages on mobile phones—is equally becoming more popular. Approximately 36 percent of cellphone users in the United States said they send text messages daily. About half of all users send messages to just two to five people; only one-fifth of all users spread SMS to more than ten people.[7] The technology particularly strengthens ties within families and close-knit groups.[8] Growth rates paint a clear picture: social technologies are evolving faster in the developing world than the mainstream press. Social news consumption and social networking highlight trust and known ties. It is likely that future military operations will take place in countries where the mobile phone penetration is significantly higher than that of the Internet and traditional press outlets. Text messaging comes into play when news consumers do not have access to mainstream media or an Internet connection. Text messaging, in other words, will be an important medium of public information. But because of its point-to-point nature—it is "narrowcasting" rather than broadcasting—texting works more like word-of-mouth, and is prone to rumor, bias, and propaganda.

Third, traditional journalism is changing. One aspect of this change is increasing market density. The landscape in the most important likely theaters has been populated by hundreds of TV channels. Al-Arabiya and al-Jazeera are only the two best-known channels in the Arab world. The local media in Afghanistan and Iraq were equally thriving despite ongoing violence there. Another more fundamental aspect of changing journalism is that user-generated content, and non-professional journalistic outlets, are gaining traction. Blogging and other venues of amateur journalism should not be overestimated as outlets on their own right. Instead the mainstream media will continue to gather experience and develop routines to tap into a dense and thick layer of user-provided material, particularly imagery both still and moving; not everybody is becoming a journalist, but many are becoming an eye-witness and agency cameraman on standby. Citizen-reporting will become more widespread. A third aspect is that consumers, particularly young consumers, are beginning to adapt their news-consumption patterns to the news supply. From an individual user's perspective, online social networks may determine the newsworthiness of a given news item more than its placement above the centerfold of a print newspaper's front page.

As an effect of these developments, fourth, the diversity of target audiences will increase by nearly all measures: by education and literacy, by level of interest, by language and cultural background, by region, by format of preferred news source, by political preferences, by world-views, and by the level of participation and activism. Although some of these groups will have rather specific views and characteristics, it will paradoxically become more difficult to target them precisely and in an isolated way. Particularly the example of Israel shows that domestically important constituents may follow ongoing operations through the foreign language press. Future wars will be reported not only in near real-time. The word on military action, and often the image as well, will be out fast and received by a bigger number of observers in real-time. The costs for secrecy will be enormous, and censorship and the control of the information flow from the battlefield almost impossible.

From this analysis follows, fifth, that the conditions for what has become known as counterpropaganda operations will change. Any monopoly on information will be more difficult to maintain in any populated area, both "propaganda" in a Saddam-style information campaign that temporarily dominated the airwaves with U.S. collateral damage in 1991 as well as "counter-propaganda" in an American-style embedded media program that dominated the coverage of the invasion of Baghdad in 2003.[9] The "noise" emitted by both more saturated traditional media markets and rumor-prone social media outlets will be more difficult to penetrate than in the past. Israel's Gaza operation in early 2009 demonstrated that many tactical details, emanating through new media outlets, do not necessarily add up to a clearer strategic picture.

These trends are already beginning to shape the operational environment of today's operations. All land forces and insurgent movements studied in this book have one more thing in common: they have been at war, under high operational stress, for an extended period of time. The Second Intifada started in September 2000 and went on for at least five years, leaving Gaza and Southern Lebanon in an agitated state; the war in Afghanistan started in October 2001 and continues; and the Iraq War was launched in March 2003 and still goes on in 2009. These stressful half-dozen years coincided with perhaps the most fundamental information revolution in human history. All six organizations analyzed here faced huge pressure to learn and adapt, and they all have their own strengths and weaknesses.

COUNTERINSURGENCY

The armies studied in this book were forced to adapt to both a new kind of enemy and a new kind of media environment as they were fighting along. Their success has been uneven. All three cases have specific strengths and specific weaknesses, but in all three cases the list is more densely populated with weak spots. We will respectively start with the strengths.

The U.S. military still is the world's best equipped force and among the best trained. Its officer corps is maintaining a lively and creative debate about the changing nature of war that remains unrivalled in any other country. It therefore is not surprising that the U.S. defense community is in many ways ahead of its peers when it comes to dealing not only with insurgencies, but also with the press and with the Web at war. Key players in the Pentagon and the services have understood some of the challenge of irregular warfare in the information age: the media will report from any operation, the information flow can't be controlled, it's therefore better to work with the media than against them, and it's best to be the "first out" with information, even with bad information. Many commanders and public affairs officers have also learned that the release authority for operational information should be as low as possible, in order to increase the reaction speed. The land forces in particular have understood that the perception of the local population can be of paramount importance in a counterinsurgency. It may be a precondition and critical building block for operational success. Therefore the local population's views might be of higher operational priority than the domestic U.S. audience, a significant departure from classic public affairs doctrine and thinking, and from the preferences of their elected political masters. Another benefit is cultural. America remains one of the most open and dynamic societies. This is mirrored in the way its soldiers deal with the new media: U.S. servicemen and women not only write online about their individual experiences to an extent that does not compare to any other army, and the Army is tolerating such blogging. The Department of Defense started to make use of its best bloggers by easing access to the troops, such as in the case of Michael Yon. The Pentagon even came to appreciate initiatives such as CompanyCommand.com, PlatoonLeader.org, or SmallWarsJournal.com. Both the engagement with local and regional Arab media and experimentation with

Web 2.0 platforms are improving. Such an attitude should be a shining example for most other NATO militaries.

But the U.S. approach also has significant weaknesses, conceptual, institutional, and political. A widespread conceptual flaw is the attempt to rival al-Qaeda's sophisticated use of media technologies. Secretaries of Defense Rumsfeld and Gates shared this view, finding it "just plain embarrassing that Al Qaeda is better at communicating its message on the Internet than America." The very attributes that distinguish government actors positively from non-state subversive movements—accountability, transparency, a sophisticated division of labor, quality control, orderly bureaucratic procedures, hierarchies and chains-of-command, adherence to laws, continuity of performance—are preventing government agencies from using the Web in the same way as irregular movements. Some of the characteristics of War 1.0, in other words, are far superior to those of War 2.0—ethically, politically, and operationally. Yet al-Qaeda's use of the Web has, often naively, been promoted as a role model.

America's dynamism and determination also has negative institutional consequences. When compared to its allies, the U.S. military has two things in abundance, a can-do attitude and money. In the field of communication, therefore, the Pentagon has both the will and the resources to create new organisms to deal with new problems. The consequence is a proliferation of agencies, departments, and new sub-organizations dealing with public affairs, strategic communication, psychological warfare, operational security, etc. What followed is duplication, confusion, and—worse—internal competition for influence and resources. The resulting PR ecosystem has reached remarkable proportions. Many insiders expressed confusion about responsibilities, chains of command, and conceptual approaches to the problem. The outcome is unintended: groupthink and inertia.

Another problem is political. The magnitude of the terrorist threat in the twenty-first century is often compared to the magnitude of the threats of the twentieth century: the "war on terror" or "long war," it has been argued time and again, would define a new era just as the Cold War once did.[10] Radical Islam, therefore, has to be confronted boldly and offensively, just as Nazi Germany had to be confronted.[11] But such comparisons, more widespread in the United States than in Europe, probably overrate their enemy's organizational, political, and military capabilities. The heightened threat perception in the United States translated into a foreign policy in the Middle East and Central Asia that in turn provided powerful raw material for jihadi propaganda and recruitment. The U.S. government's public affairs and public diplomacy officials, as a result, find their room for maneuver drastically limited. Outside the region the repercussions are most strongly felt in Europe, particularly in the United Kingdom, where radical Islam has been on a steep rise in first half-dozen years since the start of the campaigns against terrorism. Radical Islamism was by no means caused by the West. It is a century-old phenomenon that predates most of the Western policies that are sometimes mistaken for its cause.[12] But America's reaction to 9/11 has probably contributed more to strengthening Islamic extremism than to its demise.[13]

The Armed Services in the United Kingdom are more difficult to assess. Any observer of the British military and the Ministry of Defence needs to take a step back and add context: the UK's most fundamental security threat does not come from abroad; it is located inside the United Kingdom—in sharp contrast to that of the country's closest ally, the United States, where the opposite is true. Jihadi radicalization and domestic terrorism is, in several highly debated ways, loosely linked to the theaters in Afghanistan and Iraq. But it is the Home Office, the domestic intelligence services, the Metropolitan Police, and other domestic agencies that deal with the more immediate threat of radical Islam at home, not the Ministry of Defence, the agency responsible for the defense against external threats from abroad. Against this background the main weakness of the ministry's public outreach is somewhat surprising: it is predominantly focused on the domestic front. Strategic and operational thoughts on public affairs are nearly absent in the ministry's media directorate. Because the British Ministry of Defence has far less resources on strategic communications than the Pentagon, there are naturally fewer actors in uniform or civilians under the ministry's roof who interact with journalists. The ministry's predominantly civilian-staffed press office therefore has more relative power vis-à-vis the armed services than the Pentagon's press office. But the MoD's senior civilians in charge of PR have other loyalties, expertise, and emphases than senior officers: they tend to feel more faithful to the minister than to the chief of staff; they tend to professionally socialize in London's political hallways not in military mess halls; and they focus more on the domestic media than on the foreign theaters of operations. The overarching challenge for strategic communicators in Britain, however, is that the country is often seen as fighting in America's shadow. Being a staunch ally of the United States makes it more difficult to develop an independent outlook when viewed from the Middle East.

The conditions for Israel's and the Israel Defense Force's use of military power are hugely different from the situation faced by the United States and the United Kingdom in all their current and past irregular confrontations. The challenges for the Israel Defense Forces in their media operations are massive. For Israel, military conflict is happening either close to home or at home, and it is perceived as existential, as a incessantly repeated major cause for the Arab "resistance" is the very existence of the Jewish State. The Israeli political and military elites therefore have no illusions: they don't even try to win the hearts and minds of their enemies. This is not to say that the Israeli politicians and generals disregard the psychological dimension of the use of force. To the contrary. For Israel, the deterrent potential of its army—a deterrence that is not limited to nuclear weapons—has long been a crucial element of the state's security. The use of military power itself, therefore, has a symbolic intention, but airstrikes and targeted killings are seen as more powerful arguments than "armed social work" and reconstruction.

This approach has immediate consequences for the military's outreach to the public. One is that the domestic audience is—deliberately—the prime target audience of military spokespersons, not international audiences or the adversary.

Israel is a democracy in an extraordinary conflict with an army in an extraordinary role. This requires an extraordinary explanation effort in the Israeli public, even if that public already knows more about military affairs than the counterparts in other democracies, even in the United States. Another consequence is that the IDF's press office operates, particularly during ongoing operations, in a highly politicized environment where it is very difficult for military spokespersons to maintain a professional officer's nonpolitical position. Israel, in contrast to both the United States and the United Kingdom in the twenty-first century, doesn't do expeditionary warfare: war is very close, not far away. In most conflicts, but particularly during the 2006 Lebanon War, it was therefore easy for journalists to travel to forward-deployed units and get access to military sources without the ministry's press office in control. Israel's relatively small population exacerbates this problem: most defense correspondents have served in and retain extensive personal contacts with the army, and cellphone technology facilitates real-time conversations from news rooms to battalions in the field. In the 2009 operation "Cast Lead" the IDF has learned and applied many lessons. Cellphones and journalists were banned from the battlefield, while new media platforms were embraced, with the IDF opening a YouTube channel to show bomb-camera footage. From a strictly military point of view, the coverage concealed the IDF's weaknesses and highlighted its strengths. Although the coverage in the Arab and non-Israeli media largely highlighted the human costs of the operation in Gaza, Israel was successfully projecting the image of a powerful and determined defense force—an image designed to deter.

INSURGENCY

All insurgencies that face a counterinsurgent with a conventionally superior army share one starting point: attacking the security forces is more costly and dangerous than attacking soft targets, such as civilians and unprotected installations. But violence against civilians is a double-edged sword. On the one hand such attacks undermine the government's legitimacy and the authority of the counterinsurgent forces. Each explosion and each kidnapping makes the argument that the security forces are weak, that their power is limited, and that their patience is eroding. On the other hand civilian casualties make it more difficult for insurgents to argue a good cause. Each civilian casualty also makes the argument to neutral observers that the insurgents disrespect human life, that they are weak, that they are incapable of hitting real military targets, and that they are not worthy of support.

From the militants' perspective, therefore, it is truly an optimal solution to trick the opponent into killing innocents. Civilian casualties inflicted by counterinsurgents combine, from an insurgent's point of view, the best of both worlds: they damage the government's authority without damaging the insurgency's standing. In all cases studied here it was often exceedingly difficult for governmental security forces—for operational and political reasons—to counter insurgent activity with large numbers of ground troops. Counterinsurgents, therefore, habitually fall back on their conventional superiority and use mechanized units, artillery, airpower, and targeted killings. But a large military power differential—the most extreme being modern airpower—is a double-edged sword as well, this time for the counterinsurgent: airpower may minimize risk for ground troops, it may kill insurgents, and it may be politically less costly than sending large numbers of citizens into harm's way. Yet perceived injustice and inadvertent mistakes are bound to provide invaluable propaganda opportunities to irregulars. Recent technological developments and their penetration of even the globe's most remote areas have made it much easier to exploit these opportunities. So it does not come as a surprise—in fact it should have been expected—that all three violent movements studied here have greatly improved their information operations in order to exploit allied mistakes, such as civilian casualties and detainee abuse, and probably engineer events for that purpose.

Of the insurgent groups surveyed here, Hezbollah is in the best position to maximize the benefits of an evolving information environment while dealing with the inevitable challenges. The reasons are numerous. Hezbollah remains a local phenomenon. The party has a strong social base and an established constituency, the Lebanese Shia. More than al-Qaeda and the Taliban, Hezbollah is and has a vast social organization, offering services such as schools, hospitals, and agricultural assistance for large numbers of Lebanese. The Party of God has also established itself as a formidable political force that is more and more integrated into Lebanon's political system. Hezbollah's information activities precipitated and foreshadowed the party's social and political integration process, from simple everyday items to complex programs: the organization's insignia and colors can be found on banners, bracelets, pins, posters, stickers, T-shirts, lighters, key fobs, toys, and other fashion items. The group has the potential to gather massive crowds in the tens of thousands at rallies in Beirut. On the more sophisticated end of the spectrum is al-Manar, a broadly accepted source of entertainment and news with a professional support organization. Since 2000, and most recently during the thirty-four-day war against Israel, Hezbollah has demonstrated remarkable organizational prowess under the most adverse conditions across the entire spectrum of its activities, political, social, military—and in its messaging. Not only did al-Manar continue to operate, it got news out fast. The station succeeded in getting significant visibility in the Israeli news coverage even for extended periods of time during the war. Hezbollah's public and media outreach made an important contribution to the prevailing perception of what Hezbollah boasted was a "divine victory" over the Israel Defense Forces. It shows that even in the twenty-first century, old-fashioned personal methods of public outreach such as community work may be far superior to high-tech approaches.

The Taliban, at first glance, have several things in common with Hezbollah: they are a local movement with stable roots in Afghanistan's tribal communities; they deftly used their own spokespersons and the international press to highlight

the tactical blunders of their enemies; and they are skillfully connecting historical narratives of victimization in order to religiously inspire the resistance against
external aggression. But just as Afghanistan and Lebanon cannot be compared,
the differences between the two movements are overwhelming. Their information operations are a vivid illustration. There are no Taliban toys, there is no
Taliban TV channel, and there is no decent Taliban Web site for a broad audience. Instead the Taliban rely on two main venues: locally on the word-of-mouth,
enhanced by threats and night letters, and internationally on spokesmen who talk
to the press, mostly by cellphone, enhanced by a second-rate Web presence. Yet
these crude methods are working: both locally and globally, the Taliban are successfully fabricating the perception of a movement far more powerful and more
omnipresent than it is in reality. The holy warriors were also getting better at
highlighting blunders and mistakes of U.S. forces and NATO troops.

But the Taliban's challenges are noteworthy as well. The pious Afghan fighters
traditionally have been less pragmatic than those of Hezbollah. The movement is
fractured internally, with the purist Islamists attempting to steer it into one direction and the pragmatists pushing for political consolidation. One of the most difficult stages for any insurgent movement is the transition, or expansion, from a
violent militant group to a politically influential group. It takes a skillful insurgent
leader, a person with solid military skills, sound political instincts, and charisma to
manage such a transition. The Taliban never had such a leader. And it is highly
unlikely that such a figure will emerge and unify the movement. Instead the radicals run the risk of either disintegrating or turning into its former nemesis: the
Taliban are teetering toward becoming a criminal gang financed by drug money,
feared for indiscriminate violence, and protected by parochialism and corruption—
the very curses Mullah Omar once vied to eradicate from Afghanistan. With respect
to their immediate information environment, the Taliban are facing an additional
trial: they are operating in one of the world's fastest growing mobile phone markets.
This development adds an important variable with largely unknown effects into
Central Asia's great game. It is already evident that the Taliban movement, an organization that once banned all entertainment and consumer electronics, is struggling
to come to grips with their country's budding information revolution. The Taliban
do not know how SMS and more widespread Internet access will affect their local
information operations—nor do their opponents understand what twenty-first-century social technology will do to eighteenth-century social structures. More widespread mobile phone and Internet use in Afghanistan is already making it easier for
the Taliban to victimize the population; yet cellphones also are making it easier for
villagers to victimize the Taliban by reporting their whereabouts to the security
forces—with very little risk for themselves.

For al-Qaeda the picture is again rather different. The group successfully
embraced the new media as an operating platform, thus turning itself into a diffuse
movement rather than a coherent entity. Its organizational form, its tactics, and its
operational procedures approximate War 2.0 far more than Hezbollah's or the
Taliban's. From a strategic point of view, however, the Islamist movement—*because*

it approximates War 2.0—stands out in two extremes: it maximizes benefits *and* it maximizes costs. The benefit side has been discussed in detail, both here and in the counterterrorism and counterinsurgency debate: the movement is able to tap into widespread feelings of discontent and humiliation in the Muslim world, it attracts numerous and highly ambitious young individuals, it aptly recruits and runs cells, it generates an impressive strategic debate, it manages to transfer tactical and technological knowledge from one theater to another, and it is impressively nimble and adaptive on the battlefield. Al-Qaeda has developed a partly self-recruiting and highly efficient public relations campaign, with professional video productions, multiple languages, and prompt reactions. But a closer look at al-Qaeda's challenges reveals that the costs of this adaptation are more impressive and more remarkable than the benefits: the movement is so dispersed and decentralized that it has become exceedingly difficult for any leader to exert control, beyond offering mere inspiration. Al-Qaeda overplayed its hand with violence, perhaps as a result of the unbridled zeal of some of its most active self-recruited operatives, both in the Muslim world and in Europe. The movement has become a basket for the world's most frustrated and often the most backward radicals. Therefore its appeal to the broader masses, even considering the peculiarities of humiliated Muslims, will necessarily remain limited. In the information field, the movement does not even have control over who participates and who communicates in its name (in sharp contrast to Hezbollah and to some extent also the Taliban). Al-Suri wanted the jihad to become "the Islamic Nation's battle, and not the struggle of an elite."[14] Yet this is precisely what jihad in the information age is likely to become: the struggle of a small, self-recruited, and self-proclaimed "elite" at the fringes.

WAR 1.0 VERSUS WAR 2.0

Up to now, this book deliberately has not explicitly distinguished between insurgency and terrorism. Yet there are at least two different academic disciplines and professional specializations that draw a clear line between the two: the study of terrorism on the one hand and the study of modern warfare on the other hand. In national security administrations, that differentiation corresponds to counterterrorism agencies on the one side, which are predominantly in the intelligence and law enforcement communities, and military counterinsurgency on the other side. The dividing line, however, has begun to erode in the first decade of the twenty-first century, both in academia and in policy. The "global war on terror" is called "counterinsurgency" on its regional battlefields. And some have proposed to use that terminology on a global scale as well. Yet there is an important but often overlooked distinction. The concepts of terrorism and insurgency implicitly contain a set of assumptions, and these assumptions may guide or misguide analysis and political action. They should be made explicit: terrorism, it is generally understood, has the aim of inculcating fear and intimidating direct opponents as well as third persons; it may have a political, ideological, or religious motivation. Insurgency, by contrast, always has a political objective: the overthrow of established authority or the break-away from constituted government. Terrorism, in other words, is a militant tac-tic whereas insurgency is a political strategy. The latter may, but does not have to, employ the first. This difference has important repercussions both for schol-arship and policy-making. Counterinsurgency implicitly assumes that oppo-nents have a political motivation and that an adversarial movement is gaining—or at least has the potential to gain—popular appeal, reach a critical mass, and become a political force. A counterinsurgency approach is therefore susceptible to overestimating the enemy.

Irregular warfare may be a more concise and less warped way of referring to the phenomenon. Irregular forces, as opposed to regular armies, favor indirect and asymmetric approaches, though they may employ a broad range of military and political means to attack their adversary's power, influence, and will. They may have political or other objectives. Yet one feature is stable: in irregular con-flicts, public perceptions of violent action are by far more important than in con-ventional military conflicts. For Islamic extremists in Iraq, in Afghanistan, in North Africa, across the Middle East and Central Asia, but also in Europe, per-ceptions are a key driver of political violence. Views and interpretations trans-late into collective and individual motivations and therefore contribute to a discomforting equilibrium of confrontation: because foreign forces are stationed in Muslim lands, a number of outraged resistance fighters and defenders of the faith will decide to take action against what they see as infidel occupiers and col-onizers. Conversely Western states feel compelled to react militarily to what they see as ruthless terrorists who threaten international and domestic security. Two elements may have a moderating effect on this escalation: a sophisticated military strategy that successfully minimizes civilian casualties and, if possible, increases local security and living standards; and, paradoxically at first glance, an overly violent and brutal approach by the resistance, as such tactics alienate more and more people, including potential recruits, from the militants' cause.

For some violent groups, however, the new media change the rules of the game. Even if both moderating effects coincide, as they did locally for instance in al-Anbar province in Iraq in late 2006 and 2007, the desired effect may still not be achieved globally. An equilibrium that keeps the circulation system of global jihad pumping will, with a high likelihood, remain functional. In other words, measures to increase moderation regionally, which is what successful counterin-surgency is, are highly unlikely to end global terrorism. Islamism connects a robust ideological cause to frustrated fringe groups in a huge mass of potential supporters.[15] Telecommunication technology, we argued in this book, is one addi-tional variable that has affected the conditions of this equilibrium. Extremists will continue to find grievances, bellicose know-how, money, and each other online. For individuals, the barrier of entry into the business of terrorism will remain lower than it used to be in the past, while for groups the terminal break-ing point will be more difficult to reach.

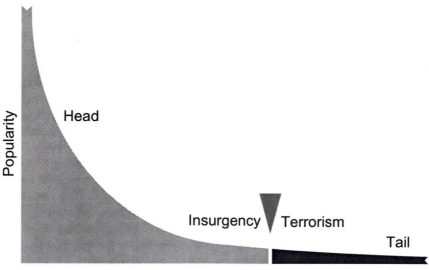

Figure 1   The Long Tail

A set of ideas that were devised to understand business in the information age also help to understand political violence and radical extremism in the information age. Chris Anderson of *Wired* magazine developed the concept of the "Long Tail" to fathom that in the new business environment the future of commerce was "selling less of more." He illustrated his argument with companies such as Amazon, Netflix, and Apple's iTunes: these firms made profit out of selling small numbers of previously hard-to-find items to a large number of customers, instead of selling big volumes of a low number of popular products. The high-volume head of the traditional demand curve of course remained profitable. But the flat tail of the same curve, the low-volume end, now became lucrative as well, driven by increased efficiencies in distribution, manufacturing, and marketing. "Suddenly, popularity no longer has a monopoly on profitability," Anderson wrote.[16] A similar logic applies to ideologically and politically driven niche violence: it doesn't require a high-volume to survive and endure over time—that is, a large popular following attracted by a broadly appealing cause. Instead extremists can bring to bear the curve's low-volume end—that is, relatively small numbers of highly-motivated, partly self-recruited, entrepreneurial, geographically dispersed, and diverse radicals, all subscribing to a shared extreme cause without broader popular appeal. New media have popularized the means of production, shrunk the distribution costs, and improved the connection of supply and demand for extreme political, religious, or ideological positions, thus making niche terrorism viable. As a result, the critical mass of people necessary to pass the threshold to an enduring terrorist movement has shrunk. Suddenly, popularity no longer has a monopoly on feasibility. Popular support is more and more disconnected from resilience. The effect of this development is somewhat paradoxical.

The new media drive a wedge between terrorism and insurgency: the critical mass necessary to surpass the threshold for a political insurgent movement has not shrunk. Insurgents, even when they started out as terrorists, have traditionally tried, at some stage of their development, to present their cause in a way that attracted followers at the head-end of the popular demand curve, or even moved more supporters toward that end. Insurgencies tried to win over the mainstream population to become a more legitimate political force. The ultimate objective for insurgents was to assume power or realize a political agenda, an immutable logic that remains true of successful insurgency in the information age. But just the opposite applies to global jihadi terrorism: by approximating War 2.0, modern terrorist movements inadvertently move toward the far and flat end of the curve's tail, away from popular appeal and away from the possibility of consolidating and assuming political power. And here lies the paradox that characterizes War 2.0: more popularly accessible justifications for violence and technical know-how make less popular causes viable. The "democratization" of the distribution and production of ideology and tactics, in other words, uplifts the most fervently antidemocratic fringe groups.

The consequences of this new dynamic are as overlooked as they are overpowering: Web-enhanced organizational setups boost terrorism but bridle insurgency. The new media, in conjunction with ideology, change political extremism into precisely the opposite of "population-centric." For transnational terrorist groups, the future will likely be "recruiting less of more," to paraphrase Anderson. The recruitment market for terrorists is now global. If a movement such as al-Qaeda recruits a small number of operatives in a large number of countries, it can still manage to survive and do harm. But it will not be able to mature into a global insurgency. New technologies, and new ideologies, have recalibrated an old equilibrium of armed conflict: it is now easier for insurgents and terrorists to enter the game. But at the same time it is more difficult for War 2.0–approximating irregulars to evolve into a political movement and to assume power, because of the internal weaknesses of this approach, because of a lack of popular support, and because their War 1.0–resembling conventional and democratic opponents are far too powerful—militarily, economically, culturally, and politically. Modern-day Islamic extremists, in other words, cannot win—and they probably cannot be defeated. The global jihad, therefore, is self-limiting.[17] It may not be possible to terminate the phenomenon at all in the foreseeable future; it is only possible to manage its costs. This insight informs our recommendations.

RECOMMENDATIONS

Governments in NATO countries should redefine the political purpose of local campaigns that were launched initially to eradicate global terrorism. It is unlikely that global Islamic terrorism can be eliminated entirely. The consequences are wide-ranging.

It seems equally unlikely that the idealistic, ambitious, and costly strategy of transforming entire societies into different systems—perhaps even democracies—within mere years or decades will succeed. But even if "nation building" would succeed, and Afghanistan could be stabilized, global terrorism would most likely be weakened, not terminated.

A cost-minimization strategy should be explored. If the attempt to occupy, transform, and "reconstruct" large swathes of previously ungoverned or badly governed land in Afghanistan, Iraq, and elsewhere does not bring the desired results, alternatives should be explored. If steering toward the hearts-and-minds aspect of War 2.0 doesn't bring the desired results for the intervening governments over the long term, some aspects of War 1.0 might have to be reconsidered: unclear political objectives could be replaced by a more clearly defined military mission: neutralizing emerging terrorist targets would require fewer ground troops and, if done in an appropriate way, might cause less alienation in theater and at home. But unpleasant political and military compromises might be necessary. Yet, depending on the particular case, such a strategy could turn out to be the most realistic one possible.

Counterinsurgency experts should reconsider the role of the population. It has become accepted wisdom of the strategic debate in the first decade of the twenty-first century that irregular war is "population-centric." Such an assumption may be adequate in local settings, such as in Lebanon, and to a certain extent in Iraq. It may not be true for global jihadism. Only a small segment of what is commonly described as al-Qaeda is "population-centric." Counterinsurgency methods, therefore, may be an inadequate instrument against global terrorism.

The phrase "war on terror" should be dropped. Terminologies have political consequences. From a communication point of view, it is very much in the interest of jihadists to lump various groups together into one artificial category, Islamic fundamentalists or just "terrorists." As a result of such a lack of differentiation, the power and the coherence of the jihadi movement is easily overestimated, fear of "al-Qaeda" is blown out of proportion, and inappropriately strong countermeasures are adopted. The effect may be that the counterinsurgent's legitimacy is undermined and that the extremists' appeal is bolstered.

Disaggregate. All three groups studied in the second half of this book are usually named as enemies in the "war on terror." The imperative, to the contrary, should be to disaggregate and to differentiate. There are, we tried to make clear, vast differences between Hezbollah, the Taliban, and al-Qaeda. Even within these groups differences abound: the Taliban themselves are a diverse cluster, with local subgroups and diverging tribal interests. Not all Taliban put a jihadi agenda first, but instead local or economic interests; they therefore should not be treated as a unitary actor. Nor should Hezbollah or al-Qaeda be treated as monolithic. The vital interest of the counterinsurgent is to highlight and exploit disparities, not to ignore them or help remove them.

General Web trends should be closely watched. It should be a prime objective of the world's armed forces to avoid groupthink and misguided concepts, such as the

U.S. Air Force's confusion with respect to "cyberwar." The Internet affects most forms of social and business interaction, far beyond the confines of the IT industry: travel, literature, the creative arts, project management, research and development, supply chains, retail, and, of course journalism. Almost every industry is struggling to understand and use the new tools and trends. The learning and adaptation speed varies greatly across industries, and it does not come as a surprise that governments and armies tend to be on the slower end of that spectrum. Governments should therefore try to avoid reinventing the wheel or, even worse, reinventing something that was already proven wrong.

New technologies should not be overrated. New technologies, particularly those with a social utility or fast video support, may mesmerize novices. The Dot-com bubble in the IT industry and on the technology markets as well as the hype for military "transformation" in the defense establishments during the late 1990s and early 2000s highlight this risk. So it seems prudent to be wary. Just as the fog of war will not be lit, mainstream journalism will not be superseded by blogs, and the use of the Web for jihad has important limits.

Conversely, the Web and mobile phones should not be underestimated. New technologies affect social interaction in the developed world. The same technologies are increasingly being marketed and spread to regions and countries that never had access to a free press or a vibrant book market, let alone the Internet. How this will affect tribal communities and traditional societies is largely unknown—a fact that will add an unpredictable new aspect to irregular conflict in the future, particularly from the insurgent's point of view.

User-driven initiatives and technologies should be supported internally. Even in hierarchical organizations, the social interactive media can be constructively used to update organizational routines. Examples are CompanyCommand.com, a protected community Web site for U.S. Army captains; Intellipedia, a classified intelligence-wiki used across the U.S. government; platforms such as The Small Wars Journal that enhance expert debates; collective blogs such as ARRSE that foster a community spirit; and even individual milblogs on off-the-shelf blogging platforms. The principles embodied in blogging (freedom of expression, democratic involvement, debate) are the same principles Western armies are purportedly sent fighting for. Supporting such initiatives, for many armed forces, will involve a significant change in organizational culture: decision authority needs to be delegated, deep-seated reflexes for secrecy need to be overcome (particularly in the largest European countries), the merits of—metaphorically speaking—open-source collaboration have to be recognized, and trust sometimes has to replace an order.

Declassification procedures should be revised. The speed of PR responses to tactical events tends to be too slow. Declassification procedures often stand in the way of getting information out quickly, made worse by any military culture's tendency to ask superiors for permission in order to protect oneself against potential negative consequences. Most video material, imagery, and written reports get stamped classified in a standard operating routine. Declassification authority and a general attitude to routinely classifying material should be reconsidered, for instance, by shifting the default question from "why unclassify?" to "why classify?"

Military public affairs should be upgraded in ministries of defense. Senior officers, not civil servants, are a better choice for the heads of communication units, even in civilian headquarters. This is so for at least five reasons: on all military questions, generals have more credibility with the press and the public; they add critical value to the career field of media operations inside the officer corps; they have better and more up-to-date knowledge and insights on all things military; they have better access to senior commanders; they may have clout among other officers; and they therefore can access the right information faster than a civilian would be able to do. If a civilian should be the public face, it should be considered to have a civilian work for a senior general or to have a double-headed structure.

Service competition should be managed constructively. The different armed services will compete for media visibility and a better public image; this has long been a fact of military life. Civilian spokespersons and their staffs, such as in Britain or in Israel, cannot and should not avoid this competition. Within limits, the competition between the military services may be healthy mainly for three reasons: it highlights the significance of media operations to senior officers, it remedies complacency in the face of a fast-changing environment, and it creates an incentive for the services to experiment and innovate in public affairs.

A culture of error tolerance should be fostered. In media affairs, mistakes are bound to happen. If one out of ten messages backfires, nine were successful. If restriction and micromanagement succeeded in avoiding that one mistake, there's a high chance that it also avoided the nine successful operations. It is often better to have a message out promptly instead of polished.

Chronology

1 January 2009	Worldwide mobile phone usage is estimated at 4 billion, roughly double the number of TV sets worldwide. IBM projects that number to grow to 5.8 billion by 2013. The fastest-growing segment of the mobile phone market consists of Internet-capable smartphones.
	More than 1.5 billion people have Internet access.
27 December 2008	Israel launches operation "Cast Lead" against Hamas in Gaza. All sides employ a wide range of Web 2.0 platforms to cover the ongoing operations, while the press is largely blocked from reporting.
1 January 2008	The global number of instant messaging accounts is estimated at 1 billion (the five largest services are Skype, QQ, Windows Live Messenger, AIM, and Jabber).
27 December 2007	Benazir Bhutto, a Pakistani politician, is killed in a terrorist attack in Rawalpindi, Pakistan.
29 November 2007	3.3 billion mobile phone users are registered worldwide, a number equivalent to half the global population.
1 November 2007	ASUS launches Eee PC, a robust low-cost notebook, with solid state memory and a low energy consumption (its initial cost was $399).
14 May 2007	The Pentagon bans a number of popular interactive Web sites on its computers, including YouTube and MySpace.
7 March 2007	MNF-Iraq opens YouTube channel.
10 December 2006	An American oil company is attacked in Bouchaoui, Algeria. The video of the attack shows that Google Earth was used to prepare the operation.
11 September 2006	Ayman al-Zawahiri announces in a video the affiliation of the Algerian Groupe Salafiste pour la Prédication et le Combat (GSPC) to al-Qaeda.

11 September 2006	Facebook opens its networking service to the general public.
12 July 2006	Israel launches the thirty-three-day 2006 Lebanon War against Hezbollah. The IDF clumsily manages the PR side of the war.
7 June 2006	Abu Musab al-Zarqawi is killed in a U.S. Air Force strike in Iraq.
September 2005	2 billion mobile phone users are registered worldwide.
7 July 2005	Four suicide bombers kill fifty-two commuters in the London Tube Bombings, 700 people are injured.
15 February 2005	YouTube is launched in the United States.
7 May 2004	Nicholas Berg is killed in Iraq. His beheading is widely distributed on the Internet.
28 April 2004	The first pictures of abuses of prisoners in Abu Ghraib are broadcast on CBS.
11 March 2004	The Madrid Train bombings kill 191 people and wound 1,755, three days before Spain's general elections.
August 2003	Skype is released as a first public beta version.
20 March 2003	A U.S.-led coalition invades Iraq.
3 March 2003	Al-Arabiya, an Arabic news channel, is launched by the Saudi-controlled pan-Arab satellite TV pioneer MBC.
April 2002	1 billion mobile phone users are registered worldwide.
23 January 2002	Daniel Pearl, a journalist, is abducted in Karachi, Pakistan. He is killed a few days later. A video of his assassination is posted on the web.
7 October 2001	The United States launches a "war on terrorism" in Afghanistan.
11 September 2001	Al-Qaeda attacks the United States.
15 January 2001	Wikipedia is launched.
12 October 2000	Seventeen American sailors die in the USS Cole bombing in the Yemeni port of Aden.
10 March 2000	The Dot-com bubble is at its height, with the NASDAQ peaking at 5132.52.
23 August 1999	Blogger, one of the earliest blog publishing tools, is launched by Pyra Labs.
24 March 1999	NATO's campaign against Serbia in the Kosovo War begins.
9 October 1998	U.S. Department of Defense publishes its first Joint Doctrine on Information Operations, JP3-13.
7 August 1998	U.S. Embassy bombings kill 220 people in simultaneous explosions in Dar es Salaam, Tanzania, and Nairobi. Osama bin Laden becomes a household name in the Muslim world and the West.
23 February 1998	Al-Qaeda, as the World Islamic Front, publishes its manifesto "Jihad against Jews and Crusaders."
15 September 1997	Google.com is registered as a domain, one week after Google, Inc. was founded in Menlo Park, California.
1 November 1996	The satellite channel al-Jazeera is launched by the emirate of Qatar.

4 October 1996	The U.S. Department of Defense creates the Defense Science Board Task Force on Information Warfare.
August 1996	Al-Qaeda publishes its "Declaration of War on the United States." It is accessible at http://www.yaislah.org.
4 July 1996	Hotmail, the first Web-based e-mail service opens (not yet owned by Microsoft).
25 June 1996	The Khobar Towers bombings in Saudi Arabia, executed by Hezbollah Al-Hijaz (Party of God in the Hijaz), kill nineteen U.S. servicemen.
3 September 1995	eBay is founded in San Jose, California.
13 October 1994	The world's first widely used Web browser, Netscape Navigator, is released. The Pentagon's Web site, DefenseLink.mil, goes online the same month.
22 April 1993	Mosaic 1.0, the world's first popular Web browser, is released at the National Center for Supercomputing Applications (NCSA).
26 February 1993	World Trade Center bombing: A 1,500-lb (680-kg) car bomb fails to fell the World Trade Center's North Tower in New York City. Al-Qaeda is behind the attack.
21 December 1992	DoD Directive TS3600.1 on Information Warfare is published internally as a top secret document, hampering open discussion from the outset.
March 1991	The WorldWideWeb application, an early browser, is released at CERN, a lab in Switzerland.
28 February 1991	A U.S.-led coalition begins liberating Kuwait after Iraq attacked and occupied the country.
24 November 1989	Abdallah Azzam, a founding figure of modern jihad, is killed in an explosion in Peshawar, Pakistan.
15 February 1989	The defeated Soviet Union ends its withdrawal from Afghanistan.
11 August 1988	Osama bin Laden founds al-Qaeda in Peshawar, Pakistan.
20 November 1985	Microsoft releases its first retail version of Microsoft Windows.
22 January 1984	Apple launches the Macintosh, the first commercially viable personal computer.
1 June 1980	The Cable News Network, CNN, is launched by Ted Turner.
25 December 1979	The Soviet Union's 40th Army invades Afghanistan.
30 April 1975	The Vietnam War ends.
5 December 1969	The initial four-node ARPANET, a precursor of the Internet, is established.

Abbreviations

3G	Third Generation
ABC	American Broadcasting Company
AIVD	Algemene Inlichtingen- en Veiligheidsdienst [Dutch General Intelligence and Security Service]
AO	area of operations
AP	Associated Press
ARPA	Advanced Research Projects Agency
ARPANET	Advanced Research Projects Agency Network
ARRSE	Army Rumour Service
ASD(PA)	Assistant Secretary of Defense for Public Affairs
BAFF	British Armed Forces Federation
BBC	British Broadcasting Corporation
BFT	Blue Force Tracker
BKA	Bundeskriminalamt [German Federal Crime Office]
BMI	Bundesministerium des Innern [Interior Ministry in Germany or Austria]
CALL	Center for Army Lessons Learned
CBS	Columbia Broadcasting System
CD	Compact Disc
CERN	European Organization for Nuclear Research
CIA	Central Intelligence Agency
CJSOTF - A	Combined Joint Special Operations Task Force - Afghanistan
CNN	Cable News Network
COIN	Counterinsurgency
CP	Command post
CPJ	Committee to Protect Journalists
CRIF	Conseil Représentatif des Institutions Juives de France

D Def PR	Directorate for Defence Public Relations
D News	Directorate for News
DARPA	Defense Advanced Research Projects Agency
DASD(JC)	Deputy Assistant Secretary of Defense for Joint Communications
DCC	Director of Corporate Communications
DCP	Directorate for Communication and Planning
DFID	Department for International Development
DGCC	Directorate General for Corporate Communications
DGMC	Directorate General Media and Communications
DGSE	Direction Générale de la Sécurité Extérieure [Directorate-General for External Security]
DISA	Defense Information Systems Agency
DMOC	Defence Media Operations Centre
DoD	Department of Defense
DVD	Digital Versatile Disc/Digital Video Disc
ETA	Euskadi Ta Askatasuna [Basque Homeland and Freedom]
EU	European Union
FCO	Foreign and Commonwealth Office
FLN	Front de Libération National [National Liberation Front]
FM 3-0	Field Manual 3-0
FM 3-24	Field Manual 3-24
FOB	Forward Operating Base
GBU-31	Guided Bombing Unit 31
GDP	Gross Domestic Product
GIA	Groupe Islamique Armé [Armed Islamic Group]
GPO	Government Press Office
GPS	Global Positioning System
GSM	Global System for Mobile Communications
GZ	Green Zone
HMMWV	High Mobility Multipurpose Wheeled Vehicle
HMS	His/Her Majesty's Ship
IAF	Israeli Air Force
IBM	International Business Machines Corporation
ICCC	International Computer Communication Conference
ID	Identification
IDF	Israel Defense Forces
IED	Improvised Explosive Device
IJU	Islamic Jihad Union
IM	Instant Messaging
IO	Information Operation
IP	Internet Protocol
IRA	Irish Republican Army
ISAF	International Security Assistance Force
ISI	Inter-Services Intelligence (Pakistan)
IT	Information Technology
JIOWC	Joint Information Operations Warfare Command

JOA	Joint Operational Area
JSTARS	Joint Surveillance Target Attack Radar System
LAN	Local Area Network
LIFG	Libyan Islamic Fighting Group
MBC	Middle East Broadcasting Center
MI5	Military Intelligence, Section 5 (UK)
MIT	Massachusetts Institute of Technology
MNF-I	Multi-National Force–Iraq
MoD	Ministry of Defence
NASDAQ	National Association of Securities Dealers Automated Quotations
NATO	North Atlantic Treaty Organization
NBC	National Broadcasting Company
NCO	Non-commissioned Officer
NCSA	National Center for Supercomputing Applications
NGO	Nongovernmental Organization
NIE	National Intelligence Estimate
NPR	National Public Radio
OODA Loop	Observe, Orient, Decide, and Act Loop
OOTW	Operations Other Than War
OPSEC	Operations Security
P4	"Personal For" message
PA	Public Affairs
PAO	Public Affairs Officer
PC	Personal Computer
PDA	Personal Digital Assistant
PET	Politiets Efterretningstjeneste [Danish Security and Intelligence Services]
PhD	Doctor of Philosophy
PKK	Kurdistan Workers' Party
PR	Public Relations
PSYOP	Psychological Operation
Q&A	Questions and Answers
QDR	Quadrennial Defense Review
R&D	Research & Development
RPG	Rocket-propelled Grenade
RUF	Revolutionary United Front
SAS	Special Air Service
SC	Strategic Communication
SCIG	Strategic Communication Integration Group
SECDEF	United States Secretary of Defense
SIPR	Secret Internet Protocol Router
SIPRNET	Secret Internet Protocol Router network
SMS	Short Message Service
SSG	Staff Sergeant
STD	Sexually Transmitted Disease
TATP	Tricycloacetone Triperoxide

TBS	The Basic School
TCP/IP	Transmission Control Protocol/Internet Protocol
TNT	Trinitrotoluene
TRADOC	Training and Doctrine Command
TTPs	Tactics, Technics and Procedures
TV	Television
UAV	Unmanned Aerial Vehicles
UK	United Kingdom
UN	United Nations
UNDCP	United Nations International Drug Control Program
UNIFIL	United Nations Interim Force in Lebanon
UNRWA	United Nations Relief and Works Agency for Palestine Refugees in the Near East
U.S.	United States
USS	United States ship
USSF	United States Special Forces
VoIP	Voice over Internet Protocol

Notes

Introduction, pages 1–8

1. "Modern," for the purposes of this book, refers to the historical period from the Industrial Revolution—or more relevant here, the French Revolution—to the present.

2. The "instruments of national power," the U.S. military's top publication says, are "diplomatic, informational, military, and economic." Department of Defense, *Dictionary of Military and Associated Terms*, JP 1-02, 2007, p. x.

3. FM 3-0, p. viii.

4. Daniel Kimmage and Kathleen Ridolfo, "Iraqi Insurgent Media," *RFE/RL Special Report*, 2007.

5. Henry G. Gole, "Don't Kill the Messenger: Vietnam War Reporting in Context," *Parameters*, Winter 1996, p. 152.

6. Anton A. Huurdeman, *The Worldwide History of Telecommunications*, New York: Wiley, 2003, p. 3.

7. Jack London, *The Shrinkage of the Planet*, New York: Mondial, 1910, p. 97.

8. Huurdeman, *The Worldwide History of Telecommunications*, p. 3.

9. Clive Thompson, "Brave New World of Digital Intimacy," *The New York Times Magazine*, 7 September 2008.

10. Piers Robinson, "The CNN Effect: Can the News Media Drive Foreign Policy?" *Review of International Studies*, 25, 1999, 301–9; Frank J. Stech, "Winning CNN Wars," *Parameters*, Autumn 1994, 37–56; Margaret Belknap, "The CNN Effect: Strategic Enabler or Operational Risk?" *Parameters*, 3, 2002, pp. 100–114.

11. Vernon Loeb, "'Guerilla' War Acknowledged," *Washington Post*, 17 July 2003, p. A1.

12. His much-quoted report from Iraq was initially published at http://smallwarsjournal.com/blog/2007/06/understanding-current-operatio/.

13. Nadya Labi, "Jihad 2.0," *The Atlantic Monthly*, July/August 2006.

14. Dialogue quoted in "A World Wide Web of Terror," *The Economist*, 12 July 2007. On Tsouli see also Marc Sageman, *Leaderless Jihad*, Philadelphia: University of Pennsylvania Press, 2008, pp. 119–20.

15. Marc Prensky, "Listen to the Natives," *Educational Leadership*, 63, 4, 2005, pp. 8–13.

16. Marc Leibovich, "McCain: The Analog Candidate," *The New York Times*, 3 August 2008, http://www.nytimes.com/2008/08/03/weekinreview/03leibovich.html, 8 January 2009.

17. See also John Palfrey and Urs Gasser, *Born Digital: Understanding the First Generation of Digital Natives*, New York: Basic Books, 2008.

18. John Nagl, interview (with T. Rid), 17 March 2008.

19. Andrew Tilghman, "The Army's Other Crisis. Why the Best and the Brightest Young Officers are Leaving," *The Washington Monthly*, 2007, vol. 39, 12, pp. 44–53.

20. Clausewitz wrote, in German: "[E]s ist ihre [der Theorie] Pflicht, die absolute Gestalt des Krieges obenan zu stellen und sie als einen allgemeinen Richtpunkt [general gauge] zu brauchen." Author's translation: "It is the obligation of theory to use the absolute form of war as a general gauge." See Carl von Clausewitz, *Vom Kriege*, Berlin: Ullstein, 1832 (1980), p. 654. On Clausewitz and German Idealism see Peter Paret, *Clausewitz and the State*, Princeton: Princeton University Press, 2007 (1976), especially pp. 380–81; Lennart Souchon, *Romantik, Deutscher Idealismus, Hegel und Clausewitz*, Hamburg: Führungsakademie der Bundeswehr, 2007.

21. "Idealtypus" was Weber's expression. He did not use the term "friction." Max Weber, *Wirtschaft und Gesellschaft*, Tübingen: Mohr Siebeck, 1922 (1977), p. 10. On the comparison, see Christopher Daase, "Clausewitz in the Twenty-First Century," in Hew Strachan and Andreas Herberg-Rothe (eds.), *Clausewitz in the Twenty-First Century*, pp. 182–95, Oxford: Oxford University Press, 2007, especially pp. 185–86.

Chapter 1

1. One of the best histories of war reporting is Phillip Knightley, *The First Casualty. From the Crimea to Vietnam: The War Correspondent as Hero, Propagandist and Myth Maker*, New York: Harcourt Brace Jovanovich, 1975. See also Susan L. Carruthers, *The Media at War*, New York: St. Martin's Press, 2000; Frank Aukofer and William P. Lawrence, *America's Team, the Odd Couple: A Report on the Relationship between the Military and the Media*, Nashville: The Freedom Forum First Amendment Center, 1995; Daniel C. Hallin, *The 'Uncensored War.' The Media and Vietnam*, Oxford: Oxford University Press, 1986; John J. Fialka, *Hotel Warriors. Covering the Gulf War*, Baltimore: Johns Hopkins University Press, 1991; William M. Hammond, *Public Affairs: The Military and the Media, 1962–1968*, Washington: Center of Military History, 1988; William M. Hammond, *Public Affairs: The Military and the Media, 1968–1973*, Honolulu: University Press of the Pacific, 2002; Thomas Rid, *War and Media Operations. The U.S. Military and the Press from Vietnam to Iraq*, London: Routledge, 2007. For armies in the information age, see Alvin Toffler and Heidi Toffler, *War and Anti-War*, New York: Little, Brown and Company, 1993; John Arquilla and David Ronfeldt, *In Athena's Camp: Preparing for Conflict in the Information Age*, Santa Monica: Rand, 1997; Thomas X. Hammes, *The Sling and the Stone: On War in the 21st Century*, Osceola, WI: Zenith Press, 2006, and specifically the debate on military "transformation"; a good critique is Williamson Murray, "Clausewitz out, Computer in. Military Culture and Technological Hubris," *The National Interest*, vol. 48, Summer, 1997, pp. 57–64; a good introduction to war blogs is John Hockenberry, "The Blogs of War," *Wired* 13 August 2005.

2. On the history of telecommunications, see George P. Oslin, *The Story of Telecommunications*, Macon, GA: Mercer University Press, 1992; Anton A. Huurdeman, *The Worldwide History of Telecommunications*, New York: Wiley, 2003.

3. Peter Drucker, "Beyond the Information Revolution," *The Atlantic*, October, 1999.

4. U.S. Department of Defense, *Joint Doctrine for Information Operations*, JP 3-13, 2006.

5. Conseil du Département de la Moselle, "Proclamation des Représentans du Peuple près l'armée de la Moselle," Metz: Antoine & fils, 23 September 1793, p. 1.

6. Incidentally it helped trigger one of Europe's most violent insurrections in the Vendée. Peter Paret, *Internal War and Pacification: the Vendée, 1789–96*, Princeton: Princeton University Press, 1961.

7. Jeremy M. Norman, *From Gutenberg to the Internet: A Sourcebook on the History of Information Technology*, Novato, CA: Historyofscience.com, 2005, p. 173; Gerard J. Holzmann and Björn Pehrson, *The Early History of Data Networks*, Washington: IEEE Computer Society Press, 1995, p. 64. An excellent history is Huurdeman, *The Worldwide History of Telecommunications*, p. 24.

8. Ignace Urbain Jean Chappe, *Histoire de la télégraphie*, Paris: Chez l'auteur, 1824, p. 130. On optical telegraphs, see Alexander J. Field, "French Optical Telegraphy, 1793–1855: Hardware, Software, Administration," *Technology and Culture*, vol. 35, 2, 1994, pp. 315–47; Duane Koenig, "Telegraphs and Telegrams in Revolutionary France," *The Scientific Monthly*, vol. 59, 6, 1944, pp. 431–37.

9. Chappe, *Histoire de la télégraphie*, pp. 129–31.

10. Quoted in Norman, *From Gutenberg to the Internet: A Sourcebook on the History of Information Technology*, p. 3.

11. "Die Leitung der grossen Armeen ist durch den Telegraphen ungemein erleichtert." Albrecht von Boguslawski, *Der kleine Krieg und seine Bedeutung für die Gegenwart*, Berlin: Friedrich Luckhardt, 1881, p. 17.

12. Dennis Showalter, "Soldiers into Postmasters? The Electric Telegraph as an Instrument of Command in the Prussian Army," *Military Affairs*, vol. 37, 2, 1973, pp. 48–52, p. x.

13. Helmuth von Moltke, *Militärische Werke*, ed. Großer Generalstab, *Kriegsgeschichtliche Abteilung I* (13 vols.), Berlin: E. S. Mittler (1892–1912), 3. Abt., Kriegsgeschichtliche Arbeiten, III, 11.

14. R. Smith, *The Utility of Force: The Art of War in the Modern World*, Harlow, Essex, UK: Allen Lane, 2005, p. 70.

15. The anecdote comes from Boguslawski, *Der kleine Krieg und seine Bedeutung für die Gegenwart*, p.21–22, footnote.

16. Huurdeman, *The Worldwide History of Telecommunications*, p. 100; Oslin, *The Story of Telecommunications*, p. 112.

17. Robert V. Bruce, *Bell*, Ithaca: Cornell University Press, 1990, p. 181.

18. Bell's specification is reproduced in George Bartlett Prescott, *The Speaking Telephone, Talking Phonograph, and Other Novelties*, New York: D. Appleton & Company, 1878, p. 205 following.

19. Annual Reports of the War Department for the Fiscal Year Ended June 30, 1901, Washington: Government Printing Office, 1901, p. 1009.

20. T. E. Lawrence, *Seven Pillars of Wisdom*, London: Bernard Shaw, 1926, p. 620.

21. Ibid., p. 208.

22. Hew Strachan, *The First World War*, Oxford: Oxford University Press, 2001, pp. 231–34.

23. Ibid., p. 233.

24. Peter Paret (ed.) *Makers of Modern Strategy: From Machiavelli to the Nuclear Age*, Oxford: Clarendon Press, 1990, p. 314.

25. William R. Blair, "Army Radio in Peace and War," *Annals of the American Academy of Political and Social Science*, vol. 142, March, 1929, pp. 86–89, p. 86.

26. Ibid., p. 87.

27. Dean Juniper, "The First World War and Radio Development," *History Today,* vol. 54, 5, 2004, pp. 32–38, p. 36.

28. Martin Gilbert, *The First World War: A Complete History,* London: Macmillan, 2004, pp. 111, 165, 431.

29. John Keegan, *The First World War,* New York: A. Knopf, 1999, p. 48.

30. Juniper, "The First World War and Radio Development," p. 36.

31. Alistair Horne, *A Savage War of Peace. Algeria 1954–1962,* New York: NYRB Classics, 1977 (2006), p. 85. For a general history of propaganda, see Philip M. Taylor, *Munitions of the Mind,* Manchester: Manchester University Press, 2003. For a specific analysis on the media in small wars (mainly from the government's point of view), see Susan L. Carruthers, *Winning Hearts and Minds: British Governments, the Media and Colonial Counter-Insurgency 1944–1960,* Leicester: Leicester University Press, 1995.

32. Juniper, "The First World War and Radio Development"; Blair, "Army Radio in Peace and War."

33. Amrom H. Katz, *Some Notes on the History of Aerial Reconnaissance (Part 1),* Santa Monica: RAND Corporation, 1966, pp. 8–13; Air Material Command, *Reconnaissance Aircraft and Aerial Photographic Equipment 1915–1945,* Wright Field, OH: Historical Division, 1946.

34. Herbert E. Ives, *Airplane Photography,* Philadelphia: J. B. Lippincott, 1920, p. 16.

35. Ibid., p. 16.

36. "Airborne Television," *Science News Letter,* vol. 49, 30 March 1946, pp. 195–96.

37. Constance Babington-Smith, *Air Spy. The Story of Photo-Intelligence in World War II,* New York: Harper, 1957.

38. A. Abramson, *The History of Television, 1942 to 2000,* Jefferson, NC: McFarland & Co. Inc. Pub., 2003, pp. 3–11.

39. "Airborne Television," p. 195.

40. Abramson, *The History of Television,* p. 18.

41. In fact the expression "battle for the hearts and minds" originated in that war. Anthony Short, *The Communist Insurrection in Malaya, 1948–1960,* New York: Crane, Russak, and Co., 1975, p. 416.

42. Yves Courrière, *La guerre d'Algérie,* Paris: Fayard, 2001.

43. For a more detailed treatment, see Peter Braestrup, *Big Story: How the American Press and Television Reported and Interpreted the Crisis of Tet 1968 in Vietnam and Washington,* Novato, CA: Presidio, 1994.

44. Don Oberdorfer, *Tet!* New York: Garden City, 1971, p. 105.

45. Colin L. Powell and Joseph E. Persico, *My American Journey,* New York: Random House, 1995, p. 120.

46. Walter Cronkite, quoted in Oberdorfer, *Tet!* p. 158.

47. Walter Cronkite, on CBS News Special, 27 February 1968, ibid., pp. 250–51.

48. Lyndon B. Johnson, quoted in Johanna Neuman, *Lights, Camera, War,* New York: St. Martin's Press, 1996, p. 179.

49. Tin Bui, *Following Ho Chi Minh: Memoirs of a North Vietnamese Colonel,* translated by J. Strowe and D. Van, Honolulu: University of Hawaii Press, 1995, p. 62.

50. Tin Bui, "How North Vietnam Won the War," *The Wall Street Journal,* 3 August 1995, p. A8.

51. In early 2008, the British military had 7,800 forces in Afghanistan and 4,100 troops in Iraq. For more details on Northern Ireland see the chapter on the United Kingdom.

52. Mike Jackson, *Operation Banner,* vol. Army Code 71842, London: British Army, 2006, pp. 2–7.

53. Ibid., pp. 2–8.

54. David B. Stockwell, *Press Coverage in Somalia: A Case for Media Relations to be a Principle of Military Operations Other Than War,* Master's Thesis, Ft. Meade, MD: Defense Information School, Issue 1995, p. 21; Nik Gowing, *Real Time Television Coverage of Armed Conflicts and Diplomatic Crises: Does it Pressure or Distort Foreign Policy Decisions?,* Working Paper, Boston: The Shorenstein Center, Issue 1994, p. 48.

55. Information as given by Stockwell, who interviewed Hassan in October 2003, Stockwell, *Press Coverage in Somalia,* Issue, p. 21.

56. Phil Gramm, quoted in Neuman, *Lights, Camera, War,* p. 14.

57. John McCain, quoted in Bill Clinton, *My Life,* London: Random House, 2004, p. 551.

58. Anthony Lake, quoted in Gowing, *Real Time Television Coverage* Issue, p. 48.

59. Clinton, *My Life,* pp. 551–54.

60. Michael Gordon and Bernard Trainor, *Cobra II. The Inside Story of the Invasion and Occupation of Iraq,* London: Atlantic Books, 2006, p. 66.

61. J. C. R. Licklider and W. Clark, "On-Line Man-Computer Communication," *Proceedings Spring Joint Computer Conference,* vol. 21, 1962, pp. 113–28, p. 114.

62. B. M. Leiner, V. G. Cerf, D. D. Clark, R. E. Kahn, L. Kleinrock, D. C. Lynch, J. Postel, L. G. Roberts, and S. Wolf, "A Brief History of the Internet," *Arxiv preprint cs.NI/9901011,* 1999.

63. Tim Berner-Lee's original message can be found at http://groups.google.com/group/alt.hypertext/msg/395f282a67a1916c.

64. The link, which is not pointing to the original document any more, was http://info.cern.ch/hypertext/WWW/TheProject.html.

65. Andreessen, quoted in Thomas L. Friedman, *The World is Flat. A Brief History of the Twenty-first Century,* New York: Farrar, Straus, Giroux, 2004, p. 58.

66. Ibid., p. 60.

67. Ibid., p. 67.

68. "Here We Go Again?" *The Economist,* 22 May 2008.

69. Friedman, *The World is Flat. A Brief History of the Twenty-first Century,* p. 69.

70. Internet World Stats, www.internetworldstats.com, 9 January 2009.

71. Drucker was actually using an analogy that was already made in more detail by Herbert A. Simon, an influential social scientist, in 1987. Drucker, "Beyond the Information Revolution."

72. For current figures, broken down by country, see Alexa's traffic rankings, http://www.alexa.com.

73. See Tim O'Reilly, "What is Web 2.0?" http://www.oreillynet.com/pub/a/oreilly/tim/news/2005/09/30/what-is-web-20.html. Mike Wesch, an anthropologist, created a short introduction to Web 2.0 for one of its most popular platforms, YouTube: "Web 2.0 . . . The Machine is Us/ing Us," http://youtube.com/watch?v=6gmP4nkoEOE, 30 May 2008.

74. http://en.wikipedia.org/wiki/New_media, 24 February 2008.

75. Yochai Benkler, "Coase's Penguin, or Linux and the Nature of the Firm," *Yale Law Journal,* 112, 2002; see also Yochai Benkler and Helen Nissenbaum, "Commons-based Peer Production and Virtue," *Journal of Political Philosophy* vol. 14, 4, 2006, pp. 394–419.

76. Linux and similar projects have attracted a huge interest in organizational sciences; see, for instance, Bruce M. Kogut and Anca Metiu, "Open-Source Software Development and Distributed Innovation," *Oxford Review of Economic Policy,* vol. 17, 2, 2001, pp. 248–64; Eric von Hippel and Georg von Krogh, "Open Source Software and the 'Private–Collective'

Innovation Model: Issues for Organization Science, *Organization Science,* vol. 14, 2, 2003, pp. 209–23; Eric von Hippel and Georg von Krogh, "Free Revealing and the Private-collective Model for Innovation Incentives," *R&D Management,* vol. 36, 3, 2006, pp. 295–306.

77. The phrase was coined by *Wired* magazine's Chris Anderson. Chris Anderson, *The Long Tail: Why the Future of Business Is Selling Less of More,* New York: Hyperion, 2006.

78. Quoted in "Hollywood and the Internet," *The Economist,* 23 February 2008, p. 88.

79. Eric von Hippel, in a milestone article, used the example of high-performance wind-surfing. Eric von Hippel, "Learning from Open-Source Software," *MIT Sloan Management Review,* vol. 42, 4, 2001, pp. 82–86; see also Hippel and Krogh, "Open Source Software and the 'Private–Collective' Innovation Model: Issues for Organization Science."

80. Prensky, "Listen to the Natives"; more recently, see Palfrey and Gasser, *Born Digital: Understanding the First Generation of Digital Natives.*

Chapter 2

1. One of the best histories of war reporting, starting with the Crimean War, is Knightley, *The First Casualty.*

2. For a comprehensive treatment of military–media relations, see Carruthers, *The Media at War.* Specifically on propaganda, see Taylor, *Munitions of the Mind.* For a detailed look at the U.S. learning experience, see Rid, *War and Media Operations.*

3. In unconventional, small wars, insurgents had always tried getting favorable press coverage, but they did not have a self-sufficient information infrastructure to communicate to mass audiences (see Chapter 6, War 2.0).

4. William A. Owens, *Lifting the Fog of War,* Baltimore: Johns Hopkins University Press, 2001, p. 14.

5. Ibid., p. 15. For an equally optimistic view, see Tommy R. Franks, *American Soldier,* New York: HarperCollins, 2004.

6. See Gordon and Trainor, *Cobra II;* Thomas E. Ricks, *Fiasco. The American Military Adventure in Iraq,* New York: Penguin, 2006.

7. Murray, "Clausewitz out, Computer in."

8. TRADOC pamphlet 525-69, Concept for Information Operations, 1 August 1995, Department of the Army.

9. William A. Owens, "The Emerging U.S. System-of-Systems," Strategic Forum, 63, February 1996, National Defense University.

10. Donald Rumsfeld, "Transforming the Military," *Foreign Affairs,* vol. 81, 3, 2002, p. 20.

11. Ibid., p. 20.

12. U.S. Department of Defense, *JP 1-02,* p. 436.

13. JP 3-57.

14. JP 3-07.3.

15. Mike Birmingham, interview (T. Rid), 6 April 2004, Pentagon.

16. Nigel Aylwin–Foster, "Changing the Army for Counterinsurgency Operations," *Military Review,* November–December, 2005, pp. 2–15.

17. Ricks, *Fiasco. The American Military Adventure in Iraq.*

18. Military subordination to civilian authority is a cornerstone of Western democracies; see Samuel Huntington, *The Soldier and the State,* Cambridge, MA: Harvard University Press, 1957; and Eliot A. Cohen, *Supreme Command. Soldiers, Statesmen, and Leadership in Wartime,* New York: The Free Press, 2002.

19. See Galula's analysis of the "strategic criteria for a cause." David Galula, *Counterinsurgency Warfare: Theory and Practice,* New York: Praeger, 1964.

20. For a good discussion of the role of language in revolutionary war, see John Shy and Thomas W. Collier, "Revolutionary War," in Peter Paret (ed.), *Makers of Modern Strategy: from Machiavelli to the Nuclear Age,* pp. 815–62, Oxford: Clarendon Press, 1990, p. 821.

21. This raises the question of language for this book, too. The authors believe that it is impossible to stay neutral, but that a constant attempt should be made to remain as objective as possible, even when analyzing views that deny the values and principles that allow objective research.

22. David H. Petraeus, John A. Nagl, James F. Amos, and Sarah Sewall, *The U.S. Army/Marine Corps Counterinsurgency Field Manual FM 3-24,* Chicago: Chicago University Press, 2007, p. 2.

23. The entire passage, which has been somewhat liberally translated by Paret and Howard, reads as follows: "Hören denn mit den diplomatischen Noten je die politischen Verhältnisse verschiedener Völker und Regierungen auf? Ist nicht der Krieg bloß eine andere Art von Schrift und Sprache ihres Denkens? Er hat freilich seine eigene Grammatik, aber nicht seine eigene Logik." Clausewitz, *Vom Kriege,* p. 683 (book 8, chapter 6).

24. Charles Richard was one of the first commanders of a so-called *Bureau arabe.* "Quand on veut conquérir, dans le vrai sens du mot, un pays, il y a deux espèces de conquêtes à exécuter: celle du terrain qui est la conquête matérielle, et celle du peuple qui est la conquête morale." Charles Richard, *Etude sur l'insurrection du Dhara,* Alger: A. Besancenez, 1846, p. 7. See also Douglas Porch, "Bugeard, Galliéni, Lyautey: The Development of French Colonial Warfare," in Peter Paret (ed.), *Makers of Modern Strategy,* pp. 376–407, Princeton: Princeton University Press, 1986; Douglas Porch, *The March to the Marne. The French Army 1871–1914,* Cambridge: Cambridge University Press, 1981.

25. Jacques Frémeaux, *Les Bureaux arabes dans l'Algérie de la conquête,* Paris: Denoël, 1993; for later applications, see Robin Bidwell, *Morocco under Colonial Rule. French Administration of Tribal Areas 1912–1956,* London: Frank Cass, 1973; Vincent Monteil, "Les Bureaux arabes au Maghreb (1833–1961)," *Esprit,* vol. 29, 300, 1961, pp. 575–606.

26. Joseph-Simon Galliéni, *Galliéni au Tonkin (1892–1896),* Paris: Berger–Levrault, 1941, pp. 47, 218, 328. For a comparison to earlier methods, see Albert Ringel, *Les bureaux arabes de Bugeaud et les cercles militaires de Galliéni,* Paris: E. Larose, 1903.

27. Hubert Lyautey, *Du rôle colonial de l'armée,* Paris: Armand Colin, 1900, p. 11.

28. Hubert Lyautey, *Lettres du Tonkin et de Madagascar: 1894–1899,* Paris: A. Colin, 1921, p. 334.

29. For a detailed outline of this doctrinal evolution, see Thomas Rid, "The 19th Century Origins of Counterinsurgency Doctrine," *Journal of Strategic Studies,* 2009 (forthcoming).

30. "David Galula, 48, French Army Aide," *The New York Times,* 12 May 1967, p. 47.

31. His two best-known writings are David Galula, *Pacification in Algeria 1956–1958, MG-478-1,* Santa Monica: Rand Corporation, 1963 (2006); Galula, *Counterinsurgency Warfare: Theory and Practice.*

32. Petraeus, Nagl, Amos, and Sewall, *FM 3-24,* p. xix.

33. Max Boot, "Keys to a Successful Surge," *Los Angeles Times,* 7 February 2007.

34. Lesley Blanch, *The Sabres of Paradise,* London: John Murray, 1960.

35. Bernard Lewis, *The Crisis of Islam: Holy War and Unholy Terror,* New York: Modern Library, 2003, p. 61.

36. Walter Laqueur, *Guerrilla. A Historical and Critical Study,* vol. 4, Boston: Little, Brown, 1976, p. 390.

37. Thomas L. Friedman, *From Beirut to Jerusalem,* New York: Farrar, Straus, Giroux, 1989.
38. Petraeus, Nagl, Amos, and Sewall, *FM 3-24,* p. lii.

Chapter 3

1. Some of the chapter's historical findings were presented in more detail in War and Media Operations.
2. Thomas A. Keaney and Eliot A. Cohen (eds.), *Gulf War Air Power Survey,* 1993, vol. 1, p. 332.
3. Molly Moore, *A Woman at War,* New York: Scribner's, 1993, p. 142.
4. Neil Munro, "The Pentagon's New Nightmare: An Electronic Pearl Harbor," *Washington Post,* 16 July 1995, p. C3.
5. "Cornerstones of Information Warfare," 1995, U.S. Air Force, Government Printing Office, Washington, DC.
6. JP 3-13, 1998, p. vii.
7. William Gibson, *Neuromancer,* New York: Ace Books, 1984, p. 69.
8. Some philosophers were obviously even more confused by new technologies and their social effects than the armed forces. In direct relation to the Gulf War, the writings of Paul Virilio and Jean Baudrillard stand out in this respect. Paul Virilio and Sylvère Lothringer, *Pure War,* New York: Semiotext(e), 1997; Jean Baudrillard, *The Gulf War Did Not Take Place,* Bloomington: Indiana University Press, 1991.
9. John J. Kruzel, "Cyber Warfare a Major Challenge, Deputy Secretary Says," American Forces Press Service, 3 March 2008.
10. "SECAF/CSAF Letter to Airmen: Mission Statement," 7 December 2005, http://www.af.mil/library/viewpoints/jvp.asp?id=192, 9 March 2008.
11. The "Cyber Command" was suspended in August 2008. See Noah Shachtman's Danger Room blog, especially http://blog.wired.com/defense/2008/08/air-force-suspe.html.
12. General Kevin P. Chilton, Statement before the House Armed Services Committee, 27 February 2008, p. 14.
13. Ibid., p. 14.
14. JP 3-13, p. x.
15. Quoted in Eric Schmitt and Thom Shanker, "U.S. Adapts Cold-War Idea to Fight Terrorists," *The New York Times,* 18 March 2008, p. 1.
16. Quoted in ibid.
17. Quoted in Tom Vanden Brook, "Air Force Trains Warriors to Defend Cyberspace from Terror," *USA Today,* 29 February 2008, p. 10A.
18. Quoted in Biller Gertz, "General Foresees 'Generational War' against Terrorism; Worries over Sustaining U.S. 'Will,'" *The Washington Times,* 13 December 2006, p. A3.
19. The technical dimension of cyberwar may be hugely overrated. By far the most quoted example is Russia's alleged attack on the Estonian government's Web sites and data centers. The small Baltic country had one of the technologically most sophisticated governments in the world, and thus was a vulnerable target. "Estonia's attacks were less sophisticated than previous 'cyberwars,'" said Kevin Poulsen, a hacker turned *Wired*-editor. Cyber conflicts between Israeli and Palestinian hackers, between India and Pakistan, or China and the U.S., Poulsen argued, were more elaborate. But "[e]ven those attacks fell short of a cyber war, at least as experts have defined the term. I'm sceptical that real cyber war, or cyber terrorism, will ever take place." Even if electronic attacks on U.S. infrastructure or government organizations would occur on a major scale, the network administrators are

likely to turn to their contractors for sophisticated IT-security and support, not to the Air Force. Quoted in Bobbie Johnson, "Nato says cyber warfare poses as great a threat as a missile attack," *The Guardian,* 6 March 2008, p. 2.

20. FM 3-0, 2008, p. 7-1.

21. FM 3-0, 2008, p. 7-3.

22. FM 3-0, 2008, p. 7-4.

23. Bernard Trainor, "The Military and the Media: A Troubled Embrace," *Parameters,* December, 1990, pp. 2–11, p. 2.

24. Gen. William C. Westmoreland, "Vietnam in Perspective," *Military Review,* vol. 59, 1, 1979, pp. 34–43, p. 35.

25. Sean Naylor, coauthor of *Clash of Chariots,* a book on great tank battles, was unable to find any firsthand photographs of the fight. Sean Naylor, interview (T. Rid), Washington, DC, 30 March 2004.

26. Moore, *A Woman at War,* p. 142.

27. James DeFrank, interview (T. Rid), Pentagon, 27 February 2004.

28. Melanie Reeder, quoted in Tammy L. Miracle, "The Army and Embedded Media," *Military Review,* September–October, 2003, pp. 41–45, p. 42.

29. Rick Thomas, interview (T. Rid), by telephone, 5 May 2004.

30. Terry McCreary, interview (T. Rid), by telephone, 12 May 2006.

31. Terry McCreary, quoted in Johanna Neuman, "Pentagon Plans to Deploy Journalists in Iraq," *Los Angeles Times,* 4 December 2002, p. A14.

32. McCreary, interview.

33. Mike Birmingham, interview (T. Rid), Washington, DC, 6 April 2004.

34. James Mann, *Rise of the Vulcans: The History of Bush's War Cabinet,* New York: Penguin, 2004, pp. 43–44.

35. DeFrank, interview.

36. Ibid.

37. T. McCreary, "Command Support of Public Affairs Activities in Potential Future Military Operations," *SECDEF-CJCS P4 Message,* 2003.

38. FM 3-0, 2008, foreword by William Wallace. The U.S. Army, in this respect, was slower than many of its European counterparts. The British, French, and German land forces had elevated stability operations to a core mission in their respective doctrinal updates, most published or internally issued before FM 3-0's publication.

39. FM 3-0, 2008, p. vii.

40. Isambard Wilkinson, "Taliban Invaders Ambushed in the Mountains," *The Daily Telegraph,* 12 January 2007, p. 6.

41. Pamela Constable, "Scores of Insurgents Killed in Afghan Border Area; NATO Forces Tracked Groups from Pakistan," *The Washington Post,* 11 January 2007, p. A10. Hanif was captured one week later.

42. David S. Cloud, "U.S. Sees a Surge in Cross-Border Attacks in Afghanistan," *International Herald Tribune,* 17 January 2007, p. 4.

43. Robert Gates, quoted in Thom Shanker, "Defense Secretary Urges More Spending for U.S. Diplomacy," *The New York Times,* 27 November 2007.

44. Performance Budget FY 2007–2008, GPRA Plan, p. 89.

45. Michael Mullen, "Memorandum for the Deputy Secretary of Defense," CM-0087-07, 14 December 2007.

46. One of the authors (T. Rid) participated and presented at a 4-day workshop with representatives of many of the DoD agencies concerned with strategic communication. "The New Media and the Warfighter," U.S. Army War College, Carlisle Barracks, 15–17 January 2008.

47. The spokesperson of the Israel Defense Forces, for instance, the head of Dover Tsahal, is traditionally an officer with the rank of major general who reports directly to the top commander, the chief of staff. The spokesperson in Tel Aviv is therefore in a more powerful position. See our chapter on Israel.

48. Mike Mullen, "Strategic Communication," *Department of Defense Memorandum CM-0087-07,* 14 December 2007.

49. For more details, see Sarah Boxer, "Blogs," *The New York Review of Books,* vol. 55, 2, 2008.

50. Yon's blog originally was at michaelyon.blogspot.com. As Yon became more professional, his site moved to michaelyon-online.com.

51. http://michaelyon.blogspot.com/2005/08/gates-of-fire.html.

52. http://armyofdude.blogspot.com/2008/03/photo-story-monday-one-year-later.html.

53. Cami McCormick, "'Brothers For Life' Remember Slain Soldier," CBS News, 19 March 2008. McCormick's audio-report is at http://audio.cbsnews.com/2008/03/19/audio3949287.mp3.

54. Ryan W. Brus, Army Public Affairs, Media Relations Division, in e-mail to author (T. Rid), "RE: Question on Blogs (UNCLASSIFIED)," 7 May 2007, 11.28.

55. MNF-Iraq's YouTube channel, including video-specific statistics, is at http://www.youtube.com/mnfiraq.

56. General Caldwell, posting as Frontier 6, at http://smallwarsjournal.com/blog/2008/02/changing-the-organizational-cu-1/.

57. http://www.alexa.com/data/details/traffic_details/smallwarsjournal.com, 10 January 2009 (comparison with the CSIS and the Stiftung Wissenschaft und Politik in Berlin).

58. http://smallwarsjournal.com/blog/2009/03/thoughts-on-the-new-media/, 2 March 2009.

59. Dan Baum, "What the Generals Don't Know," *The New Yorker,* vol. 80, 43, 2005, p. 42.

60. Pete Kilner, interview (T. Rid), by telephone, 27 January 2007.

61. Sandra I. Erwin, "Washington Pulse," *National Defense,* vol. 90, 627, 2006.

62. Andrew P. Schilling, "Peers," *Marine Corps Gazette,* vol. 90, 5, 2006, p. 56.

63. Mullen, "Strategic Communication."

Chapter 4

1. The IRA had some publications in Gaelic.

2. Except those in support of UK civil authority during natural disasters, UK Ministry of Defence, *Joint Doctrine Publication (JDP) 01,* 2004, pp. 1–11.

3. Ian Frederick William Beckett, *Modern Insurgencies and Counter-Insurgencies,* London: Routledge, 2001.

4. Senior Public Affairs officer, interview with author (T. Rid), London, 14 December 2003.

5. For the Navy the Falkland/Malvinas War was the more important conflict. R. Harris, *Gotcha!: The Media, the Government, and the Falklands Crisis,* London: Faber and Faber, 1983; Paul Dixon, "Britain's 'Vietnam Syndrome'? Public Opinion and British Military Intervention from Palestine to Yugoslavia," *Review of International Studies,* vol. 26, 2000, pp. 99–121.

6. In early 2008, the British military had 7,800 forces in Afghanistan and 4,100 troops in Iraq.

7. Jackson, *Operation Banner,* pp. 1–3.

8. Maria McGuire, *To Take Arms,* Belfast: Viking Press, 1973, p. 74.

9. Jackson, *Operation Banner,* pp. 2–7.

10. Ibid., pp. 2–8.

11. Britain's most senior public affairs officers, for instance, were of higher military rank than their French or German counterparts. In the United States, for instance, in the Marine Corps, the picture is more nuanced. See Rid, *War and Media Operations*, p. 83.

12. Lawrence Freedman, *The Official History of the Falklands Campaign*, vol. II, London: Routledge, 2005, p. 34.

13. Joseph Metcalf, III, "The Mother of the Mother," *United States Naval Institute Proceedings*, vol. 118, 8, 1991, pp. 56–58.

14. Knightley, *The First Casualty*, p. 53.

15. Freedman, *The Official History of the Falklands Campaign*, p. 35.

16. Jason Burke, "Rebels' Defiance Makes Sierra Leone Rescue Mission More Likely," *The Observer*, 3 September 2000, p. 3.

17. Sam Kiley, Daniel McGrory, and Richard Beeston, "Paras Fly out Ready to Rescue Jungle Hostages," *The Times*, 6 September 2000.

18. Lord Hutton, *Report of the Inquiry into the Circumstances Surrounding the Death of Dr. David Kelly C.M.G.*, London: House of Commons, 2004, p. 7.

19. "Naval Captives Can Sell Stories," *BBC News*, 8 April 2007.

20. Dan Sabbagh, "It was an outrage, that Faye Turney was allowed to sell her story," *The Times*, 13 April 2007, p. 58.

21. Tony Hall, *Review of Media Access to Personnel*, London: Ministry of Defence, 2007, p. 1.

22. Ibid., p. 2.

23. Quoted in Sarah Sands, "Sir Richard Dannatt: A Very Honest General," *Daily Mail*, 12 October 2006; quoted below as "Honest General."

24. Quoted in "Honest General."

25. Dannatt also questioned the prudence of the treasury in his interview: "Twenty-nine per cent of government spending is on social security. Five per cent is on defence. Others can take the view on whether that proportion is right," *Honest General*.

26. See *The Independent* on Saturday, 14 October 2006, p. 1.

27. Terri Judd, "Forces Round on Jackson for Failing to Criticise MoD Earlier," *The Independent*, 8 December 2006, p. 22

28. Matthew Hickley, "'General Hypocrite'," *Daily Mail*, 8 December 2006, p. 10.

29. MoD, *JDP*, pp. 1–2.

30. Hall, *Review of Media Access to Personnel*, p. 3.

31. Christina Lamb, "Taking the Fight to the Taliban," *The Sunday Times*, 18 June 2006, p. 19.

32. Michael Evans, interview with authors, London, 18 September 2007.

33. Peter Barron, "Talking to the Enemy?" BBC News, 26 October 2006.

34. UK Ministry of Defence, *The Green Book*, 2007, p. i.

35. The document's current version is at: www.mod.uk/DefenceInternet/About Defence/CorporatePublications/DoctrineOperationsandDiplomacyPublications/The GreenBook/.

36. MoD, *The Green Book*, p. i.

37. Terri Judd, interview with authors, London, 18 September 2007.

38. Andrew Ritchie, interview with authors, London, 20 September 2007.

39. Nick Gurr, *The Defence Communications Strategy*, London: Ministry of Defence, Issue, 27 February 2007; the document is not published under the author's name; Nick Gurr, interview with authors, London, 20 September 2007.

40. Ibid., Issue, Annex A.

41. Ibid., Issue.

42. Ibid., Issue, Annex A.

43. http://www.rumration.co.uk/.

44. BadCo, interview with authors, London, 19 September 2007.

45. Quoted in Sean Rayment, "Troops Warned off Social Websites for Fear of Terror Attack," *The Sunday Telegraph,* 11 November 2007, p. 13.

46. Robin Riley, interview with authors, London, 20 September 2007.

47. Sean Rayment, "Troops Warned off Social Websites for Fear of Terror Attack," *The Sunday Telegraph,* 11 November 2007, p. 13.

48. Hall, *Review of Media Access to Personnel,* p. 3.

49. Ibid., p. 4.

50. Ministry of Defence, *Contact with the Media and Communicating in Public,* Defence Instruction and Notices 2007, DIN03-006, August, 2007.

51. The regulation "applies to all members of the regular Armed Forces, the Volunteer Reserve Forces and members of the Regular Reserves undertaking Service duties, cadets and civilian volunteers when on duty, and to MoD Civil Servants regardless of where they work, and Crown Servants within the Regional Forces and Cadets Associations and their Council." in ibid., pp. 1–2.

52. Ibid., p. 3.

53. Michael Evans, "Deadly Stalkers Follow Patrols in 'Bomb Alley'," *The Times,* 15 December 2005, p. 40; also interview with authors.

54. So said both the MoD's civil servant responsible for internet activities, Robin Riley, and the ARRSE administrators in interviews with authors, London, 19 and 20 September 2007.

55. Robin Riley, interview with authors, London, 20 September 2007.

56. Hall, *Review of Media Access to Personnel,* p. 15.

57. The British one-star ranks are Brigadier (Army), Commodore (Navy), and Air Commodore (Air Force). Half-stars are Colonel, Captain, and Group Captain.

58. Ritchie, interview. The last directors of corporate communications were for the Army Brigadier Matthew Sykes, Commodore Alan Adair for the Navy, and Air Commander Paul Thomas for the Royal Air Force.

59. The OF-4 (lieutenant colonel) equivalents in Britain are, respectively, Lieutenant Colonel (Army), Commander (Navy), Wing Commander (Air Force). OF-3 (major) equivalents are Major, Lieutenant Commander, Squadron Leader.

60. Ritchie, interview.

61. Ritchie, interview.

62. Job posting "Director General Media and Communications," closing date 26 March 2008, Elizabeth Smith, Corporate Capability Directorate, Level 6 Zone N, Desk 26, Ministry of Defence, Main Building, Whitehall, SW1A 2HB.

63. Gurr, *The Defence Communications Strategy,* Issue.

64. Steve Tatham, *Losing Arab Hearts and Minds: The Coalition, Al Jazeera and Muslim Public Opinion,* London: Hurst & Company, 2006, £15.00, 239 pp.

65. *JDP,* pp. 1–7.

66. Ibid., pp. 5–4.

67. Ibid., pp. 5–14.

68. Ibid., pp. 5–14.

69. Gurr, *The Defence Communications Strategy,* Issue, Annex B.

70. Judd, interview.

71. Dannatt, *Daily Mail.*

72. "UK Troops 'under Enormous Pressure'," *Guardian,* 14 November 2007.

Chapter 5

1. See, for instance, the remarks by Moshe Yaalon, former IDF chief of staff, in Yoram Peri, *Generals in the Cabinet Room. How the Military Shapes Israeli Policy,* Washington, DC: U.S. Institute of Peace, 2006, p. 140. Also Efraim Inbar, "The 'No Choice War' Debate in Israel," *Journal of Strategic Studies,* vol. 12, March 1989, pp. 22–37.

2. Noam Ohana, *Journal de guerre: De Sciences Po aux unités d'élite de Tsahal,* Paris: Denoël, 2007, pp. 46–47.

3. Numbers as provided by the Israeli Ministry of Foreign Affairs, http://paris1.mfa.gov.il/mfm/Data/62925.pdf, accessed 17 October 2008.

4. David Lahmi, "Tous sous les drapeaux . . . d'Israël," *Guysen Israel News,* 15 July 2002. For a different point of view, see Benjamin Barthe, "En Israël, les pro et les anti-armée s'affrontent sur le web," *Le Monde,* 27 February 2008.

5. Pierre Razoux, *Tsahal,* Paris: Perrin, 2006, pp. 594–95.

6. Olivier Rafowicz, interview (M. Hecker), 13 March 2008, Jerusalem.

7. Yoram Peri, "Intractable Conflict and the Media," *Israel Studies,* vol. 12, 1, 2007, pp. 79–102, p. 88; and Or Heller, interview (M. Hecker), 28 February 2008, by telephone.

8. Ibid., p. 87.

9. Ruth Yaron, interview with authors, 30 March 2008, Jerusalem; Moshe Yaalon, interview with authors, Jerusalem, 3 April 2008.

10. Arieh O'Sullivan, "The thankless task of the IDF Spokesman. Ruth Yaron steps down, warning her successor it won't be 'a rose garden,'" *The Jerusalem Post,* 2 June 2005.

11. Yigal Palmor, interview (M. Hecker), 18 March 2008, Jerusalem.

12. Amotz Asa-El, "The IDF's PR: What Went Wrong?" *The Jerusalem Post,* 15 February 2007.

13. Emmanuel Navon, "Soft Powerlessness: Arab Propaganda and the Erosion of Israel's International Standing," Working Paper, Herzliya Conference, 21–24 January 2006.

14. Ron Schleifer, *Psychological Warfare in the Intifada: Israeli and Palestinian Media Politics and Military Strategies,* East Sussex, UK: Sussex Academic Press, 2006, p. 106.

15. Stephanie Gutmann, *The Other War. Israelis, Palestinian, and the Struggle for Media Supremacy,* Lanham, MD: Encounter Books, 2005, p. 250.

16. See Yehiel Limor and Hillel Nossek, "The Military and the Media in the Twenty-First Century: Towards a New Model of Relations," *Israel Affairs,* vol. 12, 3, 2006, pp. 484–510.

17. Oren Meyers, *Israeli Journalists as an Interpretive Community,* Haifa: University of Haifa, 2004.

18. Martin van Creveld, *The Transformation of War,* New York: The Free Press, 1991, p. 21.

19. Abba, his assumed name, means "father" in Hebrew. Joel Leyden, "Israel Public Relations Directory," *Israel News Agency,* 18 May 2007.

20. Avi Shlaim, "Interview with Abba Eban, 11 March 1976," *Israel Studies,* vol. 8, 1, 2003, pp. 153–77.

21. Avi Kober, "The Intellectual and Modern Focus in Israeli Military Thinking as Reflected in Ma'arachot Articles, 1948–2000," *Armed Forces and Society,* vol. 30, 1, 2003.

22. Yoel Cohen, "Nuclear Ambiguity and the Media: The Israeli Case," *Israel Affairs,* vol. 12, 3, 2006, pp. 529–45.

23. Limor and Nossek, "The Military and the Media in the Twenty-First Century: Towards a New Model of Relations," ibid., pp. 484–510, p. 493.

24. Schleifer, *Psychological Warfare in the Intifada: Israeli and Palestinian Media Politics and Military Strategies,* pp. 112–21.

25. Nir Noiman and Naama Peri, "The Secrets of Sima. Part One," *Bamahane,* February 2008.

26. For instance, Yuval Karniel, "The Committee against Freedom of Expression," *Haaretz,* 7 February 2008.

27. Limor and Nossek, "The Military and the Media in the Twenty-First Century: Towards a New Model of Relations," *Israel Affairs,* vol. 12, 3, 2006, pp. 484–510, p. 494.

28. See, for instance, James Fallows, "Who Shot Mohammed al-Dura?" *The Atlantic Monthly,* June 2003.

29. Gutmann, *The Other War,* p. 61.

30. Aviv Lavie, "Trying to Buck the News Blackout," *Haaretz,* 18 March 2002.

31. Sandro Contenta, "Israel Bans TV Crews from Filming Army Raids," *The Toronto Star,* 21 March 2002.

32. Lavie, "Trying to Buck the News Blackout," *Haaretz,* 18 March 2002.

33. Contenta, "Israel Bans TV Crews from Filming Army Raids," *The Toronto Star,* 21 March 2002.

34. See http://www.cpj.org/protests/02ltrs/Israel02apr02pl.html, accessed 17 October 2008.

35. Aviv Lavie, "Beyond the Hills of Darkness," *Haaretz,* 8 April 2002.

36. Senior military officer, interview (M. Hecker), 29 January 2008, Paris; senior diplomat, interview (M. Hecker), 18 February 2008, Paris.

37. Jacob Dallal, "Bad Information. The Lesson of Jenin," *The New Republic,* August 2005.

38. James Bennet and Joel Greenberg, "Israel Seizes Ship It Says Was Arming Palestinians," *The New York Times,* 5 January 2002, p. 1.

39. Senior military official, interview.

40. For instance, "But the official version, as told by Israeli spokesmen and spoon-fed to selected journalists, makes little sense when it moves on to the questions of who did it and why," reported *The Guardian;* Brian Whitaker, "The Strange Affair of Karine A," *The Guardian,* 21 January 2002.

41. State of Israel Comptroller's Report #53A, 7 October 2002, p. 42, #27, 29, translated by Dan Diker, "Why Are Israel's Public Relations So Poor?" 9-26 Heshvan 5763, October/November 2002.

42. Gutmann, *The Other War,* p. 251.

43. Sara Leibovich-Dar, "In the Eye of the Beholder," *Haaretz,* 24 February 2002.

44. "Why Israel's Image Suffers," interview with GPO Director Danny Seaman, *Kol Ha'Ir,* 11 October 2002.

45. Gutmann, *The Other War,* p. 254.

46. Mitch Potter, interview (M. Hecker), 21 February 2008, Paris.

47. Patrick Anidjar, interview (M. Hecker), 13 March 2008, Jerusalem.

48. "Why Israel's Image Suffers," *Kol Ha'Ir,* 11 October 2002.

49. "Seaman lets it slip. Israel's bully has nothing to boast about," *The Guardian,* 17 October 2002.

50. Anat Balint, "Let the Journalists Suffer," *Haaretz,* 21 July 2003.

51. "Israel Supreme Court Orders GPO to Accredit Palestinian Journalists," *Associated Press,* 6 August 2004; see also Gutmann, *The Other War,* pp. 256–57.

52. Ruth Yaron, interview (T. Rid and M. Hecker), 30 March 2008, Jerusalem.

53. Ibid.

54. Miri Regev, interview with authors, 2 April 2008, Tel Aviv.

55. O'Sullivan, "The Thankless Task of the IDF Spokesman."

56. "Response by Commissioner-General Peter Hansen to Allegations Regarding Misuse of a UN Vehicle," *UNRWA Press Release,* 2 October 2004.

57. "Israel's 'Malicious Propaganda' Endangers UN Staff," *UNRWA Press Release,* 4 October 2004.

58. Amos Harel, "Spinning Past the Point," *Haaretz,* 5 October 2004.

59. Amos Harel, "Stretcher Case," *Haaretz,* 7 October 2004.

60. Aluf Benn, "How Israel Created Another PR Disaster," *Haaretz,* 6 October 2004.

61. "Senior Israeli Commander Resigns Following Leaks to Media," *Associated Press Newswires,* 4 November 2004; "Sealing Leaks," *The Jerusalem Post,* 11 November 2004.

62. Senior military officer, interview (M. Hecker), 30 January 2008, Paris; Arieh O'Sullivan and Nina Gilbert, "Mofaz: No More Polygraphs in IDF," *The Jerusalem Post,* 10 November 2004.

63. Anshell Pfeffer, "Behind the Lines," *The Jerusalem Post,* 12 November 2004.

64. Fischman, quoted in ibid.

65. Arieh O'Sullivan, "Gaza Division Commander Resigns," *The Jerusalem Post,* 5 November 2004.

66. O'Sullivan and Gilbert, "Mofaz: No More Polygraphs in IDF."

67. Heller, interview.

68. Vered Levy-Barzilai, "The High and the Mighty," *Haaretz,* 21 August 2002.

69. Yuval Yoaz, "Halutz Battles in Court for His New IDF Post," *Haaretz,* 29 December 2004.

70. "IDF spokeswoman: I thought of resigning after Dan Halutz gave me false information," www.news-israel.net, 8 March 2005.

71. Aluf Benn, "Image-Maker for the IDF," *Haaretz,* 12 June 2002.

72. Arieh O'Sullivan, "Colonel Miri Regev to be Chief Censor," *The Jerusalem Post,* 7 January 2004.

73. David Weizmann, interview (M. Hecker), 7 February 2008, Paris.

74. Joel Leyden, "Israel Defense Forces PR Lacks Professionals for Gaza Disengagement," *Israel News Agency,* 21 August 2005.

75. Hirsh Goodman, "The Disengagement and Israel's Media Strategy," Jaffee Center for Strategic Studies, *Strategic Assessment,* 8, 3, November 2005.

76. Ibid.

77. Anat Balint, "At the IDF Spokesman's Office, Trial by Fire, Lessons in Openness," *Haaretz,* 28 August 2005.

78. Ibid.

79. Heller, interview.

80. Anshel Pfeffer, "Analysis: Losing the Propaganda War," *The Jerusalem Post,* 11 June 2006.

81. For instance, "Israel: More Evidence on Beach Killings Implicates IDF," *Human Rights Watch*, 15 June 2006.

82. For instance, Chris McGreal, "The Battle of Huda Ghalia—Who Really Killed Girl's Family on Gaza Beach?" *The Guardian*, 17 June 2006.

83. Yaacov Katz, "IDF Not Responsible for Gaza Blast," *The Jerusalem Post*, 13 June 2006.

84. Senior French journalist, interview (M. Hecker), 15 February 2008, Paris.

85. Mitch Potter, interview (M. Hecker), 21 February 2008, Paris.

86. Potter, interview.

87. Zev Furst, "The Second Lebanon War: Military Strategy and the Battle for Public Opinion," *The Israel Journal of Foreign Affairs*, vol. 1, 2, 2007; Gideon Alon, "Ex-IDF Chief: Lebanon War Was Fought without Clear Objective," *Haaretz*, 16 January 2007.

88. Aluf Benn, "PM Meets with Spokespeople to Sharpen PR Message," *Haaretz*, 7 August 2006.

89. Gil Hoffman, "Israel Calls up Media 'Reserves' to Get Its Message to the World," *The Jerusalem Post*, 17 July 2006.

90. Meron Medzini, "Hasbara in the Second Lebanon War: A Rebuttal", *The Israel Journal of Foreign Affairs*, vol. 1, 3, 2007; on the disagreements within the armed forces, see an interview with General Shimon Naveh, published by the *Combat Studies Institute*, Fort Leavenworth, Kansas, 1 November 2007.

91. Schleifer, *Psychological Warfare in the Intifada: Israeli and Palestinian Media Politics and Military Strategies*, p. 108; Nachman Shai, "Bye-Bye Hasbara, Say Hello to Public Diplomacy," *The Jerusalem Post*, 5 March 2008.

92. Dan Diker, *Why Are Israel's Public Relations so Poor?* Jerusalem Center for Public Affairs, Issue, 15 October 2002.

93. Senior correspondent, interview (M. Hecker), 28 February 2008, by telephone.

94. Anshel Pfeffer, "Fighting under the Media Glare," *The Jerusalem Post*, 28 July 2006.

95. "I have an obligation to deal with the Israeli audience, not with the foreign press," Regev, interview. See also Amotz Asa-El, "The IDF's PR: What Went Wrong?" *The Jerusalem Post*, 15 February 2007.

96. Potter, interview.

97. Matthias Gebauer, "All-inclusive-Paket für Kriegsberichter," *Spiegel Online*, 28 Juli 2006.

98. Charles Enderlin, interview with authors, 30 March 2008, Jerusalem.

99. Ze'ev Schiff, "The Scoop Is All," *Haaretz*, 28 April 2007.

100. "The Media Is Not to Blame," *Haaretz*, 20 April 2007.

101. Amnon Lévy, "La trahison des médias," *Yediot Aharonot*, translated from the Hebrew in *Courrier International*, 10 May 2007.

102. Daniel Ben-Simon, interview (M. Hecker), 17 March 2008, Jaffa.

103. Alon Ben-David, interview (T. Rid), 26 October 2008, by telephone.

104. Ben-David, interview.

105. Amos Harel, "IDF Officers to Get Polygraphs over War Leaks," *Haaretz*, 22 October 2006.

106. Amos Harel, "Chief IDF Lawyers Orders Probe into Possible Leaks during Lebanon War," *Haaretz*, 19 October 2006.

107. Ben-David, interview.

108. Not a precise translation, the caption was explained in an interview with a former Israeli soldier, 21 February 2008, Paris.

109. http://www.idf2000.co.il; see also Uri Blau, "Kill, Then Shoot," *Kol Ha'Ir,* 5 October 2001.

110. Nir Noiman et Naama Peri, "The Secrets of Sima. Part One," *Bamahane,* February 2008.

111. Former official of *Dover Tsahal,* interview (M. Hecker), 13 March 2008, Jerusalem.

112. Calev Ben David, "What We Have Here Is a Failure to Communicate," *The Jerusalem Post,* 23 November 2007.

113. , *JP 1-02,* p. 160.

114. Marc Hecker, "Du bon usage de la terreur," *Focus stratégique,* April 2008, pp. 1–31

115. Samuel M. Katz, *The Hunt for the Engineer,* New York: The Lyons Press, 2002, pp. 253–56.

116. Yaalon, interview.

117. Yaron, interview.

118. An excellent real-time documentation of the IDF's innovative uses of new technology is at Noah Shachtman's blog archive, http://blog.wired.com/defense.

Chapter 6

1. Mao Tse-Tung, *Selected Works,* vol. 1, Peking: Foreign Language Press, 1965, p. 150.

2. Laqueur, *Guerrilla,* pp. 361–64. Gérard Chaliand, "Au maquis avec Amilcar Cabral," in ibid., Stratégies de la guérilla. Anthologie historique de la longue marche à nos jours, Paris: Gallimard, 1984 (1979), pp. 153–84.

3. General V. N. Giap, *Guerre du peuple, armée du peuple,* Hanoi: Editions en langues étrangères, 1961 (1973); Che Guevara, *Guerrilla Warfare,* New York: Monthly Review Press, 1961.

4. Carlos Marighella, *Manual do Guerrilheiro Urbano [Le mini-manuel du guérillero rubain],* Paris: Seuil, 1973. Recently see Marc Hecker, "De Marighella à Ben Laden. Passerelles stratégiques entre guérillos et jihadistes," *Politique étrangère,* 2, 2006, pp. 385–96.

5. Brynjar Lia, *Architect of Global Jihad: The Life of al-Qaida Strategist Abu Musab al-Suri,* New York: Columbia University Press, 2008, p. 373.

6. Lawrence, *Seven Pillars of Wisdom,* p. 186.

7. Bruce Watson, *Sieges,* Westport, CT: Greenwood, 1993, pp. 150–51.

8. George Crile, *Charlie Wilson's War,* New York: Grove Press, 2004, p. 448.

9. Mao Tse-Tung, "Problems of Strategy in China's Revolutionary War," in *Selected Works,* vol. 1, pp. 179–254, Peking: Foreign Language Press, 1965, p. 186.

10. Ibid., p. 179.

11. The entire passage, which has been somewhat liberally translated by Paret and Howard, reads as follows: "Hören denn mit den diplomatischen Noten je die politischen Verhältnisse verschiedener Völker und Regierungen auf? Ist nicht der Krieg bloß eine andere Art von Schrift und Sprache ihres Denkens? Er hat freilich seine eigene Grammatik, aber nicht seine eigene Logik." Clausewitz, *Vom Kriege,* p. 683 (book 8, chapter 6), translation adopted by author.

12. Ibid., p. 31.

13. Absolute war frequently is confused with total war. The two ideas are entirely unrelated. Confusion may result from a superficial reading (or in fact no reading at all) of *On War* or an intentionally misconstrued argument.

14. Clausewitz contradicts himself between book 1 and book 8 of *Vom Kriege*. In book 8 he says that Bonaparte had pushed the war to its absolute form. But book 8 was not considered finished by the author; book 1 was. See Raymond Aron, *Clausewitz. Den Krieg denken*, translated by Irmela Arnsperger, Frankfurt a.M.: Fischer, 1980 (1986).

15. This limitation of *On War* becomes evident in the context of Clausewitz's discussion of the trinity. Two of the trinity's three fix elements—the government and the army (the third is the population)—are absent on the insurgent side in revolutionary war. See book 1, chapter 1, section 28. "Peoples' war" as a "revolutionary means," Clausewitz explicitly wrote in his *magnum opus*, "does not concern us here at all." See book 6, chapter 26.

16. A remark on terminology: the present study will use the term media operations as an umbrella term. The official classification in public affairs, psychological operations, information operations, public diplomacy, or more recently strategic communications and occasionally "winning hearts and minds" is imprecise. It reflects an evolved but increasingly obsolete bureaucratic structure that has been overtaken by technological and cultural changes. It structures information strategies by source, not by utility. The term *media operations* is broader and more narrow: we define media operations as the intentional representation of force or the threat of force to affect decisions. It therefore excludes the actual use of force without a representation on a medium as well as the use of any media without the use or the threat of force.

17. For a detailed discussion, see Rid, *War and Media Operations*, p. 109.

18. For a contemporary reinterpretation, see Herfried Münkler, *Der Wandel des Krieges. Von der Symmetrie zur Asymmetrie*, Weilerswist: Velbrück Wissenschaft, 2006.

19. Galula, *Counterinsurgency Warfare: Theory and Practice*, p. 16.

20. Ibid., p. 4.

21. Ibid., p. 9.

22. Peter Neumann and Brooke Rogers, *Recruitment and Mobilisation for the Islamist Militant Movement in Europe*, London: King's College London, 2008, p. 38.

23. For a detailed discussion of peer production, see Yochai Benkler's seminal article: Benkler, "Coase's Penguin, or Linux and the Nature of the Firm."

24. Omar Nasiri, *Inside the Jihad: My Life with Al Qaeda*, New York: Basic Books, 2008, p. 76.

25. http://www.internetworldstats.com/stats.htm, 10 January 2009.

26. Mao Tse-Tung, *On Guerilla Warfare*, London: Cassell, 1965, p. 93.

Chapter 7

1. See a conversation with Mohammad Raad reproduced in Walid Charara and Frédéric Domont, *Le Hezbollah, un mouvement islamo-nationaliste*, Paris: Fayard, 2004, pp. 99–101.

2. Victoria Fontan, "Le discours d'Al-Manar, vecteur de 'glasnost' du Hezbollah," *Questions de communication*, 8, 2005, pp. 51–66, p. 55.

3. Judith Palmer Harik, *Hezbollah: The Changing Face of Terrorism*, New York: I.B. Tauris, 2004, p. 43.

4. Joseph Elie Alagha, *The Shift in Hizbullah's Ideology*, Amsterdam: Amsterdam University Press, 2006, p. 29. On Amal, see Augustus Richard Norton, *Amal and the Shi'a: Struggle for the Soul of Lebanon*, Austin: University of Texas Press, 1987.

5. Yann Richard, *L'islam chi'ite,* Paris: Fayard, 1991, p. 162.

6. Norton, *Amal and the Shi'a: Struggle for the Soul of Lebanon,* p. 100.

7. Ibid., Annex B, pp. 167–87.

8. Palmer Harik, *Hezbollah,* p. 66.

9. Naim Qassem, *Hizbullah: The Story from Within,* London: Saqi Books, 2005, p. 62.

10. Jean-Loup Samaan, *Les métamorphoses du Hezbollah,* Paris: Karthala, 2007, p. 128.

11. Charara and Domont, *Le Hezbollah, un mouvement islamo-nationaliste,* p. 164.

12. The date varies, see ibid., p. 163; Judith Palmer Harik, "Hizballah's Public and Social Services and Iran," in Houchang E. Chehabi (ed.), *Distant Relations: Iran and Lebanon in the Last 500 Years,* London: Tauris, 2006, pp. 259–86, p. 273; also Qassem, *Hizbullah,* pp. 83–84.

13. Palmer Harik, "Hizballah's Public and Social Services and Iran," p. 273.

14. Palmer Harik, *Hezbollah,* p. 83.

15. Palmer Harik, "Hizballah's Public and Social Services and Iran," p. 273; Giles Trendle, "Hizballah Pragmatism and Popular Standing," in Rosemary Hollis and Nadim Shehadi (eds.), *Lebanon on Hold. Implications for Middle East Peace,* London: Royal Institute for International Affairs, 1996, p. 65.

16. Qassem, *Hizbullah,* p. 84.

17. Charara and Domont, *Le Hezbollah, un mouvement islamo-nationaliste,* p. 164.

18. Rula Jurdi Abisaab, "The Cleric as Organic Intellectual: Revolutionary Shi'ism in the Lebanese Hawzas," in Houchang E. Chehabi (ed.), *Distant Relations: Iran and Lebanon in the Last 500 Years,* London: Tauris, 2006, p. 248.

19. Jeffrey Stinson, "Lebanon Relief Effort Raises Houses, Questions," *USA Today,* 17 December 2006.

20. Palmer Harik, "Hizballah's Public and Social Services and Iran," p. 278.

21. Samaan, *Les métamorphoses du Hezbollah,* p. 156.

22. Ibid., p. 127.

23. The full electoral program is reproduced in the annex of Qassem, *Hizbullah.*

24. Palmer Harik, *Hezbollah,* pp. 73–75.

25. International Crisis Group, *Lebanon: Hizbollah's Weapons Turn Inward,* Middle East Briefing 23, 2008.

26. Hassan Nasrallah, "Hezbollah: y a-t-il une vie après le retrait d'Israël?" *Politique Internationale,* vol. 88, 2000.

27. Palmer Harik, *Hezbollah,* pp. 70–72.

28. Augustus Richard Norton, *Hezbollah: A Short History,* Princeton, NJ: Princeton University Press, 2007, pp. 91–92.

29. Ibid., p. 93.

30. Ash-Sharq al-Awsat (London), 14 December 2001, quoted in Avi Jorisch, "Al-Manar: Hizbullah TV, 24/7," *Middle East Quarterly,* vol. 11, 1, 2004, pp. 17–31.

31. Tom Perry, "Hezbollah brings Israel War to Computer Screen," *Reuters,* 16 August 2007.

32. Helena Cobban, "Hizbullah's New Face," *Boston Review,* April–May 2005.

33. Adrien Jaulmes, "Au Liban, le Hezbollah accentue sa propaganda," *Le Figaro,* 23 August 2006.

34. Kinda Chaib, "Le Hezbollah libanais à travers ses images: la représentation du martyr," in Sabrina Mervin (ed.), *Les mondes chiites et l'Iran,* Paris: Karthala, 2007, p. 115.

35. Ibid., pp. 113–31.

36. Ibid., p. 121.

37. "Hizbullah's Broadcasting Arms Garner Awards," *Lebanon Brief News,* 12 July 2002.

38. Nicholas Blanford, "Hizbullah Sharpens Its Weapons in Propaganda War," *Christian Science Monitor,* 28 December 2001.

39. Jorisch, "Al-Manar: Hizbullah TV, 24/7."

40. Kim Ghattas, "Al-Manar Network Feels World's Heat," *Boston Globe,* 21 December 2004; Daniel McGrory, "The Underground Voice of Hezbollah That Israel Is Still Unable to Silence," *The Times* (London), 5 August 2006, p. 7.

41. José-Alain Fralon, "48 heures pour faire cesser les hostilités entre Israéliens et Palestiniens. Les défis de la télévision du Hezbollah libanais," *Le Monde,* 20 October 2000.

42. Mona Harb, "La banlieue du Hezbollah: images alternatives du Beyrouth d'après-guerre," *Annales de la Recherche Urbaine,* 96, 2004, pp. 53–61.

43. Avi Jorisch, *Beacon of Hatred: Inside Hizballah's Al-Manar Television,* Washington, DC: Washington Institute for Near East Policy, 2004, pp. 31–33.

44. McGrory, "The Underground Voice of Hezbollah That Israel Is Still Unable to Silence."

45. Fontan, "Le discours d'Al-Manar," p. 56.

46. Palmer Harik, *Hezbollah,* p. 161.

47. Marie-Laure Cittanova, "Al-Manar," *Les Echos,* 15 December 2004, p. 28.

48. Jorisch, *Beacon of Hatred,* p. 21.

49. Ron Schleifer, "Psychological Operations: A New Variation on an Age Old Art: Hezbollah versus Israel," *Studies in Conflict & Terrorism,* vol. 29, 1, 2006, pp. 1–19, pp. 6, 12.

50. Palmer Harik, *Hezbollah,* p. 130.

51. Ibid., p. 131.

52. Quoted in Jorisch, "Al-Manar: Hizbullah TV, 24/7."

53. A transcript of Nasrallah's speech is at http://www.alwihdah.com/view.php?cat=2&id=33, accessed 10 October 2008.

54. Ibid.

55. "Poll: Palestinians view Al-Jazeera TV, Al-Quds Newspaper and Voice of Al-Aqsa Radio as the most reliable sources of news," Jerusalem Media and Communications Center, 3 April 2007.

56. Fontan, "Le discours d'Al-Manar."

57. Also spelled *vilayat-e faqih;* see Amal Saad-Ghorayeb, *Hizbu'llah: Politics and Religion,* London: Pluto Press, 2002, pp. 59–68.

58. See *as-Safir,* 5 March 2003.

59. *An-Nahar,* 12 May 2003.

60. "US complains about 'anti-Semitic' programming on Hezbollah TV," *The Daily Star,* 30 October 2003; Sam F. Ghattas, "Israel, U.S. Criticize Hezbollah TV Show," *Associated Press,* 29 October 2003.

61. Charara and Domont, *Le Hezbollah, un mouvement islamo-nationaliste,* p. 171.

62. Avi Jorisch, "Hezbollah Hate With a U.S. Link," *Los Angeles Times,* 13 October 2002, p. M5.

63. Mark Dubowitz and Roberta Bonazzi, "Advertising on Terror TV," *National Post* (Canada), 18 October 2005, p. A23; also published in the *The Wall Street Journal.*

64. Daniel McGrory, "The Underground Voice of Hezbollah That Israel Is Still Unable to Silence," *The Times* (London), 5 August 2006, p. 7.

65. "Al-i'lam zaman al-hurub wa al-tahadiyyat," al-Jazeera, 16 July 2007.

66. Adellat Bitar, "Kayfa istata'a i'lam hizballah ta'min istimrariyat al-'amal fi marhalat al-'odwan," al-Diyar, 22 September 2006.

67. Fatima al-Aissaoui, "Batul Ayyub: kontu artadi 'iba'a khaliyiya kay la ya'rifunani," as-Sharq al-Awsat, 18 July 2007.

68. Al-Manar Television Web site, Beirut, in Arabic, 27 May 2008, translated by BBC Monitoring International Reports.

69. Marilyn Khalife, "Kayfa yufakkir jomhur Hizb Allah? Wa ma housa sirr Hassan Nasrallah?," an-Nahar, 2 September 2006.

70. In 2007, Ahmed Majed published (in Arabic) one of the most comprehensive collections of Hassan Nasrallah's more than 120 speeches delivered between May 2000 and July 2006. Ahmed Majed, *Al Khitâb 'Inda as-Sayyed Hassan Nasrallah: Dirâsa fi al Bonya al-Chakliyya, al Madâmîn, al Nidâm, al Marja'iyyât [Le discours chez Sayyed Hassan Nasrallah: Etude de la structure formelle, des contenus, de l'organisation et des références]*, Beirut: Collection Adabiyyât al Nouhoud, 2007.

71. Excerpt from Nasrallah's speech (16 July 2006), translated from the Arabic by Meriam Daadouche.

72. "15 Handicapped Children Killed in Qana Raid: MP," AFP, 30 July 2006.

73. "Most Israelis back continuing Lebanon attacks after Qana: poll," *Agence France Presse*, 1 August 2006.

74. Al-Manar Television, Beirut, in Arabic 1432 GMT, 22 September 2006, quoted in "Hezbollah Leader Hails 'Divine Victory' over Israel," BBC Monitoring Middle East, 22 September 2006.

75. "Doghout Isrâ'iliyya li Ikâf Batth Qanât al Manâr Fi Ostrâlia," *Syria Days*, 21 August 2008, http://www.syriadays.com/?p=6115, accessed 28 October 2008.

76. Thanks to Andrew Exum, who visited the exhibition, for his remarks on the House of the Spider. Zvika Krieger, "Exhibition Game: Inside Hezbollah's Museum of Hate," *The New Republic*, 27 August 2007.

77. http://conflictblotter.com/2007/08/01/the-house-of-spiders/, accessed 28 October 2008.

78. Nayef Krayem, quoted on CNN, 13 October 2001, 2300 ET.

Chapter 8

1. http://www.hrw.org/reports/2007/afghanistan0407/1a.htm, accessed 7 February 2008.

2. http://www.iacasualties.org, accessed 7 February 2008.

3. Doris Buddenburg and Hakan Demirbuken, *Afghanistan Opium Survey 2006*, Kabul: United Nations Office on Drugs and Crime, Issue, September 2006.

4. Christina Oguz and Shirish Ravan, *Afghanistan Opium Survey 2007*, Kabul: United Nations Office on Drugs and Crime, Issue, October 2007.

5. Jonathan Landay, "Islamic Militants' Influence Spreading," *The Seattle Times*, 3 February 2008.

6. Ann Scott Tyson, "NATO's Not Winning in Afghanistan, Report Says," *Washington Post*, 31 January 2008, p. A18.

7. Quoted in Richard Norton-Taylor, "Browne Says BBC Interview Endangered Lives of Troops," *The Guardian*, 12 July 2006, p. 9.

8. http://www.defenselink.mil/transcripts/transcript.aspx?transcriptid=4138.

9. Ahmad Rashid, *Taliban*, New Haven: Yale University Press, 2001.

10. Ibid., p. 25.

11. An excellent analysis of jihad's shift from the "near" to the "far" enemy is Guido Steinberg, *Der nahe und der ferne Feind. Das Netzwerk des islamistischen Terrorismus,* München: Beck, 2005. See also Fawaz A. Gerges, *The Far Enemy: Why Jihad Went Global,* Cambridge: Cambridge University Press, 2005.

12. Rashid, *Taliban,* p. 24.

13. Waliullah Rahmani, "Combating the Ideology of Suicide Terrorism in Afghanistan," *Terrorism Monitor,* vol. 4, 21, 2006.

14. Sean Naylor, *Not a Good Day to Die,* New York: Penguin, 2005.

15. Schmidle speaks of a "next generation," Giustozzi uses the prefix "neo." Nicholas Schmidle, "Next-Gen Taliban," *The New York Times Magazine,* 6 January 2008; Antonio Giustozzi, *Koran, Kalashnikov, and Laptop. The Neo-Taliban Insurgency in Afghanistan,* New York: Columbia University Press, 2008.

16. Ahmad Rashid, *Descent into Chaos,* New York: Viking, 2008, p. xxii.

17. When we refer to "the Taliban" in the following pages, we refer to a loosely defined movement of several groups. Therefore we also decided to use the plural.

18. Lawrence Wright, *The Looming Tower. Al-Qaeda and the Road to 9/11,* New York: Alfred A. Knopf, 2006.

19. Jos J. L. Gommans, *The Rise of the Indo-Afghan Empire, C. 1710–1780,* Leiden: E.J. Brill, 1995, pp. 65–66.

20. Rashid, *Taliban,* p. 42.

21. Quoted in Jane Perlez, "Frontier Years Give Might to Ex-Guerrilla's Words," *The New York Times,* 5 July 2008.

22. Quoted in Rashid, *Taliban,* p. 50.

23. Quoted in ibid, p. 5.

24. Philip Smucker, "Taliban Learns Tactics, PR from al Qaeda," *Washington Times,* 30 May 2007, p. A1.

25. Rashid, *Descent into Chaos,* p. 250.

26. Sami Yousafzai, "Afghanistan: Want to Meet the Taliban? No Prob," *Newsweek,* vol. 148, 25 December 2006, p. 14.

27. U.S. Department of State, "Country Reports on Terrorism," 30 April 2007, http://www.state.gov/s/ct/rls/crt/2006/82734.htm, accessed 26 June 2008.

28. "The Importance of Media Activities to the Taliban Islamic Movement," *Al-Somood Magazine,* January 2008.

29. Dan Nystedt, "Mobile Phone Use Grows in Afghanistan," *IDG News Service,* 23 June 2008.

30. Marcus Gee, "Calling up a Brighter Future; The Cellphone Craze has Helped Seed the Hard Soil of Afghanistan's Economy," *The Globe and Mail,* 8 June 2007, p. A25.

31. The Asia Foundation, *Afghanistan in 2007,* Kabul, 2007, p. 97.

32. Taimoor Shah, "Taliban Threatens Afghan Cellphone Companies," *The New York Times,* 26 February 2008.

33. Allison Lampert, "In Kabul's Pul-e-Charkhi, Cellphones Can Be Deadly," *The Gazette (Montreal),* 6 December 2007, p. A1.

34. Elizabeth Rubin, "In the Land of the Taliban," *The New York Times Magazine,* 22 October 2006.

35. Sami Yousafzai and Urs Gehriger, "Der Kodex der Taliban," *Weltwoche,* 46, 2006.

36. Ahmad Rashid, "Letter from Afghanistan: Are the Taliban Winning?" *Current History,* January 2007, pp. 17–20.

37. Thomas Johnson provided an excellent analysis of night letters. Thomas H. Johnson, "The Taliban Insurgency and an Analysis of Shabnamah (Night Letters)," *Small Wars & Insurgencies*, vol. 18, 3, 2007, pp. 317–44.

38. Kathy Gannon, "Secret 'Night Letters' Condemn Afghan Government as Traitors of Islam, Urge War on U.S." *Associated Press Worldstream,* 20 March 2002.

39. "Taliban Communications, Old and New," *Jane's Terrorism & Security Monitor,* 12 November 2007.

40. Translated and reproduced in "Lessons in Terror. Attacks on Education in Afghanistan," *Human Rights Watch,* vol. 18, 6(C), 2006, p. 53.

41. Ibid., p. 56.

42. The Order of Malta, the NGO's roof organization, made its name during the first crusade in Jerusalem in 1099. Its motto remains *tuitio fidei et obsequium pauperum,* or defense of the faith and assistance to the poor.

43. Quoted in Human Rights Watch, "Lessons in Terror," p. 57.

44. Ibid., p. 12.

45. The letter is reproduced in Johnson, "The Taliban Insurgency and an Analysis of Shabnamah (Night Letters)," p. 322. Johnson provides an excellent and detailed analysis of this and other night letters.

46. *Afghanistan in 2007,* p. 97.

47. Ivan Watson, "Taliban Enlists Video in Fight for Afghanistan," *National Public Radio,* 2 November 2006.

48. International Crisis Group, *Taliban Propaganda: Winning the War of Words,* Asia Report 158, 24 July, 2008, p. 18.

49. Schmidle, "Next-Gen Taliban."

50. *Taliban Propaganda,* p. 19.

51. Ibid., p. 14.

52. Urs Gehriger, "Layeha (Regelbuch) für die Mudschaheddin," *Die Weltwoche,* vol. 46, 6, 2006.

53. Ibid.

54. Human Rights Watch, "Taliban Night Letter from Helmand Province," http://www.hrw.org/campaigns/afghanistan/2006/education/letter2.htm, accessed 28 June 2008.

55. Ibid.

56. Declan Walsh, "Headteacher Decapitated by Taliban," *Guardian,* 5 January 2006.

57. For a more detailed critique, see Tim Foxley, *The Taliban's Propaganda Activities,* Stockholm: SIPRI, Issue, June 2007.

58. Jane's, "Taliban Communications, Old and New."

59. The Crisis Group provided examples: alemarah.net, alemarah.org, alemarah.cjb.net, alemarah.r8.org, alemarah.i67.org, alemarah.110mb.com, and alemara.110mb.com, *Taliban Propaganda,* p. 15.

60. "Taliban Communications, Old and New."

61. The ITU reported that Pakistan has 17,500,000 Internet users as of March 2008, a penetration of 10.4 percent. Afghanistan had 580,000 Internet users, a penetration of 1.8 percent. http://www.internetworldstats.com/asia.htm.

62. Jane's, "Taliban Communications, Old and New."

63. *Taliban Propaganda,* p. 13.

64. On *al-Somood,* see Ibid., pp. 9, 13.

65. http://www.alsomood.r8.org, where the magazine was originally published, was banned by ne1.net, a host company. On 30 January 2008, the magazine was accessible on http://www.freewebtown.com/tokhi/index%20alsomood.html; as well as: http://xrl.us/bcz4h.

66. *Taliban Propaganda,* p. 13.

67. Rashid, *Taliban,* p. 25.

68. Lisa Myers, "An Interview with a Taliban Commander," NBC, 27 December 2005, http://www.msnbc.msn.com/id/10619502/.

69. BBC News, "Tories Criticise BBC over Taleban," 26 October 2006.

70. http://www.defenselink.mil/news/newsarticle.aspx?id=47196.

71. Kevin Maurer, "Taliban Show Media Savvy," *The Fayetteville Observer,* 12 January 2008.

72. Ibid, p. 8.

73. Quoted in Sean Naylor, "Insurgents in Afghanistan Have Mastered Media Manipulation," *Armed Forces Journal,* 2008.

74. The report could not be verified by third sources. Information here is given as quoted by ibid.

75. "200 Civilian Casualties Feared in Coalition Air Raid," Pajhwok Afghan News, 3 August 2007.

76. Naylor, "Media Manipulation."

77. "Airstrikes Target Taliban Commanders in Southern Afghanistan, Casualties Reported," AP, 3 August 2007.

78. Abdul Waheed Wafa, and Taimoor Shah, "U.S. Airstrike on 2 Taliban Commanders in South Wounds at Least 18 Civilians, Afghans Say," *The New York Times,* 4 August 2007, p. A6

79. Naylor, "Media Manipulation."

80. Smucker, "Taliban learns tactics, PR from al Qaeda."

81. Rashid, *Descent into Chaos,* p.241.

82. *Taliban Propaganda,* p. i.

Chapter 9

1. Nasiri, *Inside the Jihad,* p. 179. On the Taliban as innovators, see p. xii, 37, 192, 212, as well as Gerges, *The Far Enemy,* p. 83.

2. Steve Coll, *The Bin Ladens: An Arabian Family in the American Century,* New York: Penguin, 2008, pp. 14–15.

3. Lawrence Wright, "The Rebellion," *The New Yorker,* 2008, pp. 38–39.

4. Wright, *The Looming Tower.* This selective interpretation of history was, and remains, a source of an unrealistic belief in al-Qaeda's own strength and the weakness of their opponents.

5. Osama bin Laden, "Declaration of War against the Americans Occupying the Land of the Two Holy Places," 23 August 1996, reproduced in Gilles Kepel and Jean-Pierre Milelli, *Al-Qaeda in Its Own Words,* Cambridge, MA: Belknap Press, 2008.

6. Ibid., pp. 53–56.

7. Katrin Brettfeld and Peter Wetzels, *Muslime in Deutschland: Integration, Integrationsbarrieren, Religion sowie Einstellungen zu Demokratie, Rechtsstaat und politisch-religiös motivierter Gewalt,* Berlin: Bundesministerium des Innern, 2007.

8. Michael Scheuer, "Al-Qaeda's Media Doctrine: Evolution from Cheerleader to Opinion-Shaper," *Terrorism Focus,* vol. 4, 15, 2007, p. 5.

9. The bombing plot was hatched in the Khaldan training camp, near the Afghanistan–Pakistan border. National Commission on Terrorist Attacks, *The 9/11 Commission Report*, 2004, p. 73.

10. The four Saudi nationals convicted—and executed—for the attack said on Saudi Television that they were inspired by Osama bin Laden and al-Qaeda. Kenneth Katzman, *Al-Qaeda: Profile and Threat Assessment*, Washington, DC: CRS Report for Congress, Issue, 17 August 2005, p. 4; *The 9/11 Commission Report*, p. 60.

11. The operation was principally executed by Saudi Hezbollah. Al-Qaeda's involvement remains unclear. The 9/11 Commission, based on classified reports, indicated that al-Qaeda might have had a hand in the Khobar Tower bombings, *The 9/11 Commission Report*, pp. 60, 468.

12. The majority of Salafi intellectuals are concerned not with operational and strategic questions such as al-Suri, but with legal and religious doctrine; among the most influential are Azzam al-Zawahiri, Dr. Fadl, bin Laden, and Abu Qatada.

13. An ambiguity between a descriptive and a normative style characterizes many of the most influential texts of strategic theory, for instance, Clausewitz, Jomini, Mao, and Galula.

14. Paul Cruickshank and Mohannad Hage Ali, "Abu Musab Al Suri: Architect of the New Al Qaeda," *Studies in Conflict & Terrorism*, vol. 30, 1, 2007, pp. 1–14.

15. Omar Nasiri was also involved in the *al-Ansar* production. He describes how the journal was distributed and received by jihadists worldwide. Nasiri, *Inside the Jihad*.

16. On criticism of bin Laden from within al-Qaeda, see Gerges, *The Far Enemy*, p. 102.

17. Alan Cullison, "Inside Al-Qaeda's Hard Drive," *Atlantic Monthly*, September 2004.

18. Quoted in "Architect of New War on the West," *Washington Post*, 23 May 2006, p. A1.

19. Both quotes, Bergen and Khashoggi, are from Lawrence Wright, "The Master Plan," *The New Yorker*, 11 September 2006.

20. Lia, *Architect of Global Jihad*, pp. 359, 63.

21. Ibid., p. 420.

22. Brynjar Lia, "Al-Suri's Doctrines for Decentralized Jihadi Training," *Terrorism Monitor*, vol. V, 1, 2007, pp. 1–4, p. 372.

23. Ibid., p. 379.

24. Al-Suri distinguishes between morally good and bad terrorism, "praiseworthy" and "blameworthy" terrorism. Lia, *Architect of Global Jihad*, p. 383; on individual jihad, see pp. 392–93.

25. Lia, "Al-Suri's Doctrines for Decentralized Jihadi Training," p. 421.

26. Ibid., p. 441.

27. Ibid., p. 437.

28. Ibid., p. 17.

29. Lia, *Architect of Global Jihad*, p. 420.

30. Lia, "Al-Suri's Doctrines for Decentralized Jihadi Training," p. 443, emphasis in original.

31. Lia, *Architect of Global Jihad*, p. 364.

32. Ibid., p. 371.

33. Ibid., p. 226.

34. Ibid., p. 373.

35. Quoted in Lia, "Al-Suri's Doctrines for Decentralized Jihadi Training," p. 3; Abu Mus'ab Al-Suri, *The Call to Global Islamic Resistance*, 2005, p. 1420.

36. Al-Suri, *The Call to Global Islamic Resistance*, p. 1421.

37. Kimmage, an expert on extremist media, collected the material primarily from the al-Ikhlas and al-Fallujah forums, based on "official" affiliation with known armed groups or media production companies as identified by a logo. His objective was to study one representative month of jihadist media production. Daniel Kimmage, "The al-Qaeda Media Nexus," *RFE/RL Special Report,* 2008, p. 18.

38. Mohammad bin Ahmad al-Salem, *39 Ways to Serve and Participate in Jihad*: online publication, 2003, quoted from chapter 34 "electronic jihad."

39. Wright, *The Looming Tower,* pp. 122–25.

40. Wright, "The Rebellion," pp. 41–42.

41. Ayman al-Zawahiri, "Advice of One Concerned," 5 July 2007, quoted in Jarret Brachman, "Leading Egyptian Jihadist Sayyid Imam Renounces Violence," *CTC Sentinel,* vol. 1, 1, 2007, pp. 12–14, p. 13.

42. The authors want to thank Yassin Musharbash for raising this counter-argument.

43. Abdul Hameed Bakier, "Al-Qaeda's al-Zawahiri Repudiates Dr. Fadl's 'Rationalization of Jihad'," *Terrorism Focus,* vol. 5, 17, 2008, pp. 3–4, p. 3.

44. The newly sworn-in undersecretary of state for public diplomacy, Glassman, named al-Sahrif as an example in James K. Glassman, "How To Win The War of Ideas," *Wall Street Journal,* 24 June 2008, p. 19.

45. Wright, "The Rebellion"; Peter Bergen and Paul Cruickshank, "The Unraveling," *The New Republic,* 2008; Michael Scheuer, "Rumor's of al-Qaeda's Death May be Highly Exaggerated," *Terrorism Focus,* vol. 5, 21, 2008.

46. Jarret Brachman, Brian Fishman, and Joseph Felter, *The Power Of Truth: Questions For Ayman Al-Zawahiri,* West Point, NY: Counter Terrorism Center, Issue, 21 April 2008, http://www.ctc.usma.edu/questions/CTC-Power_of_Truth_4-21-2008.pdf, accessed 26 June 2008.

47. Ayman al-Zawahiri, *The Open Meeting with Shaykh Ayman al-Zawahiri,* As-Sahab Media, Issue, 2008.

48. Samir Amghar, Amel Boubekeur, and Michael Emerson, *European Islam. Challenges for Public Policy and Society,* Brussels: Centre for European Policy Studies, 2007, p. 1.

49. Ibid., pp. 14–62; Marieke Slootman and Jean Tillie, *Processes of Radicalisation,* Amsterdam: University of Amsterdam, 2006.

50. Brettfeld and Wetzels, *Muslime in Deutschland,* p. 494.

51. Algemene Inlichtingen- en Veiligheidsdienst, *Jaarverslag 2007,* April 2008, p. 42.

52. EUROPOL, *EU Terrorism Situation and Trend Report (TE-SAT),* The Hague: European Police Office, 2008, p. 21; EUROPOL, *EU Terrorism Situation and Trend Report (TE-SAT),* The Hague: European Police Office, 2007.

53. Bundesministerium des Innern (Germany), *Verfassungsschutzbericht 2007,* May 2008, p. 182.

54. AIVD, *Jaarverslag 2007,* p. 47.

55. Sageman, *Leaderles Jihad,* p. 111.

56. BMI, *Verfassungsschutzbericht 2007,* p. 106.

57. Wright, "The Master Plan."

58. AIVD, *Jaarverslag 2007,* p. 47; BMI, *Verfassungsschutzbericht 2007,* p. 181.

59. Labi, "Jihad 2.0."

60. Dialogue quoted in "A World Wide Web of Terror," *The Economist.*

61. "UK Terrorism Convictions," *Jane's Terrorism & Security Monitor,* 2007.

62. Quoted in "British Muslim Computer Geek, Son of Diplomat, Revealed as Al-Qaeda's Top Cyber Terrorist," *The Daily Mail,* 16 January 2008.

63. EUROPOL, *EU Terrorism Situation and Trend Report (TE-SAT)*, p. 22.

64. Scheuer, "Al-Qaeda's Media Doctrine," p. 5.

65. Bruce Hoffman, "The Myth of Grass-Roots Terrorism. Why Osama bin Laden Still Matters" *Foreign Affairs*, May/June 2008; Elaine Sciolino and Eric Schmitt, "A Not Very Private Feud over Terrorism," *The New York Times*, 8 June 2008; Marc Sageman and Bruce Hoffman, "Does Osama Still Call the Shots? Debating the Containment of al-Qaeda's Leadership," *Foreign Affairs*, July/August 2008.

66. Kimmage, "Nexus"; on Somalia, see EUROPOL, *EU Terrorism Situation and Trend Report (TE-SAT)*.

67. Al-Suri, *The Call to Global Islamic Resistance*, p. 1419.

68. Ibid., p. 1424.

69. Written Statement of Dr. Thomas Fingar, Deputy Director of National Intelligence for Analysis, before the U.S. House of Representatives, Committee on Armed Services, 13 February 2008, pp. 9–10.

70. BMI, *Verfassungsschutzbericht 2007*, pp. 180–81.

71. "Crawley Boy Who Kept Bomb Kit in a Garage; Terror Gang Leader Dreamed of Carnage on the Scale of 9/11," *Evening Standard*, 30 April 2007.

72. Elaine Sciolino and Stephen Grey, "British Terror Trial Traces a Path to Militant Islam," *The New York Times*, 25 November 2006, p. 1.

73. Duncan Gardham and Philip Johnston, "'Revenge' for Rushdie Honour, Boasts Web Site," *The Daily Telegraph*, 30 June 2007, p. 1.

74. Chris Greenwood and Caroline Gammell, "Terror Car Bomb Was Primed to Cause Carnage among Revellers in Late-Night Club," *The Western Mail*, 30 June 2007, p. 8.

75. Claus Blok Thomsen and Morten Skjoldager, "Fotografier Belaster Terrorsigtet," *Politiken*, 18 January 2008, p. 1.

76. EUROPOL, *EU Terrorism Situation and Trend Report (TE-SAT)*, p. 18.

77. Ibid., p. 18; Guido Steinberg, "Die Islamische Jihad Union," *SWP-Aktuell*, 23, 2008.

78. http://www.spiegel.de/video/video-21405.html, accessed 10 May 2008.

79. Numerous counterinsurgency studies by the RAND Corporation, for instance, are quick to compare a large number of irregular conflicts over history. But a thorough comparison of insurrections may be more problematic; see Walter Laqueur's highly detailed analysis, "The Great Differences in the Prevailing Conditions [of political violence] Are Too Deep and Too Numerous to Be Digested in Cross-National Surveys," in Laqueur, *Guerrilla*, p. 389.

80. Scheuer, "Al-Qaeda's Media Doctrine," p. 4.

81. Quoted in Michael Scheuer, "Al-Qaeda's Insurgency Doctrine: Aiming for a 'Long War'," *Terrorism Focus*, vol. III, 8, 2006, pp. 4–6.

82. Peter Bergen, quoted in "Al Qaeda's Media Strategy," CNN, 30 January 2006.

83. Scheuer, "Al-Qaeda's Insurgency Doctrine."

84. "Let It Rise," *The Economist*, A special report on corporate IT, 25 October 2008, pp. 3–4.

85. Numbers according to the IntelCenter, http://www.washingtonpost.com, accessed 23 June 2008.

86. Kimmage, "Nexus."

87. Ibid., p. 5.

88. Ibid., p. 5, footnote 4.

89. Hassan M. Fattah, "Al Qaeda Increasingly Reliant on Media," *The New York Times*, 30 September 2006.

90. http://www.youtube.com/islamicstate, 10 February 2008. After more than four months, however, the channel had merely 8,900 views. A tiny number. Multi-National Force–Iraq, the U.S.-led coalition, opened its YouTube channel, http://www.youtube.com/mnfiraq, on 7 March 2007; after 11 months, it had nearly 400,000 channel views. As a comparison, Barack Obama, at the height of his campaign a week after Super Tuesday in February 2008 had nearly 12 million YouTube channel views, an impressive number even when compared to TV shows; the Republican CNN/YouTube debate, a debate broadcast on CNN that featured videotaped questions from ordinary people, was the highest-rated cable debate in campaign history. More than 4.4 million people watched the single event. See also Daniel Kimmage, "Fight Terror with YouTube," ibid., 26 June 2008, p. A23.

91. AFP (Dubai), "Zawahiri Urges Attacks on Western Targets in North Africa," 3 November 2007.

Conclusion

1. Israel may be the exception to this rule.

2. http://www.internetworldstats.com, 10 January 2009.

3. GSMA Press Release, 16 April 2008, London, UK. The GSM Association (GSMA) is a trade association representing more than 700 GSM mobile phone operators worldwide.

4. GSMA fact sheet, Wireless Intelligence, http://www.gsmworld.com/news/statistics/index.shtml.

5. "The Meek Shall Inherit the Web," *The Economist,* Technology Quarterly, 4 September 2008.

6. See AOL's Third Annual Instant Messaging Survey, 2005.

7. "Wirefly Survey Finds 36% of Cell Phone Users Now Send Text Messages Daily," Reuters, Business Wire, 8 April 2008; a Cingular market survey published in August 2006 and a Samsung survey published in April 2008 both find that parent-child relationships tighten as a result of text messaging.

8. Sixty-eight percent of American parents communicate with their kids through text message. Fifty-six percent of teens (ages thirteen–nineteen) communicate more often with their parents since they began text messaging. See Samsung's *Mobile Matters* Survey, 2008.

9. For a detailed account, see Rid, *War and Media Operations.*

10. For instance, "Victory will come, but it will take time and require the kind of focused and sustained national commitment that we saw during the Cold War." Michael V. Hayden, Director, CIA, Duquesne University Commencement Ceremony, 4 May 2007.

11. For example, "Like the fascism our nations defeated six decades ago, terrorism is designed to make us afraid of today, afraid of tomorrow, and afraid of each other. It is a battle based not on territory, but on ideology—on freedom versus fear, on tolerance versus tyranny." Robert S. Mueller, III, Director, FBI, Chatham House, London, 7 April 2008.

12. For a detailed argument, see Lewis, *The Crisis of Islam.*

13. This certainly is the view of some radical Islamists: "Israel creates a motive for a global Islamic cause, and the American occupation adds a revolutionary dimension, which is an excellent key to jihad." Lia, *Architect of Global Jihad,* p. 380.

14. Ibid., p. 420.

15. For a variation of this argument, see Olivier Roy, *Globalised Islam: The Search for a New Ummah*, London: C Hurst & Co, 2004.

16. Anderson, *The Long Tail: Why the Future of Business Is Selling Less of More*, p. 24. For a concise summary, see pp. 52–57. Anderson considered the application of the Long Tail to political violence as well (p. 50). For a different interpretation of the argument, see John Robb, *Brave New War: The Next Stage of Terrorism and the End of Globalization*, New York: Wiley, 2007. The author comes to different conclusions: he highlights the benefit of the Long Tail for irregulars and recommends countering networks with networks.

17. Against this background, the equation or even the comparison of the jihadi movement with Germany during the Third Reich or the Soviet Union during the Cold War seems particularly odd.

Bibliography

OFFICIAL DOCUMENTS

Algemene Inlichtingen- en Veiligheidsdienst, *Jaarverslag 2007*, April 2008.

Katrin Brettfeld and Peter Wetzels, *Muslime in Deutschland: Integration, Integrationsbarrieren, Religion sowie Einstellungen zu Demokratie, Rechtsstaat und politisch-religiös motivierter Gewalt*, Berlin: Bundesministerium des Innern, 2007.

Doris Buddenburg and Hakan Demirbuken, *Afghanistan Opium Survey 2006*, Kabul: United Nations Office on Drugs and Crime, September 2006.

Bundesministerium des Innern (Germany), *Verfassungsschutzbericht 2007*, May 2008.

Department of Defense (U.S), *Joint Doctrine for Information Operations*, JP 3-13, 2006.

Department of Defense (U.S.), *Dictionary of Military and Associated Terms*, JP 1-02, 2007.

EUROPOL, *EU Terrorism Situation and Trend Report (TE-SAT)*, The Hague: European Police Office, 2007.

EUROPOL, *EU Terrorism Situation and Trend Report (TE-SAT)*, The Hague: European Police Office, 2008.

Nick Gurr, *The Defence Communications Strategy*, London: Ministry of Defence, Issue, 27 February 2007.

Tony Hall, *Review of Media Access to Personnel*, London: Ministry of Defence, 2007.

Mike Jackson, *Operation Banner*, vol. Army Code 71842, London: British Army, 2006.

Ministry of Defence (UK), *Joint Doctrine Publication (JDP) 01*, 2004.

Ministry of Defence (UK), *Contact with the Media and Communicating in Public*, Defence Instruction and Notices 2007DIN03-006, August 2007.

Ministry of Defence (UK), *The Green Book*, 2007.

Mike Mullen, "Strategic Communication," *Department of Defense Memorandum CM-0087-07*, 14 December 2007.

National Commission on Terrorist Attacks (U.S.), *The 9/11 Commission Report*, 2004

Christina Oguz and Shirish Ravan, *Afghanistan Opium Survey 2007*, Kabul: United Nations Office on Drugs and Crime, Issue, October 2007.

David H. Petraeus, John A. Nagl, James F. Amos, and Sarah Sewall, *The U.S. Army/Marine Corps Counterinsurgency Field Manual FM 3-24*, Chicago: Chicago University Press, 2007.

REPORTS

The Asia Foundation, *Afghanistan in 2007,* Kabul, 2007.

Samir Amghar, Amel Boubekeur, and Michael Emerson, *European Islam. Challenges for Public Policy and Society,* Brussels: Centre for European Policy Studies, 2007.

John Arquilla and David Ronfeldt, *In Athena's Camp: Preparing for Conflict in the Information Age,* Santa Monica, CA: Rand Corporation, 1997.

Frank Aukofer and William P. Lawrence, *America's Team, the Odd Couple: A Report on the Relationship between the Military and the Media,* Nashville, TN: The Freedom Forum First Amendment Center, 1995.

Jarret Brachman, Brian Fishman, and Joseph Felter, *The Power Of Truth: Questions For Ayman Al-Zawahiri,* Report, West Point, NY: Combating Terrorism Center, Issue, 21 April 2008.

Dan Diker, *Why Are Israel's Public Relations So Poor?* Jerusalem Center for Public Affairs, Issue, 15 October 2002.

Tim Foxley, *The Taliban's Propaganda Activities,* Stockholm: SIPRI, Issue, June 2007.

David Galula, *Pacification in Algeria 1956–1958, MG-478-1,* Santa Monica, CA: Rand Corporation, 1963 (2006).

Nik Gowing, *Real Time Television Coverage of Armed Conflicts and Diplomatic Crises: Does it Pressure or Distort Foreign Policy Decisions?* Working Paper, Boston: The Shorenstein Center, Issue, 1994.

Lord Hutton, *Report of the Inquiry into the Circumstances Surrounding the Death of Dr David Kelly C.M.G.,* London: House of Commons, 2004.

International Crisis Group, *Lebanon: Hizbollah's Weapons Turn Inward,* Middle East Briefing 23, 2008.

International Crisis Group, *Taliban Propaganda: Winning the War of Words,* Asia Report 158, 24 July 2008.

Avi Jorisch, *Beacon of Hatred: Inside Hizballah's Al-Manar Television,* Washington, DC: Washington Institute for Near East Policy, 2004.

Amrom H. Katz, *Some Notes on the History of Aerial Reconnaissance (Part 1),* Santa Monica, CA: RAND Corporation, 1966.

Kenneth Katzman, *Al-Qaeda: Profile and Threat Assessment,* Washington, DC: CRS Report for Congress, Issue, 17 August 2005.

Thomas A. Keaney and Eliot A. Cohen (eds.) *Gulf War Air Power Survey,* Washington, DC: U.S. Government Printing Office, 1993.

Daniel Kimmage, "The al-Qaeda Media Nexus," RFE/RL Special Report, 2008.

Daniel Kimmage and Kathleen Ridolfo, "Iraqi Insurgent Media," RFE/RL Special Report, 2007.

"Lessons in Terror. Attacks on Education in Afghanistan," *Human Rights Watch,* vol. 18, 6(C), 2006.

Oren Meyers, *Israeli Journalists as an Interpretive Community,* Haifa: University of Haifa, 2004.

Peter Neumann and Brooke Rogers, *Recruitment and Mobilisation for the Islamist Militant Movement in Europe,* London: King's College London, 2008.

Lennart Souchon, *Romantik, Deutscher Idealismus, Hegel und Clausewitz,* Hamburg: Führungsakademie der Bundeswehr, 2007.

Guido Steinberg, "Die Islamische Jihad Union", *SWP-Aktuell,* 23, 2008.

David B. Stockwell, *Press Coverage in Somalia: A Case for Media Relations to be a Principle of Military Operations Other Than War,* Master's Thesis, Fort Meade, MD: DINFOS, Issue, 1995.

BOOKS AND BOOK CHAPTERS

Rula Jurdi Abisaab, "The Cleric as Organic Intellectual: Revolutionary Shi'ism in the Lebanese Hawzas," in Houchang E. Chehabi (ed.), *Distant Relations: Iran and Lebanon in the Last 500 Years*, London: Tauris, 2006.

Albert Abramson, *The History of Television, 1942 to 2000*, Jefferson, NC: McFarland & Co. Inc. Pub., 2003.

Air Material Command, *Reconnaissance Aircraft and Aerial Photographic Equipment 1915–1945*, Wright Field, OH: Historical Division, 1946.

Joseph Elie Alagha, *The Shift in Hizbullah's Ideology*, Amsterdam: Amsterdam University Press, 2006.

Chris Anderson, *The Long Tail: Why the Future of Business Is Selling Less of More*, New York: Hyperion, 2006.

Raymond Aron, *Clausewitz. Den Krieg denken*, translated by Irmela Arnsperger, Frankfurt am Main: Fischer, 1980 (1986).

Constance Babington-Smith, *Air Spy. The Story of Photo-Intelligence in World War II*, New York: Harper, 1957.

Jean Baudrillard, *The Gulf War Did Not Take Place*, Bloomington, IN: Indiana University Press, 1991.

Ian Frederick William Beckett, *Modern Insurgencies and Counter-Insurgencies*, London: Routledge, 2001.

Robin Bidwell, *Morocco under Colonial Rule. French Administration of Tribal Areas 1912–1956*, London: Frank Cass, 1973.

Lesley Blanch, *The Sabres of Paradise*, London: John Murray, 1960.

Albrecht von Boguslawski, *Der kleine Krieg und seine Bedeutung für die Gegenwart*, Berlin: Friedrich Luckhardt, 1881.

Peter Braestrup, *Big Story: How the American Press and Television Reported and Interpreted the Crisis of Tet 1968 in Vietnam and Washington*, Novato, CA: Presidio, 1994.

Robert V. Bruce, *Bell*, Ithaca, NY: Cornell University Press, 1990.

Tin Bui, *Following Ho Chi Minh: Memoirs of a North Vietnamese Colonel*, translated by J. Strowe and D. Van, Honolulu: University of Hawaii Press, 1995.

Susan L. Carruthers, *The Media at War*, New York: St. Martin's Press, 2000.

Susan L. Carruthers, *Winning Hearts and Minds: British Governments, the Media and Colonial Counter-Insurgency 1944–1960*, Leicester, UK: Leicester University Press, 1995.

Kinda Chaib, "Le Hezbollah libanais à travers ses images: La représentation du martyr," in Sabrina Mervin (ed.), *Les mondes chiites et l'Iran*, Paris: Karthala, 2007.

Gérard Chaliand, "Au maquis avec Amilcar Cabral," in Gérard Chaliand, *Stratégies de la guérilla. Anthologie historique de la longue marche à nos jours*, Paris: Gallimard, 1984 (1979).

Ignace Urbain Jean Chappe, *Histoire de la télégraphie*, Paris: Chez l'auteur, 1824.

Walid Charara and Frédéric Domont, *Le Hezbollah, un mouvement islamo-nationaliste*, Paris: Fayard, 2004.

Carl von Clausewitz, *Vom Kriege*, Berlin: Ullstein, 1832 (1980).

Bill Clinton, *My Life*, London: Random House, 2004.

Eliot A. Cohen, *Supreme Command. Soldiers, Statesmen, and Leadership in Wartime*, New York: The Free Press, 2002.

Steve Coll, *The Bin Ladens: An Arabian Family in the American Century*, New York: Penguin, 2008.

Yves Courrière, *La guerre d'Algérie,* Paris: Fayard, 2001.

George Crile, *Charlie Wilson's War,* New York: Grove Press, 2004.

Christopher Daase, "Clausewitz in the Twenty-First Century," in Hew Strachan and Andreas Herberg-Rothe (eds.), *Clausewitz in the Twenty-First Century,* Oxford: Oxford University Press, 2007, pp. 182–195.

John J. Fialka, *Hotel Warriors. Covering the Gulf War,* Baltimore: Johns Hopkins University Press, 1991.

Tommy R. Franks, *American Soldier,* New York: HarperCollins, 2004.

Lawrence Freedman, *The Official History of the Falklands Campaign,* vol. II, London: Routledge, 2005.

Jacques Frémeaux, *Les Bureaux arabes dans l'Algérie de la conquête,* Paris: Denoël, 1993.

Thomas L. Friedman, *From Beirut to Jerusalem,* New York: Farrar, Straus, Giroux, 1989.

Thomas L. Friedman, *The World Is Flat. A Brief History of the Twenty-first Century,* New York: Farrar, Straus and Giroux, 2004.

Joseph-Simon Galliéni, *Galliéni au Tonkin (1892–1896),* Paris: Berger-Levrault, 1941.

David Galula (as Jean Caran), *The Tiger's Whiskers,* New York: Walker, 1965.

David Galula, *Counterinsurgency Warfare: Theory and Practice,* New York: Praeger, 1964.

Fawaz A. Gerges, *The Far Enemy: Why Jihad Went Global,* Cambridge, UK: Cambridge University Press, 2005.

General V. N. Giap, *Guerre du peuple, armée du peuple,* Hanoi: Editions en langues étrangères, 1961 (1973).

William Gibson, *Neuromancer,* New York: Ace Books, 1984.

Martin Gilbert, *The First World War: A Complete History,* London: Macmillan, 2004.

Antonio Giustozzi, *Koran, Kalashnikov, and Laptop. The Neo-Taliban Insurgency in Afghanistan,* New York: Columbia University Press, 2008.

Jos J. L. Gommans, *The Rise of the Indo-Afghan Empire, C.1710–1780,* Leiden: E. J. Brill, 1995.

Michael Gordon and Bernard Trainor, *Cobra II. The Inside Story of the Invasion and Occupation of Iraq,* London: Atlantic Books, 2006.

Ernesto "Che" Guévara, *Guerrilla Warfare,* New York: Monthly Review Press, 1961.

Stephanie Gutmann, *The Other War. Israelis, Palestinians, and the Struggle for Media Supremacy,* Lanham, MD: Encounter Books, 2005.

Daniel C. Hallin, *The "Uncensored War." The Media and Vietnam,* Oxford: Oxford University Press, 1986.

Thomas X. Hammes, *The Sling and the Stone: On War in the 21st Century,* Osceola, WI: Zenith Press, 2006.

William M. Hammond, *Public Affairs: The Military and the Media, 1962–1968,* Washington, DC: Center of Military History, 1988.

William M. Hammond, *Public Affairs: The Military and the Media, 1968–1973,* Honolulu: University Press of the Pacific, 2002.

R. Harris, *Gotcha!: The Media, the Government, and the Falklands Crisis,* London: Faber and Faber, 1983.

Gerard J. Holzmann and Björn Pehrson, *The Early History of Data Networks,* Washington, DC: IEEE Computer Society Press, 1995.

Alistair Horne, *A Savage War of Peace. Algeria 1954–1962,* New York: NYRB Classics, 1977 (2006).

Samuel Huntington, *The Soldier and the State,* Cambridge, MA: Harvard University Press, 1957.

Anton A. Huurdeman, *The Worldwide History of Telecommunications,* New York: J. Wiley, 2003.

Herbert E. Ives, *Airplane Photography,* Philadelphia: J. B. Lippincott, 1920.

Samuel M. Katz, *The Hunt for the Engineer,* New York: The Lyons Press, 2002.

John Keegan, *The First World War,* New York: A. Knopf, 1999.

Gilles Kepel and Jean–Pierre Milelli, *Al-Qaeda in Its Own Words,* Cambridge, MA: Belknap Press, 2008.

Phillip Knightley, *The First Casualty. From the Crimea to Vietnam: The War Correspondent as Hero, Propagandist and Myth Maker,* New York: Harcourt Brace Jovanovich, 1975.

Walter Laqueur, *Guerrilla. A Historical and Critical Study,* vol. 4, Boston: Little, Brown, 1976.

T. E. Lawrence, *Seven Pillars of Wisdom,* London: Bernard Shaw, 1926.

Bernard Lewis, *The Crisis of Islam: Holy War and Unholy Terror,* New York: Modern Library, 2003.

Brynjar Lia, *Architect of Global Jihad: The Life of al-Qaida Strategist Abu Mus'ab al-Suri,* New York: Columbia University Press, 2008.

Hubert Lyautey, *Du rôle colonial de l'armée,* Paris: Armand Colin, 1900.

Hubert Lyautey, *Lettres du Tonkin et de Madagascar: 1894–1899,* Paris: A. Colin, 1921.

Ahmed Majed, *Al Khitâb 'Inda as-Sayyed Hassan Nasrallah: Dirâsa fi al Bonya al-Chakliyya, al Madâmîn, al Nidâm, al Marja'iyyât [Le discours chez Sayyed Hassan Nasrallah: Etude de la structure formelle, des contenus, de l'organisation et des références],* Beirut: Collection Adabiyyât al Nouhoud, 2007.

James Mann, *Rise of the Vulcans: The History of Bush's War Cabinet,* New York: Penguin, 2004.

Carlos Marighella, *Manual do Guerrilheiro Urbano [Le mini-manuel du guérillero urbain],* Paris: Seuil, 1973.

Maria McGuire, *To Take Arms,* Belfast: Viking Press, 1973.

Molly Moore, *A Woman at War,* New York: Scribner's, 1993.

Herfried Münkler, *Der Wandel des Krieges. Von der Symmetrie zur Asymmetrie,* Weilerswist: Velbrück Wissenschaft, 2006.

Omar Nasiri, *Inside the Jihad: My Life with Al Qaeda,* New York: Basic Books, 2008.

Sean Naylor, *Not a Good Day to Die,* New York: Penguin, 2005.

Johanna Neuman, *Lights, Camera, War,* New York: St. Martin's Press, 1996.

Jeremy M. Norman, *From Gutenberg to the Internet: A Sourcebook on the History of Information Technology,* Novato, CA: Historyofscience.com, 2005.

Augustus Richard Norton, *Amal and the Shi'a: Struggle for the Soul of Lebanon,* Austin: University of Texas Press, 1987.

Augustus Richard Norton, *Hezbollah: A Short History,* Princeton, NJ: Princeton University Press, 2007.

Don Oberdorfer, *Tet!,* New York: Garden City, 1971.

Noam Ohana, *Journal de guerre: De Sciences Po aux unités d'élite de Tsahal,* Paris: Denoël, 2007.

George P. Oslin, *The Story of Telecommunications,* Macon, GA: Mercer University Press, 1992.

William A. Owens, *Lifting the Fog of War,* Baltimore: Johns Hopkins University Press, 2001.

John Palfrey and Urs Gasser, *Born Digital: Understanding the First Generation of Digital Natives,* New York: Basic Books, 2008.

Judith Palmer Harik, *Hezbollah: The Changing Face of Terrorism,* New York: I. B. Tauris, 2004.

Judith Palmer Harik, "Hizballah's Public and Social Services and Iran," in Houchang E. Chehabi (ed.), *Distant Relations: Iran and Lebanon in the Last 500 Years,* London: Tauris, 2006, pp. 259–286.

Peter Paret, *Internal War and Pacification: the Vendée, 1789–96*, Princeton, NJ: Princeton University Press, 1961.

Peter Paret (ed.), *Makers of Modern Strategy: from Machiavelli to the Nuclear Age*, Oxford: Clarendon Press, 1990.

Peter Paret, *Clausewitz and the State*, Cambridge, MA: Princeton University Press, 2007 (1976).

Yoram Peri, *Generals in the Cabinet Room. How the Military Shapes Israeli Policy*, Washington, DC: U.S. Institute of Peace, 2006.

Douglas Porch, "Bugeaud, Galliéni, Lyautey: The Development of French Colonial Warfare," in Peter Paret (ed.), *Makers of Modern Strategy*, Princeton, NJ: Princeton University Press, 1986, pp. 376–407.

Douglas Porch, *The March to the Marne. The French Army 1871–1914*, Cambridge, UK: Cambridge University Press, 1981.

Colin L. Powell and Joseph E. Persico, *My American Journey*, New York: Random House, 1995.

George B. Prescott, *The Speaking Telephone, Talking Phonograph, and Other Novelties*, New York: D. Appleton & Company, 1878.

Naim Qassem, *Hizbullah: The Story from Within*, London: Saqi Books, 2005.

Ahmad Rashid, *Descent into Chaos*, New York: Viking, 2008.

Ahmad Rashid, *Taliban*, New Haven: Yale University Press, 2001.

Pierre Razoux, *Tsahal*, Paris: Perrin, 2006.

Charles Richard, *Etude sur l'insurrection du Dhara*, Alger: A. Besancenez, 1846.

Yann Richard, *L'islam chi'ite*, Paris: Fayard, 1991.

Thomas E. Ricks, *Fiasco. The American Military Adventure in Iraq*, New York: Penguin, 2006.

Thomas Rid, *War and Media Operations. The U.S. Military and the Press from Vietnam to Iraq*, London: Routledge, 2007.

Albert Ringel, *Les bureaux arabes de Bugeaud et les cercles militaires de Galliéni*, Paris: E. Larose, 1903.

John Robb, *Brave New War: The Next Stage of Terrorism and the End of Globalization*, New York: Wiley, 2007.

Olivier Roy, *Globalised Islam: The Search for a New Ummah*, London: C. Hurst & Co., 2004.

Amal Saad-Ghorayeb, *Hizbu'llah: Politics and Religion*, London: Pluto Press, 2002.

Marc Sageman, *Leaderles Jihad*, Philadelphia: University of Pennsylvania Press, 2008.

Mohammad bin Ahmad al-Salem, *39 Ways to Serve and Participate in Jihad*, online publication, 2003.

Jean–Loup Samaan, *Les métamorphoses du Hezbollah*, Paris: Karthala, 2007.

Ron Schleifer, *Psychological Warfare in the Intifada: Israeli and Palestinian Media Politics and Military Strategies*, East Sussex, UK: Sussex Academic Press, 2006.

Anthony Short, *The Communist Insurrection in Malaya, 1948–1960*, New York: Crane, Russak, and Co., 1975.

John Shy and Thomas W. Collier, "Revolutionary War," in Peter Paret (ed.), *Makers of Modern Strategy: from Machiavelli to the Nuclear Age*, Oxford: Clarendon Press, 1990, pp. 815–862.

Marieke Slootman and Jean Tillie, *Processes of Radicalisation*, Amsterdam: University of Amsterdam, 2006.

Rupert Smith, *The Utility of Force: The Art of War in the Modern World*, Harlow, Essex, UK: Allen Lane, 2005.

Guido Steinberg, *Der nahe und der ferne Feind. Das Netzwerk des islamistischen Terrorismus*, München: Beck, 2005.

Hew Strachan, *The First World War,* Oxford: Oxford University Press, 2001.

Philip M. Taylor, *Munitions of the Mind,* Manchester, UK: Manchester University Press, 2003.

Alvin Toffler and Heidi Toffler, *War and Anti-War,* New York: Little, Brown and Co., 1993.

Giles Trendle, "Hizballah Pragmatism and Popular Standing," in Rosemary Hollis and Nadim Shehadi (eds.), *Lebanon on Hold. Implications for Middle East Peace,* London: Royal Institute for International Affairs, 1996.

Mao Tse-Tung [Zedong], *On Guerilla Warfare,* London: Cassell, 1965.

Mao Tse-Tung, "Problems of Strategy in China's Revolutionary War," in *Selected Works,* vol. 1, Peking: Foreign Language Press, 1965, pp. 179–254.

Martin van Creveld, *The Transformation of War,* New York: The Free Press, 1991.

Paul Virilio and Sylvère Lothringer, *Pure War,* New York: Semiotext(e), 1997.

Bruce Watson, *Sieges,* Westport, CT: Greenwood, 1993.

Max Weber, *Wirtschaft und Gesellschaft,* Tübingen: Mohr Siebeck, 1922 (1977).

Lawrence Wright, *The Looming Tower. Al-Qaeda and the Road to 9/11,* New York: Alfred A. Knopf, 2006.

JOURNAL ARTICLES

Nigel Aylwin–Foster, "Changing the Army for Counterinsurgency Operations," *Military Review,* November–December, 2005, 2–15.

Margaret Belknap, "The CNN Effect: Strategic Enabler or Operational Risk?" *Parameters,* 3, 2002, 100–114.

Yochai Benkler, "Coase's Penguin, or Linux and the Nature of the Firm," *Yale Law Journal,* 112, 2002.

Yochai Benkler and Helen Nissenbaum, "Commons-Based Peer Production and Virtue," *Journal of Political Philosophy,* vol. 14, 4, 2006, 394–419.

William R. Blair, "Army Radio in Peace and War," *Annals of the American Academy of Political and Social Science,* vol. 142, March 1929, 86–89.

Yoel Cohen, "Nuclear Ambiguity and the Media: The Israeli Case," *Israel Affairs,* vol. 12, 3, 2006, 529–545.

Paul Cruickshank and Mohannad Hage Ali, "Abu Musab Al Suri: Architect of the New Al Qaeda," *Studies in Conflict & Terrorism,* vol. 30, 1, 2007, 1–14.

Paul Dixon, "Britain's 'Vietnam syndrome'? Public opinion and British military intervention from Palestine to Yugoslavia," *Review of International Studies,* vol. 26, 2000, 99–121.

Sandra I. Erwin, "Washington Pulse," *National Defense,* vol. 90, 2006, 627.

Alexander J. Field, "French Optical Telegraphy, 1793–1855: Hardware, Software, Administration," *Technology and Culture,* vol. 35, 2, 1994, 315–347.

Victoria Fontan, "Le discours d'Al-Manar, vecteur de 'glasnost' du Hezbollah," *Questions de communication,* 8, 2005, 51–66.

Zev Furst, "The Second Lebanon War: Military Strategy and the Battle for Public Opinion," *The Israel Journal of Foreign Affairs,* vol. 1, 2, 2007.

Henry G. Gole, "Don't Kill the Messenger: Vietnam War Reporting in Context," *Parameters,* Winter 1996, 148–153.

Mona Harb, "La banlieue du Hezbollah: Images alternatives du Beyrouth d'après-guerre," *Annales de la Recherche Urbaine,* 96, 2004, 53–61.

Marc Hecker, "De Marighella à Ben Laden. Passerelles stratégiques entre guérillos et jihadistes," *Politique étrangère*, 2, 2006, 385–396.

Marc Hecker, "Du bon usage de la terreur," *Focus stratégique*, April 2008, 1–31.

Eric von Hippel, "Learning from Open-Source Software," *MIT Sloan Management Review*, vol. 42, 4, 2001, 82–86.

Eric von Hippel and Georg von Krogh, "Open Source Software and the 'Private–Collective' Innovation Model: Issues for Organization Science," *Organization Science*, vol. 14, 2, 2003, 209–223.

Eric von Hippel and Georg von Krogh, "Free Revealing and the Private–Collective Model for Innovation Incentives," *R&D Management*, vol. 36, 3, 2006, 295–306.

Bruce Hoffman, "The Myth of Grass-Roots Terrorism. Why Osama bin Laden Still Matters," *Foreign Affairs*, May/June 2008.

Efraim Inbar, "The 'No Choice War' Debate in Israel," *Journal of Strategic Studies*, vol. 12, March 1989, 22–37.

Thomas H. Johnson, "The Taliban Insurgency and an Analysis of Shabnamah (Night Letters)," *Small Wars & Insurgencies*, vol. 18, 3, 2007, 317–344.

Avi Jorisch, "Al-Manar: Hizbullah TV, 24/7," *Middle East Quarterly*, vol. 11, 1, 2004, 17–31.

Dean Juniper, "The First World War and Radio Development," *History Today*, vol. 54, 5, 2004, 32–38.

Avi Kober, "The Intellectual and Modern Focus in Israeli Military Thinking as Reflected in Ma'arachot Articles, 1948–2000," *Armed Forces and Society*, vol. 30, 1, 2003.

Duane Koenig, "Telegraphs and Telegrams in Revolutionary France," *The Scientific Monthly*, vol. 59, 6, 1944, 431–437.

Bruce M. Kogut and Anca Metiu, "Open-Source Software Development and Distributed Innovation," *Oxford Review of Economic Policy*, vol. 17, 2, 2001, 248–264.

J. C. R. Licklider and W. Clark, "On-Line Man-Computer Communication," *Proceedings Spring Joint Computer Conference*, vol. 21, 1962, 113–128.

Yehiel Limor and Hillel Nossek, "The Military and the Media in the Twenty-First Century: Towards a New Model of Relations," *Israel Affairs*, vol. 12, 3, 2006, 484–510.

Meron Medzini, "Hasbara in the Second Lebanon War: a Rebuttal," *The Israel Journal of Foreign Affairs*, vol. 1, 3, 2007.

Joseph Metcalf III, "The Mother of the Mother," *United States Naval Institute Proceedings*, vol. 118, 8, 1991, pp. 56–58.

Tammy L. Miracle, "The Army and Embedded Media," *Military Review*, September–October 2003, 41–45.

Vincent Monteil, "Les Bureaux arabes au Maghreb (1833–1961)," *Esprit*, vol. 29, 300, 1961, 575–606.

Williamson Murray, "Clausewitz out, Computer in. Military Culture and Technological Hubris," *The National Interest*, vol. 48, Summer 1997, 57–64.

Hassan Nasrallah, "Hezbollah: y a-t-il une vie après le retrait d'Israël?" *Politique Internationale*, vol. 88, 2000.

Sean Naylor, "Insurgents in Afghanistan Have Mastered Media Manipulation," *Armed Forces Journal*, 2008.

Hillel Nossek and Yehiel Limor, "The Military and the Media in the Twenty-First Century: Towards a New Model of Relations," *Israel Affairs*, vol. 12, 3, 2006, 484–510.

Yoram Peri, "Intractable Conflict and the Media," *Israel Studies*, vol. 12, 1, 2007, 79–102.

Marc Prensky, "Listen to the Natives," *Educational Leadership*, vol. 63, 4, 2005.

Ahmad Rashid, "Letter from Afghanistan: Are the Taliban Winning?" *Current History,* January 2007, 17–20.

Thomas Rid, "The 19th Century Origins of Counterinsurgency Doctrine," *Journal of Strategic Studies,* forthcoming.

Piers Robinson, "The CNN Effect: Can the News Media Drive Foreign Policy?" *Review of International Studies,* vol. 25, 1999, 301–309.

Donald Rumsfeld, "Transforming the Military," *Foreign Affairs,* vol. 81, 3, 2002.

Marc Sageman and Bruce Hoffman, "Does Osama Still Call the Shots? Debating the Containment of al-Qaeda's Leadership," *Foreign Affairs,* July/August 2008.

Andrew P. Schilling, "Peers," *Marine Corps Gazette,* vol. 90, 5, 2006, 56.

Ron Schleifer, "Psychological Operations: A New Variation on an Age Old Art: Hezbollah versus Israel," *Studies in Conflict & Terrorism,* vol. 29, 1, 2006, 1–19.

Avi Shlaim, "Interview with Abba Eban, 11 March 1976," *Israel Studies,* vol. 8, 1, 2003, 153–177.

Dennis Showalter, "Soldiers into Postmasters? The Electric Telegraph as an Instrument of Command in the Prussian Army," *Military Affairs,* vol. 37, 2, 1973, 48–52.

Frank J. Stech, "Winning CNN Wars," *Parameters,* Autumn 1994, 37–56.

Bernard Trainor, "The Military and the Media: A Troubled Embrace," *Parameters,* December 1990, 2–11.

Gen. William C. Westmoreland, "Vietnam in Perspective," *Military Review,* vol. 59, 1, 1979, 34–43.

PRESS ARTICLES

"A World Wide Web of Terror," *The Economist,* 12 July 2007.

"Airborne Television," *Science News Letter,* vol. 49, 30 March 1946, pp. 195–196.

Ayman al-Zawahiri, "The Open Meeting with Shaykh Ayman al-Zawahiri," *As-Sahab Media,* Issue, 2008.

Abdul Hameed Bakier, "Al-Qaeda's al-Zawahiri Repudiates Dr. Fadl's 'Rationalization of Jihad,'" *Terrorism Focus,* vol. 5, 17, 2008, pp. 3–4.

Dan Baum, "What the Generals Don't Know," *The New Yorker,* vol. 80, 43, 2005, p. 42.

Peter Bergen and Paul Cruickshank, "The Unraveling," *The New Republic,* 2008.

Nicholas Blanford, "Hizbullah Sharpens Its Weapons in Propaganda War," *Christian Science Monitor,* 28 December 2001.

Max Boot, "Keys to a Successful Surge," *Los Angeles Times,* 7 February 2007.

Sarah Boxer, "Blogs," *The New York Review of Books,* vol. 55, 2, 2008.

Jarret Brachman, "Leading Egyptian Jihadist Sayyid Imam Renounces Violence," *CTC Sentinel,* vol. 1, 1, 2007, pp. 12–14.

Tin Bui, "How North Vietnam Won the War," *The Wall Street Journal,* 3 August 1995, p. A8.

Marie–Laure Cittanova, "Al-Manar," *Les Echos,* 15 December 2004.

Helena Cobban, "Hizbullah's New Face," *Boston Review,* April–May 2005.

"Crawley boy who kept bomb kit in a garage; Terror gang leader dreamed of carnage on the scale of 9/11," *Evening Standard,* 30 April 2007.

Alan Cullison, "Inside Al-Qaeda's Hard Drive," *Atlantic,* September 2004.

Jacob Dallal, "Bad Information. The Lesson of Jenin," *The New Republic,* August 2005.

"David Galula, 48, French Army Aide," *The New York Times,* 12 May 1967, p. 47.

Peter Drucker, "Beyond the Information Revolution," *The Atlantic Monthly,* October 1999.

Michael Evans, "Deadly Stalkers Follow Patrols in 'Bomb Alley,'" *The Times* (London), 15 December 2005, p. 40.

James Fallows, "Who Shot Mohammed al-Dura?" *The Atlantic Monthly,* June 2003.

Hassan M. Fattah, "Al Qaeda Increasingly Reliant on Media," *The New York Times,* 30 September 2006.

José-Alain Fralon, "48 heures pour faire cesser les hostilités entre Israéliens et Palestiniens. Les défis de la télévision du Hezbollah libanais," *Le Monde,* 20 October 2000.

Kathy Gannon, "Secret 'Night Letters' Condemn Afghan Government as Traitors of Islam, Urge War on U.S.," *Associated Press Worldstream,* 20 March 2002.

Duncan Gardham and Philip Johnston, "'Revenge' for Rushdie Honour, Boasts Website," *The Daily Telegraph,* 30 June 2007.

Marcus Gee, "Calling up a Brighter Future; The Cellphone Craze Has Helped Seed the Hard Soil of Afghanistan's Economy," *The Globe and Mail,* 8 June 2007.

Urs Gehriger, "Layeha (Regelbuch) für die Mudschaheddin," *Die Weltwoche,* vol. 46, 6, 2006.

Kim Ghattas, "Al-Manar Network Feels World's Heat," *Boston Globe,* 21 December 2004.

James K. Glassman, "How To Win The War Of Ideas," *Wall Street Journal,* 24 June 2008.

Chris Greenwood and Caroline Gammell, "Terror car bomb was primed to cause carnage among revellers in late-night club," *The Western Mail,* 30 June 2007.

John Hockenberry, "The Blogs of War," *Wired Magazine,* 13 August 2005.

Adrien Jaulmes, "Au Liban, le Hezbollah accentue sa propagande," *Le Figaro,* 23 August 2006.

Terri Judd, "Forces Round on Jackson for Failing to Criticise MoD Earlier," *The Independent,* 8 December 2006, p. 22.

Daniel Kimmage, "Fight Terror with YouTube," *The New York Times,* 26 June 2008.

Zvika Krieger, "Exhibition Game: Inside Hezbollah's Museum of Hate," *The New Republic,* 27 August 2007.

Nadya Labi, "Jihad 2.0," *The Atlantic Monthly,* July/August 2006.

Allison Lampert, "In Kabul's Pul-e-Charkhi, Cellphones Can Be Deadly," *The Gazette (Montreal),* 6 December 2007.

Jonathan Landay, "Islamic Militants' Influence Spreading," *The Seattle Times,* 3 February 2008.

Brynjar Lia, "Al-Suri's Doctrines for Decentralized Jihadi Training," *Terrorism Monitor,* vol. 5, 1, 2007, pp. 1–4.

Kevin Maurer, "Taliban Show Media Savvy," *The Fayetteville Observer,* 12 January 2008.

Daniel McGrory, "The Underground Voice of Hezbollah That Israel Is Still Unable to Silence," *The Times* (London), 5 August 2006, p. 7.

Johanna Neuman, "Pentagon Plans to Deploy Journalists in Iraq," *Los Angeles Times,* 4 December 2002.

Richard Norton–Taylor, "Browne Says BBC Interview Endangered Lives of Troops," *The Guardian,* 12 July 2006.

Dan Nystedt, "Mobile Phone Use Grows in Afghanistan," *IDG News Service,* 23 June 2008.

Arieh O'Sullivan, "The thankless task of the IDF Spokesman. Ruth Yaron steps down, warning her successor it won't be 'a rose garden,'" *The Jerusalem Post,* 2 June 2005.

Jane Perlez, "Frontier Years Give Might to Ex-Guerrilla's Words," *The New York Times,* 5 July 2008.

Tom Perry, "Hezbollah Brings Israel War to Computer Screen," *Reuters,* 16 August 2007.

Waliullah Rahmani, "Combating the Ideology of Suicide Terrorism in Afghanistan," *Terrorism Monitor,* vol. 4, 21, 2006.

Elizabeth Rubin, "In the Land of the Taliban," *The New York Times Magazine*, 22 October 2006.

Michael Scheuer, "Al-Qaeda's Insurgency Doctrine: Aiming for a 'Long War,'" *Terrorism Focus*, vol. III, 8, 2006, pp. 4–6.

Michael Scheuer, "Al-Qaeda's Media Doctrine: Evolution from Cheerleader to Opinion-Shaper," *Terrorism Focus*, vol. 4, 15, 2007.

Michael Scheuer, "Rumors of al-Qaeda's Death May Be Highly Exaggerated," *Terrorism Focus*, vol. 5, 21, 2008.

Nicholas Schmidle, "Next-Gen Taliban," *The New York Times Magazine*, 6 January 2008.

Eric Schmitt and Thom Shanker, "U.S. Adapts Cold-War Idea to Fight Terrorists," *The New York Times*, 18 March 2008, p. 1.

Elaine Sciolino and Stephen Grey, "British Terror Trial Traces a Path to Militant Islam," *The New York Times*, 25 November 2006.

Elaine Sciolino and Eric Schmitt, "A Not Very Private Feud Over Terrorism," *The New York Times*, 8 June 2008.

Taimoor Shah, "Taliban Threatens Afghan Cellphone Companies," *The New York Times*, 26 February 2008.

Philip Smucker, "Taliban Learns Tactics, PR from al Qaeda," *Washington Times*, 30 May 2007.

Jeffrey Stinson, "Lebanon Relief Effort Raises Houses, Questions," *USA Today*, 17 December 2006.

"Taliban Communications, Old and New," *Jane's Terrorism & Security Monitor*, 12 November 2007.

Claus Blok Thomsen and Morten Skjoldager, "Fotografier Belaster Terrorsigtet," *Politiken*, 18 January 2008.

Andrew Tilghman, "The Army's Other Crisis. Why the Best and the Brightest Young Officers are Leaving," *The Washington Monthly*, 2007.

Ann Scott Tyson, "NATO's Not Winning in Afghanistan, Report Says," *Washington Post*, 31 January 2008.

"UK Terrorism Convictions," *Jane's Terrorism & Security Monitor*, 2007.

Abdul Waheed Wafa and Taimoor Shah, "U.S. Airstrike on 2 Taliban Commanders in South Wounds at Least 18 Civilians, Afghans Say," *The New York Times*, 4 August 2007, p. A6.

Declan Walsh, "Headteacher Decapitated by Taliban," *The Guardian*, 5 January 2006.

Ivan Watson, "Taliban Enlists Video in Fight for Afghanistan," *National Public Radio*, 2 November 2006.

Lawrence Wright, "The Master Plan," *The New Yorker*, 11 September 2006.

Lawrence Wright, "The Rebellion," *The New Yorker*, 2008.

Sami Yousafzai, "Afghanistan: Want to Meet the Taliban? No Prob," *Newsweek*, vol. 148, 25 December 2006, p. 14.

Sami Yousafzai and Urs Gehriger, "Der Kodex der Taliban," *Die Weltwoche*, 46, 2006.

Index

About the Authors

THOMAS RID is a research fellow at the Center for Transatlantic Relations in the School for Advanced International Studies, Johns Hopkins University. Previously he worked at the RAND Corporation, the Institut français des relations internationales, and the Stiftung Wissenschaft und Politik. He is author of *War and Media Operations* and co-editor of *Understanding Counterinsurgency Warfare*.

MARC HECKER is a research fellow at the Security Studies Center of the Institut français des relations internationales in Paris. Among his publications are *La presse française et la première guerre du Golfe*, *La défense des intérêts de l'Etat d'Israël en France*, and *Une vie d'Afghanistan*.

LaVergne, TN USA
24 December 2009
168052LV00002B/15/P